ENERGY SECURITY, TRANSITION, AND ECONOMIC GROWTH

ENERGY SECURITY, TRANSITION, AND ECONOMIC GROWTH

Editors

Farhad Taghizadeh-Hesary
Tokai University, Japan

Youngho Chang
Singapore University of Social Sciences, Singapore

Naoyuki Yoshino
Keio University, Japan

World Scientific

NEW JERSEY • LONDON • SINGAPORE • BEIJING • SHANGHAI • TAIPEI • CHENNAI

Published by

World Scientific Publishing Co. Pte. Ltd.
5 Toh Tuck Link, Singapore 596224
USA office: 27 Warren Street, Suite 401-402, Hackensack, NJ 07601
UK office: 57 Shelton Street, Covent Garden, London WC2H 9HE

Library of Congress Control Number: 2025010516

British Library Cataloguing-in-Publication Data
A catalogue record for this book is available from the British Library.

ENERGY SECURITY, TRANSITION, AND ECONOMIC GROWTH

ISBN 978-981-98-1259-2 (hardcover)
ISBN 978-981-98-1260-8 (ebook for institutions)
ISBN 978-981-98-1261-5 (ebook for individuals)

For any available supplementary material, please visit
https://www.worldscientific.com/worldscibooks/10.1142/14296#t=suppl

Desk Editors: Aanand Jayaraman/Yulin Jiang

Typeset by Stallion Press
Email: enquiries@stallionpress.com

https://doi.org/10.1142/9789819812608_fmatter

About the Editors

Dr. Farhad Taghizadeh-Hesary is an associate professor at the Tokai University Research Institute for Environment and Sustainability (TRIES) in Tokyo, Japan, the vice-president and co-founder of the International Society for Energy Transition Studies (ISETS) and Chief Economist of the Climate Finance Asia. In 2023, he received the Medal and Commendation for Science and Technology from the Minister of Education, Culture, Sports, Science, and Technology of Japan for his contribution to renewable energy finance research. He was recognized as a Highly Cited Researcher by Clarivate Analytics. Dr. Taghizadeh-Hesary is the editor-in-chief of the *Journal of Environmental Assessment Policy and Management*, and an associate editor/board member for several scholarly journals. His extensive research includes over 350 academic journal papers and book chapters, along with editing 25 books published by Springer Nature, Elsevier, Routledge, World Scientific, Edward Elgar, and the Asian Development Bank Institute. He led dozens of consulting and capacity building and training projects for international organizations and governments of various countries. He holds a Ph.D. in economics from Keio University with a scholarship from the Japanese government (MEXT).

Dr. Youngho Chang is an Associate Professor and Head, Minor in Applied Economics at the School of Business, the Singapore University of Social Sciences (SUSS), Singapore. He specializes in the economics of climate change, economic-energy-environmental modeling, energy and security, oil and macroeconomy, the economics of electricity market deregulation, and green finance and sustainability. He has published over 70 papers in internationally referred academic journals and nine edited books. Apart from publications, as a consultant, he has carried out a cost-benefit analysis that examined the economics of carbon emissions reductions for a small open economy, analyzed market power in a deregulated electricity market, forecasted global demand for methanol, and examined the impact of carbon control on operations and supply chain. He has taught at the National University of Singapore and Nanyang Technological University, Singapore. He received his Ph.D. in Economics (Environmental and Resource Economics) from the University of Hawaii at Manoa, U.S.A.

Dr. Naoyuki Yoshino is a distinguished economist with expertise in public finance, infrastructure development, and financial systems. He is currently the Chief Advisor at the Financial Research Center of Japan's Financial Services Agency and a Professor Emeritus at Keio University. From 2014 to 2020, he served as Dean and CEO of the Asian Development Bank Institute (ADBI). Dr. Yoshino earned his Ph.D. from Johns Hopkins

University under the mentorship of Sir Alan Walters. He has been a visiting scholar at MIT and has held visiting professorships at institutions worldwide. His research focuses on infrastructure financing, SME development, and green finance, and he has authored over 100 publications, including books and academic journal articles. Recognized for his contributions to sustainable finance, Dr. Yoshino received the International Green Finance Lifetime Achievement Scientific Award from the Central Bank of Hungary in 2021.

https://doi.org/10.1142/9789819812608_fmatter

Acknowledgments

This book results from the collective efforts of many senior experts in energy economics and policy, dedicated to advancing the understanding of energy security, sustainable transitions, and economic growth. A select number of chapters are revised and updated versions of papers originally published in a special issue of *The Singapore Economic Review*. We extend our heartfelt thanks to Professor Euston Quah, Editor-in-Chief, for his support throughout the completion of the special issue. We also wish to express our gratitude to World Scientific Publishing, whose suggestion to develop this book has helped bring these insights to a wider audience. Finally, we are grateful to all the contributors who shared their expertise and perspectives, enriching the analyses presented in this book.

https://doi.org/10.1142/9789819812608_fmatter

Contents

https://doi.org/10.1142/9789819812608_fmatter

Introduction

FARHAD TAGHIZADEH-HESARY,[*,§], YOUNGHO CHANG[†] and NAOYUKI YOSHINO[‡]

[*]*TOKAI Research Institute for Environment and Sustainability (TRIES), Japan*

[†]*School of Business, Singapore University of Social Sciences, Singapore*

[‡]*Keio University, Tokyo, Japan*

[§]*farhad@tsc.u-tokai.ac.jp*

Energy security, energy transition, and economic growth are among the most pressing global challenges today. As nations seek to secure reliable, affordable, and sustainable energy systems, the need to balance economic development with environmental responsibility is more critical than ever. Energy security, in particular, is fundamental for ensuring economic growth, prosperity, and resilience against external shocks, especially in the context of fluctuating global energy markets and increasing environmental concerns. The transition to renewable energy sources is essential for reducing dependence on fossil fuels, curbing carbon emissions, and mitigating the impact of climate change, all while fostering economic growth.

This book, *Energy Security, Transition, and Economic Growth,* provides a timely and comprehensive analysis of these interconnected issues. It brings together insights from a range of regional and country-level case studies, offering new perspectives on how different nations are navigating the complex landscape of energy security and transition. The book is structured into two parts: regional-level analyses and country-level studies, comprising ten chapters. Each chapter presents empirical research, practical policy recommendations, and innovative solutions that can be applied to different energy contexts around the world.

What distinguishes this book from existing literature is its novel approach to understanding the energy transition. While many studies focus on either energy security or economic growth in isolation, this book integrates these themes, exploring how they shape and influence one another. The research presented here uses a variety of advanced econometric models and data analysis techniques to offer fresh insights into the complex relationships between energy consumption, economic performance, and environmental sustainability. The book covers a wide range of topics related to energy security from different regions, from the promotion of renewable energy in Southeast Asia to the challenges faced by fossil fuel-dependent economies like Kazakhstan in Central Asia. It also addresses the critical role of green finance, technological innovations such as virtual power plants and solar water pumps, and the need for targeted energy policies to drive sustainable transitions.

The findings in this book are particularly valuable for policymakers, energy practitioners, and researchers looking for practical solutions to the challenges of energy security and transition. Each chapter contributes to a broader understanding of how countries can navigate the transition to renewable energy while maintaining or enhancing their energy security and economic growth. The book not only provides policy recommendations but also offers empirical evidence that can help shape future energy strategies on both regional and country levels, making it a valuable resource for anyone involved in the energy sector.

Section one focuses on regional studies and comprises five chapters.

In Chapter 1, Taghizadeh-Hesary *et al.* utilize the Green Power Index to assess sustainable power markets in nine Southeast Asian countries. It finds that economic growth, foreign direct investment, R&D, good governance, and privatization promote energy security while rising electricity prices hinder progress. The study recommends reforms in electricity tariffs, fostering green growth, and enhancing regional and global cooperation to strengthen energy security in the short and long term.

In Chapter 2, Amin *et al.* analyze the relationship between energy intensity and capital efficiency across different income groups in South Asia. It finds that lower-income countries have higher technical inefficiencies and energy intensity, while high-income nations use capital more efficiently, reducing energy intensity. The study highlights the need for optimizing capital utilization in developing economies to enhance energy efficiency and resilience, offering policy recommendations for energy security and sustainable growth.

In Chapter 3, Sun *et al.* examine pathways to sustainable growth in OECD countries, focusing on energy security and environmental efficiency. It reveals significant variations in energy efficiency across nations. The study advocates for tailored policies promoting renewable energy integration and increased efficiency, aligning economic growth with environmental sustainability for a resilient energy transition.

In Chapter 4, Rahmani *et al.* discuss the adoption of solar water pumps as a driver of energy security in the agricultural sectors of developing economies. They highlight the role of financial incentives and supportive policies in promoting solar technology in rural areas. Their findings indicate that widespread adoption of solar pumps reduces dependence on grid electricity and enhances agricultural productivity and energy resilience in rural communities.

In Chapter 5, Taghizadeh-Hesary *et al.* assess the link between energy security, pollution, and health in selected Asian developing economies. The chapter highlights the health risks associated with fossil fuel dependency and emphasizes the role of renewable energy in mitigating these issues. Their findings underscore that a shift toward clean energy sources can reduce pollution-related health problems while enhancing energy security and contributing to a healthier population.

The second section, which is on the country-level analyses, consists of five chapters:

In Chapter 6, Rasoulinezhad and Taghizadeh-Hesary examine the role of green finance in promoting energy efficiency, sustainable transitions, and emissions reduction. The authors discuss how green finance mechanisms like green bonds support energy-efficient projects and contribute to a low-carbon economy. Their findings suggest that greater access to green finance is crucial for enabling countries to meet long-term sustainability and energy security objectives.

In Chapter 7, Huang and Kim examine Japan's post-2011 energy strategy, focusing on reducing nuclear power dependence through an optimal energy mix. The results show that renewable energy can replace nuclear power with capital-use subsidies. Virtual power plants (VPP) can reduce fiscal costs for wind and solar power and social costs, emphasizing the importance of VPPs alongside renewable energy policies for efficient power allocation and overcapacity management.

In Chapter 8, Panthamit *et al.* investigate the economic drivers of energy security in Lao PDR, focusing on electricity consumption and the transition to renewables. Their findings suggest that increasing electricity demand requires a sustainable energy strategy. The authors recommend policies that support renewable energy development to enhance energy security and economic growth in Lao PDR.

In Chapter 9, Mukan *et al.* explore the impact of oil price volatility on Kazakhstan's stock market and the implications for energy security in the context of an energy transition. Their analysis highlights that diversifying Kazakhstan's energy sources can mitigate the risks associated with oil price fluctuations, creating a stable path toward a more secure energy system.

In Chapter 10, Tu *et al.* examine the relationship between energy security and exchange rate dynamics in Vietnam. They assess how fluctuations in exchange rates influence energy imports and overall economic stability. Their findings reveal that stabilizing exchange rates is essential for maintaining affordable energy access and supporting energy security and economic stability in Vietnam.

Section 1

Regional-Level Analyses

https://doi.org/10.1142/9789819812608_0001

Chapter 1

Advancing Access to Renewable Energy in Southeast Asia to Enhance Energy Security

FARHAD TAGHIZADEH-HESARY[*,¶], EHSAN RASOULINEZHAD[†,‖], PHOUMIN HAN[‡,**], and LILU VANDERCAMME[§,††]

[*]*Tokai University Research Institute for Environment and Sustainability (TRIES), Tokai University, Tokyo, Japan*

[†]*Faculty of World Studies, Tehran University, Tehran, Iran*

[‡]*Economic Research Institute for ASEAN and East Asia, Indonesia*

[§]*Faculty of Economics, Keio University, Tokyo, Japan*

[¶]*farhad@tsc.u-tokai.ac.jp*

[‖]*e.rasoulinezhad@ut.ac.ir*

[**]*han.phoumin@eria.org*

[††]*liluvandercamme@keio.jp*

This study introduces a multidimensional dependent variable, the green power index (GPI), as a relevant indicator for evaluating sustainable power markets and examines its key drivers. Using a product lifecycle management estimator within an Autoregressive Distributive Lag panel model, the analysis covers nine Southeast Asian countries. The findings suggest that economic growth, higher foreign direct investment (FDI), increased research and development (R&D) efforts, enhanced governance, and privatization are significant contributors to fostering a sustainable power market and ensuring energy security in the short and long term. Conversely, rising electricity prices may impede progress. The empirical results highlight critical policy recommendations, including reforming electricity tariffs, promoting green growth, and enhancing trade, investment, and cooperation among Southeast Asian nations and other global economic players to strengthen energy security.

Keywords: Renewable energy, GPI, energy security, ASEAN, sustainability.

1. Introduction and Background

In recent years, the discourse surrounding the need for comprehensive reforms in electricity markets has gained considerable traction due to persistent challenges such as environmental degradation and energy security concerns. Policymakers face the complex task of increasing market efficiency while ensuring widespread access to affordable, market-driven electricity tariffs. Although such reforms hold the potential to steer countries toward cleaner energy systems and broader electricity access, progress has been impeded by various obstacles, including the COVID-19 pandemic (Norouzi *et al.*, 2020), insufficient financial resources (Nelson, 2020), and outdated regulatory frameworks (Zsiboracs *et al.*, 2020). Historical data from B.P. (2020) indicate that, despite gas and coal dominating electricity generation from 1985 to 2019, there has been a marked shift in global efforts to transition away from fossil fuels toward renewable energy sources. Notably, the United Kingdom was among the first to initiate substantial electricity market reforms in 1988, transitioning toward a liberalized system (Tsay and Chen, 2019). Similarly, several Latin American countries, such as Chile, Argentina, and Peru, pursued reforms in the 1980s and 1990s to reduce public debt and attract private investment (Dussan, 1996). Several nations embarked on electricity market reforms in Asia during the mid-1990s, with Turkey commencing liberalization efforts in 2001 (Senerdem and Akkemik, 2020).

Singapore led Southeast Asia in establishing a competitive electricity market, followed by the Philippines, which introduced the Wholesale Electricity Spot Market. However, these reforms were hampered mainly by limited capital, sluggish technological adoption, and insufficient private sector participation (Sharma, 2005; Sarangi *et al.*, 2019; Delina, 2021; Mohsin *et al.*, 2021). According to the International Energy Agency (IEA, 2020), Southeast Asia is one of the most rapidly expanding regions in terms of electricity demand. Malaysia, Thailand, Vietnam, and Indonesia account for over 80% of the region's total demand. The region has set ambitious targets, including achieving universal access to electricity by 2030 and doubling its generation capacity by 2040 (Weatherby, 2020). Despite substantial progress in expanding electricity access since 2000, a significant portion of the population remains underserved (IEA, 2019). Thus, achieving universal access while improving market efficiency is crucial to the region's economic development. However, this must be achieved alongside the transition to green energy systems to reduce dependence on fossil fuels. In response to these challenges, several Southeast Asian countries have implemented electricity market reforms over the past few decades. Malaysia undertook reforms in 1992 to liberalize its electricity supply industry, while Singapore began its electricity market liberalization process in 1995. Taiwan also initiated electricity market reform policies in 1990 (Tsay and Chen, 2019).

Given the urgency of electricity market reforms in Southeast Asia and the factors that influence the pace of these reforms, this study examines their impact on sustainable power markets. Specifically, the research evaluates how macroeconomic variables, electricity tariffs, and governance structures influence the GPI within ASEAN economies. The GPI, a novel contribution of this study, serves as the dependent variable and is designed to measure the sustainability of power markets through indicators such as electrification rates, the share of renewable energy in total generation, and carbon dioxide emissions from energy production. The study further investigates the effects of key explanatory variables, including real gross domestic product (GDP), FDI, R&D expenditures in the energy sector, electricity prices, privatization, deregulation, and green policies, on the GPI.

Previous studies, including those by Kundu and Mishara (2011), Urpelainen and Yang (2019), and Zheng (2021), have explored the effects of these factors on electrification rates, CO_2 emissions, and renewable energy adoption in other regions. However, to our knowledge, prior research has yet to examine the impact of these factors on the GPI within ASEAN specifically. This study, therefore, makes two critical contributions to the literature: first, by introducing the multidimensional GPI, and second, by providing the first comprehensive analysis of the ASEAN region's progress toward achieving sustainable electricity markets.

The structure of this chapter is as follows: Section 2 reviews the relevant literature, identifying the gaps that this research aims to address. Section 3 details the data sources and model specifications used in this study. Section 4 presents the results of the econometric analysis and Section 5 offers concluding remarks and policy recommendations.

2. Literature Review

2.1. *Challenges in achieving sustainable electricity markets*

Scholars have widely discussed the transition to sustainable electricity markets, focusing on identifying and addressing key obstacles to reform. Early work by Dussan (1996) emphasized the role of electricity market reforms in attracting private sector investment, which is crucial for developing efficient power systems. This theme has been further explored by Sarangi *et al.* (2019), Nasr Esfahani *et al.* (2021), and Hao *et al.* (2021), who underscored the importance of reforms for achieving energy security, particularly in developing countries where the need for a stable and sustainable power supply is critical.

Several barriers continue to impede the implementation of effective power sector reforms. Foster and Rana (2020) identify critical elements such as institutional governance, financial sustainability, and sector liberalization as fundamental for successful reform efforts. The report emphasizes that creating an enabling environment for private sector participation, alongside effective regulation, is essential to drive service quality improvements and economic growth in developing economies. Meanwhile, IRENA (2019) highlights the role of dynamic pricing models in facilitating the integration of renewable energy. By adjusting electricity prices based on demand, these tariffs can incentivize consumers to use power during periods of high renewable energy availability, thus enhancing grid efficiency and reducing costs. Furthermore, the Renewable Power Generation Costs report by IRENA (2021) demonstrates the declining costs of renewable technologies, underscoring the importance of incorporating these cost dynamics into tariff models to support the broader adoption of clean energy.

Environmental and climate-related factors have also emerged as significant considerations in reform discussions. Defeuilley (2019) argued that international collaborations to combat climate change could create greener electricity markets. Akrami *et al.* (2019) suggested that existing electricity market reforms often create operational uncertainties that must be revisited to promote more stable energy supplies. Yin *et al.* (2019) stressed the importance of market liberalization for enhancing efficiency and sustainability, particularly in regions with developing economies.

Southeast Asia faces its own unique set of challenges. Senderdem and Akkemik (2020) pointed to integrating public and private sector efforts as a crucial factor for fostering efficient regional electricity markets. Mier and Weissbart (2020) observed that the inefficiencies in current power markets undermine progress toward decarbonization targets. In the case of China, Guo *et al.* (2020) concluded that electricity market reforms are influenced by many factors, making the reform process highly complex. Sorknaes *et al.* (2020) highlighted the macroeconomic barriers to establishing a smart energy market in Southeast Asia, emphasizing the need for policies that attract FDI and encourage private sector involvement in renewable energy projects. Southeast Asia faces unique challenges in transforming its energy sector. The IEA's Southeast Asia Energy Outlook 2022 emphasizes the need for substantial investment in infrastructure to support renewable energy integration, stressing that the region's diverse energy landscape requires tailored strategies to attract private investment and enhance energy security. Despite growing commitments, a gap persists between current investments and the level needed to meet clean energy targets, with a projected requirement of USD 130 billion annually by 2030 to align with sustainability goals. IEA (2024) highlights that most countries in the region still depend heavily on public funds for infrastructure, making it essential to engage private capital through public–private partnerships, long-term concessions, and build-operate-transfer arrangements. Successful implementation of these models hinges on establishing a stable, transparent regulatory environment that attracts and retains foreign investment. Additionally, CSIS (2023) underscores that macroeconomic and policy-related barriers, such as inadequate infrastructure and market inefficiencies, continue to hinder the full-scale deployment of renewables in Southeast Asia. It recommends improving policy coherence and reducing regulatory uncertainties to integrate private sector efforts better and advance the region's energy transition.

A persistent challenge, as identified by studies such as Taghizadeh-Hesary and Yoshino (2019), Nelson (2020), and Tsao *et al.* (2021), is the lack of adequate capital to finance green energy projects. The low return on investment for green energy initiatives often discourages private investors, further hampering the expansion of renewable energy infrastructure. This financial barrier is one of the most significant obstacles to increasing the share of renewable energy in the region's power generation mix.

2.2. *Strategies for advancing electricity market reforms*

To overcome these challenges, scholars have proposed various strategies to advance electricity market reforms. Past literature indicates that the success of market reforms depends heavily on the specific conditions of each country, as the factors driving reform can vary widely (Newbery, 1999). Poudineh *et al.* (2020) argued that the success of market reforms is contingent upon the specific conditions of each country, as the factors driving reform vary widely. One commonly discussed strategy is the privatization of electricity markets, which has been shown to attract more significant investment and improve efficiency. Pineau (2002) used the example of Cameroon to demonstrate how privatization can bring about much-needed reforms in the power sector by injecting new capital and introducing more efficient production methods. Newbery (1999) demonstrated that the privatization and restructuring of the U.K. electricity market led to increased competition and efficiency, serving as a benchmark for other reforms globally. Similarly, Joskow (2008) illustrated how liberalization in Europe and North America improved operational efficiency and investment in the energy sector. Similarly, Kundu and Mishara (2011) illustrated the positive effects of privatization in Orissa, India, which resulted in a more reliable electricity supply. In developing countries, studies have also observed positive effects; for instance, Izaguirre (1998) reported that private sector involvement helped enhance electricity access and reliability in several regions, while Jamasb *et al.* (2004) noted that successful reforms in Latin America led to significant improvements in service delivery and infrastructure development.

Another critical factor in advancing electricity market reform is R&D investment. Sirin and Erdogan (2013) highlighted that technological innovation, driven by increased R&D expenditures, is essential for overcoming the challenges faced by the energy sector. Pollitt (2019) reinforced this view, asserting that developing and deploying new technologies are critical for the successful reform of electricity markets.

FDI has also been recognized as a key driver of electricity market reform, particularly in regions with insufficient local capital. Xuegong *et al.* (2013) emphasized the role of FDI in encouraging private sector involvement, which can significantly boost the pace of reform. Zheng (2021) similarly demonstrated the positive impact of FDI on electricity market efficiency, particularly in developing countries where FDI is pivotal in financing large-scale energy projects.

In Southeast Asia, privatization, enhanced R&D investment, and FDI are critical to addressing the financial and technological barriers that have slowed the progress of electricity market reforms. These strategies help to overcome the immediate challenges of financing and implementing green energy projects and provide a foundation for achieving long-term sustainability in the region's electricity markets.

2.3. *Literature gap*

Evaluating the effects of macroeconomic variables on sustainable electricity markets provides critical insights for policymakers and researchers globally. Despite numerous studies on electricity market reforms, limited attention has been given to the impacts of FDI, privatization, and R&D expenditure, specifically in Southeast Asia. While research has addressed similar issues in other regions, Southeast Asia's unique policy and economic environment still needs to be explored. Moreover, no existing academic work, to the authors' knowledge, has employed a comprehensive measure like the GPI to assess the progress of these reforms in fostering sustainable and efficient electricity markets. This lack of focused analysis on the region's specific challenges and drivers, such as FDI, R&D, and privatization, leaves policymakers with insufficient guidance on accelerating the transition to sustainable energy. Thus, this study seeks to fill these literature gaps by evaluating these macroeconomic factors in the context of Southeast Asia and by introducing the GPI as a novel, multidimensional tool for assessing market sustainability and energy security.

3. Data and Methodology

3.1. *Theoretical background*

To assess the sustainable energy market, this study employs a top-down model within the power generation sector, utilizing macroeconomic theory and variables for market interpretation (Cieplinski *et al.*, 2021). This model follows an optimization-based framework, represented by the Bellman equation (Eq. 1), as outlined by Taghizadeh-Hesary *et al.* (2022):

$$V(x_0) = max_{a_0}[F(x_0, \alpha_0) + \beta V(x_1)] \tag{1}$$

where V represents the best possible value of the objective. The first-order condition for Eq. (1) can be conducted, resulting in Eq. (2):

$$\frac{\vartheta}{\vartheta a_0}(V(x_0)=max_{a_0}[F(x_0,\alpha_0)+\beta V(x_1)]) \tag{2}$$

Under the envelope condition, the derivative of the value function is Eq. (3):

$$\frac{\vartheta}{\vartheta x_0}(V(x_0)=max_{a_0}[F(x_0,\alpha_0)+\beta V(x_1)]) \tag{3}$$

In conclusion, several economic variables (X_1, X_2) influence optimizing a sustainable electricity market, which may either positively or negatively affect the advancement of such a market within a country. The selection of these variables is grounded in existing literature, including studies by Pineal (2002), Kundu and Mishara (2011), Urpelainen and Yang (2019), Pollitt (2019), and Zheng (2011).

3.2. *Data description*

The primary aim of this chapter is to explore the relationship between sustainable power markets and macroeconomic variables in Southeast Asian countries. A multidimensional dependent variable, the GPI, is introduced as a suitable proxy for measuring sustainable power markets. We will use principal component analysis (PCA) to construct the GPI, a statistical technique commonly used for data reduction. PCA enables extracting key data, eliminating redundant information, identifying hidden patterns, and visualizing the primary relationships among observations. This method simplifies complex datasets by reducing their dimensions for more straightforward analysis. The PCA approach will consolidate the three dependent variables outlined in the first equation (Eq. 4) into a single dependent component GPI:

$$GPI = f(ELECT, CARBON, RE) \tag{4}$$

Equation 4 demonstrates that the GPI is a function of three variables: *ELECT* (electrification ratio), *CARBON* (energy-related carbon dioxide emissions), and *RE* (share of renewable energy in total power generation). However, to confirm the reliability of using PCA for efficiently factorizing these three variables, we apply the Kaiser–Meyer–Olkin (KMO) measure of sampling adequacy.

Additionally, the explanatory variables in our model are categorized into four groups: macroeconomic variables, price levels, governance related to the power market, and a general governance indicator. Following Balza *et al.* (2013), we use privatization in the power market as a proxy for governance in this sector. Moreover, the general governance indicator comprises three distinct governance variables, political stability, regulatory quality, and government effectiveness, all derived from the Worldwide Governance Indicators, as detailed in Table 1.

Table 1. Definition of the variables.

Group	Category	Symbol	Definition	Unit
Dependent variable GPI	GPI	ELECT	Electrification ratio	%
	GPI	RE	Share of renewable energy in the total power generation	%
	GPI	CO_2	Energy-related carbon emission level	Million metric tons (Mmt)
Independent variable	Macroeconomic	GDP	Gross domestic product in real-term	Constant 2010 USD
	Macroeconomic	FDI	Foreign direct investment, net inflow	% of GDP
	Macroeconomic	R&D	R&D expenditure in the energy sector	% of GDP
	Price	TAR	Average of electricity tariff	USD per kWh
	Governance relation to the power market	PRIV	Privatization of the power sector	Percentage of the average gross fixed capital formation
	General governance	P.S.	Political stability	Estimate
	General governance	R.Q.	Regulatory quality	Estimate
	General governance	G.E.	Government effectiveness	Estimate

Note: kWH = kilowatt-hour.

3.3. *Empirical model specification*

The primary econometric equation of our model is provided in Eq. (5) (Taghizadeh-Hesary *et al.* 2022):[1]

$$GPI_{it} = \alpha_0 + \alpha_1 GDP_{it} + \alpha_2 FDI_{it} + \alpha_3 RD_{it} + \alpha_4 TAR_{it} + \alpha_5 PRIV_{it} + \alpha_6 DEREG_{it} + \alpha_7 GREEN_{it} + \varepsilon t \tag{5}$$

To analyze how the GPI is determined in Southeast Asian countries, we will conduct panel data estimation using Eq. (5), utilizing data from 2000 to 2019 across nine nations: Cambodia, Indonesia, the Lao People's Democratic Republic (Lao PDR), Malaysia, the Republic of the Union of Myanmar (referred to as Myanmar), the Philippines, Singapore, Thailand, and Vietnam. The time-series data will be sourced from several databases, including the World Bank, the Purnomo Yusgiantoro Center (PYC) Data Center, the ASEAN Centre for Energy, the Private Participation in Infrastructure database, the

[1]The model and the empirical study in this chapter are based on Taghizadeh-Hesary *et al.* (2022).

Worldwide Governance Indicators report, B.P.'s 2020 Statistical Energy Review, and respective national energy authorities, such as the Federation of Malaysian Manufacturers and the Council for the Development of Cambodia.

In terms of the estimation strategy, given that the period (2000-2019) exceeds the number of cross-sections (nine countries), the suitable econometric method is the panel ARDL (Autoregressive Distributed Lag) approach, as proposed by Pesaran and Smith (1995). This approach includes the mean group (MG) estimator, the pooled mean group (PMG) estimator, and the dynamic fixed effects (DFE) estimator. The ARDL representation of Equation 5 is expressed in Eq. (6):

$$\Delta lnGPI_{i,t} = \sum_{j=1}^{p-1} \beta_j^i \Delta lnGPI_{i,t-j} + \sum_{j=0}^{q-1} \rho_j^i lnX_{i,t-j} + \delta^i [lnGPI_{i,t-1} - \{\theta_0^i + \theta_1^i X_{i,t-1}\}] + \mu_{it} \quad (6)$$

In this context, GPI represents the green power index. At the same time, X denotes the vector set of all explanatory variables, including macroeconomic indicators such as GDP, FDI, and R&D expenditure in the energy sector, the average electricity tariff, power sector privatization, and the governance index (GI). The coefficients β and ρ correspond to the short-run effects of the lagged GPI and the regressors, respectively, whereas θ and δ represent the long-run coefficients and the speed of adjustment to the long-run equilibrium. Lastly, i and t refer to a Southeast Asian country and the years 2000–2019, respectively.

Econometrically, the MG estimator calculates the coefficients for each country individually and averages them across the group, while the PMG estimator allows short-run coefficients and intercepts to vary across countries. In contrast, the DFE estimator assumes that both short- and long-run coefficients are constant across all countries in the panel. Following the findings of Lau *et al.* (2019) and Smolovic *et al.* (2020), who demonstrated that the PMG estimator outperforms the other two and is more robust to outliers and lag order, we apply the Hausman test to assess the significance of the PMG estimator compared to MG and DFE. Additionally, we perform tests for cross-sectional dependence, including the Breusch–Pagan LM (Lagrange Multiplier), Pesaran Scaled LM, and Pesaran CD tests, to examine the presence of cross-sectional dependency among the sample countries.

Next, panel unit root tests are applied to determine the stationarity of the variables. These tests include first-generation unit root tests, such as those proposed by Levin *et al.* (2002), Im *et al.* (2003), and Breitung (2001), as well as the cross-sectionally augmented IPS (Im, Pesaran, and Shin) test by Pesaran (2007). Let us suppose that these preliminary tests confirm the integration of variables. In that case, the long-run relationship between the series is examined using three cointegration tests: Pedroni (1999) and Kao (1999) as first-generation cointegration tests, and Westerlund (2007) as the second-generation test accounting for structural dynamics.

Once the series is confirmed to be cointegrated in the long run, the next step is to assess the signs and magnitudes of the long-run relationships between the variables. To achieve this, we employ a PMG estimation within the ARDL framework and the M.G. and

DFE estimators as a comparison to ensure the robustness and reliability of our empirical findings.

The conceptual framework of the methodological procedure can be shown in Fig. 1.

4. Empirical Results

4.1. *Applying the PCA technique*

In the first stage, we construct the multidimensional variables for the GPI and the GI using PCA. Before running the PCA, we ensure that the data suit this technique. The observed KMO statistics are 0.661 and 0.692, indicating that the sample is adequate for PCA. Applying PCA to the three variables—electrification ratio, the share of renewable energy in total power generation, and energy-related carbon emissions—reveals that only one component is significant (eigenvalue > 1), which we define as the GPI (Fig. 2(a)). Similarly, the GI is determined by the first PCA component with an eigenvalue greater than 1.

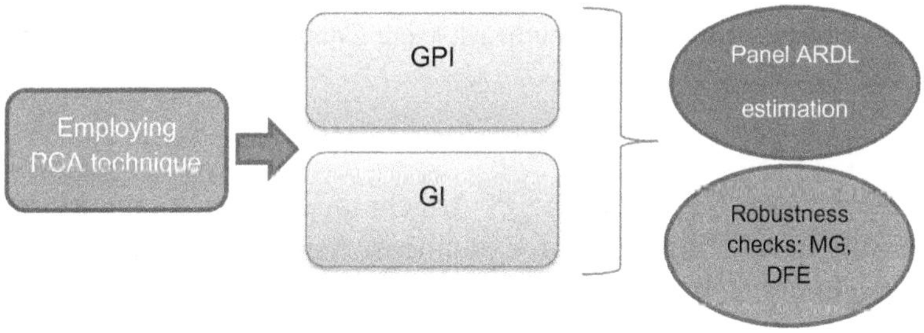

Figure 1. Conceptual framework of research.

Source: Taghizadeh-Hesary *et al.* (2022).

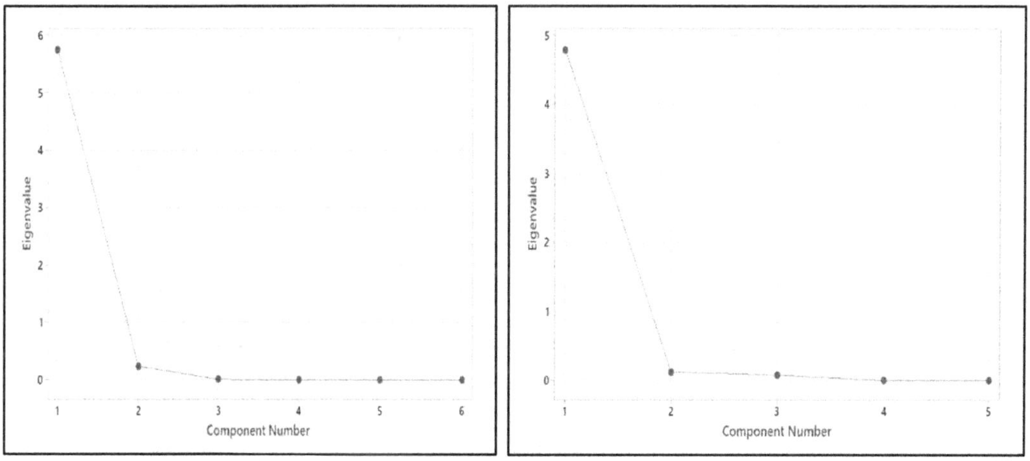

Figure 2. Screen plot, PCA technique: (a) GPI and (b) GI.

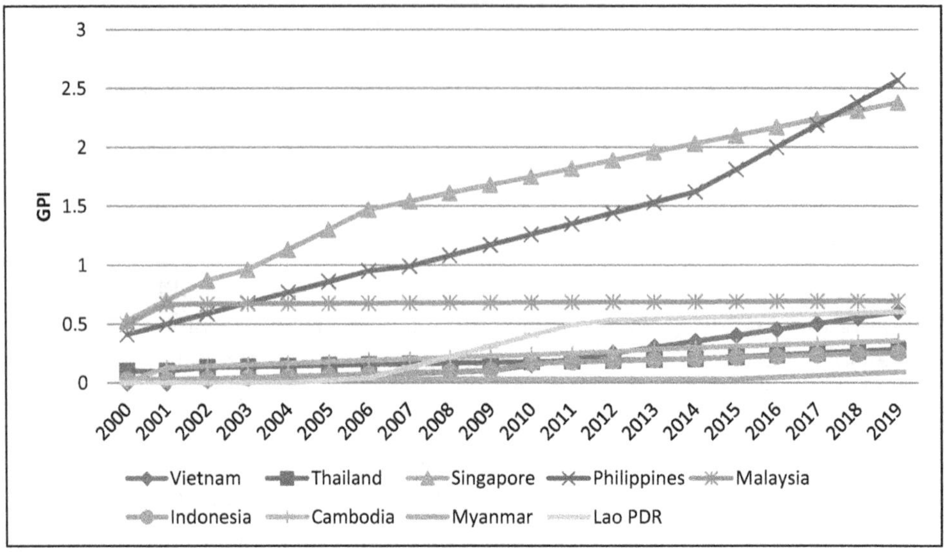

Figure 3. (Color available online) GPI, Southeast Asian Countries, 2000–2019.
Note: Lao PDR = the Lao People's Democratic Republic.

We can calculate the GPI using the PCA technique for each country in our sample. Figure 3 shows the trend of this index for Southeast Asia.

As illustrated in Fig. 3, the GPI has improved with steeper positive slopes for countries such as Singapore and the Philippines. Notably, in 2018, the GPI for the Philippines surpassed that of Singapore, highlighting the effectiveness of policies and legislation in driving a transition toward a greener economy. Another important observation is that GPI trends show distinct turning points after introducing key environmental plans or regulations in each country. Examples include Vietnam in 2011 and 2012, following the implementation of the Vietnam Climate Change Strategy in 2011 and the Vietnam National Green Growth Strategy in 2012; Thailand in 2015 with its Attractive Energy Development Plan; Singapore in 1999 with the Environmental Protection & Management Act; Indonesia in 2009 with Law No. 32 on the Management & Protection of the Environment; Cambodia with its Law on Environmental Protection & Natural Resource Management in 1996 and the National Policy on Green Growth in 2013; Myanmar in 2015 with its National Electrification Program; Lao PDR in 2012 with its Law on Environmental Protection; the Philippines with the Clean Air Act of 1999 and the Environmental Education Act of 2008; and Malaysia with the Environmental Quality Act of 1974, the 1989 Regulations, and the Efficient Management of Electrical Energy Regulations in 2008. The maturity of these regulations aimed at greening the economy over time has significantly driven higher GPI scores. Countries such as Singapore and the Philippines, which enacted relevant policies and legislation before 2000, exhibit higher GPI levels than other Southeast Asian economies.

The average GPIs of Southeast Asian countries are higher than those of India, where challenges such as electrification and the transition from coal to renewable energy sources

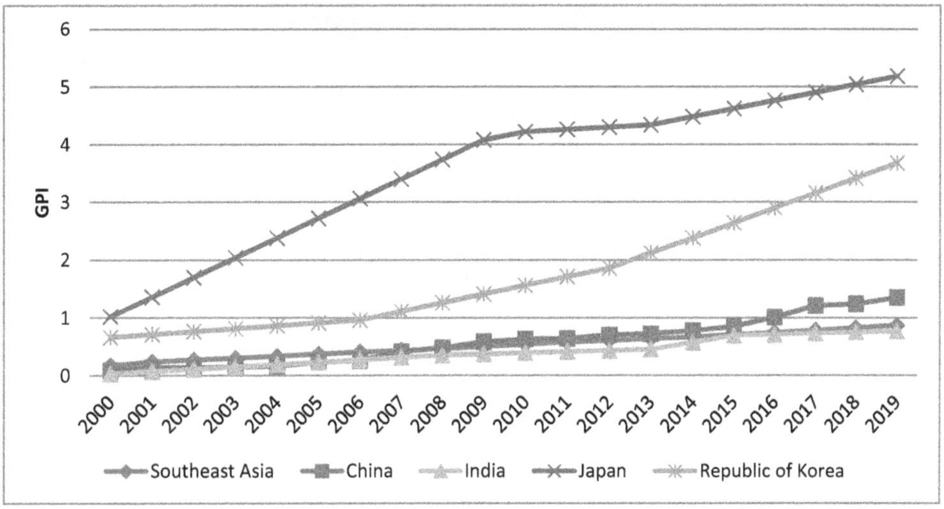

Figure 4. (Color available online) GPI, Southeast Asia, and other Asian countries, 2000–2019.

persist (Thomas *et al.*, 2020). However, Southeast Asia lags behind the GPI levels of China, Japan, and the Republic of Korea (Fig. 4). Despite some policy setbacks in China in 2019 (Lin and Purra, 2019), the country has made numerous successful strides toward greening its economy. These include implementing the Electric Power Law of the People's Republic of China in 1995, the Renewable Energy Law in 2005, Electricity Sector Reforms in 2015, and the 13th Five-Year Plan for Electricity (2016–2020).

4.2. *Running preliminary tests*

Preliminary tests must be conducted prior to performing empirical estimations. For the first test, the cross-sectional dependency among variables is explored through three tests: Breusch–Pagan LM, Pesaran Scaled LM, and Pesaran CD. The results are provided in Table 2. According to the probability values, we cannot accept the H0 (no cross-sectional dependency between countries).

Given the presence of cross-sectional dependency, it is essential to use second-generation panel unit root tests to assess the stationarity of the series. Consequently, we employ both first-generation panel unit root tests (Levin *et al.*, 2002; Breitung, 2001; Breitung and Das, 2005; Im *et al.*, 2003; and Fisher-ADF tests) and second-generation tests, such as the cross-sectionally augmented IPS test. The test results, shown in Table 3, indicate that all

Table 2. Results of cross-sectional dependency tests.

	Breush–Pagan LM	Pesaran Scaled LM	Pesaran CD
Cross-sectional stat.	20.443	30.103	1.803
P-value	0.0277*	0.000*	0.081**

Notes: *Significant levels at 5%.
**Significant levels at 1%.

Table 3. Results of panel unit root tests.

	First-Generation Panel Unit Root Test				Second-Generation Panel Unit Root Test
Variable	LLC	Breitung	IPS	Fisher-ADF	CIPS
GPI	–0.864	3.658	1.943	5.684	–1.493
D(GPI)	–6.740*	4.804**	–7.019*	65.593*	–2.768**
GDP	–0.792	3.485	1.800	3.447	–2.443
D(GDP)	–5.903*	–2.800*	–6.986*	63.855*	–2.815*
FDI	–1.015	2.285	0.204	9.855	–0.704
D(FDI)	–3.650*	–5.411**	–5.474**	50.185*	–2.954*
R&D	–0.617	6.985	3.011	3.940	–2.243
D(R&D)	–6.905**	–2.006**	–4.048*	36.594*	–2.911*
TAR	–0.416	3.327	1.803	9.118	–1.365
D(TAR)	–4.019*	4.500*	–7.044*	50.059*	–2.766*
PRIV	–0.1	2.343	1.803	5.473*	–2.400
D(PRIV)	–6.549*	–5.377*	–6.899*	67.522*	–2.816*
GI	–0.741	3.793	3.057	3.659	–2.150
D(GI)	–6.496*	5.019*	–4.053*	61.700**	–2.776*

Notes: *significant levels at 5%.
**significant levels at 1%.
PRIV = privatization, TAR = power tariff.

series become stationary after first differencing or are integrated at I(1), meaning they achieve stationarity at the first level of differences. This finding underscores the necessity of performing a panel cointegration test.

To investigate any long-run relationship among the model's variables, we conducted two-panel cointegration tests: the Pedroni (1997) and Westerlund (2007) tests, which have a null hypothesis of no cointegration. The Pedroni cointegration test is limited in accounting for structural breaks and cross-country correlations as a first-generation test. Therefore, this chapter also employs the Westerlund test, a second-generation method that accounts for structural dynamics, providing a more robust assessment.

Table 4 presents the results of the Pedroni cointegration test, which generates seven cointegration statistics—four-panel statistics and three-group-panel statistics—based on assumptions of homogeneity and heterogeneity. In all cases, the null hypothesis is the absence of cointegration. The results in Table 4 indicate that there is indeed cointegration among the series in our model, confirming a long-run relationship between the variables.

We also conducted the Kao cointegration test further to verify the reliability of the Pedroni cointegration test. As shown in Table 5, the null hypothesis of no cointegration among the series is firmly rejected. Consequently, we can conclude that the sustainable power markets and the other variables in our model exhibit a long-run relationship and move together over time.

Considering the probability of structural breaks over a time period, the Westerlund test—the second-generation panel cointegration test—is employed. The results in Table 6 depict a long-run cointegration between variables.

Table 4. Panel cointegration test results, Pedroni test.

Trend Assumption	Deterministic Intercept and Trend	No Deterministic Trend
Panel v-statistics	–0.254 (0.611)	–0.411 (0.670)
Panel-rho statistics	–1.900 (0.031)	–0.215 (0.438)
Panel PP-statistics	–3.776 (0.00)	–1.100 (0.151)
Panel ADF-statistics	–3.019 (0.00)	–1.584 (0.117)
Group rho-statistics	–0.708 (0.276)	0.880 (0.710)
Group PP-statistics	–3.476 (0.00)	–0.432 (0.375)
Group ADF-statistics	3.294 (0.00)	–2.500 (0.00)

Table 5. Panel cointegration test results, Kao test.

	t-stat.	P-value
ADF	–2.654	0.00

Table 6. Panel cointegration test results, Westerlund test.

Statistics	Value	Prob.	Robust Prob.
G_t	–4.694	0.00	0.00
G_a	–20.101	0.00	0.00
P_t	–7.868	0.00	0.00
P_a	–17.540	0.00	.000

4.3. *Estimation findings*

To investigate the signs and magnitudes of the coefficients, the PMG estimator, using the ARDL approach, is employed to assess the effects of various variables on the GPI, which serves as a proxy for the sustainable power market. The long- and short-run estimation results are presented in Tables 7 and 8, respectively.

In the context of the long-run sustainable power market, the results in Table 7 show that GDP has a positive and statistically significant impact, indicating that a 1% increase in the economic size of Southeast Asian countries could lead to an approximate 1.7% rise in the GPI. This positive effect is primarily attributed to the expansion of green project financing and the increased fiscal capacity of governments under favorable growth conditions, as supported by previous research, such as Saufi et al. (2016). Additionally, FDI and R&D expenditures exhibit positive effects, underscoring the importance of policies promoting investment and increasing the share of R&D in national budgets across Southeast Asia.

Interestingly, electricity tariffs negatively impact GPI, with a 1% rise in power prices potentially reducing GPI by around 0.5%. Furthermore, privatization and governance quality positively influence power market sustainability. A 1% increase in private sector

Table 7. PMG findings, long-run coefficients.

Independent Variable	Coefficient	t-stat.
Speed of adjustment	–0.188**	–3.60
GDP	1.703*	4.76
FDI	0.795**	3.94
R&D	0.800*	4.91
TAR	–0.231**	–3.830
PRIV	0.065*	5.131
GI	0.139*	4.819

Notes: *Significant levels at 5%.
**Significant levels at 1%.

Table 8. PMG findings, short-run coefficients.

Independent Variable	Coefficient	t-stat.
ΔGDP	0.048*	6.303
ΔFDI	0.313*	4.794
ΔR&D	0.011*	5.189
ΔTAR	–0.519**	–3.140
ΔPRIV	0.003*	6.103
ΔGI	0.261*	6.175

Notes: *Significant levels at 5%.
**Significant levels at 1%.

involvement in the power market could enhance sustainability by approximately 0.06%, while improved governance may raise sustainability by 0.13%. The long-run estimations highlight that economic growth and governance quality are two of the most significant factors driving power market sustainability in the Southeast Asian countries examined.

Regarding the short-run estimated coefficients in Table 8, the signs of the coefficients align with those found in the long-run relationship. Specifically, GDP, FDI, R&D, PRIV, and GIs all positively impact the GPI, while increases in electricity tariffs negatively affect power market sustainability. An intriguing observation is that while the signs of the coefficients remain consistent between the short and long runs, the magnitudes of the effects on power market sustainability are more pronounced in the long run. Moreover, in the short run, the influence of FDI and governance indicators appears more significant than the other variables. This suggests that while these factors are crucial in the short and long terms, their immediate impact on the sustainable power market is especially prominent.

The reason for the larger magnitudes of coefficients, in the long run, is that government policies and macroeconomic changes generally require time for implementation and maturation before their full effects are realized. In the short term, these initiatives may not immediately yield significant results. This observation of more substantial long-run effects aligns with the findings of Braid (2003) and Dressler (2016) but contrasts with Galinato and Galinato (2013), who observed more significant short-run impacts. In Southeast Asian power markets, scholars such as Holden *et al.* (2014) argue that achieving sustainability is a long-term process. Governments must introduce reforms and policies that will take time to deliver lasting results. Therefore, changes in macroeconomic variables, electricity tariffs, and governance have a more pronounced impact in the long run. This underscores the importance of developing a clear, strategic vision and long-term planning to achieve sustainable power markets.

4.4. *Robustness check*

To conduct a thorough robustness check and ensure the reliability of the estimated coefficients, we employ two additional estimators: the MG and DFE estimators. These are used to assess the sensitivity of the empirical results to alternative ARDL panel estimators. The results of these two estimators are presented in Table 9, allowing for a comparison with the primary findings and ensuring the robustness of the conclusions.

The results from the robustness check confirm that all the variables in our model maintain consistent signs as estimated through the PMG estimator. This supports the positive impacts of GDP, FDI, power market privatization, and governance on power market sustainability while confirming that an increase in electricity tariffs reduces sustainability in both the short and long runs. Additionally, estimations from both the MG and DFE approaches indicate that the long-term impacts of the variables on the sustainable power

Table 9. Robustness check.

	MG Estimator		DFE Estimator	
Long-run estimation	Coefficient	t-stat.	Coefficient	t-stat.
Speed of adjustment	–0.014**	–2.980	–0.131*	–5.492
GDP	0.672**	3.101	0.031**	2.850
FDI	0.026*	5.185	0.024*	4.157
R&D	0.043*	4.695	0.019*	3.804
TAR	–0.011**	–3.414	–0.002**	2.933
PRIV	0.013*	4.906	0.019*	5.094
GI	0.213*	7.594	0.025*	4.731
Short-run estimation				
ΔGDP	0.483*	5.193	0.029*	4.584
ΔFDI	0.258**	2.685	0.018*	5.696
ΔR&D	0.194*	4.937	0.014**	2.388
ΔTAR	–0.014**	–2.994	–0.000*	6.110
ΔPRIV	0.009*	5.685	0.015*	4.770
ΔGI	0.118*	5.145	0.017**	3.19

Notes: *significant levels at 5%.
**significant levels at 1%.

market are larger than their short-term effects, aligning with our earlier findings from the PMG estimation. This consistency across different estimators further strengthens the reliability of our results.

5. Conclusions and Policy Implications

This research addresses the pressing issue of power market reform in Southeast Asia, where countries strive for more competitive operations, sustainability, and increased private sector participation. We compiled annual data for various variables, classified into macroeconomic indicators, general governance, power market governance, and power prices, for the period 2000–2019 across the region. The analysis was conducted using the ARDL panel technique, employing the PMG estimator and two additional estimators, MG and DFE, for robustness checks. Notably, this study proposes, for the first time, a multidimensional GPI as a proxy for a sustainable power market. This index was constructed using the PCA technique based on three key variables: electrification ratio, the share of renewable energy in total power generation, and energy-related carbon emissions. Additionally, we introduced a general GI, created by combining three governance variables—political stability, regulatory quality, and government effectiveness—through PCA.

The findings of this study, which introduced the GPI, suggest that Southeast Asian governments can enhance power market sustainability by focusing on critical factors such as economic growth, improved FDI inflows, increased R&D budgets, better governance quality, and power market privatization. These variables positively influence sustainability in the short and long runs, while increases in electricity prices may slow the progress toward sustainability over both time horizons. Additionally, the results show that the impacts of these variables are more substantial in the long run, emphasizing the importance of governments developing strategic plans and roadmaps with clear visions and missions to support long-term sustainability in the power market.

The findings of this research carry policy implications not only for Southeast Asian countries but also for other developing nations globally. These significant policy recommendations can assist governments in implementing green energy policies that align with universal electrification goals. The critical practical policy implications are as follows:

1. Southeast Asian countries need to adapt their economic strategies in response to the challenges posed by the COVID-19 pandemic to ensure the sustainability of their power markets. Governments can focus on building more resilient and sustainable economies by adopting innovative approaches like the "build back better" strategy proposed by Moore and Collins (2021). Integrating sustainability into recovery efforts, such as promoting eco-tourism and reducing the carbon footprint of industries, will enable the region to stimulate economic growth while working toward long-term power market sustainability. The tourism sector, a vital part of Southeast Asia's economy, can play a significant role in this green recovery if revitalized through sustainable practices, as Scarlett (2021) highlighted.

2. The role of FDI is crucial in driving sustainability in Southeast Asia's power markets. To attract more foreign capital, governments must implement regulatory reforms that facilitate and simplify FDI. Strengthening bilateral investment agreements and partnerships with other economic powers across Asia and beyond can also promote the flow of capital needed for renewable energy projects. Expanding Special Economic Zones (SEZs) is another effective strategy, as these zones provide attractive conditions for investors, such as tax incentives and streamlined regulations. Previous studies by Wahyuni *et al.* (2013) and Teangsompong and Sirisunhirun (2018) have demonstrated the importance of SEZs in boosting economic growth, making their expansion a key tool for attracting investment in green energy.
3. Governments should consider implementing a progressive electricity tariff classification (ETC) system to address rising electricity prices, which can hinder power market sustainability. This system would allow targeted subsidies to support low-income households, ensuring affordability while promoting efficient energy use. Malaysia's successful implementation of ETC, managed by Tenaga Nasional Berhad, especially during the COVID-19 pandemic, can serve as a model for other nations. Moreover, Malaysia's introduction of the green electricity tariff (GBT) in December 2021, which encourages the use of renewable electricity, provides an example of how to promote green energy adoption across various sectors. Southeast Asian countries could benefit from adopting similar approaches tailored to their specific economic contexts.
4. Another priority should be accelerating the privatization and liberalization of power markets. Governments need to facilitate greater private sector participation by offering financial incentives, such as tax exemptions and temporary subsidies, to stimulate investments in green energy projects. Providing private investors more autonomy and ensuring transparent, predictable regulatory environments will encourage investment in renewable energy infrastructure. Creating an open, competitive power market will attract domestic and international investors, driving innovation and the development of sustainable energy solutions.
5. The post-pandemic recovery period allows Southeast Asian countries to pursue green growth strategies that align with long-term sustainability goals. Governments should integrate sustainable electricity generation into their recovery plans, focusing on expanding renewable energy sources such as solar, wind, and hydropower. This transition will not only support environmental objectives, including carbon emission reduction and climate change mitigation, but also contribute to the long-term stability of the region's energy supply. Power market sustainability can be a central pillar of green recovery strategies, helping economies emerge more substantially and more resilient to future disruptions.
6. Enhanced regional collaboration and policy alignment are essential for successfully transitioning to sustainable power markets in Southeast Asia. Given the interconnected nature of energy markets, governments should foster greater cooperation, leading to more effective cross-border energy projects, such as shared renewable energy grids and joint investments in green technologies. Developing a unified regional framework for energy policy, where regulatory standards, investment incentives, and

environmental goals are aligned, can strengthen energy security and accelerate the transition to a sustainable, resilient energy system across the region.

Despite the new insights from this research on power market sustainability in Southeast Asia, several gaps and areas warrant further investigation. For instance, assessing the impact of various variables on the Southeast Asian power market in the post-COVID era remains a subject of debate. Future research should also consider exploring the effects of additional factors, such as bilateral exchange rates, electricity price–cost margins, cross-subsidy levels, and income inequality, on power market sustainability in Southeast Asia. These areas of study could provide a more comprehensive understanding of the dynamics influencing sustainable energy transitions in the region.

References

Akrami, A, M Doostizadeh and F Aminifar (2019). Power system flexibility: An overview of emergence to evolution. *Journal of Modern Power Systems and Clean Energy*, 7, 987–1007.

Anh Tu, C and E Rasoulinezhad (2021). Energy efficiency financing and the role of green bond: Policies for a post-Covid period. *China Finance Review International*, ahead-of-print, https://doi.org/10.1108/CFRI-03-2021-0052.

Balza, L, R Jimenez and J Mercado (2013). Privatisation, institutional reform, and performance in the Latin American electricity sector. IDB Technical Note, TN-599, https://publications.iadb.org/publications/english/document/Privatisation-Institutional-Reform-and-Performance-in-the-Latin-American-Electricity-Sector.pdf.

Braid, R (2003). A three-input model of the spatial effects of a central-city wage tax. *Journal of Urban Economics*, 54(1), 89–109.

Breitung, J (2001). The local power of some unit root tests for panel data. *Nonstationary Panels, Panel Cointegration, and Dynamic Panels*, Emerald Group Publishing Limited, 161–177.

Cieplinski, A, S D'Alessandro and F Marghella (2021). Assessing the renewable energy policy paradox: A scenario analysis for the Italian electricity market. *Renewable and Sustainable Energy Reviews*, 142, 110838, https://doi.org/10.1016/j.rser.2021.110838.

CSIS (2023). Clean energy and decarbonization in Southeast Asia: Overview, obstacles, and opportunities. Center for Strategic and International Studies, https://www.csis.org/analysis/clean-energy-and-decarbonization-southeast-asia-overview-obstacles-and-opportunities.

Defeuilley, C (2019). Energy transition and the future(s) of the electricity sector. *Utilities Policy*, 57, 97–105.

Delina, L (2021). Promises and pitfalls of China-Southeast Asia energy connectivity. *Energy Strategy Reviews*, 33, 1–14, https://doi.org/10.1016/j.esr.2020.100574.

Dodd, T, A Rai, and K Caught (2020). Electricity markets in flux: The importance of a just transition. *The Electricity Journal*, 33(9), 1–6, https://doi.org/10.1016/j.tej.2020.106835.

Dressler, S (2016). A long-run, short-run, and politico-economic analysis of the welfare costs of inflation. *Journal of Macroeconomics*, 47(B), 255–269.

Dussan, M (1996). Electric power sector reform in Latin America and the Caribbean. IDB Working Paper Series, IFM-104, https://publications.iadb.org/publications/english/document/Electric-Power-Sector-Reform-in-Latin-America-and-the-Caribbean.pdf.

Foster, V and A Rana (2020). *Rethinking Power Sector Reform in the Developing World.* International Bank for Reconstruction and Development / The World Bank.

Galinator, G and S Galinator (2013). The short-run and long-run effects of corruption control and political stability on forest cover. *Ecological Economics*, 89, 153–161.

Guo, H, M Davidson, Q Chen, D Zhang, N Jiang, Q Xia, C Kang, and X Zhang (2020). Power market reform in China: Motivations, progress, and recommendations. *Energy Policy*, 145, 1–13, https://doi.org/10.1016/j.enpol.2020.111717.

Hao, W, Q Abbas, I Ahmad, M Alharthi, I Hanif and F Taghizadeh-Hesary (2021). Institutional efficiency and utility reform performance: An evidence from electricity performance in South & East Asia. *Economic Analysis and Policy*, 72, 549–561, https://doi.org/10.1016/j.eap.2021.09.013.

Holden, E, K Linnerud and D Banister (2014). Sustainable development: Our common future revisited. *Global Environmental Change*, 26, 130–139.

IEA (2022). *Southeast Asia Energy Outlook 2022*, International Energy Agency, https://iea.blob.core.windows.net/assets/e5d9b7ff-559b-4dc3-8faa-42381f80ce2e/SoutheastAsiaEnergyOutlook2022.pdf.

IEA (2024). *World Energy Investment 2024*. IEA, Paris, https://www.iea.org/reports/world-energy-investment-2024.

International Energy Agency (2019). *Southeast Asia Energy Outlook 2019: Comprehensive Review of a Region on the Rise*. Paris: IEA Publications.

International Energy Agency (2020). *2020 Electricity Market Report–December 2020*, https://www.iea.org/reports/electricity-market-report-december-2020/2020-regional-focus-southeast-asia.

Im, KS, M Pesaran and Y Shin (2003). Testing for unit roots in heterogeneous panels. *Journal of Econometrics*, 115, 53–74.

IRENA (2022). *Renewable Power Generation Costs in 2021*, https://www.irena.org/-/media/Files/IRENA/Agency/Publication/2022/Jul/IRENA_Power_Generation_Costs_2021.pdf.

IRENA (2019). *Innovation Landscape Brief: Time-of-Use Tariffs*, https://www.irena.org/-/media/Files/IRENA/Agency/Publication/2019/Feb/IRENA_Innovation_ToU_tariffs_2019.pdf.

Izaguirre, AK (1998). Private participation in the electricity sector—recent trends. Washington, D.C.: The World Bank, https://documents1.worldbank.org/curated/pt/769261468780006587/pdf/18714-Replacement-file-154IZAGU.pdf.

Jamasb, T, R Mota, D Newbery and M Pollitt (2004). Electricity sector reform in developing countries: A survey of empirical evidence on determinants and performance. Cambridge Working Papers in Economics, Cambridge: University of Cambridge.

Joskow, PL (2008). Lessons learned from electricity market liberalization. *The Energy Journal*, 29(Special Issue 2), 9–42, https://doi.org/10.5547/ISSN0195-6574-EJ-Vol29-NoSI2-3.

Kao, C (1999). Spurios regression and residual-based tests for cointegration in panel data. *Journal of Econometrics*, 90, 1–44.

Kundu, G and B Mishra (2011). Impact of reform and privatisation on consumers: A case study of power sector reform in Orissa, India. *Energy Policy*, 39(6), 3537–3549.

Lau, L, C Ng, S Cheah and C Choong (2019). Chapter 9: Panel data analysis (stationarity, cointegration and causality). In B Ozan and I Ozturk (eds), *Environmental Kuznets Curve*, 101–13, Turkey: Academic Press, https://doi.org/10.1016/C2018-0-00657-X.

Levin A, C Lin and C Chu (2002). Unit root tests in panel data: Asymptotic and finite-sample properties. *Journal of Econometrics*, 108, 1–24.

Lin, K and M Purra (2019). Transforming China's electricity sector: Politics of institutional change and regulation. 124, 401–410.

Mier, M and C Weissbart (2020). Power markets in transition: Decarbonization, energy efficiency, and short-term demand response. *Energy Economics*, 86, 1–13, https://doi.org/10.1016/j.eneco.2019.104644.

Mohsin M, I Hanif, F Taghizadeh-Hesary, Q Abbas and W Iqbal (2021). Nexus between energy efficiency and electricity reforms: A DEA-based way forward for clean power development. *Energy Policy*, 149, 112052, https://doi.org/10.1016/j.enpol.2020.112052.

Moore, H and H Collins (2021). Rebuilding the post-Covid-19 economy through an industrial strategy that secures livelihoods. *Social Sciences & Humanities Open*, 3(1), 1–6, https://doi.org/10.1016/j.ssaho.2021.100113.

Nasr Esfahani, A, N Moghaddam, A Maleki and A Nazemi (2021). The knowledge map of energy security. *Energy Reports*, 7, 3570–3589.

Nelson, J (2020). Australia's national electricity market: Financing the transition. *The Electricity Journal*, 33(9), 1–6, https://doi.org/10.1016/j.tej.2020.106834.

Newbery, D (1999). *Privatization, Restructuring, and Regulation of Network Utilities*. Cambridge: MIT Press.

Norouzi, N, G Rubens, P Enevoldsen and AB Forough (2020). The impact of COVID-19 on the electricity sector in Spain: An econometric approach based on prices. *International Journal of Energy Research*, 45(4), 6320–6332.

Pedroni, P (1999). Critical values for cointegration tests in heterogeneous panels with multiple regressors. *Oxford Bulletin of Economics and Statistics*, 61, 653–670.

Pesaran, MH (2007). A simple panel unit root test in the presence of cross-section dependence. *Journal of Applied Econometrics*, 22, 265–312.

Pesaran, MH and R Smith (1995). Estimating long-run relationships from dynamic heterogeneous panels. *Journal of Econometrics*, 68, 79–113.

Pineau, P (2002). Electricity sector reform in Cameroon: Is privatisation the solution? *Energy Policy*, 30(11–12), 999–1012.

Pollitt, M (2019). The European single market in electricity: An economic assessment. *Review of Industrial Organization*, 55, 63–87.

Poudineh, R, A Sen and B Fattouh (2020). An integrated approach to electricity sector reforms in the resource-rich economies of the MENA. *Energy Policy*, 138, 111236, https://doi.org/10.1016/j.enpol.2019.111236.

Sarangi, GK, A Mishra, Y Chang and F Taghizadeh-Hesary (2019). Indian electricity sector, energy security and sustainability: An empirical assessment. *Energy Policy*, 135(110964), https://doi.org/10.1016/j.enpol.2019.110964.

Saufi, N, S Daud and H Hassan (2016). Green growth and corporate sustainability performance. *Procedia Economics and Finance*, 35, 374–78.

Scarlett, H (2021). Tourism recovery and the economic impact: A panel assessment. *Research in Globalization*, 3, 1–7, https://doi.org/10.1016/j.resglo.2021.100044.

Senerdem, E and K Akkemik (2020). Evaluation of the reform in the Turkish electricity sector: A CGE analysis. *International Journal of Economic Policy Studies*, 14, 389–419.

Sharma, D (2005). Electricity reforms in the ASEAN: A panoramic discourse. *Economic and Political Weekly*, 40(50), 5318–5326.

Sirin, S and F Erdogen (2013). R&D expenditures in liberalisation of electricity markets: The case of Turkey. *Renewable and Sustainable Energy Reviews*, 24, 491–498.

Smolovic, J, M Muhadinovic, M Radonjic and J Duraskovic (2020). How does renewable energy consumption affect economic growth in the traditional and new member states of the European Union? *Energy Reports*, 6(6), 505–513.

Sorknas, P, H Lund, I Skov, S Sjorup, K Skytte, P Morthorst and F Fausto (2020). Smart energy markets- future electricity, gas, and heating markets. *Renewable and Sustainable Energy Reviews*, 119, 109655, https://doi.org/10.1016/j.rser.2019.109655.

Taghizadeh-Hesary, F and N Yoshino (2019). The way to induce private participation in green finance and investment. *Finance Research Letters*, 31, 98–103, https://doi.org/10.1016/j.frl.2019.04.016.

Taghizadeh-Hesary, F, N Yoshino, E Rasoulinezhad and C Rimaud (2021). Power purchase agreements with incremental tariffs in local currency: An innovative green finance tool. *Global Finance Journal*, 50, 100666, https://doi.org/10.1016/j.gfj.2021.100666.

Taghizadeh-Hesary, F, E Rasoulinezhad and H Phoumin (2022). Ways to achieve universal access to sustainable electricity in Southeast Asia. *Economic Change and Restructuring*, 55, 2031–2050, https://doi.org/10.1007/s10644-022-09386-4.

Teangsompong, T and S Sirisunhirun (2018). Multi-level structural equation modeling for city development based on the expectations of the local population in a special border economic zone in western Thailand. *Kasetsart Journal of Social Sciences*, 39(3), 534–541.

Thomas, D, S Harish, R Kennedy and J. Urpelainen (2020). The effects of rural electrification in India: An instrumental variable approach at the household level. *Journal of Development Economics*, 146, 1–10, https://doi.org/10.1016/j.jdeveco.2020.102520.

Tsao, Y, T Vu and J Lu (2021). Pricing, capacity and financing policies for investment of renewable energy generations. *Applied Energy*, 303, 117664, https://doi.org/10.1016/j.apenergy.2021.117664.

Tsay, I and P Chen (2019). A dual market structure design for the reform of an independent power grid system—the case of Taiwan. *Energy Reports*, 5, 1603–1615.

Tran, QH (2021). The impact of green finance, economic growth and energy usage on CO_2 emission in Vietnam – a multivariate time series analysis. *China Finance Review International*, ahead-of-print, https://doi.org/10.1108/CFRI-03-2021-0049.

Urpelainen, J and J Yang (2019). Global patterns of power sector reform, 1982–2013. *Energy Strategy Reviews*, 23, 152–162.

Weatherby, C (2020). Renewable energy in Southeast Asia. NBER Working Paper No.89, https://www.nbr.org/publication/renewable-energy-in-southeast-asia/.

Westerlund, J (2007). Testing for error correction in panel data. *Oxford Bulletin of Economics and Statistics*, 69, 709–748.

Xuegong, S, G Liyan and Z Zhen (2013). Market entry barriers for foreign direct investment and private investors: Lessons from China's electricity market. *Energy Strategy Reviews*, 2(2), 169–175.

Yin, J, Q Yan, K Lei, T Balezentis and D Streimikiene (2019). Economic and efficiency analysis of China electricity market reform using computable general equilibrium model. *Sustainability*, 11, 350, https://www.mdpi.com/2071-1050/11/2/350.

Wahyuni, S, E Astuti and K Utari (2013). Critical outlook at special economic zone in Asia: A comparison between Indonesia, Malaysia, Thailand, and China. *Journal of Indonesian Economy and Business*, 28(3), 336–346.

Wang, F, H Yin and S Li (2010). China's renewable energy policy: Commitments and challenges. *Energy Policy*, 38(4), 1872–1878.

Zheng, W (2021). Effects of China's market-oriented economic reform, FDI inflows on electricity intensity. *Energy*, 220, 1–12, https://doi.org/10.1016/j.energy.2021.119934.

Zsiborács, H, N Baranyai, L Zentkó, A Mórocz, I Pócs, K Máté and G Pintér (2020). Electricity market challenges of photovoltaic and energy storage technologies in the European Union: Regulatory challenges and responses. *Applied Sciences*, 10(4), 1–26, https://www.mdpi.com/2076-3417/10/4/1472.

https://doi.org/10.1142/9789819812608_0002

Chapter 2

Energy Security and Growth: Linking Energy Intensity with Capital Efficiency in South Asia

SAKIB BIN AMIN[*,§], FARHAD TAGHIZADEH-HESARY[†,¶], FOQORUDDIN AL KABIR[*,‖], FARHAN KHAN[*,**], and LILU VANDERCAMME[‡,††]

[*]*North South University, Bangladesh*
[†]*TOKAI Research Institute for Environment and Sustainability (TRIES), Tokai University, Japan*
[‡]*Keio University, Japan*
[§]*sakib.amin@northsouth.edu*
[¶]*farhad@tsc.u-tokai.ac.jp*
[‖]*foqoruddin.al@northsouth.edu*
[**]*farhan.khan008@northsouth.edu*
[††]*liluvandercamme@keio.jp*

Energy security, energy transition, and economic growth are interconnected components of sustainable development. This chapter empirically analyzes the relationship between energy intensity (EI) and capital efficiency across varying income groups, measured through the incremental capital–output ratio (ICOR). Utilizing a comprehensive dataset covering South Asian lower- and middle-income, and high-income countries (HICs) from 1990 to 2018, this study explores the differential impacts of energy transition policies on economic growth and energy efficiency (EE). The analysis reveals significant disparities in how ICOR affects EI, with higher technical inefficiencies observed in lower-income nations, resulting in greater EI. In contrast, HICs demonstrate a more efficient use of capital, leading to lower EI. These findings underscore the importance of optimizing capital utilization in developing economies to facilitate energy transitions, reduce energy inefficiencies, and enhance economic resilience. The study offers targeted policy recommendations to promote energy security through improved EE, accelerated technological adoption, and strategic energy transitions, ultimately contributing to sustainable economic growth and development. These insights are particularly relevant for policymakers in developing nations, where balancing economic growth and EE remains critical for achieving long-term sustainability goals.

Keywords: ICOR, EI, causality, elasticity, sustainability.

1. Introduction

Energy plays a fundamental role in driving economic development and is often called the lifeblood of any economy (Batra, 2023). As a critical factor of production, energy powers modern economies and is heavily utilized in household activities, particularly in durable goods (Zheng *et al.*, 2024). Despite its importance, the significance of energy in economic activities was only fully acknowledged following the global oil price shocks of the 1970s. Since then, energy security has become a central focus in contemporary research (Kraft and Kraft, 1978; Munir, 2020; Amin *et al.*, 2020; Ozturk and Acaravci, 2020). For instance, the World Bank (2000) asserts that access to a primary energy level is essential for economies at subsistence levels of development. Likewise, Stošić-Mihajlović and Trajković (2018) and Sanguino *et al.* (2020) highlight the crucial role of energy in economic growth. Therefore, energy consumption and access are vital components of modern economies.

Given energy's critical role, policymakers closely monitor various energy sector indicators when formulating and implementing energy policies, recognizing the sector's influence on economic performance and environmental sustainability. EI is a critical indicator that allows policymakers to assess and compare countries' EE, capital usage, technical efficiency, and environmental impacts (Amin *et al.*, 2023). Studies have shown that energy-intensive nations tend to produce higher levels of CO_2 emissions (Wang *et al.*, 2024). Consequently, identifying the factors that drive EI at sectoral and national levels is crucial for effective policymaking (Chu and Le, 2022).

The existing literature highlights the multifaceted effects of energy on the economy. The primary focus is the relationship between EI and economic development, which is explained by two main hypotheses (Deichmann *et al.*, 2018). The first hypothesis suggests that EI rises in the early stages of development and declines as economies advance (Rajbhandari and Zhang, 2018; Agovino *et al.*, 2019). The second hypothesis posits that economic development has a negative impact on EI, with economic progress enabling the adoption of more efficient production techniques and technological advancements, thereby reducing EI.

Another line of research explores how distortions in energy markets affect the broader economy. One subcategory examines the impact of these distortions on the aggregate economy, focusing on market structure and price rigidities (Zhu *et al.*, 2024; She, 2023). A second subcategory suggests that technical factors and energy prices are more reliable indicators of market responses to energy sector distortions than market structure alone (Pindyck and Rotemberg, 1983; Atkeson and Kehoe, 1999; Diaz *et al.*, 2004; Diaz and Puch, 2017). In this context, energy and capital are considered complementary or less substitutable. Both are closely tied to technology in producing goods, with energy playing a critical role in maximizing capital efficiency through advanced technologies (Jahanger *et al.*, 2023).

Furthermore, Sun *et al.* (2021) argue that energy prices and other external factors, such as technology and knowledge, influence returns on capital investments. Building on this perspective, the ICOR is recognized as a critical metric for evaluating EI or EE, as it reflects how effectively capital is utilized as firms gradually improve their technical efficiency (GED, 2019).

The originality of this study lies in two key aspects. First, it takes a unique approach by investigating the relationship between EI and ICOR, which has yet to be addressed in energy research. Second, the study employs cross-sectionally augmented robust panel methodologies to compare the EI–ICOR relationship across five South Asian countries (SAC), 34 lower- and middle-income countries (LMIC), and 52 HIC. The analysis includes an ordinary least squares (OLS) regression using cross-sectional (CS) data from 129 countries over six intervals (1990, 1995, 2000, 2005, 2010, and 2015). This research diverges from previous studies by explicitly modeling EI in relation to ICOR and other relevant variables. Moreover, it uniquely demonstrates how technical factors captured through ICOR can influence the behavior of EI, setting it apart from earlier works.

The remainder of this chapter is structured as follows: Section 2 offers a brief review of the relevant literature, Section 3 outlines the model, methodology, and data used in the analysis, Section 4 presents the study's results, and Section 5 provides the concluding remarks.

2. Literature Review

The nexus between energy security, energy transition, and economic growth is becoming more critical as global economies face increasing pressure to balance energy needs with sustainability goals. For many developing economies, mainly those reliant on fossil fuels, transitioning to cleaner energy sources is essential to meet growing energy demands while reducing carbon emissions (Amin *et al.*, 2021). This literature review addresses critical aspects such as EI, capital efficiency, technological innovations, governance, financial markets, and the social dimensions of energy transitions while grounding these discussions in empirical and theoretical frameworks.

2.1. *EI, capital efficiency, and economic growth*

EI, the amount of energy consumed per unit of gross domestic product (GDP), is a fundamental measure of how efficiently an economy uses energy (Rudenko and Tanasov, 2022). The concept is rooted in the Environmental Kuznets Curve (EKC) hypothesis, which suggests that environmental degradation, including energy use, initially increases with economic growth but declines as economies mature and adopt more efficient technologies (Deichmann *et al.*, 2018). This pattern is especially evident in HICs, where technological advancements have decoupled energy use from economic growth (Voigt *et al.*, 2014).

One crucial factor influencing EI is capital efficiency, often measured through the ICOR, which reflects the amount of capital needed to produce additional economic output. A lower ICOR indicates more efficient use of capital, which correlates with reduced energy consumption. Taguchi and Lowhachai (2014) showed that in Asian economies, higher capital efficiency is linked to lower EI. Similarly, Dong *et al.* (2022) identified that inefficiencies in capital deployment contribute to higher EI in LMICs, emphasizing the need for targeted investments in energy-efficient technologies.

From a theoretical perspective, the Harrod–Domar model underpins much of the analysis on ICOR, suggesting that the relationship between capital utilization and economic growth is central to understanding how economies can optimize energy use. However, while developed countries have seen improvements in EE and reduced ICOR, many LMICs still struggle with capital inefficiencies, limiting their ability to achieve sustainable economic growth.

2.2. *Renewable energy, technological innovation, and policy effectiveness*

The transition to renewable energy is critical to reducing global reliance on fossil fuels and ensuring long-term energy security. Renewable energy sources (RES), such as solar, wind, and hydropower, can reduce carbon emissions and lower EI by diversifying the energy mix. The global push toward renewable energy was accelerated by the 2022 Russia–Ukraine conflict, which exposed vulnerabilities in fossil fuel-dependent economies, particularly in Europe. Ateed (2024) documented how this geopolitical event prompted nations to hasten their renewable energy transitions to mitigate energy insecurity.

In HICs, robust policy frameworks like the European Green Deal have supported renewable energy adoption, which sets ambitious targets for reducing carbon emissions and expanding renewable energy infrastructure. Pehlivanoglu *et al.* (2021) found that investments in renewable energy reduce EI and contribute to long-term economic growth. However, the success of these policies is highly context-dependent. For instance, in LMICs, where financial resources and infrastructure are limited, the transition to renewable energy faces significant barriers (Isah *et al.*, 2023).

Technological innovations, such as green hydrogen, energy storage systems, and smart grids, are pivotal in enabling the large-scale deployment of renewable energy. Oyekale *et al.* (2020) argue that these technologies can help overcome the challenges of integrating renewable energy into existing grids, particularly in regions where energy infrastructure is underdeveloped. However, the effectiveness of these policies varies greatly depending on a country's governance capacity, institutional frameworks, and financial resources. This disparity underscores the need for targeted, context-specific policy interventions to maximize the benefits of renewable energy transitions globally.

2.3. *EE, the rebound effect, and quantitative data*

Improving EE is one of the most cost-effective strategies for reducing EI and emissions. EE refers to using less energy to perform the same task or produce the same output, and it has been a cornerstone of energy policies globally. However, the rebound effect complicates the outcomes of efficiency improvements. The rebound effect occurs when gains in EE lead to increased energy consumption in other areas, offsetting the overall reduction in energy use (Wei *et al.*, 2019).

To mitigate this effect, Creutzig *et al.* (2024) suggest integrating EE policies with broader sustainability initiatives, such as carbon pricing and demand-side management. These policies help ensure that energy savings from efficiency improvements are not eroded by increased consumption elsewhere. In addition, Gielen *et al.* (2023) highlight how digital energy management systems can optimize real-time energy use, further reducing operational inefficiencies.

From a quantitative perspective, the growing body of meta-analyses and systematic reviews provides valuable empirical insights into the impact of EE policies (Wang *et al.*, 2023). For instance, studies show that countries with stricter EE standards for buildings, transportation, and industrial equipment have substantially reduced their overall EI

(Pehlivanoglu *et al.*, 2021). Integrating such quantitative data strengthens the case for the widespread adoption of EE measures across various sectors.

2.4. *Governance structures, financial markets, and multilateral cooperation*

Effective governance structures are essential for implementing successful energy transitions. Governance refers to the systems and processes for implementing decisions and policies (Kjaer, 2023). In many developing economies, weak governance structures and institutional fragmentation slow the adoption of renewable energy and energy-efficient technologies (Khan *et al.*, 2024). Tani (2023) emphasizes that countries with centralized governance, clear policy frameworks, and solid regulatory enforcement, such as the European Union, have made significant progress in energy transitions.

Green finance has emerged as a critical enabler of energy transitions, mainly through instruments such as green bonds, carbon credits, and sustainability-linked loans. Alharbi *et al.* (2023) documented how the expansion of green finance in Europe has accelerated the deployment of renewable energy projects, driving reductions in EI. In contrast, many LMICs need financing gaps that hinder their ability to scale up renewable energy investments. Mühlich and Zucker-Marques (2023) argue that international financial institutions like the World Bank and the International Monetary Fund (IMF) must expand their support for green finance initiatives in developing countries to bridge these gaps.

Multilateral institutions, including the United Nations and the International Energy Agency (IEA), also play a pivotal role in shaping global energy policies (Tobni, 2024). Through frameworks such as the Paris Agreement, countries are encouraged to commit to reducing their carbon emissions and transitioning to sustainable energy systems. However, the effectiveness of these multilateral efforts depends on domestic political will and institutional capacity, particularly in LMICs where governance structures may be less robust.

2.5. *Social equity, energy poverty, and climate resilience*

A just and equitable energy transition must prioritize addressing energy poverty and ensuring that the benefits of energy transitions are distributed fairly across society. Energy poverty refers to the lack of access to modern and affordable energy services, disproportionately affecting rural and underserved populations in LMICs. Nsafon *et al.* (2023) highlight the need for inclusive energy policies that expand access to clean energy technologies, particularly in areas that lack grid connectivity. Otsuka and Goto (2017) also stress that energy policies must address regional disparities to avoid exacerbating social inequality during energy transitions.

The concept of a just transition is gaining importance in academic and policy discussions. It emphasizes that energy transitions should address environmental and economic concerns and prioritize social equity. Boone *et al.* (2023) argue that retraining and reskilling workers in fossil-fuel-dependent sectors and creating green jobs is essential for ensuring that the shift to renewable energy does not disproportionately harm certain groups.

Finally, the role of climate resilience in energy infrastructure is becoming more critical as the effects of climate change intensify. Perera and Hong (2023) discuss how extreme weather events, such as floods, droughts, and hurricanes, increasingly disrupt energy systems, particularly in vulnerable regions. Investing in climate-resilient infrastructure ensures that energy systems can withstand these challenges while providing reliable energy services.

3. Data, Model, and Methodology

3.1. *Data*

Through a comprehensive approach, this research explores the connections between EI, the ICOR, and GDP. It intends to empirically assess the long-term relationships between these variables and provide policy recommendations for the future. The data were sourced from the 2020 World Development Indicators (WDI) edition (Amin *et al.*, 2022).[1]

3.2. *Model selection*

The following theoretical identity equation can indicate *ICOR*[2]:

$$ICOR = \frac{I}{\Delta Y} = \frac{\Delta K + \mu^* K}{\Delta Y} = \frac{\Delta K}{\Delta Y} + \frac{\mu^* K}{\Delta Y} \tag{1}$$

Economic growth can be defined as

$$g = \frac{\Delta Y}{Y} \tag{2}$$

From Eq. (2), $DY = gY$. Therefore, we can rewrite Eq. (1) as

$$\frac{\Delta K}{\Delta Y} + \frac{\mu^*}{g}\left(\frac{K}{Y}\right) \tag{3}$$

Therefore, for the selected SAC, LMIC, and HIC, we consider the following panel model from the literature:

$$EI_{it} = f(Y_{it}, Y_{it}^2, ICOR_{it}, P_{it}) \tag{4}$$

where EI = energy intensity, Y = gross domestic product (GDP) or national income, $ICOR$ = incremental capital–output ratio, P = energy price, and Y^2 = square term of Y.

The transmission pathways of the effects arising from changes in the dependent variables are rooted in various economic theories. The nonlinear impact of Y on EI is conveyed through the structural characteristics of the economy, which can be explained using the *EI*

[1] The model and the empirical study of this chapter is based on Amin *et al.* (2022).

[2] The formulation resonates with the Harrod–Domar model.

Kuznets curve and its inverse (Deichmann *et al.*, 2018). In later stages of development, the economy's transition toward more service-based activities may lower *EI* from its elevated levels seen in earlier stages due to a larger industrial sector. Conversely, development might begin with a focus on the service sector and later shift toward the industrial sector, leading to an increase in *EI* during the later stages of development.

The influence of *P* on *EI* occurs through the firm's consumption behavior, which is driven by input substitution for efficiency purposes. Based on production theory, firms would reduce their energy consumption in the production process (lowering *EI*) by substituting different inputs, such as capital, labor, or other relevant resources, to maximize the output bundle within resource constraints. Hence, there should be a negative correlation between *P* and *EI*. According to the theoretical identity in Eq. (1), a higher *ICOR* reduces capital investment returns, suggesting that firms are experiencing technical inefficiencies. If new capital installations are delayed, more energy would be consumed alongside capital to enhance returns on investment, given their interdependency, thus increasing *EI*. Therefore, a positive relationship between *EI* and *ICOR* is anticipated.

3.3. *Econometric methodology*

CS dependence[3] tests were conducted to assess the interdependence among the variables. While earlier studies assumed uniform slopes, recent research, such as Amin and Khan (2021), disputes this and suggests that slopes vary across different sections. Panel data, in general, tend to exhibit interdependence across sections, making traditional unit root tests insufficient for accurate statistical inference. This study employs Pesaran and Yamagata's (2008) test to address slope heterogeneity. Additionally, we utilized second-generation unit root tests, including the cross-sectionally augmented IPS (CIPS) and cross-sectionally augmented ADF (CADF), to evaluate the stationary properties of the data. Pesaran (2007) contends that these unit root tests account for the CS dependence hypothesis. The testing procedures were broadly similar, with the vital distinction being that CIPS incorporates the CS average from the CADF test. The LM-Bootstrap (LM-B) and Durbin–Hausman (DH) panel cointegration tests were applied for cointegration analysis.

The pool mean group (PMG) panel ARDL model was also considered for panel estimation. Pesaran *et al.* (1999) proposed that this model captures heterogeneous coefficients of variables while accounting for their interdependencies (Mensah *et al.*, 2019). It assumes that long-run (LR) parameters remain constant across the selected countries but allows short-run (SR) parameters, error variances, and intercepts to vary (Mensah *et al.*, 2019; Amin and Khan, 2021). One of the key advantages of the PMG panel ARDL model is its ability to provide robust results for variables with different integration orders.

The variables' Granger causality was examined after assessing the cointegrating properties and LR coefficients. The causality test proposed by Dumitrescu and Hurlin (2012) was used, as it allows for parameter variation within panel sections and effectively addresses CS dependence. This test is also suitable for small sample sizes.

[3]We use Pesaran CD, Breusch–Pagan LM, and Pesaran Scaled LM to check this paper's cross-sectional dependency.

4. Results and Discussions

Table 1 displays the outcomes of the CS dependence tests, as outlined in the previous section. The findings indicate that the variables exhibit CS dependence. Additionally, the slope homogeneity test results, shown in Table 2, further confirm the significant heterogeneity of the variables within the model.

Table 1. CS dependency tests.

		SAC			
Criteria	*EI*	*Y*	Y^2	*ICOR*	*P*
Breusch–Pagan LM	151.27***	172.98***	172.96***	20.60***	171.14***
Pesaran Scaled LM	40.78***	47.05***	47.04***	3.06***	46.52***
Pesaran CD	12.30***	13.15***	13.15***	1.78*	13.08***
		LMIC			
Criteria	*EI*	*Y*	Y^2	*ICOR*	*P*
Breusch-Pagan LM	5088.56***	9234.42***	24248.20***	678.89***	351.52***
Pesaran Scaled LM	135.17***	258.94***	510.23***	3.51***	351.52***
Pesaran CD	20.98***	86.24***	102.31***	0.47	108.33***
		HIC			
Criteria	*EI*	*Y*	Y^2	*ICOR*	*P*
Breusch-Pagan LM	24575.42***	29307.46***	29248.46	1950.16***	33277.79***
Pesaran Scaled LM	451.47***	543.35***	542.21***	12.12***	620.45***
Pesaran CD	99.82***	152.99***	152.86***	4.33***	180.92

Note: ***, **, and * refer to significance levels at 1, 5, and 10%, respectively.

Table 2. Pesaran–Yamagata slope homogeneity test.

	SAC	
Test	Statistics	P-value
Delta	–2.83***	0.01
Delta adj.	–2.24**	0.03
	LMIC	
Test	Statistics	P-value
Delta	25.83***	0.000
Delta adj.	29.46***	0.000
	HIC	
Test	Statistics	P-value
Delta	36.74***	0.000***
Delta adj.	41.77***	0.000***

Note: ***, **, and * refer to significance levels at 1, 5, and 10%, respectively.

Furthermore, the slope homogeneity test (Table 7) also confirms the highly heterogeneous variables in the model.

The CIPS and CADF tests (Tables 3–5) confirmed that the variables considered in the model were stationary at I (1). This gives us scope for further investigating the LR relationship among the variables by applying the cointegration test.

The LM-B and DH tests confirmed the LR relationship between the variables (Table 6). Confirming the cointegration test further allows us to estimate the cointegrating factors through the PMG panel ARDL.

Table 7 demonstrates that the *ICOR* coefficient is highly significant and inelastic for both SAC and LMIC groups. This suggests that a 1% rise in *ICOR* leads to a 0.15% and 0.11% increase in *EI* for SAC and LMIC, respectively, in the long run. However, the *ICOR* coefficient for HIC is extremely inelastic at 0.003 in the long run, indicating that ICOR has a minimal impact on *EI* in HIC.

The primary reason for the positive correlation between *EI* and *ICOR* is technical inefficiency, which can influence the production process through various mechanisms. When firms cannot use capital effectively due to technical inefficiencies, energy consumption per unit of production rises, leading to an increase in *EI* over the long term. Some common examples of technically inefficient factors in the LMIC and SAC regions include insufficient mechanical expertise, lack of technological and operational efficiency, and poor scale efficiency.

Furthermore, the coefficient for *Y* is positive and significant, with elasticities of 0.80 and 0.83 for the LMIC and HIC, respectively. This suggests that a 1% rise in *Y* leads to an increase in *EI* by 0.80% and 0.83% in these regions. However, the Y^2 term is negative

Table 3. Panel unit root tests for SAC.

CIPS				
	Level		First-Difference	
Variable	I	I and T	I	I and T
EI	−1.70	−2.93**	−5.56***	−5.78***
Y	−1.68	−2.709	−4.15***	−4.39***
Y^2	−2.06	−2.79	−4.12***	−4.31***
ICOR	−3.66***	−3.68***	–	–
P	−1.27	−2.65	−3.93***	−4.33***
CADF				
	Level		First-Difference	
Variable	Intercept	Intercept & Trend	Intercept	Intercept & Trend
EI	1.78	−2.62	4.00***	−4.55***
Y	−1.69	−2.22	−2.99***	−3.51***
Y^2	−1.38	−1.43	−3.03***	−3.51***
ICOR	−1.19	−1.29	−4.55***	4.57***
P	−1.50	−2.28	−4.05***	−4.65***

Note: ***, **, and * refer to significance levels at 1, 5, and 10%, respectively.

Table 4. Panel Unit Root Tests for LMIC

CIPS				
	Level		First-Difference	
Variable	I	I and T	I	I and T
EI	−1.96	−2.01	−4.98***	−5.14***
Y	−1.92	−1.99	−3.82***	−4.04***
Y^2	1.92	−1.98	−3.78***	−4.01***
ICOR	−1.84	−2.20	−5.69***	−6.04***
P	−1.96	−2.12	−4.06***	−4.05***
CADF				
	Level		First-Difference	
Variable	Intercept	Intercept & Trend	Intercept	Intercept & Trend
EI	−0.33	2.65	−4.29***	−2.11***
Y	−2.08**	2.11	−3.09***	−1.50*
Y^2	−0.06	2.17	−2.98***	−1.38**
ICOR	−0.78	−0.46	−4.17***	−6.63***
P	−2.30**	−1.28	−5.26***	−3.69***

Note: ***, **, and * refer to significance levels at 1, 5, and 10%, respectively. Critical values are not reported for brevity but can be delivered on request.

Table 5. Panel unit root tests for HIC.

CIPS				
	Level		First-Difference	
Variable	I	I and T	I	I and T
EI	−1.83	−1.98	−5.44***	−5.66***
Y	−1.95	−2.04	−3.98***	−4.06***
Y^2	−1.91	−2.03	−3.98***	−4.04***
ICOR	−1.90	−1.95	−6.01***	−6.13***
P	−1.63	−1.98	−3.98***	−4.27***
CADF				
	Level		First-Difference	
Variable	I	I and T	I	I and T
EI	−0.20	2.96	−9.17***	−6.32***
Y	−1.17	0.12	−5.48***	2.48***
Y^2	−1.04	3.15	−5.41***	−2.45***
ICOR	0.74	0.39	−9.99***	−5.58***
P	2.47	−0.10	−8.13***	−5.96***

Note: ***, **, and * refer to significance levels at 1, 5, and 10%, respectively

Table 6. Panel cointegration test results.

SAC			
LM-B Test		DH Test	
Intercept	Intercept & Trend	DH_Group	DH_Panel
5.88	9.15	9.08***	12.59***
LMIC			
Intercept	Intercept & Trend	DH_Group	DH_Panel
1410.56	1853.89	−15.85	3.55***
HIC			
Intercept	Intercept & Trend	DH_Group	DH_Panel
2186.12	2876.94	262.05***	500.92***

Note: ***, **, and * refer to significant levels at 1, 5, and 10%, respectively.

Table 7. Estimation of cointegration factors.

SAC	
Variable	ARDL (PMG)
Y	1.39(4.00)
Y^2	−0.03(0.08)
ICOR	0.15(0.04)***
P	−0.33(0.07)**
ECT	−0.21***
P-CD	0.38
N	102
LMIC	
Variable	ARDL (PMG)
Y	0.80 (0.05)***
Y^2	−0.16(0.01)***
ICOR	0.11(0.02)***
P	0.15(0.03)***
ECT	0.10***
P-CD	0.74
N	850

(*Continued*)

Table 7. (*Continued*)

HIC	
Variable	ARDL (PMG)
Y	0.83 (0.0003)***
Y^2	–0.13(3.73E-06)***
ICOR	0.003 (0.0001)***
P	–0.80(0.0003)***
ECT	–0.79***
P-CD	1.13
N	1196

Note: ***, **, and * refer to significance levels at 1, 5, and 10%, respectively. Standard errors are in parenthesis. For HIC, we have included the second and third lags of *ICOR* to address the prevailing strong CS dependence in the errors.

(–0.16 and –0.13), reflecting a nonlinear trajectory toward *EE* over time. These findings align with the traditional *EI* Kuznets curve hypothesis (Deichmann *et al.*, 2018). As economies advance, *EI* initially increases due to a higher industrial share but eventually declines as the focus shifts to more service-oriented activities.

In contrast, the coefficient for *Y* in SAC is positive but not statistically significant. Similarly, while the squared term of *Y* shows the expected sign, it lacks statistical significance. This result may be attributed to these countries' developmental positions. Since there is no evident nonlinearity in the *EI*–*Y* relationship, these countries are likely near the midpoint of their developmental transition, where changes in *Y* have minimal impact on *EI* due to a flatter slope at this stage.

Additionally, *P* is negatively correlated with *EI* across all regions in the long run, with a 1% rise in price reducing *EI* by an average of 0.42%. The inelasticity of the price coefficient across regions suggests that consumers are generally hesitant to adjust their energy consumption levels. As energy is a normal good and essential for most activities, increases in energy prices do not significantly reduce the quantity demanded. Consequently, fluctuations in energy prices are not closely tied to substantial changes in *EI*. Moreover, the differing impact of energy prices on *EI* across regions is evident. In the SAC and LMIC, EI is more inelastic in response to price changes than the HIC. When energy prices increase, firms tend to lower their energy consumption per production unit. However, they focus on optimizing other inputs to maintain the desired production levels (i.e., staying on the same isoquant). However, input efficiencies in the SAC and LMIC are lower than in HIC due to slow technological advancements, reliance on outdated capital, skills mismatch in the labor force, managerial challenges, and regulatory constraints. As a result, higher energy prices in SAC and LMIC do not significantly reduce energy use per output unit due to the lag in efficiency improvements.

Finally, the post-estimation test for CS dependence confirmed no interdependency among the errors across sections. The robustness of the results was further tested using CS-augmented dynamic OLS (DOLS) with heterogeneous variance and pooled weighted

Table 8. Robustness check of the estimated cointegration factors.

SAC	
Variable	DOLS
Y	–4.31(3.41)
Y^2	0.42(127.24)
ICOR	0.13(0.02)**
P	–0.15(0.07)**
P-CD	–0.19
N	74
LMIC	
Variable	DOLS)
Y	0.96 (0.03)***
Y^2	–0.21(0.01)***
ICOR	0.06(0.02)***
P	–0.08(0.02)***
ECT	–0.10***
P-CD	1.37
N	850
HIC	
Variable	DOLS
Y	0.66 (0.04)***
Y^2	–0.09(0.005)***
ICOR	0.002 (0.006)
P	–0.32(0.0003)***
ECT	–0.79***
P-CD	–0.09
N	1040

Note: ***, **, and * refer to significance levels at 1, 5, and 10%, respectively. Standard errors are in parenthesis. For HIC, we have included the second, fifth, and tenth lags of *ICOR* to address the prevailing strong CS dependence in the errors.

CS. The results in Table 8 show no significant sensitivity in the signs of the critical variables. While some of the coefficients have minor variations, these can be disregarded due to the differing parameter estimation techniques used in the two models. Notably, the *ICOR* coefficient for HIC in the DOLS model is insignificant, indicating that *ICOR* has no impact on *EI*. This finding aligns with the conclusions drawn from the ARDL (PMG) estimation, further reinforcing that *ICOR* does not influence *EI*, regardless of the significance level, as both methods ultimately lead to the same conclusion.

3.3. *A global cross-section analysis*

Building on the analysis of *ICOR*'s impact on *EI* within the SAC, LMIC, and HIC regions, this study seeks to extend the investigation to a global scale by examining CS data from 129 countries. A conventional OLS regression was employed to conduct this analysis. The data were divided into six five-year intervals: 1990, 1995, 2000, 2005, 2010, and 2015. As illustrated in Table 9, *ICOR* had a negative effect on *EI* in 1990, although this effect lacked statistical significance. However, over time, beginning in 1995, the impact of ICOR steadily diminished, suggesting an improvement in EE within production processes as the years progressed.

3.4. *Causality analysis*

The results of the panel causality tests, as shown in Tables 10–12, indicate varying relationships across different regions. In the SAC, the test reveals a unidirectional causality

Table 9. Cross-section estimation with OLS.

Year	*ICOR*	*Y*	Y^2	*P*
1990	–0.09(0.23)	0.40(0.38)	–0.07(0.05)	–0.14(0.09)
1995	0.10(0.03)***	–0.17(0.06)***	0.01(0.01)	–0.38(0.12)***
2000	0.05(0.03)*	–0.24(0.08)***	0.02(0.01)	–0.47(0.14)***
2005	0.04(0.02)*	–0.14(0.06)	0.01(0.01)	–0.71(0.06)***
2010	0.04(0.02)*	–0.22(0.08)**	0.01(0.1)	–0.61(0.06)***
2015	0.005(0.03)	–0.18(0.07)**	–0.002(0.01)	–0.59(0.07)***

Note: ***, **, and * refer to significance levels at 1, 5, and 10%, respectively. Standard errors are in parenthesis.

Table 10. Dumetrescu–Hurlin panel causality test for SAC.

Null Hypothesis	W-Statistic
$EI \rightarrow ICOR$	1.97
$ICOR \rightarrow EI$	8.62**
$GDP \rightarrow EI$	10.36***
$EI \rightarrow GDP$	1.12
$GDP^2 \rightarrow EI$	10.49***
$EI \rightarrow GDP^2$	1.08
$EI \rightarrow P$	3.13
$P \rightarrow EI$	9.87***

Note: ***, **, and * refer to significance levels at 1, 5, and 10%, respectively.

Table 11. Dumetrescu–Hurlin panel causality test for LMIC.

Null Hypothesis	W-Statistic
$EI \rightarrow ICOR$	5.01***
$ICOR \rightarrow EI$	19.20***
$GDP \rightarrow EI$	6.34***
$EI \rightarrow GDP$	3.08***
$GDP^2 \rightarrow EI$	2.32**
$EI \rightarrow GDP^2$	2.87***
$EI \rightarrow P$	13.16***
$P \rightarrow EI$	5.05***

Note: ***, **, and * refer to significance levels at 1, 5, and 10%, respectively.

Table 12. Dumetrescu–Hurlin panel causality test for HIC.

Null Hypothesis	W-Statistic
$EI \rightarrow ICOR$	7.49
$ICOR \rightarrow EI$	9.12***
$GDP \rightarrow EI$	13.38***
$EI \rightarrow GDP$	9.05**
$GDP^2 \rightarrow EI$	13.29***
$EI \rightarrow GDP^2$	8.95**
$EI \rightarrow P$	14.47***
$P \rightarrow EI$	12.76***

running from *ICOR* to *EI* in the long run. Additionally, within the SAC, unidirectional causality is observed from *P* to *EI* in the long run. The findings differ for the LMIC, where bidirectional causality is detected between *ICOR* and *EI* in the long run. However, this bidirectional relationship is absent in the HIC, where the causality results between *ICOR* and *EI* resemble those found in the SAC. Lastly, the tests show bidirectional causality between *P* and *EI* in the long run for both the LMIC and HIC.

4. Conclusion and Policy Implication

The relationship between energy consumption and economic growth has been widely studied in the literature (Taghizadeh-Hesary *et al.*, 2016), with energy identified as a critical factor in facilitating efficient capital utilization. Diaz and Puch (2017) suggest that capital efficiency is significantly influenced by energy prices, EI, technological advancement, and knowledge. The ICOR is an essential metric for evaluating EI, as it reflects the efficiency with which capital is used to generate output, particularly as firms enhance their technological capabilities. Based on the principles of the Harrod–Domar model, it is evident that ICOR substantially impacts EI, with EI—measured as the ratio of energy consumption to GDP—being sensitive to fluctuations in ICOR.

The analysis reveals that ICOR unidirectionally affects EI in South Asian countries (SAC), with an elasticity of 0.15. In LMIC, a bidirectional relationship between ICOR and EI is observed, with an elasticity of 0.11, though this is statistically lower than in SAC. For HIC, ICOR influences EI unidirectionally, but the elasticity is considerably lower at 0.003. These results suggest that the impact of ICOR on EI is significantly weaker in developed economies, likely due to higher levels of technical efficiency, which allows for more effective capital deployment and lower EI.

The findings indicate that inefficiencies in technical attributes lead to higher ICOR, which, in turn, increases EI. To address this, both SAC and LMIC must implement frameworks to enhance technical efficiency within firms. Sector-specific ICOR assessments will be essential for identifying industries with higher ICOR, providing policymakers with the insights needed to design targeted, time-sensitive technical efficiency policies. Depending on the severity of ICOR, governments should consider introducing policies that focus on workforce skill development, which may include training programs, foreign collaboration for technology transfer, resource optimization strategies, and investment in technology adoption to improve efficiency. Amin *et al.* (2021) advocate for the rapid introduction of energy service companies (ESCOs), which can offer critical technical assistance across various sectors, helping firms enhance their energy use and invest capital more efficiently.

Given the inherent delays associated with such processes, achieving technical efficiency in SAC and LMIC will require time. Additionally, many of these countries remain heavily reliant on fossil fuels, which exacerbates the environmental impacts of high EI. Therefore, in conjunction with efforts to improve technical efficiency, it is recommended that renewable energy production be scaled up. Policies encouraging installing solar rooftop net metering systems, developing renewable-energy-based captive power plants, and creating medium-scale solar plants in industrial zones are strongly recommended. Promoting innovative, sector-specific approaches to introducing renewable energy solutions and enhancing EE at the firm level will further support these efforts.

Institutional barriers, particularly in developing nations such as SAC and LMIC, often obstruct the implementation of EE initiatives. Excessive centralization within governance structures creates institutional inefficiencies that slow the progress of energy-efficiency agendas. As such, regulatory reforms to establish institutional legitimacy should begin with key public entities and gradually extend to the private sector. Reforms in financial institutions, technology, infrastructure development, and decision-making processes will be essential to driving this transition.

To align energy policies with sustainability objectives and ensure that energy security, transition, and economic growth work in harmony, several policy recommendations are proposed:

1. *Enhance capital efficiency through targeted investments in technology*: The relationship between ICOR and EI demonstrates that improving capital efficiency is crucial for reducing energy consumption and achieving sustainable economic growth. Policymakers should prioritize investments in energy-efficient technologies, particularly in LMIC, where capital inefficiencies are more severe. Providing financial incentives for adopting advanced technologies in energy-intensive industries can significantly reduce energy consumption while boosting productivity. Additionally, international cooperation should be fostered to bridge the technological gap between HIC and developing countries. Programs focusing on technology transfer and capacity building could allow LMIC to bypass traditional, energy-inefficient stages of industrialization and adopt cleaner, more efficient production processes (Dong *et al.*, 2022).
2. *Promote renewable energy deployment and energy diversification*: To strengthen energy security and reduce reliance on fossil fuels, governments must accelerate the deployment of RES such as solar, wind, and hydropower. Pehlivanoglu *et al.* (2021) demonstrated that investments in renewable energy reduce EI and contribute to long-term economic growth. HICs should continue to lead by example by setting ambitious renewable energy targets while developing countries should receive financial and technical support to expand their renewable energy capacities. Moreover, as Ateed (2024) highlights, the energy disruptions caused by the Russia–Ukraine conflict have underscored the importance of energy diversification for reducing vulnerabilities to external shocks. Policymakers must adopt a multi-pronged energy security strategy that includes renewable energy deployment and diversification of energy import sources.
3. *Strengthen EE programs*: Improving EE is a cost-effective strategy for reducing EI and emissions. EE programs should focus on upgrading outdated infrastructure, particularly in industrial sectors that consume large amounts of energy. Governments should introduce stricter EE standards for buildings, transportation, and industrial equipment, as suggested by Bertoldi (2022). Digital technologies can further enhance EE by optimizing energy use in real time, helping to reduce both EI and operational costs. In addition, the rebound effect, as Subramanian (2023) discussed, must be carefully managed. Policymakers should implement complementary measures to ensure that EE improvements do not inadvertently lead to higher energy consumption elsewhere. Integrating EE policies with broader sustainability initiatives, such as carbon pricing or energy conservation campaigns, can achieve this.
4. *Address income inequality and energy poverty through inclusive energy policies*: Energy poverty and income inequality are critical barriers to achieving a just energy transition, particularly in developing economies. Policymakers should prioritize policies that improve access to affordable, reliable, and clean energy. Dong *et al.* (2022) emphasize the need for inclusive energy policies that address the needs of vulnerable populations. These policies should focus on expanding access to renewable energy in rural and underserved areas, creating green jobs, and ensuring that low-income households benefit from energy transition initiatives. Targeted subsidies, microfinancing options for renewable energy systems, and investment in decentralized energy

infrastructure (e.g., off-grid solar systems) are critical measures for alleviating energy poverty and promoting inclusive growth.

5. *Foster international collaboration for a global energy transition*: The global energy transition requires a coordinated effort among countries to meet climate targets while ensuring economic stability. International financial institutions like the World Bank and the IMF should increase their support for green finance and sustainable energy projects in developing countries. Pandey *et al.* (2022) recommended that international collaboration is necessary to help LMIC overcome financial and technological barriers to energy transition. Furthermore, multilateral agreements should focus on sharing best practices in EE, renewable energy deployment, and energy diversification strategies. These efforts can help ensure that all countries, regardless of income level, contribute to global energy security and climate resilience.

Despite these recommendations, it is crucial to acknowledge that many developing countries, particularly in SAC and LMIC, face institutional barriers that hinder the implementation of EE programs. Excessive fragmentation within centralized governance structures often results in institutional inefficiencies that slow down the progress of energy-efficiency initiatives. Therefore, regulatory reforms to establish institutional legitimacy should begin with key public entities and gradually extend to the private sector. Overhauling financial institutions, fostering technology and infrastructure development, and improving decision-making processes will facilitate this transition.

Going forward, this study could be extended to a more granular level to provide industry-specific insights to assist policymakers in SAC and LMIC in crafting more tailored energy policies. Country-specific analyses are also recommended to better assess different contexts' distinct challenges and opportunities. The anticipated findings from these analyses help align energy policies with broader sustainability goals, ensuring that energy security, transition, and economic growth work together to support sustainable development.

References

Agovino, M, S Bartoletto and A Garofalo (2019). Modelling the relationship between energy intensity and GDP for European countries: An historical perspective (1800–2000). *Energy Economics*, 82, 114–134, https://doi.org/10.1016/j.eneco.2018.02.017.

Alharbi, SS, M Al Mamun, S Boubaker and SKA Rizvi (2023). Green finance and renewable energy: A worldwide evidence. *Energy Economics*, 118, 106499.

Amin, SB and F Khan (2021). Tourism and renewable energy in South Asia: A panel study. *Tourism and Hospitality Management*, 27(3), 555–579.

Amin, SB, FA Kabir and F Khan (2021). Socioeconomic and institutional barriers for accelerating biogas generation in Asia. In *Reference Module in Earth Systems and Environmental Sciences*, https://doi.org/10.1016/B978-0-12-819727-1.00042-X.

Amin, SB, F Al Kabir and F Khan (2020). Energy-output nexus in Bangladesh: A two-sector model analysis. *Energy Strategy Reviews*, 32, 100566, https://doi.org/10.1016/j.esr.2020.100566.

Amin, SB, F Taghizadeh-Hesary, F Al Kabir and F Khan (2022). Nexus between energy intensity and capital-output ratio: A holistic approach. *Energy & Environment*, 34(7), 2721–2739.

Ateed, EH (2024). The impact of Russia-Ukraine war on the global energy crisis. In *Analyzing Energy Crises and the Impact of Country Policies on the World*, 119–138, IGI Global.

Atkeson, A and PJ Kehoe (1999). Models of energy use: Putty-putty versus putty-clay. *American Economic Review*, 89(4), 1028–1043, https://doi.org/10.1257/aer.89.4.1028.

Batra, G (2023). Renewable energy economics: Achieving harmony between environmental protection and economic goals. *Social Science Chronicle*, 2(2), 1–32.

Bertoldi, P (2022). Policies for energy conservation and sufficiency: Review existing policies and recommendations for new and effective policies in OECD countries. *Energy and Buildings*, 264, 112075.

Boone, CG, E Bromaghim and AR Kapuscinski (2023). Sustainability careers. *Annual Review of Environment and Resources*, 48(1), 589–613.

Chu, LK and NTM Le (2022). Environmental quality and the role of economic policy uncertainty, economic complexity, renewable energy, and energy intensity: The case of G7 countries. *Environmental Science and Pollution Research*, 29(2), 2866–2882.

Creutzig, F, SG Simoes, S Leipold, P Berrill, I Azevedo, O Edelenbosch, T Fishman, H Haberl, E Hertwich, V Krey and AT Lima (2024). Demand-side strategies key for mitigating material impacts of energy transitions. *Nature Climate Change*, 14, 561–572, https://doi.org/10.1038/s41558-024-02016-z.

Deichmann, U, A Reuter, S Vollmer and F Zhang (2018). Relationship between energy intensity and economic growth: New evidence from a multi-country multi-sector data. World Bank Policy Research Working Paper No. 8322.

Diaz, A and LA Puch (2017). Vintage capital, energy intensity and the medium-term business cycle. UC3M Working Papers on Economics.

Diaz, A, LA Puch and MD Guillo (2004). Costly capital reallocation and energy use. *Review of Economic Dynamics*, 7(2), 494–518.

Dong, K, Y Dou and Q Jiang (2022). Income inequality, energy poverty, and energy efficiency: Who cause who and how? *Technological Forecasting and Social Change*, 179, 121622.

Dumitrescu, EI and C Hurlin (2012). Testing for Granger non-causality in heterogeneous panels. *Economic Modelling*, 29(4), 1450–1460.

GED (2019). Study on employment, productivity and sectoral investment in Bangladesh. Planning Commission, Government of Bangladesh.

Isah, A, MO Dioha, R Debnath, MC Abraham-Dukuma and HM Butu (2023). Financing renewable energy: Policy insights from Brazil and Nigeria. *Energy, Sustainability and Society*, 13(1), 2.

Jahanger, A, I Ozturk, JC Onwe, TE Joseph and MR Hossain (2023). Do technology and renewable energy contribute to energy efficiency and carbon neutrality? Evidence from top ten manufacturing countries. *Sustainable Energy Technologies and Assessments*, 56, 103084.

Khan, MI, Y Bicer, M Asif, TA Al-Ansari, M Khan, TA Kurniawan and SG Al-Ghamdi (2024). The GCC's path to a sustainable future: Navigating the barriers to the adoption of energy efficiency measures in the built environment. *Energy Conversion and Management: X*, 100636.

Kjaer, AM (2023). *Governance*. John Wiley & Sons.

Kraft, J and A Kraft (1978). On the relationship between energy and GNP. *The Journal of Energy and Development*, 3(2), 401–403, http://www.jstor.org/stable/24806805.

Mensah, IA, M Sun, C Gao, AY Omari-Sasu, D Zhu, BC Ampimah and A Quarcoo (2019). Analysis on the nexus of economic growth, fossil fuel energy consumption, CO_2 emissions and oil price in Africa based on a PMG panel ARDL approach. *Journal of Cleaner Production*, 228, 161–174.

Munir, Q, HH Lean and R Smyth (2020). CO_2 emissions, energy consumption and economic growth in the ASEAN-5 countries: A cross-sectional dependence approach. *Energy Economics*, 85, 104571, https://doi.org/10.1016/j.eneco.2019.104571.

Mühlich, L and M Zucker-Marques (2023). Closing the global crisis finance gap: Why and how the IMF should address weaknesses in the global financial safety net.

Nsafon, BEK, NN Same, AO Yakub, D Chaulagain, NM Kumar and JS Huh (2023). The justice and policy implications of clean energy transition in Africa. *Frontiers in Environmental Science*, 11, 1089391.

Otsuka, A and M Goto (2018). Regional determinants of energy intensity in Japan: the impact of population density. *Asia-Pacific Journal of Regional Science*, 2, 257–278, https://doi.org/10.1007/s41685-017-0045-1.

Oyekale, J, M Petrollese, V Tola and G Cau (2020). Impacts of renewable energy resources on effectiveness of grid-integrated systems: Succinct review of current challenges and potential solution strategies. *Energies*, 13(18), 4856.

Ozturk, I and A Acaravci (2010). CO_2 emissions, energy consumption and economic growth in Turkey. *Renewable and Sustainable Energy Reviews*, 14, 3220–3225.

Pandey, N, H de Coninck and AD Sagar (2022). Beyond technology transfer: Innovation cooperation to advance sustainable development in developing countries. *Wiley Interdisciplinary Reviews: Energy and Environment*, 11(2), 422.

Pehlivanoglu, F, O Kocbulut, S Akdag and AA Alola (2021). Toward a sustainable economic development in the EU member states: The role of energy efficiency-intensity and renewable energy. *International Journal of Energy Research*, 45(15), 21219–21233.

Perera, ATD and T Hong (2023). Vulnerability and resilience of urban energy ecosystems to extreme climate events: A systematic review and perspectives. *Renewable and Sustainable Energy Reviews*, 173, 113038.

Pesaran, MH (2007). A simple panel unit root test in the presence of cross-section dependence. *Journal of Applied Econometrics*, 22, 265–312.

Pesaran, MH and T Yamagata (2008). Testing slope homogeneity in large panels. *Journal of Econometrics*, 142(1), 50–93.

Pesaran, MH, Y Shin and RP Smith (1999). Pooled mean group estimation of dynamic heterogeneous panels. *Journal of American Statistics Association*, 94(446), 621–634.

Pindyck, RS and JJ Rotemberg (1983) Dynamic factor demands and the effects of energy price shocks. *The American Economic Review*, 73(5), 1066–1079, http://www.jstor.org/stable/1814672.

Rajbhandari, A and F Zhang (2018). Does energy efficiency promote economic growth? Evidence from a multicounty and multisectoral panel dataset. *Energy Economics*, 69, 128–139, https://doi.org/10.1016/j.eneco.2017.11.007.

Rudenko, D and G Tanasov (2022). The determinants of energy intensity in Indonesia. *International Journal of Emerging Markets*, 17(3), 832–857.

Sanguino, R, A Barroso, S Fernández-Rodríguez and MI Sánchez-Hernández (2020). Current trends in economy, sustainable development, and energy: A circular economy view. *Environmental Science and Pollution Research*, 27, 1–7, https://doi.org/10.1007/s11356-019-07074-x.

Sha, R (2023). Coordinating economic growth and carbon emission reduction in China: Evidence from the optimal levels of energy price distortions. *Frontiers in Energy Research*, 11, 1301266.

Stošić-Mihajlović, L and S Trajković (2018). The importance of energy for the economy, sustainable development and environmental protection: An economic aspect. *Journal of Process Management. New Technologies*, 6(1), 20–26.

Subramanian, M (2023). Leveraging digitalization for improving energy efficiency. *The Handbook of Energy Policy*, 483–508.

Sun, H, BK Edziah, AK Kporsu, SA Sarkodie and F Taghizadeh-Hesary (2021). Energy efficiency: The role of technological innovation and knowledge spillover. *Technological Forecasting and Social Change*, 167, 120659.

Taghizadeh-Hesary, F, N Yoshino, MM H Abadi and R Farboudmanesh (2016). Response of macro variables of emerging and developed oil importers to oil price movements. *Journal of the Asia Pacific Economy*, 21(1), 91–102, https://doi.org/10.1080/13547860.2015.1057955.

Taguchi, H and S Lowhachai (2014). A revisit to the incremental capital-output ratio: The case of Asian economies and Thailand. *International Journal of Economic Policy in Emerging Economies*, 7(1), 35–54.

Tani, M (2023). Environmental and energy policies in promoting energy efficiency: A case study of some European Union states.

Tibni, H (2024). Assessing the effectiveness of the 10 United Nations global and multilateral climate treaties. *European Journal of Development Studies*, 4(4), 41–55.

Voigt, S, E De Cian, M Schymura and E Verdolini (2014). Energy intensity developments in 40 major economies: Structural change or technology improvement? *Energy Economics*, 41, 47–62.

Wang, J, Y Shan, C Cui, C Zhao, J Meng and S Wang (2024). Investigating the fast energy-related carbon emissions growth in African countries and its drivers. *Applied Energy*, 357, 122494.

Wang, Y, D Wang, L Yu and J Mao (2023). What really influences the development of renewable energy? A systematic review and meta-analysis. *Environmental Science and Pollution Research*, 30(22), 62213–62236.

Wei, T, J Zhou and H Zhang (2019). Rebound effect of energy intensity reduction on energy consumption. *Resources, Conservation and Recycling*, 144, 233–239.

World Bank (2000). Energy services for the world's poor. ESMAP Energy and Development Report, Washington.

Zheng, J, Y Dang and U Assad (2024). Household energy consumption, energy efficiency, and household income–Evidence from China. *Applied Energy*, 353, 122074.

Zhu, Q, C Xu, Q Chen and L Wu (2024). Oil price distortion and its impact on green economic efficiency in China's transportation: A spatial effect perspective. *Renewable and Sustainable Energy Reviews*, 191, 114148.

https://doi.org/10.1142/9789819812608_0003

Chapter 3

Energy Security and Environmental Efficiency in OECD Countries: Pathways to Sustainable Growth[#]

HUAPING SUN[*,¶], MUHAMMAD IKRAM[†], MUHAMMAD MOHSIN[‡] and QAISER ABBAS[§,|]

[*]*School of Economics and Management, University of Science and Technology Beijing, Beijing, China, 100083*

[†]*College of Economics and Management Nanjing University of Aeronautics and Astronautics Nanjing 211106, P. R. China*

[‡]*School of Finance and Economics, Jiangsu University, Zhenjiang, Jiangsu, P. R. China*

[§]*China Institute of Development Strategy and Planning, School of Economics and Management, Centre for Industrial Economics, Wuhan University, Wuhan, China*

[¶]*shp797@163.com*

[|]*Qabbas@gudgk.edu.pk*

This chapter investigates the pathways toward sustainable growth in OECD countries, focusing on the dual goals of energy security and environmental efficiency as critical responses to climate change and increasing energy demands. Balancing economic development with environmental sustainability remains a significant challenge, necessitating policies that support energy resilience while mitigating ecological impact. Leveraging comprehensive datasets from the International Energy Agency, British Petroleum, and the World Bank, this study employs a nonradial Data Envelopment Analysis (DEA) model to assess environmental and energy efficiency metrics across OECD nations. Results reveal substantial variations in energy efficiency performance, with countries such as Iceland and Greece achieving near-optimal efficiency, while others, including Ireland, show significant room for improvement. The findings emphasize the importance of diverse policy approaches tailored to each nation's unique energy landscape, promoting renewable energy integration and increased efficiency to enhance energy security. This study's policy implications advocate for integrated strategies aligning economic growth objectives with environmental sustainability targets, fostering a resilient energy transition. Through this framework, the research provides critical insights for policymakers to facilitate sustainable growth by improving environmental efficiency and securing energy pathways in the OECD context.

Keywords: Assessment; DEA; environment; economy; energy; OECD.

JEL Classification: F14, O56, Q43.

[‡]Corresponding author.

[#]This Chapter is the updated version of the paper published in the *Singapore Economic Review*, Vol. 66, No. 2, doi: 10.1142/S0217590819430033. © 2021 World Scientific Publishing.

1. Introduction

Growing concerns about climate change have intensified the need for a robust energy strategy that balances economic development with environmental sustainability. For countries in the OECD, achieving this balance means addressing the dual objectives of energy security and environmental efficiency. Energy security is increasingly critical as global energy demand continues to rise, driving interest in alternative energy solutions that can reduce dependence on fossil fuels while meeting economic demands (Mohsin *et al.*, 2018; Ikram *et al.*, 2019). As the primary source of carbon emissions, fossil fuel-driven electricity production remains a pressing challenge worldwide. Although renewable energy has become a viable alternative, fossil fuels still account for most global power generation (Bang *et al.*, 2018; Sun *et al.*, 2019a). This reliance on non-renewable energy sources underscores the urgency of transitioning to greener technologies to reduce carbon footprints and mitigate climate vulnerabilities (Taghizadeh-Hesary *et al.*, 2013; Kolodko, 2018).

The recent volatility in energy prices and supply disruptions due to geopolitical tensions have further highlighted the risks associated with fossil fuel dependence, reinforcing the strategic importance of diversifying energy sources to improve resilience. This situation is spurring interest in alternative sources, such as wind, solar, and hydrogen, which offer lower risks of price volatility and greater environmental benefits (Zhao *et al.*, 2023; Ibekwe *et al.*, 2024). Energy security is now closely tied to the transition to renewables, as seen in recent studies that emphasize the need for diversified, reliable, and sustainable energy infrastructures that can withstand external shocks (Rasoulinezhad *et al.*, 2023). Increasingly, researchers highlight the importance of secure renewable energy supply chains, including the technological capacity to generate renewable energy and the logistical infrastructure required to store and distribute it effectively.

Policy initiatives to curb emissions, such as CO_2 reduction targets and advancing renewable energy technologies, are now key components of energy frameworks among OECD nations. These efforts, driven by international agreements and increasing climate awareness, reflect a growing consensus that strategic innovation and investment in cleaner energy sources are essential for long-term sustainability (Zhang *et al.*, 2018a; Taghizadeh-Hesary and Yoshino, 2015). For example, recent studies suggest that optimizing the integration of renewable energy systems requires technological improvements and methods that support the selection and combination of renewable sources to stabilize national energy systems (Ouyang and Lin, 2014). Emerging research on grid modernization indicates that advances in energy storage technologies and smart grid systems are essential for accommodating the intermittency of renewable energy, which is increasingly seen as vital to ensure both energy security and efficient distribution in OECD nations (Ourahou *et al.*, 2020).

Green growth has also become an integral focus within energy policy discussions, with new research showing that investing in green infrastructure can stimulate economic growth while reducing emissions. Studies indicate that green growth strategies — such as expanding the green job sector and improving energy efficiency — contribute positively to economic stability, particularly during global transitions toward decarbonization (Sadiq *et al*., 2022). Research on the economic impacts of green growth suggests that promoting energy efficiency, sustainable infrastructure, and low-carbon technologies can enhance economic resilience by creating jobs and encouraging private investment, even as nations strive to meet carbon reduction targets (Fernandes *et al*., 2021; Dell'Anna, 2021).

Despite notable progress, empirical research demonstrates that achieving a low-carbon society remains challenging, hindered by the complex interdependence of energy production, economic growth, and environmental impacts. Studies reveal that CO_2 emissions, driven by fossil fuel combustion, have risen sharply alongside industrial growth, with emissions currently at approximately 35.7 billion tons globally. This trend indicates a positive correlation between CO_2 emissions and economic expansion, posing a fundamental obstacle to environmentally sustainable growth (Zhang *et al*., 2015; Guo *et al*., 2018). Recent assessments show that decoupling economic growth from emissions remains limited, with a need for new decarbonization policies that account for sector-specific emission patterns, particularly in heavy industry and transport sectors where fossil fuel reliance remains high (Gbadeyan *et al*., 2024).

Furthermore, the transition away from high-emission energy sources varies widely across OECD countries, driven by regional differences in policy adoption, economic constraints, and the availability of natural resources. While some countries have made significant strides toward decarbonization, others continue to struggle with the economic and logistical challenges of reducing fossil fuel dependence (Mollahosseini *et al*., 2017; Olivier *et al*., 2016). For example, countries such as the United States and China still rely heavily on coal and natural gas for energy, whereas European nations have seen emission reductions due to lower demand for space heating and reduced fossil fuel consumption in energy production (Jing *et al*., 2018; Nejat *et al*., 2015). A recent comparative study on energy transitions across OECD nations highlights that economic and geographic disparities influence the pace and effectiveness of the transition, underscoring the need for country-specific policies that address unique national constraints and opportunities in renewable energy adoption (Ma *et al*., 2023).

This study aims to contribute to the growing body of literature on energy and environmental efficiency by evaluating the performance of OECD countries using a nonradial Data Envelopment Analysis (DEA) model. Unlike traditional approaches, DEA provides a comprehensive framework to assess both desirable and undesirable outputs, thereby offering a nuanced view of energy efficiency across diverse economies (Sueyoshi and Wang, 2018; Egilmez *et al*., 2016). By incorporating environmental and energy performance indicators, this study seeks to identify areas where improvements in policy and practice can drive OECD nations closer to achieving sustainable growth. Recent applications of DEA models in environmental studies demonstrate their utility in capturing complex, multi-dimensional data, allowing for a more comprehensive assessment of sustainability that includes both energy efficiency and environmental impact metrics (Arana-Jiménez *et al*., 2024).

The rest of the paper is organized as follows: Section 2 contains methodology, Section 3 explains results and discussion, and Section 4 contains the conclusion and policy framework.

2. Methodology

Most pollution and contamination problems occur from the combined production of undesirable bad outputs during the production of desirable good outputs (Färe and Grosskopf, 2004). For example, the continuous emissions of nitrous oxide, carbon dioxide, and sulfur dioxide are unexpected when the electricity is produced from burning coal and thermal sources. We now consider a production process in which desirable good outputs and undesirable bad outputs are generated together. Let us assume the vector of undesirable outputs, desirable outputs, and inputs — $U \in R_+^J$, $Y \in R_+^M$ and $X \in R_+^N$. The production technology can be expressed as follows:

$$T = \{(X, Y, U) : X \text{ can produce } (Y, U)\}. \tag{1}$$

In consideration of production theory, T is often regarded as bounded and a closed set, which is the assurance of the output closeness, and it means that limited number of inputs can merely generate the limited outputs (Zhou *et al.*, 2014; Zhou and Fan, 2010). Also, desirable outputs and inputs in T are considered to be freely disposable or robust. Specifically, if $(X, Y, U) \in T$ and $X' \geq X$ or $Y' \leq Y$, then $(X', Y, U) \in T$ or $(X, Y', U) \in T$. To facilitate the suitable model, a production technology can generate the undesirable and desirable outputs, then the succeeding two assumptions proposed by Zhou *et al.* (2012) are imposed on T.

P.1. Outputs are weakly disposable, i.e., if $(X, Y, U) \in T$ and $0 \leq \theta \leq 1$, then $(X, \theta Y, \theta U) \in T$.

P.2. Undesirable bad outputs and desirable good outputs are null-joint, i.e., if $(X, Y, U) \in T$, and $\mathbf{Y} = \mathbf{0}$ then $\mathbf{U} = 0$.

Assumption P. 1 indicates that the deterioration of undesirable bad outputs is not free, and the comparative decrease in undesirable bad outputs and desirable good outputs is possible. Assumption P.2 explains that a few undesirable bad outputs must also be generated during the production of desirable outputs. Specifically, the only way to eradicate undesirable bad outputs is to end the process of production of desirable outputs. Until now, the polluting technology, also called the weak dispose-off capability reference technology, conceptually modeled by Färe *et al.* (2005), for the concurrent generation of both undesirable and desirable outputs, is explained by the following output formula:

$$P(X) = \{(Y, U) : (X, Y, U) \in T\}. \tag{2}$$

$P(\mathbf{x})$ contains all feasible outputs which have the vector of $\mathbf{x}$ inputs and then it may be expressed as $(X, Y, U) \in T \Longleftrightarrow (Y, U) \in P(X)$ (Färe and Grosskopf, 2000). $P(x)$ is a bounded and closed set and its equivalent production technology, while T represents an "environmental output set". Even though the production technology is conceptually well-defined, it cannot be used in the empirical application. Usually, first, it is essential to construct the equivalent relationships among the Shephard distance function, directional distance function and T; after that, it can be generalized as a conventional single-output-oriented production function (*Charnes et al.*, 1994). The distance functions can be used to assess on the basis of parametric or nonparametric conditions. For measurement of nonparametric properties, Färe *et al.* (1989) presented the linear production technology, constant returns to scale (CRS), and Zhou *et al.* (2006) claimed that this type of production techniques can be used as environmental DEA technology because it is originated in DEA framework. Suppose that there are $k = 1, 2, ..., K$, DMU. Let our supposition be true for DMU_k the observed data on the vectors of inputs, undesirable bad outputs and desirable good outputs (Färe and Logan, 1983).

$$X_k = (X_{1k}, X_{2k}, \ldots, X_{Nk}),\quad Y_k = (Y_{1k}, Y_{2k}, \ldots, Y_{Mk}),\quad \text{and}\quad XU_k = (U_{1k}, U_{2k}, \ldots, U_{Jk})$$

$$\sum_{j=1}^{J} U_{Jk} > 0 \quad \text{and} \quad \sum_{k=1}^{K} U_{Jk} > 0$$

$$F: (V_{k1}, \ldots, V_{kn}) \rightarrow (f_1(V_{k1})$$

$$T_{\text{CSR}} = \left\{ (X, Y, U): \sum_{k=1}^{K} Z_k X_{nk} \leq X_n, n = 1, 2, \ldots, N \right\}$$

$$\sum_{k=1}^{K} Z_k Y_{mk} \geq Y_m, \quad m = 1, 2, \ldots, M$$

$$\sum_{k=1}^{K} Z_k U_{Jk} = U_{IJ}, \quad J = 1, 2, \ldots, J$$

$$Z_k \geq 0, \quad k = 1, 2, \ldots, K. \tag{3}$$

The construction of T_{CSR} provides a solid foundation for analysts and researchers in order to conduct an empirical estimation such as construction environmental performance index when production technology shows the approximation of CRS. T_{CSR}, i.e., (3), follows the properties of the weak dispose-off capability of null jointness and outputs between undesirable outputs and desirable outputs (Mohsin *et al.*, 2018). CRS environmental DEA technology and T_{CSR} can be applied after the availability of suitable evidence of the consideration of production technology CRS. Various scholars have investigated the application and effectiveness of CRS environmental DEA technology in different schemes as well as in the assessment of productive efficiency and measurement of environmental performance having undesirable outputs (Charnes and Cooper, 1984; Zhou *et al.*, 2008). However, in practical cases, the reference technology does not always show CRS, while in other cases, VRS might be observed in the actual situation (Färe and Lovell, 1978). Several researchers have proposed the studies with regard to the assessment of the returns to scale property e.g., Färe and Grosskopf (1997) and Rogge (2012). Consequently, it is logical to differentiate between various environmental DEA technologies, and the equivalent DEA-based models for measuring environmental performance. Zhou *et al.* (2012) concluded that the reference technology revealing CRS, and VRS or NRIS is particularly attractive in assessing studies. Hence, it is essential to demonstrate the environmental DEA technologies which validate NIRS and VRS. Like the conventional framework of DEA, NIRS environmental DEA technology (TNIRS) could be developed by imposing the restrictions on the variables of intensity on the CRS environmental DEA technology to reduce data uncertainty (Carstensen and Lindegarth, 2016).

$$T_{\text{NIRS}} = \left\{ (X, Y, U)\colon \sum_{k=1}^{K} Z_k X_{nk} \le X_n, n = 1,2,\ldots,N \right\},$$

$$\sum_{k=1}^{K} Z_k Y_{mk} \ge Y_m, \quad m = 1,2,\ldots,M,$$

$$\sum_{k=1}^{K} Z_k U_{Jk} = U_{IJ}, \quad J = 1,2,\ldots,J,$$

$$Z_k \ge 0, \quad k = 1,2,\ldots,K. \tag{4}$$

In VRS DEA, unlike the traditional DEA framework, the VRS environmental DEA technology (T_{NIRS}) could not remain structured via imposing the limitations due to yielded technology that might infringe environmental DEA technology. Therefore, it is essential to develop a differentiation between traditional DEA and the concept of environmental DEA technology. To endure it, we first make a slight modification on P.1 and P.2, whereby P.1 outputs are weakly disposable, i.e., if $(X, Y, U) \in T$ and $0 \le \theta \le 1$, then $(X, \theta Y, \theta U) \in T$, P.2 undesirable bad outputs and desirable good outputs and are null-joint, i.e., if $(X, Y, U) \in T$. Here P1 still shows the weak dispose-off capability reference technology for the concurrent generation of both undesirable and desirable outputs.

P.2 implies that the desirable good outputs are necessarily insignificant if undesirable bad outputs are insignificant. P3 is to some extent weaker than the previous one, and it can be considered as environmental DEA technology. VRS environmental DEA technology is possibly derived by multiplying the adjusting parameter not less than 1 with the right-hand side of the constraints of undesirable bad outputs. We follow the similar suggestions proposed by Färe *et al.* (1989), but multiply the right-hand side of desirable good outputs constraints with the same parameter. The resultant environmental output is given as follows:

$$T_{\text{VRS}} = \left\{ (X,Y,U)\colon \sum_{k=1}^{K} Z_k X_{nk} \le X_n, n = 1,2,\ldots,N \right\},$$

$$\sum_{k=1}^{K} Z_k Y_{mk} \ge \propto Y_m, \quad m = 1,2,\ldots,M,$$

$$\sum_{k=1}^{K} Z_k U_{Jk} = \propto U_{IJ}, \quad J = 1,2,\ldots,J,$$

$$\propto \ge 1, \quad Z_k \ge 0, \quad k = 1,2,\ldots,K. \tag{5}$$

There is a small difference between (5) and the model proposed by Scheel (2001) whereas model (5) is naturally more similar to DEA. T_{VRS} shows the VRS environmental DEA technology, and it does not have an effect on its assessing property of environmental performance.

3. Results and Discussion

Global assessments of fossil fuel consumption indicate an overall positive evaluation trend despite persisting uncertainties. China, for instance, currently emits approximately twice the amount of CO_2 compared to the United States, although projections suggest that their emissions could converge over the next decade. China's high CO_2 emission level is largely due to its expansive economic growth, significant population size, and strong reliance on coal-based energy sources (Branger & Quirion, 2015). On a global scale, Brazil and South Korea contribute about 1.4% and 1.7% of emissions, respectively, while Mexico accounts for around 1.3% (Yin *et al.*, 2015). Notably, global CO_2 emissions surged by 5.2% in 2010, with fluctuations in subsequent years, reaching 1.9% in 2012, 1.8% in 2013, and 2.2% in 2014. Regionally, Mexico reduced its emissions by 1.6%, while Brazil, South Korea, and other countries, including Indonesia and Iran, reported increases during this period (Olivier *et al.*, 2016). For developing nations, the Paris Agreement has set a clear agenda to focus on reducing greenhouse gas emissions and improving energy efficiency to support environmental sustainability.

As shown in Table 1, energy consumption (Koe capita) varies considerably, with Israel leading at 14,462.19, followed by Norway (8,160.52), Sweden (6,002.32), Germany (6,568.5), and Australia (5,636.01). Chile, however, recorded the lowest energy consumption. The primary energy supply also shows vast differences, from Luxembourg's 482.79 million tons down to Norway's 4.01 million tons. Renewable energy consumption is highest in Iceland (77.03%), followed by Norway (57.77%), Sweden (53.25%), Finland (43.24%), and Chile (24.88%). Conversely, Korea and Israel exhibit the lowest renewable energy shares at 2.71% and 3.71%, respectively. Regarding greenhouse gas emissions per capita, Australia ranks highest at 24.61 kg per capita, while the Netherlands has the lowest value of 5.28 kg per capita.

It is generally recognized that emission reductions could impact economic growth and may introduce externalities. Countries with faster economic growth tend to have higher energy consumption, often accompanied by increased greenhouse gas emissions. According to a World Bank report (2015), between 1960 and 1990, environmental indicators showed significant degradation, with greenhouse gases, particularly CO_2 from fossil fuel combustion, accounting for approximately 56.6% of emissions. The International Energy Outlook also highlights the worsening impact of fossil fuel-related CO_2 emissions on climate change (Mohsin *et al.*, 2019).

3.1. *Empirical results*

According to the 2014 energy statistics, global coal consumption rose 0.4% from the previous year, mainly driven by China, accounting for 50.6% of the total world coal usage (Xie & Weng, 2016). India also saw a notable increase, with coal consumption rising to 11.1% due to high domestic production, compared to 7.3% in 2013. Conversely, lower coal usage trends were observed across several countries, including Germany (5.3%), the United Kingdom (20.3%), Italy (3.7%), Australia (2.5%), Japan (1.6%), and the United States (0.3%) (Vinci *et al.*, 2017; Hassan & Salim, 2015).

Table 1. Individual Indicators of OECD Countries

Country	EC (Koe Capita)	PES (Million Ton)	Renewable %	GHG (Kg/Capita, 000)	GHG Per Unit of EC	GDP Growth
Australia	5636.01	119.77	09.18	24.61	1395.22	3.29
Austria	3902.54	32.310	34.39	10.24	326.53	1.90
Belgium	5296.14	56.680	09.21	12.48	379.05	1.80
Canada	8033.36	267.19	22.03	21.79	1356.22	2.36
Chile	1841.08	25.940	24.88	5.360	630.28	5.20
Denmark	4183.86	43.850	33.17	13.54	503.53	1.48
Finland	3390.62	18.570	43.24	11.84	287.07	1.77
France	3979.19	5.3900	13.52	14.58	73.670	1.57
Germany	6568.50	34.870	14.21	13.44	162.98	1.44
Greece	4042.36	258.48	17.17	8.390	1930.62	1.01
Hungary	3999.74	267.24	15.56	11.84	3633.61	1.76
Iceland	2525.82	27.460	77.03	10.90	720.75	2.68
Ireland	2519.47	25.710	09.08	6.830	407.83	4.62
Israel	14462.19	21.280	03.71	14.04	4.51	5.16
Italy	3256.81	14.000	16.52	15.02	297.51	0.73
Japan	2903.28	4.6400	06.31	10.35	316.66	0.93
Korea	2928.13	170.41	02.71	8.760	2662.71	5.28
Luxembourg	3830.65	482.79	09.03	10.68	5331.77	3.68
Mexico	4677.42	234.70	09.22	12.34	1807.36	2.78
Netherlands	2022.87	4.4000	05.89	5.280	84.530	1.99
New Zealand	2548.52	8.2000	30.79	6.500	127.00	2.68
Norway	8160.52	4.0100	57.77	23.92	21.430	2.48
Poland	1553.64	177.35	11.91	5.820	4490.83	3.69
Portugal	4776.17	78.690	27.16	12.55	649.50	1.53
Spain	4255.64	18.220	16.25	18.82	281.24	2.04
Sweden	6002.32	28.640	53.25	11.46	136.76	2.04
Switzerland	2476.78	94.830	25.29	10.35	2395.62	1.55
Turkey	2295.33	24.030	13.37	7.190	492.60	4.01
UK	3287.75	17.720	08.71	8.820	216.79	2.08
US	3477.38	7.0500	08.72	9.650	84.330	2.56

Table 2 illustrates the range of energy intensity values from 0.30 to 0.93, with New Zealand and Norway at the highest values (0.93) and Ireland and Luxembourg at the lowest (0.30). In terms of energy efficiency, Iceland and Greece demonstrated top scores (0.99), while Ireland had the lowest efficiency at 0.34. Specifically, Austria, Australia, Portugal, and Spain had energy intensity values between 0.70 and 0.80, whereas the UK, Sweden, Germany, and the USA had values between 0.40 and 0.50. Detailed efficiency scores reveal

Table 2. Energy Intensity, Energy Efficiency and Environmental Index

Country	Energy Intensity	Energy Efficiency	Environmental Index
Australia	0.72	0.74	0.65
Austria	0.74	0.74	0.65
Belgium	0.62	0.63	0.54
Canada	0.62	0.71	0.62
Chile	0.69	0.69	0.60
Denmark	0.50	0.50	0.41
Finland	0.58	0.56	0.47
France	0.51	0.48	0.39
Germany	0.46	0.49	0.62
Greece	0.84	0.99	0.93
Hungary	0.59	0.58	0.51
Iceland	0.89	0.99	0.97
Ireland	0.30	0.34	0.27
Israel	0.71	0.83	0.76
Italy	0.68	0.63	0.56
Japan	0.53	0.55	0.48
Korea	0.70	0.52	0.45
Luxembourg	0.30	0.37	0.30
Mexico	0.90	0.70	0.62
Netherlands	0.57	0.78	0.71
New Zealand	0.93	0.42	0.64
Norway	0.93	0.65	0.57
Poland	0.36	0.36	0.28
Portugal	0.84	0.95	0.87
Spain	0.89	0.41	0.62
Sweden	0.45	0.46	0.37
Switzerland	0.67	0.72	0.63
Turkey	0.69	0.91	0.82
UK	0.40	0.47	0.38
USA	0.40	0.43	0.34

Australia, Austria, Mexico, and Switzerland scoring between 0.70 and 0.80, while Germany, Sweden, the UK, and the USA ranged from 0.40 to 0.50. Italy's high energy costs have encouraged conservation, while Iceland's power-intensive manufacturing has increased its energy intensity. Over the last two decades, decreasing energy intensity has aligned with improvements in energy efficiency, providing both environmental and economic advantages. Although historically higher in transition economies than in industrialized ones, energy intensity has sharply declined since the start of these countries' economic transitions.

Table 3. Summary Statistics of GHG Emission (Tons of CO_2 Equivalent Thousand)

Sum	239719948.2
Mean	6658887.45
Maximum	104703444
Minimum	65159.976

Significant differences in energy efficiency and structural economic shifts have been observed across OECD countries. Between 2000 and 2015, 24 out of 30 OECD countries saw reductions in average energy intensity thanks to energy efficiency improvements and industrial activity shifts. Countries such as Germany, Ireland, Iceland, the Netherlands, Canada, Japan, Luxembourg, the UK, and the USA achieved these reductions through structural shifts toward less energy-intensive activities. In contrast, rising energy intensity in Israel, Portugal, and New Zealand stemmed from their reallocation of energy-intensive industries. While Spain has seen limited structural improvements, nations like Israel, Greece, Iceland, and Turkey demonstrated gains in energy efficiency. Higher GDP growth rates are generally associated with increased greenhouse gas emissions, particularly in Australia, Canada, Korea, and Poland. At the same time, this relationship appears weaker in countries such as Israel, the Netherlands, New Zealand, Norway, and Denmark.

As shown in Table 3, total greenhouse gas emissions across OECD countries reached 239,719,948.2 units between 2000 and 2015, with values ranging from a high of 104,703,444 to a low of 65,159.976 and an average of 6,658,887.45. Emissions and energy costs are generally reduced by increased renewable energy use; for instance, Japan's limited domestic oil and gas resources make it heavily reliant on imports, potentially driving economic growth alongside increased GHG emissions. Germany, meanwhile, is shifting its energy demand towards renewables and supporting cross-border renewable energy trade. Improving energy efficiency can help reduce CO_2 emissions from energy consumption, a critical approach to mitigating climate change impacts. Balancing economic development with environmental sustainability remains a priority, with many countries, including Australia, Japan, Germany, and Sweden, working towards decoupling economic growth from energy consumption. Absolute decoupling, particularly through reduced fossil fuel dependence, effectively alleviates environmental pressures (Wu *et al.*, 2018). Enhanced energy efficiency, particularly when linked to renewable energy, offers a cost-effective path toward reducing CO_2 emissions.

3.2. *Sensitivity analysis*

Various uncertainty factors may affect the results when solving several linear programming models. First, the best practice frontier, developed from attainable entities, estimates the true frontier but is subject to potential variations due to sampling. Although bootstrap methods can help reduce uncertainty by assessing sample variation within the original dataset, it is important to note that constructing the best practice frontier for environmental efficiency differs significantly from frontiers in productivity and efficiency analyses. One common approach to developing environmental efficiency involves a cross-sectional study examining performance over time. This framework allows for new observations across comparable entities at different intervals, thereby refining the frontier for environmental efficiency evaluation.

While variation and sampling uncertainty in the obtained frontier is not the primary focus of this study, ensuring data accuracy in creating a new dataset is crucial for managing these factors. Regarding CO_2 data, as Zhou *et al.* (2012) observed, data accuracy and associated variation complicate the metrics of environmental efficiency assessment. Nevertheless, the sensitivity of the proposed DEA methodology concerning data changes can be theoretically evaluated. This study performs a sensitivity analysis of environmental efficiency measurements, examining observation changes. Data adjustments for all observations are made within a ±10% range to achieve this. By generating random values within the interval [−10%, 10%], we produced 20 datasets for OECD countries, enabling environmental efficiency measurements across these datasets.

Using the 20 simulated datasets, we computed the average environmental efficiency and its standard deviation to evaluate variation in the newly developed dataset. Results indicate that within the tested uncertainty range, each OECD country's average values of environmental efficiency metrics are largely stable. This limited effect of data uncertainty and variation suggests that the standard deviation of the average environmental efficiency values remains minor, as shown in Figure 1. Thus, the results appear reliable and robust,

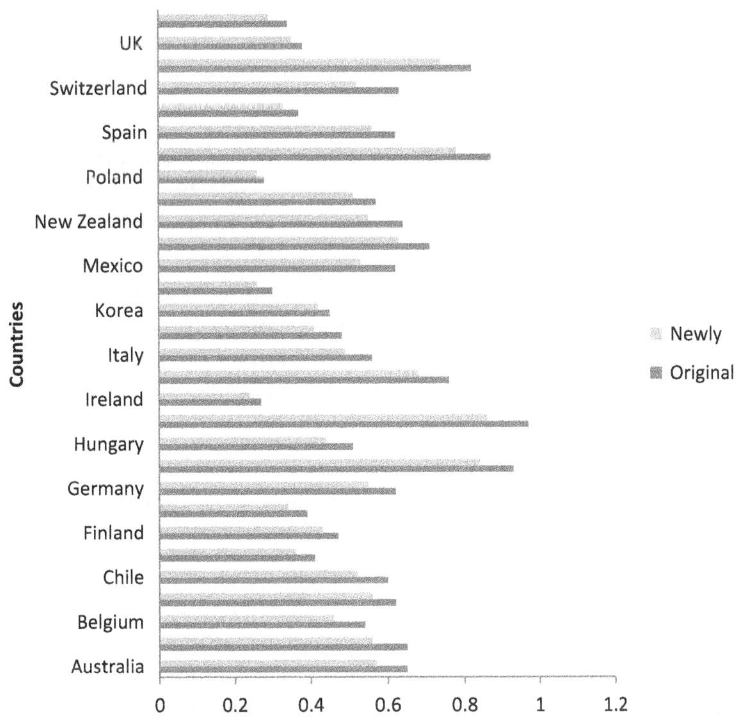

Figure 1. Original and Newly Simulated Values

with average efficiency values remaining relatively insensitive to moderate variations in data accuracy.

To examine the distribution of environmental efficiency values, significant fluctuations appeared only with higher data uncertainty. Ensuring data accuracy is critical, and comparing environmental efficiency values from the original dataset with those from newly simulated datasets is essential for sensitivity analysis. Figure 1 displays few noticeable changes, especially in the median and range of efficiency measurements, which indicates the model's insensitivity and reliable accuracy when using a substantial sample size. Minimal changes in environmental efficiency values and low standard deviation under data uncertainty demonstrate resilience, supporting the robustness of the best practice frontier under data accuracy fluctuations. This methodological approach effectively addresses data irregularities, such as numerous zero values, and adheres to desired index number properties, confirming the robustness of these results.

4. Conclusion and Policy Implications

This study examined VRS and NIRS environmental DEA methodologies, where outputs maintain weak disposability. Using a framework grounded in nonradial DEA techniques, the analysis assessed energy security and environmental efficiency. The assessment revealed energy consumption values across OECD countries ranging from 14,462.19 Israel to 1,841.08 in Chile. In terms of primary energy supply, Luxembourg registered the highest supply at 482.79 million tons, while Norway had the lowest at 4.01 million tons. Renewable energy consumption also varied widely, with Iceland leading at 77.03%, followed by Norway (57.77%), Sweden (53.25%), Finland (43.24%), and Chile (24.88%), while Korea and Israel showed the lowest renewable shares at 2.71% and 3.71%, respectively. The per capita GHG emissions also fluctuated, with Australia at the highest (24.61 kg per capita) and the Netherlands at the lowest (5.28 kg per capita). In energy efficiency, Iceland and Greece achieved the top scores of 0.99, whereas Ireland was at the lower end with a score of 0.34. Energy intensity values showed that Austria, Australia, Portugal, and Spain scored 0.70 and 0.80, while the UK, Sweden, Germany, and the USA registered between 0.40 and 0.50. Detailed efficiency scores reveal that Australia, Austria, Mexico, and Switzerland achieved values from 0.70 to 0.80, whereas Germany, Sweden, the UK, and the USA had values from 0.40 to 0.50. These findings offer actionable policy insights for governments and decision-makers. Key recommendations are outlined below.

To facilitate a low-carbon transition, OECD countries should implement carbon pricing mechanisms, such as carbon taxes or cap-and-trade, to make greenhouse gas emissions costly and incentivize businesses toward cleaner energy solutions. Additionally, reinforcing Renewable Portfolio Standards (RPS) can drive utilities to achieve specified renewable energy targets, helping to replace fossil fuels with sustainable alternatives systematically. Supporting advanced technologies like energy storage, grid modernization, and carbon capture. Financial incentives for these technologies would help stabilize renewable energy integration and reduce emissions in high-impact sectors like manufacturing. Similarly, stricter energy efficiency standards across buildings, appliances, and vehicles, supported by rebates and tax incentives, can reduce overall energy consumption, aligning economic activities with environmental goals. Green procurement policies prioritizing sustainable suppliers can further push the private sector toward eco-friendly practices. Meanwhile, green financing instruments, such as green bonds and sustainability-linked loans, could lower financing costs for eco-friendly projects, with public institutions playing a pivotal role in facilitating access to capital. Expanding subsidies and tax credits for renewable energy adoption — especially for solar, wind, and geothermal projects — can make clean energy more accessible. Decentralized renewable systems, like community solar microgrids, should be encouraged through grants and low-interest loans to enhance local energy security, particularly in remote areas. Electrification incentives for high-emission sectors, like transportation, industrial heating, and investment in EV infrastructure, are also essential for lowering carbon emissions. Finally, OECD nations should deepen regional energy cooperation through shared infrastructure and energy trade agreements to create an integrated, resilient, and efficient energy network that benefits from each country's resources and capacities.

Acknowledgments

We are grateful for the financial support provided by the National Natural Science Foundation of China (Nos. 71774071, 71690241, 71810107001 and 71673117), and Young Academic Leader Project of Jiangsu University (5521380003).

References

Bang, Y, Y Hong, NJ Sung, D Lee and SR Lim (2018). Comparative assessment of solar photovoltaic panels based on metal-derived hazardous waste, resource depletion, and toxicity potentials. *International Journal of Green Energy,* 15(10), 550–557, https://doi.org/10.1080/15435075.2018.1505618.

Benromdhane, SA (2015). Energy efficiency through integrated environmental management. *Environmental Science and Pollution Research,* 22(10), 7973–7979, https://doi.org/10.1007/s11356-015-4424-8.

Branger, F and P Quirion (2015). Reaping the carbon rent: Abatement and overallocation profits in the European cement industry, insights from an LMDI decomposition analysis. *Energy Economics,* 47, 189–205, https://doi.org/10.1016d.eneco.2014.11.008.

Bujang, AS, CJ Bern and TJ Brumm (2016). Summary of energy demand and renewable energy policies in Malaysia. *Renewable and Sustainable Energy Reviews,* 53, 1459–1467, https://doi.org/10.1016/j.rser.2015.09.047.

Carstensen, J and M Lindegarth (2016). Confidence in ecological indicators: A framework for quantifying uncertainty components from monitoring data. *Ecological Indicators,* 67, 306–317, https://doi.org/10.1016Zj.ecolind.2016.03.002.

Charnes, A and WW Cooper (1984). Preface to topics in data envelopment analysis. *Annals of Operations Research,* 2(1), 59–94, https://doi.org/10.1007/BF01874733.

Charnes, A, WW Cooper, AY Lewin and LM Seiford (1994). *Introduction. In Data Envelopment Analysis: Theory, Methodology, and Applications. Igarss 2014,* https://doi.org/10.1007/s13398-014-0173-7.2.

Chen, Y and JT Xu (2018). An assessment of energy efficiency based on environmental constraints and its influencing factors in China. *Environmental Science and Pollution Research*, pp. 1–14, https://doi.org/10.1007/s11356-018-1912-7.

Egilmez, G, S Gumus, M Kucukvar and O Tatari (2016). A fuzzy data envelopment analysis framework for dealing with uncertainty impacts of input-output life cycle assessment models on eco-efficiency assessment. *Journal of Cleaner Production,* 129, 622–636, https://doi.org/10.1016/j.jclepro.2016.03.111.

Egilmez, G, M Kucukvar and O Tatari (2013). Sustainability assessment of U.S. manufacturing sectors: An economic input output-based frontier approach. *Journal of Cleaner Production*, 53, 91–102, https://doi.org/10.1016/j.jclepro.2013.03.037.

Färe, R, D-W Nohb, W Weber and S Grosskopf (2005). Characteristics of a polluting technology: Theory and practice. *Journal of Econometrics,* 126(2), 469–492, https://doi.org/10.1016/j.jeconom.2004.05.010.

Färe, R, S Grosskopf, CAK Lovell and C Pasurka (1989). Multilateral productivity comparisons when some outputs are undesirable: A nonparametric approach. *The Review of Economics and Statistics,* 71(1), 90–98, https://doi.org/10.2307/1928055.

Färe, R and S Grosskopf (2000). Research note: Decomposing technical efficiency with care. *Management Science,* 46(1), 167, https://doi.org/10.1287/mnsc.46.L167.15125.

Färe, R and S Grosskopf (1994). Estimation of returns to scale using data envelopment analysis: A comment. *European Journal of Operational Research,* 79(2), 379–382, https://doi.org/10.1016/0377-2217(94)90366-2.

Färe, R and S Grosskopf (1997). Intertemporal production frontiers: With dynamic DEA. *Journal of the Operational Research Society,* 48(6), 656–656, https://doi.org/10.1057/palgrave.jors.2600779.

Färe, R and S Grosskopf (2004). Modeling undesirable factors in efficiency evaluation: Comment. In *European Journal of Operational Research,* 157, 242–245, https://doi.org/10.1016/S0377-2217(03)00191-7.

Färe, R and J Logan (1983). The rate-of-return regulated firm: Cost and production duality. *The Bell Journal of Economics and Management Science,* 14(1), 405–414, https://doi.org/10.2307/3003642.

Färe, R and K Lovell (1978). The measurement of efficiency of production. *Journal of Economic Theory,* 19, 150–162, https://doi.org/10.3390/ijms13056204.

Fleifle, A, O Saavedra, C Yoshimura, M Elzeir and A Tawfik (2014). Optimization of integrated water quality management for agricultural efficiency and environmental conservation. *Environmental Science and Pollution Research,* 21(13), 8095–8111, https://doi.org/10.1007/s11356-014-2712-3.

Guo, J, Y-J Zhang and K-B Zhang (2018). The key sectors for energy conservation and carbon emissions reduction in China: Evidence from the input-output method. *Journal of Cleaner Production,* 179, 180–190, https://doi.org/10.1016d.jclepro.2018.01.080.

Hassan, K and R Salim (2015). Population ageing, Income growth and CO_2 emission: Empirical evidence from high income oecd countries. *Journal of Economic Studies*, 42(1), https://doi.org/10.1108/JES-04-2013-0046.

Ikram, M, A Mahmoudi, SZA Shah and M Mohsin (2019). Forecasting number of ISO 14001 certifications of selected countries: Application of even GM (1,1), DGM, and NDGM models. *Environmental Science and Pollution Research,* https://doi.org/10.1007/s11356-019-04534-2.

Ikram, M, P Zhou, SAA Shah and GQ Liu (2019). Do environmental management systems help improve corporate sustainable development? Evidence from manufacturing companies in

Pakistan. *Journal of Cleaner Production,* 226, 628–641, https://doi.org/10.1016/j.jclepro.2019.03.265.

Jing, Q, H Bai, W Luo, B Cai and H Xu (2018). A top-bottom method for city-scale energy-related CO_2 estimation: A case study of 41 Chinese cities. *Journal of Cleaner Production*, 202, 444–455, https://doi.org/10.1016/JJCLEPRO.2018.08.179.

Kolodko, GW (2018). *Emerging Market Economies.* Routledge, https://doi.org/10.4324/9781315199382.

Mohsin, M, AK Rasheed and R Saidur (2018). Economic viability and production capacity of wind generated renewable hydrogen. *International Journal of Hydrogen Energy*, https://doi.org/10.1016/j.ijhydene.2017.12.113.

Mohsin, M, J Zhang, R Saidur, H Sun and SM Sait (2019). Economic assessment and ranking of wind power potential using fuzzy-TOPSIS approach. *Environmental Science and Pollution Research,* https://doi.org/10.1007/s11356-019-05564-6.

Mohsin, M, P Zhou, N Iqbal and SAA Shah (2018). Assessing oil supply security of South Asia. *Energy,* 155, 438–447, https://doi.org/10.1016/J.ENERGY.2018.04.116.

Molinos-Senante, M, R Sala-Garrido and M Lafuente (2015). The role of environmental variables on the efficiency of water and sewerage companies: A case study of Chile. *Environmental Science and Pollution Research,* 22(13), 10242–10253, https://doi.org/10.1007/s11356-015-4225-0.

Mollahosseini, A, SA Hosseini, M Jabbari, A Figoli and A Rahimpour (2017). Renewable energy management and market in Iran: A holistic review on current state and future demands. *Renewable and Sustainable Energy Reviews*, https://doi.org/10.1016/j.rser.2017.05.236.

Nejat, P, F Jomehzadeh, MM Taheri, M Gohari and MZ Muhd (2015). A global review of energy consumption, CO_2 emissions and policy in the residential sector (with an overview of the top ten CO_2 emitting countries). *Renewable and Sustainable Energy Reviews,* 43, 843–862, https://doi.org/10.1016/j.rser.2014.11.066.

Olivier, JGJ, G Janssens-Maenhout, M Muntean and JAHW Peters (2016). *Trends in Global CO_2 Emissions: 2016 Report. PBL Netherlands Environmental Assessment Agency & European Commission's Joint Research Centre (JRC).*

Ouyang, X and B Lin (2014). Impacts of increasing renewable energy subsidies and phasing out fossil fuel subsidies in China. *Renewable and Sustainable Energy Reviews*, 37, 933–942, https://doi.org/10.1016/j.rser.2014.05.013.

Perez, V, F Guerrero, M Gonzalez, F Perez and R Caballero (2013). Composite indicator for the assessment of sustainability: The case of Cuban nature-based tourism destinations. *Ecological Indicators,* 29, 316–324, https://doi.org/10.1016d.ecolind.2012.12.027.

Rashidi, K and R Farzipoor Saen (2015). Measuring eco-efficiency based on green indicators and potentials in energy saving and undesirable output abatement. *Energy Economics*, 50, 18–26, https://doi.org/10.1016Zj.eneco.2015.04.018.

Rogge, N (2012). Undesirable specialization in the construction of composite policy indicators: The environmental performance index. *Ecological Indicators,* 23, 143–154, https://doi.org/10.1016/j.ecolind.2012.03.020.

Scheel, H (2001). Undesirable outputs in efficiency valuations. *Omega,* 132(4), 400–410, https://doi.org/10.1016/S0377-2217(00)00160-0.

Sueyoshi, T and M Goto (2015). DEA environmental assessment in time horizon: Radial approach for Malmquist index measurement on petroleum companies. *Energy Economics,* 51, 329–345, https://doi.org/10.1016Aj.eneco.2015.07.010.

Sueyoshi, T and D Wang (2018). DEA environmental assessment on US petroleum industry: Non-radial approach with translation invariance in time horizon. *Energy Economics*, 72, 276–289, https://doi.org/10.1016/j.eneco.2018.02.003.

Sueyoshi, T and Y Yuan (2017). Social sustainability measured by intermediate approach for DEA environmental assessment: Chinese regional planning for economic development and pollution prevention. *Energy Economics,* 66, 154–166, https://doi.org/10.1016/j.eneco.2017.06.008.

Sun, H, Y Geng, L Hu, L Shi and T Xu (2018). Measuring China's new energy vehicle patents: A social network analysis approach. *Energy,* 153, 685–693, https://doi.org/10.1016/j.energy.2018.04.077.

Sun, H, T Gulzara, M Haris and M Mohsin (2019a). Evaluating the environmental effects of economic openness: Evidence from SAARC countries. *Environmental Science and Pollution Research,* https://doi.org/10.1007/s11356-019-05750-6.

Sun, H, A Samuel, Y Geng, K Fang and C Joshua (2019b). Trade openness and carbon emissions: Evidence from belt and road countries. *Sustainability,* https://doi.org/10.3390/su11092682.

Sun, M, C Gao and B Shen (2014). Quantifying China's oil import risks and the impact on the national economy. *Energy Policy,* 67, 605–611, https://doi.org/10.1016/j.enpol.2013.12.061.

Taghizadeh-Hesary, F, E Rasoulinezhadb and N Yoshino (2019). Energy and food security: Linkages through price volatility. *Energy Policy*, 128, 796–806.

Taghizadeh-Hesary, F and N Yoshino (2015). Macroeconomic effects of oil price fluctuations on emerging and developed economies in a model incorporating monetary variables. *Economic Policy Energy Environment,* 2, 51–75, https://doi.org/10.3280/EFE2015-002005.

Taghizadeh-Hesary, F and N Yoshino (2016a). Monetary policy, oil prices and the real macroeconomic variables: An empirical survey on China, Japan and the United States. *China International Journal*, 14, 46–69.

Taghizadeh-Hesary, F, N Yoshino, G Abdoli and A Farzinvash (2013). An estimation of the impact of oil shocks on crude oil exporting economies and their trade partners. *Frontiers of Economics in China,* 8(4), 571–591, https://doi.org/10.3868/s060-002-013-0029-3.

Taghizadeh-Hesary, F, E Rasoulinezhad and Y Kobayashi (2016b). Oil price fluctuations and oil consuming sectors: An empirical analysis of Japan. *Economics of Energy & Environmental Policy,* 2(19), 33–35, https://doi.org/10.3280/EFE2016-002003.

Taghizadeh-Hesary, F, N Yoshino, MMH Abadi and R Farboudmanesh (2016c). The response of macro variables of emerging and developed oil importers to oil price movements. *Journal of the Asia Pacific Economy,* 21(1), 91–102, https://doi.org/10.1080/13547860.2015.1057955.

Taghizadeh-Hesary, F, N Yoshino and Y Inagaki (2018). Empirical analysis of factors influencing the price of solar modules. *International Journal of Energy Sector Management,* https://doi.org/10.1108/IJESM-05-2018-0005.

Vidadili, N, E Suleymanov, C Bulut and C Mahmudlu (2017). Transition to renewable energy and sustainable energy development in Azerbaijan. *Renewable and Sustainable Energy Reviews,* https://doi.org/10.1016/j.rser.2017.05.168.

Vinci, S, R Boampong, MA Phillips and C Cader (2017). Nigerian Electricity Regulation Commission, Ministry of Energy, Energy access outlook 2017: From poverty to prosperity. *Energy Procedia,* 94(March), 144, https://doi.org/10.1787/9789264285569-en.

Wang, Q and R Li (2016). Impact of cheaper oil on economic system and climate change: A SWOT analysis. *Renewable and Sustainable Energy Reviews*, https://doi.org/10.1016/j.rser.2015.10.087.

World Development Report (2015). Mind, society, and behavior (Vols. 1 of 2). World development report | World development indicators. Washington, DC: World Bank Group. http://documents.worldbank.org/curated/en/645741468339541646.

Wu, Y, KW Chau, W Lu, L Shen, C Shuai and J Chen (2018). Decoupling relationship between economic output and carbon emission in the Chinese construction industry. *Environmental Impact Assessment Review,* https://doi.org/10.1016/j.eiar.2018.04.001.

Xie, Y, and Q Weng (2016). Detecting urban-scale dynamics of electricity consumption at Chinese cities using time-series DMSP-OLS (Defense Meteorological Satellite Program-Operational Linescan System) nighttime light imageries. *Energy,* 100, 177–189, https://doi.org/10.1016/j.energy.2016.01.058.

Yin, X, W Chen, J Eom, LE Clarke, SH Kim, PL Patel and GP Kyle (2015). China's transportation energy consumption and CO_2 emissions from a global perspective. *Energy Policy,* 82, 233–248, https://doi.org/10.1016Aj.enpol.2015.03.021.

Zhang, D, X Shi and Y Sheng (2015). Comprehensive measurement of energy market integration in East Asia: An application of dynamic principal component analysis. *Energy Economics,* 52, 299–305, https://doi.org/10.1016/j.eneco.2015.11.006.

Zhang, Y, Y Jin and B Shen (2018a). Measuring the energy saving and CO_2 emissions reduction potential under china's belt and road initiative. *Computational Economics,* https://doi.org/10.1007/s10614-018-9839-0.

Zhang, Y, Y Sun and J Huang (2018b). Energy efficiency, carbon emission performance, and technology gaps: Evidence from CDM project investment. *Energy Policy*, https://doi.org/10.1016/j.enpol.2017.12.056.

Zhou, P, BW Ang and KL Poh (2006). Comparing aggregating methods for constructing the composite environmental index: An objective measure. *Ecological Economics,* 59(3), 305–311, https://doi.org/10.1016/J.ECOLECON.2005.10.018.

Zhou, P, BW Ang and KL Poh (2008). A survey of data envelopment analysis in energy and environmental studies. *European Journal of Operational Research,* https://doi.org/10.1016/j.ejor.2007.04.042.

Zhou, P, BW Ang and H Wang (2012). Energy and CO_2 emission performance in electricity generation: A non-radial directional distance function approach. *European Journal of Operational Research,* 221(3), 625–635, https://doi.org/10.1016d.ejor.2012.04.022.

Zhou, P and LW Fan (2010). An extension to data envelopment analysis with preference structure for estimating overall inefficiency, 216(3), 812–818, https://doi.org/10.1016d.amc.2010.01.085.

Zhou, P, ZR Sun and DQ Zhou (2014). Optimal path for controlling CO_2 emissions in China: A perspective of efficiency analysis. *Energy Economics,* 45, 99–110, https://doi.org/10.1016/j.eneco.2014.06.019.

https://doi.org/10.1142/9789819812608_0004

Chapter 4

Enhancing Energy Security in Agriculture: Drivers of Solar Water Pump Adoption in Developing Economies

AMIR RAHMANI[*,§], ALI BONYADI NAEINI[*,¶], FARHAD TAGHIZADEH-HESARY[†,‖], and ROOHALLAH ABOOJAFARI[‡,**]

[*]*School of Management, Economics and Progress Engineering, Iran University of Science & Technology (IUST), Tehran, Iran*
[†]*Tokai University Research Institute for Environment and Sustainability (TRIES), Tokai University, Tokyo, Japan*
[‡]*Knowledge-Based Economy Department, Technology Study Institute, Tehran, Iran*
[§]*amir_rahmani@pgre.iust.ac.ir, rahmani.amir2021@gmail.com*
[¶]*bonyadi@iust.ac.ir*
[‖]*farhad@tsc.u-tokai.ac.jp*
[**]*aboojafari@tsi.ir*

Energy security remains a pressing concern for developing economies, where the agricultural sector is particularly vulnerable due to its reliance on stable and affordable energy supplies. Solar water pumps, a solar energy innovation, present a promising solution for sustainable water management in agriculture, especially in areas with abundant solar radiation. This chapter delves into the drivers behind the adoption of solar water pumps among farmers in developing economies. Through an extended Unified Theory of Acceptance and Use of Technology (UTAUT) model, this study identifies key determinants such as performance expectancy, awareness, social influence, and facilitating conditions that shape farmers' intentions to use solar water pumps. Furthermore, the study emphasizes the role of increased awareness of solar energy technologies, highlighting the need for targeted outreach programs to address knowledge gaps. The findings underscore the potential of solar water pumps to enhance energy security and offer actionable insights for policymakers and stakeholders aiming to promote the broader adoption of sustainable technologies. This study supports efforts toward more resilient agricultural practices and long-term sustainability in energy-dependent sectors by encouraging the transition to renewable energy sources.

Keywords: Energy security, solar energy adoption, energy transition, developing economies.

1. Introduction

Energy is an essential component of modern society, underpinning a wide range of human activities and serving as a key driver of economic development worldwide. It facilitates the operation of industrial, transportation, and agricultural sectors, all of which are vital for sustaining economic growth and improving quality of life (Sharvini *et al.*, 2018). However, the predominant reliance on fossil fuels for energy has resulted in significant environmental and economic challenges. Fossil fuels are responsible for approximately 89% of global CO_2 emissions, which are a major contributor to global warming and climate change (Rahmani *et al.*, 2023). This has led to a growing recognition of climate change as a critical global issue, prompting increased attention from policymakers and researchers worldwide (Aghdam *et al.*, 2020; Sadatshojaie and Rahimpour, 2020; Wall *et al.*, 2021).

The agricultural sector, a key driver of economic development in many rural economies, is heavily reliant on energy for irrigation and production processes. The agricultural sector, in particular, is a significant consumer of energy and a notable emitter of greenhouse gases (GHGs) (Rahmani and Bonyadi Naeini, 2023). Moreover, in today's rapidly evolving world, energy security is becoming an essential component for sustainable economic growth, especially in regions where reliable access to energy remains a challenge (Rahmani *et al.*, 2024b). In this context, farmers face growing concerns over fluctuating fuel prices, unreliable power supply, and environmental degradation linked to conventional energy sources. Given these challenges, there is a critical need for a transition toward cleaner energy sources in agriculture. Encouraging the adoption of renewable energies (REs), such as solar energy, in agricultural operations is a strategic response to mitigate the adverse environmental impacts associated with traditional energy sources energies (Qiao *et al.*, 2019; Shahbaz *et al.*, 2019). Solar energy technologies (SETs) present a promising alternative to fossil fuels. They offer numerous advantages, such as abundant availability, sustainability, and a significantly lower environmental footprint. Integrating SETs into agricultural practices not only supports sustainable economic development but also contributes to low-carbon production, aligning with global efforts to combat climate change. Moreover, solar energy usage directly addresses environmental pollution and provides a viable solution to the challenges posed by climate change (Li *et al.*, 2021; Rode and Weber, 2016).

An effective solution that addresses some of these challenges is the implementation of solar water pumps. These solar-powered irrigation systems provide a clean, renewable, and affordable alternative to conventional diesel or electric pumps, significantly reducing operational costs for farmers. Additionally, they contribute to climate change mitigation by lowering carbon emissions. The widespread adoption of solar water pumps strengthens energy security in rural areas, while simultaneously promoting economic growth through increased agricultural productivity and the adoption of more sustainable farming practices. By transitioning to solar-powered solutions, farmers can reduce their dependency on external energy sources, stabilizing their operations and improving their livelihoods. Moreover, the widespread use of solar water pumps aligns with national and global goals for sustainable development, emphasizing the importance of renewable energy in achieving long-term economic resilience.

Iran, one of the world's largest oil and gas producers, relies heavily on fossil fuels for its energy requirements, with renewable sources making up only about 1% of its total energy mix (Rahmani and Bonyadi Naeini, 2023). This heavy reliance has positioned Iran among the top 10 global emitters of CO_2 and the highest emitter in the Middle East.

The excessive use of fossil fuels has led to significant air quality issues, particularly in Tehran, which experiences only about 30 days of clean air annually. Despite its substantial potential for solar energy, with most regions receiving intense solar radiation for nearly 300 days/year, the adoption of solar technologies, particularly in agriculture, has been minimal in Iran (Tavana *et al.*, 2019). Many agricultural units are located far from the central power grid, necessitating a dependence on fossil fuel-based technologies like diesel generators, which are expensive and environmentally detrimental. Although solar energy pumps offer a more sustainable and cost-effective alternative, especially for remote agricultural areas, the uptake of these technologies among farmers has been limited. It is crucial to understand the factors influencing the adoption of solar energy pumps to promote their broader use and address the environmental and economic challenges the agricultural sector faces (Amutha and Rajini, 2016).

This chapter aims to address the existing knowledge gap by investigating the factors influencing the adoption of solar water pumps in Iran's agricultural sector, with a particular focus on regions characterized by high solar radiation potential but limited access to grid infrastructure. Applying the Unified Theory of Acceptance and Use of Technology (UTAUT) model (Venkatesh *et al.*, 2003) and utilizing structural equation modeling (SEM), the study examines various psychological determinants that either facilitate or hinder the adoption of solar water pumps by farmers. The analysis centers on the core constructs of the UTAUT model—performance expectancy, effort expectancy, social influence, and facilitating conditions—to assess their impact on farmers' intentions to adopt these technologies.

The insights generated from this research offer a comprehensive framework for understanding the adoption dynamics of renewable energy technologies in agricultural contexts. These findings are intended to provide policymakers and stakeholders with evidence-based guidance for developing strategies to promote the use of solar technologies in agriculture. By addressing the barriers identified and leveraging the factors that facilitate adoption, this study contributes to the broader goals of enhancing energy security, mitigating greenhouse gas emissions, and promoting sustainable economic growth in developing economies.

This chapter is structured as follows: Section 2 reviews the existing literature on renewable energy adoption in agriculture and outlines the hypotheses and models used in the study. Section 3 describes the research methodology, including the data collection and analysis methods. Section 4 presents the results of the SEM analysis, and Section 5 discusses the findings and concludes with policy implications and future research directions.

2. Literature Review

2.1. *Theoretical background*

The Unified Theory of Acceptance and Use of Technology (UTAUT) provides a comprehensive framework for understanding the factors that influence the adoption and usage of new technologies. Developed by Venkatesh *et al.* (2003), UTAUT synthesizes elements from eight prominent technology acceptance models, offering a robust theoretical foundation for examining technology adoption in various contexts. The model highlights four primary constructs: performance expectancy, effort expectancy, social influence, and facilitating conditions, all of which directly impact users' intentions to adopt and use a technology.

In the context of solar water pump adoption in agriculture, the UTAUT model serves as a valuable tool for analyzing the various factors that drive or impede the uptake of this renewable energy technology among farmers. Performance expectancy, one of the core constructs of the UTAUT model, refers to the degree to which farmers believe that using solar water pumps will enhance their agricultural productivity, reduce water management costs, and provide reliable access to water resources. If farmers perceive significant benefits from solar water pumps, their intention to adopt this technology is likely to increase.

Effort expectancy, another crucial construct, captures the perceived ease of use associated with the technology. For solar water pumps, this involves the perceived complexity or simplicity of installation, operation, and maintenance. If farmers find the technology easy to use and believe that it does not require extensive technical expertise, they are more likely to adopt it. Effort expectancy can therefore play a pivotal role in determining the adoption rate of solar water pumps in agricultural settings.

Social influence, an important factor in the UTAUT model, refers to the degree to which farmers believe that influential figures such as peers, community leaders, or agricultural experts expect them to adopt new technologies. In agricultural communities, where decisions are often shaped by collective opinions and peer dynamics, social influence plays a pivotal role in technology adoption. Farmers are more likely to embrace solar water pumps when they feel supported by their social circles and perceive that the technology is positively regarded by others around them.

Facilitating conditions, the final core construct, pertain to the degree to which farmers believe that the necessary resources and support are available to facilitate the use of solar water pumps. This includes access to financial incentives, technical support, training, and reliable supply chains for solar equipment and spare parts. Adequate facilitating conditions can lower the perceived barriers to adoption and increase the likelihood that farmers will choose to implement solar water pumps.

By applying the UTAUT model to examine the adoption of solar water pumps, this chapter delves into the psychological factors shaping farmers' decisions. The model identifies both challenges and enablers in adopting new technologies, providing valuable insights for crafting policies that encourage renewable energy solutions in agriculture. In line with the literature, awareness has been recognized as a significant variable influencing technology adoption. Thus, this study extends the UTAUT model by incorporating the awareness variable to capture its critical role in the adoption process. This inclusion enriches the model by accounting for both psychological and informational influences on farmers' decisions. Understanding these dynamics is essential for formulating strategies that bolster energy security, lower greenhouse gas emissions, and promote sustainable economic growth, particularly in developing countries. The UTAUT model, with the added awareness variable, serves as a robust theoretical foundation for investigating solar water pump adoption and offers a framework to address broader issues related to solar energy in agricultural settings.

2.2. *Formulation of hypotheses*

2.2.1. *Awareness*

Awareness refers to having a knowledge or understanding of a particular issue, concept, or situation (Aravindan *et al.*, 2022; Rahmani and Bonyadi Naeini, 2023; Wall *et al.*, 2021). It involves being conscious and informed about something, which can assist individuals in making more informed decisions and taking actions based on the information they have (Aravindan *et al.*, 2022; Rahmani and Bonyadi Naeini, 2023). Awareness refers to the level of information that consumers have on the details regarding RETs, that is, a thorough understanding of both the cost implications and the effectiveness of these technologies (Wall *et al.*, 2021). Awareness is essential because it assists individuals in understanding the benefits of using sustainable energy sources and motivates them to adopt these technologies in their daily lives (Aravindan *et al.*, 2022; Rahmani and Bonyadi Naeini, 2023). Awareness is an essential component in RE sources adoption, particularly among the younger generation who tend to be more familiar with Information Technology (IT) with higher comprehension of renewable energies (Zainudin and Ishak, 2017). In general, awareness may be derived from formal education or through exposure to technology, media, and other sources of information (Parsad *et al.*, 2020). Promoting awareness and understanding of what sustainable energy is can positively influence intentions and behaviors toward its adoption (Rahmani *et al.*, 2024a; Wall *et al.*, 2021). Researchers (Zainudin and Ishak, 2017) found that the adoption of sustainable energy in pump technology among rural farmers was based on their awareness concerning RE which had a positive influence on their intention to use. Assessing consumer attitudes regarding building-attached photovoltaic equipment (Yang *et al.*, 2021) found that increased green awareness toward PV technology highly influenced investment behavior.

Educational initiatives can promote the overall level of knowledge and understanding of sustainable energy sources (Rahmani and Bonyadi Naeini 2023). Awareness has been identified as a critical factor in the adoption of renewable energies (REs) in Malaysia. Younger generations, being more familiar with information technology, have easier access to information about REs (Zainudin and Ishak, 2017). Similarly, Parsad *et al.* (2020) found that awareness significantly and positively influences people's decisions to invest in rooftop photovoltaics (PV) and solar energy in India. Zhou and Abdullah (2017) investigated the adoption of solar pump technology among rural farmers in Pakistan and revealed that awareness, ease of use, and perceived usefulness positively affect usage intentions. In the rural areas of Zabul, southern Iran, Rezaei and Ghofranfarid (2018) demonstrated that awareness significantly enhances the intention to accept REs.

Wang *et al.* (2020) conducted research on biomass technology adoption among Pakistani farmers and found that awareness of consequences indirectly influences the acceptance of biomass. In Ghana, environmental awareness emerged as a vital factor in RE acceptance, with higher awareness levels correlating with a greater willingness to adopt REs.

Environmental awareness plays a key role in encouraging people to adopt REs. Increasing awareness about REs fosters positive attitudes and helps individuals recognize their benefits, which in turn leads to greater acceptance (Yang *et al.*, 2021). Research on consumer attitudes toward building-attached photovoltaic equipment revealed that green awareness and attitudes toward photovoltaics significantly influence purchasing behavior, with green awareness positively impacting attitudes (Tsaur and Lin, 2018). Based on these previous studies, the following hypothesis is proposed:

H1. Awareness has a positive impact on the intention to use solar water pumps.

2.2.2. *Social influence*

According to Venkatesh *et al.* (2003), social influence is especially important during the initial stages of technology adoption when individuals often look to others for validation. In the agricultural context, farmers may experience uncertainty when evaluating new technologies, especially when faced with financial constraints or limited technical knowledge. In such situations, the opinions and behaviors of peers and community leaders can play a decisive role in shaping adoption intentions.

People are influenced by subjective norms because they want to be accepted and approved by those around them while often conforming to the expectations of their social group. Subjective norms contribute to people's shaping their beliefs, attitudes, and behaviors. Social influence refers to how individuals perceive the attitudes of significant others, such as friends, family, or colleagues, toward adopting a particular technology, and how these perceptions impact their decisions (Lau *et al.*, 2020, 2021; Liang *et al.*, 2021; Rahmani and Bonyadi Naeini, 2023; Venkatesh *et al.*, 2003). This idea suggests that the influence of others can change based on their views of an individual's technology adoption. For example, if a person believes those around them view their use of solar energy positively, they are more likely to continue using it. Research from the works of Lau *et al.* (2020, 2021) and Liang *et al.* (2021) emphasizes that social influence significantly shapes people's intentions and behaviors regarding solar energy consumption. When individuals feel that others support or use solar technology, they are more inclined to follow suit. Several studies have shown the importance of social influence in renewable energy adoption. In the study by Kaur *et al.* (2024) on the adoption of solar water heaters in India, social influence was identified as the most significant factor affecting consumer behavior. The study found that individuals were more likely to adopt solar water heaters if their family, friends, or neighbors had positive perceptions or had already adopted similar technologies. This indicates that word-of-mouth recommendations and peer demonstrations of success can significantly boost adoption rates in rural and close-knit communities. Similarly, Nguyen and Hoang (2023) investigated the acceptance of solar technologies by enterprises in the Mekong Delta region of Vietnam. They found that social influence, along with effort expectancy and performance expectancy, played a decisive role in determining businesses' intentions to adopt solar technology. The support and endorsement of technology by influential figures within the community, such as local business leaders, were critical to driving adoption. In another study, Dwivedi *et al.* (2022) explored the adoption of renewable energy technologies in the Himalayan region. They found that local leaders' influence significantly affected the community's behavioral intention to adopt renewable technologies, such as solar water pumps. The study revealed that when trusted community figures advocated for the technology, the social pressure on others to adopt it increased, which in turn boosted adoption rates. Moreover, the research by Ding *et al.* (2021), which focused on solar PV systems in rural China, demonstrated the complex role of social influence. While environmental perceptions positively impacted users' satisfaction with solar energy, social influence was found to have both positive and negative effects. This highlights that social influence can vary in its effectiveness depending on the context and the way technology is perceived within a community. Rezaei and Ghofranfarid (2018), in their study on rural households' renewable energy usage in Iran, showed that although perceived behavioral control and moral norms played a more direct role, social influence was still a relevant factor. Their study emphasized the importance of communal endorsement in motivating the adoption of new technologies in rural areas, where individual decisions are often shaped by collective social dynamics. Based on the previous studies and UTAUT model, the following hypothesis is proposed:

H2. Social influence has a positive impact on the intention to use solar water pumps.

2.2.3. *Performance expectancy*

Performance expectancy plays a crucial role in shaping customers' decisions to adopt solar energy technologies (SETs), significantly influencing their purchase intentions. Consumers thoroughly evaluate the expected performance, quality, and adherence to relevant standards before committing to a purchase (Aggarwal *et al.*, 2020). People are more likely to adopt solar energy technologies if they believe these technologies will offer benefits, such as lower energy costs, reduced environmental impact, increased reliability, and enhanced convenience (Rahmani and Bonyadi Naeini, 2023). To promote the adoption of solar energy technologies, it is crucial to emphasize how these technologies can improve performance outcomes and communicate their advantages to individuals and businesses (Lau *et al.*, 2021). Performance expectancy is shaped by factors related to tasks, technology, social influence, and experience (Rahmani and Bonyadi Naeini, 2023).

Performance expectancy is influenced by task-related, technology-related, social influence, and experience-related factors. Task-related factors involve how well solar energy technologies support the user's current work tasks and how compatible the technology is with the demands of the job. Technology-related factors refer to the ease of use and compatibility of solar energy technologies with the user's needs. A solar energy technology that is user-friendly and integrates smoothly into existing workflows will score high in terms of technology-related factors. Social influence factors pertain to how peers, superiors, or other individuals affect the user's perception of the technology. Positive social influence increases the user's performance expectancy of solar energy technology (Rahmani and Bonyadi Naeini, 2023; Venkatesh *et al.*, 2003). Experience-related factors are linked to the user's prior experiences with similar technologies. If past experiences with comparable systems have been positive, the user's performance expectancy for the new solar technology will likely be higher (Venkatesh *et al.*, 2003). In the context of smart energy technologies, performance expectancy has been identified as the most influential factor driving individual adoption (Gimpel *et al.*, 2020). For example, a study examining the adoption of solar photovoltaics in Malaysia found a positive correlation between performance expectations and behavioral intentions to use the technology (Lau *et al*., 2021).

Moreover, research by Jaafar *et al*. (2020) indicates that performance expectancy not only impacts purchase intention but also has a significant positive effect on consumer attitudes. As people's expectations for the performance of these technologies rise, their overall attitudes toward them improve accordingly. This is supported by findings that show perceived quality—closely tied to performance expectations—has a direct and significant effect on individuals' attitudes toward renewable energies (REs). As positive attitudes toward REs increase so does the likelihood of adopting such technologies (Yun and Lee, 2015). Based on the previous studies and UTAUT model, the following hypothesis is proposed:

H3. Performance expectancy positively influences the intention to use solar water pumps.

2.2.4. *Effort expectancy*

Effort expectancy refers to the perceived ease of use of a technology. For farmers considering the adoption of solar water pumps, the ease of installation, maintenance, and operation of the pumps is a critical determinant of their intention to adopt. Rezaei and Ghofranfarid (2018) highlighted that effort expectancy is a significant factor influencing the adoption of renewable energy technologies in rural Iran. Their research showed that when rural households perceived solar energy systems as easy to use and maintain, their intention to adopt these technologies increased. In agricultural contexts, where farmers may have limited technical expertise, the simplicity of integrating solar water pumps into existing irrigation systems can be a major driver of adoption.

Similarly, Aravindan *et al*. (2022) found that effort expectancy played a vital role in the adoption of solar energy in Malaysia. Their study showed that when potential users perceived solar technologies as easy to install and operate, their intention to adopt these technologies was higher. The research emphasized that simplifying installation and reducing the learning curve for new users can significantly enhance adoption rates in both rural and urban settings. In a related study, Dwivedi *et al*. (2022), while investigating the adoption of renewable energy technologies in the Himalayan region, found that effort expectancy was a key mediator between local leaders' influence and behavioral intention. This indicates that while social influence can drive initial interest, the actual adoption of solar water pumps depends largely on how easy farmers perceive the technology to be in terms of everyday use and maintenance.

Kaur *et al*. (2024) also underscored the importance of effort expectancy in their study on solar water heaters in India. Their findings suggested that consumers are more likely to adopt solar technologies if they believe these systems are compatible with existing infrastructure and require minimal effort for maintenance and operation. This is particularly relevant for farmers, who may be deterred by complex systems that require significant time or effort to maintain. The study by Nguyen and Hoang (2023) found that effort expectancy, alongside social influence and performance expectancy, had a strong influence on the adoption of solar technologies by businesses in Vietnam. The study reinforced the idea that reducing the perceived complexity of using solar systems is crucial to driving higher adoption rates, particularly among users with limited technical skills. Based on the previous studies and UTAUT model, the following hypothesis is proposed:

H4. Effort expectancy positively influences the intention to use solar water pumps.

2.2.5. *Facilitating conditions*

Facilitating conditions involve creating an environment that supports the use of technology by addressing factors, such as time, cost, and adaptability (Lu *et al.*, 2003). The presence or absence of facilitating conditions as extrinsic motivators can have a significant effect on one's intention to adopt a given technology (Aravindan *et al.*, 2022; Rahmani and Bonyadi Naeini, 2023). The presence of infrastructure, enabling mechanisms, and financial support can foster the advancement of solar energy technologies (Nandal *et al.*, 2019). When facilitating conditions are absent, individuals may face restrictions concerning the adoption or effective consumption of renewable energy (Apfel and Herbes, 2021; Aravindan *et al.*, 2022; Lau *et al.*, 2020, 2021).

Government incentives have been shown to have a positive and significant impact on consumers' intentions to adopt SETs (Kesari *et al.*, 2021). Research aimed at enhancing societal readiness for renewable energy systems found that facilitating conditions indirectly influence attitudes and intentions toward RE consumption in a positive and significant way (Yun and Lee, 2015).

A study on the social acceptance of SETs highlighted concerns among Indian farmers regarding unequal access and the high costs associated with equipment operation, suggesting that the widespread adoption of sustainable energy technologies in rural areas may face challenges (Aklin *et al.*, 2018). Findings indicate that when financial-related facilitating conditions improve, individuals are more inclined to accept solar energy (O'Shaughnessy *et al.*, 2021). In the context of farmers' adoption of solar pumps, government incentives were found to significantly influence their intention to use SE pumps (Kumar *et al.*, 2020). Policymakers are encouraged to address issues related to pricing, incentives, and tax breaks in the development of solar energy, as the cost of adopting solar technologies has a positive and significant effect on their acceptance (Tanveer *et al.*, 2021). Subsidies and financial incentives have been shown to encourage investments in photovoltaic systems, underscoring the essential role policymakers play in achieving these goals (Parsad *et al.*, 2020). According to prior studies and UTAUT model, the current research is hypothesized as follows:

H5. Facilitating conditions have a positive impact on the intention to use solar water pumps.

2.2.6. *Proposed model of the research*

The literature review highlighted key variables such as usage intention, awareness, performance expectancy, effort expectancy, social influence, and facilitating conditions as

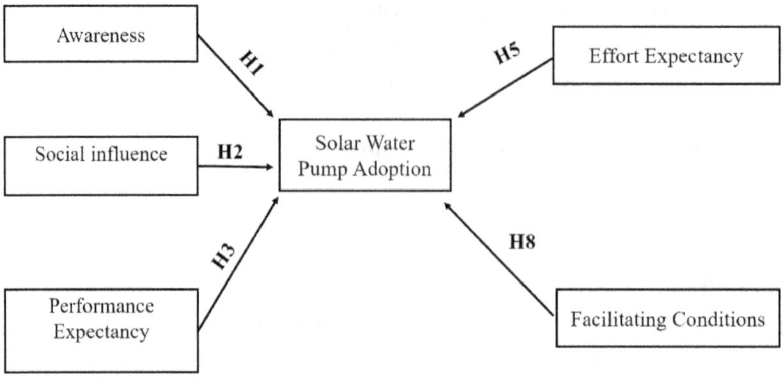

Figure 1. The proposed Model of intention to use solar water pumps in agriculture industry.

significant factors. The relationships between these variables were established through various studies, forming the foundation for the research hypotheses. Figure 1 presents the proposed research model, which aims to investigate the factors influencing the adoption of solar water pumps within the agricultural sector.

3. Methodology

3.1. *Survey design and data collection*

The survey design incorporated scale items from various established studies to measure different constructs. Specifically, five items for assessing awareness were derived from the work of Wall *et al.* (2021). Additionally, three items from the research by Venkatesh *et al.* (2003) were utilized to evaluate social influence. Effort expectancy was measured using four items based on the studies by Venkatesh *et al.* (2003). Usage intention was assessed with four items from the work of Irfan *et al.* (2021). Performance expectations were evaluated with three items from the work of Venkatesh *et al.* (2012). Lastly, facilitating conditions were measured using three items from the work of Sykes *et al.* (2009).

A structured questionnaire was developed, employing a 5-point Likert scale ranging from 1 (strongly disagree) to 5 (strongly agree). To ensure content validity, the content validity index (CVI) and content validity ratio (CVR) were calculated. The questionnaire was reviewed by 12 experts, and each item's CVI exceeded 0.85, while the CVR was above 0.70. According to Lawshe's content validity ratio table, these values confirmed the content validity of the questionnaire. The model variables and their corresponding items are detailed in Table 4.

A cross-sectional survey was conducted to gather data from farmers in Tehran province. Three hundred and forty-nine farmers were randomly selected to participate in the survey. Data collection involved a structured questionnaire and face-to-face interviews, ensuring clarity and reliability of responses. Each participant spent 45–60 minutes completing the questionnaire. If a participant declined to respond, they were replaced by the next available person. The data collection period spanned two months. Data pre-processing was carried out using SPSS (version 26). The dataset contained no missing values or responses outside the Likert scale range. The standard deviation of the samples was confirmed (STDEV.P > 0.5), and any indifferent samples were addressed. Ultimately, 21 responses were excluded, leaving 328 valid responses for analysis. Out of the 328 participants, 309 were male, making up 94.2% of the sample, while 19 were female, accounting for 5.8%. Regarding occupation, 118 participants (36.0%) were involved in arable farming, 80 participants (24.4%) were engaged in greenhouse farming, 51 participants (15.5%) were in livestock ranching, and 79 participants (24.1%) were involved in gardening. In terms of experience, 13 participants (4.0%) were at the entry level, 43 participants (13.1%) were at the intermediate level, 148 participants (45.1%) were at the mid level, and 124 participants (37.8%) were at the high level.

The data's normality was assessed and verified through skewness and kurtosis measures. The acceptable ranges for skewness are between −3 and +3, while for kurtosis, they are between −5 and +5.

3.2. *SEM and data analysis*

This study utilizes Structural Equation Modeling (SEM) to test the hypotheses, employing SPSS (version 26) and AMOS (version 26) software. SEM involves sophisticated measurement equations that simultaneously analyze a set of regression equations and the relationships between latent and observed variables (Hoyle, 2012; Tarka, 2018). Initially, confirmatory factor analysis (CFA) is conducted using the measurement model, which assesses the relationship between latent and observed variables, aiming to establish the validity and reliability of the constructs. Once the model achieves satisfactory fit and validity, the research hypotheses are tested using the structural model. This approach allows for systematic analysis of multivariate models, measurement of latent variables, and examination of the relationships between variables, ultimately revealing the outcomes of the hypotheses. SEM can also calculate measurement error and differentiate it from other errors in the model while considering the correlation between errors, a limitation in many classical methods.

Confirmatory factor analysis and SEM require adequate sample size and sphericity of relations, which are assessed using the KMO and Bartlett's Test (KMO > 0.7, Bartlett's test of sphericity: Sig < 0.05) (Allen, 2017; Mathur and Dhulla, 2014). Cronbach's alpha is commonly used to assess the reliability of latent variables. However, methodologists have suggested that McDonald's omega is a more accurate measure of reliability (Hayes and Coutts, 2020). Additionally, the reliability of observed variables is evaluated using composite reliability (CR) and factor loading coefficients. Acceptable thresholds are α > 0.7, McDonald's omega (ω) > 0.7, and CR > 0.7 (Šerbetar and Sedlar, 2016). Convergent validity of the variables is assessed through factor loading, composite reliability (CR), and average variance extracted (AVE). The acceptable values are factor loading > 0.5 with P-value < 0.05 and CR > AVE. Divergent validity is evaluated using four criteria: AVE > MSV (maximum shared variance), the Fornell–Larcker criterion, and the Heterotrait-Monotrait (HTMT) ratio (Fornell and Larcker, 1981; Henseler *et al.*, 2015). To determine the model's goodness of fit, several indices are used: chi-square divided by the degrees of freedom, root mean square error of approximation (RMSEA), comparative fit index (CFI), Tucker–Lewis index (TLI), standardized root mean square residual (SRMR), PClose, normed fit index (NFI), and parsimony normed fit index (PNFI) (Kline, 2011). After confirming reliability, validity, and goodness of fit, the hypotheses are tested within the structural model to determine the coefficient of determination (R^2).

4. Results

4.1. *Confirmatory factor* (*CFA*) *and measurement model*

The analysis indicated that both Cronbach's alpha (α) and McDonald's omega (ω) for all latent variables exceeded 0.7. Specifically, the values were as follows: awareness (α = 0.906, ω = 0.911), social influence (α = 0.822, ω = 0.824), trust (α = 0.816, ω = 0.818), intention to use (α = 0.831, ω = 0.838), effort expectancy (α = 0.898, ω = 0.901), performance expectancy (α = 0.845, ω = 0.847), and facilitating conditions (α = 0.829, ω = 0.832). Additionally, the KMO and Bartlett test results showed a KMO coefficient of 0.926, confirming the adequacy of the sample size, as it is well above the 0.7 threshold. Bartlett's test also confirmed the sphericity of the relationships (Sig = 0). The results are summarized in Tables 1 and 2.

Reliability, convergent validity, divergent validity, and goodness of fit were analyzed using CFA and measurement equations. Latent variables with their indicators, correlation coefficients, and each indicator's rank are presented in Table 2.

The analysis revealed that both Cronbach's alpha (α) and McDonald's omega (ω) for each latent construct surpassed the minimum acceptable value of 0.7, indicating strong internal consistency. Additionally, the factor loadings of all observed indicators were greater than 0.5 and statistically significant (P-value < 0.05), confirming the robustness of the measurement model.

In order to further assess the model's reliability, as well as its discriminant and convergent validity, several key indices were calculated: Composite Reliability (CR), Average Variance Extracted (AVE), Maximum Shared Variance (MSV), Maximum Reliability (MaxR(H)), the Fornell–Larcker criterion, and the Heterotrait-Monotrait (HTMT) ratio. These indicators provide a comprehensive evaluation of the model's validity. The detailed results of these assessments are presented in Tables 3 and 4.

Table 1. Kaiser–Meyer–Olkin (KMO) and Bartlett's tests.

KMO and Bartlett's Test		
Kaiser–Meyer–Olkin Measure of Sampling Adequacy.		0.921
Bartlett's Test of Sphericity	Approx. Chi-Square	4190.224
	df	231
	Sig.	0.000

Note: df: Degrees of freedom, Sig: Significance.

Table 2. Variables and factor loadings.

Latent and Observed Variables	r	r^2	P-Value
Awareness (Wall *et al.*, 2021) (α = 0.906, McDonald's omega (ω)=0.911)			
• I am aware of solar energy use and needs (aw1)	0.834	0.696	0.000
• I have enough information about solar water pump (aw2)	0.881	0.776	0.000
• I have interacted with solar energy technologies in the past (aw3)	0.797	0.635	0.000
• I know different types of solar energy technologies (aw4)	0.800	0.640	0.000
• I am aware of the benefits of solar water pump (aw5)	0.741	0.549	0.000
Social influence (Venkatesh *et al.*, 2003) (α = 0.822, (ω)=0.824)			
• People who are important to me think that I should use a solar water pump (so1)	0.823	0.677	0.000
• My friends and family support my decision to use a solar water pump (so2)	0.729	0.531	0.000
• My friends and family support my decision to use a solar water pump (so3)	0.785	0.616	0.000
Usage intention (Irfan *et al.*, 2021) (α = 0.831, McDonald's omega (ω)=0.838)			
• I intend to use solar water pumps soon (in1)	0.827	0.684	0.000
• The attitude of consuming less fossil fuels makes me use solar water pump (in2)	0.741	0.549	0.000
• I intend to shift from fossil energy to solar energy soon (in3)	0.688	0.473	0.000
• I intend to encourage others to use solar energy technologies (in4)	0.719	0.517	0.000
Effort expectancy (Venkatesh *et al.*, 2003) (α = 0.898, McDonald's omega (ω)=0.901)			
• I find the solar water pump easy to use (ee1)	0.809	0.654	0.000
• Using the solar water pump requires minimal effort (ee2)	0.891	0.794	0.000
• I do not need to exert much effort to use the solar water pump effectively (ee3)	0.849	0.721	0.000
• The solar water pump operates efficiently with little effort on my part (ee4)	0.767	0.588	0.000
Performance expectancy (Venkatesh *et al.*, 2012) (α = 0.845, McDonald's omega (ω) = 0.847)			
• I find solar energy technologies useful in my work (ex1).	0.787	0.619	0.000
• With solar energy technologies, I do my work more quickly (ex2)	0.811	0.658	0.000
• My business productivity rises by using solar energy (ex3)	0.818	0.669	0.000
Facilitating conditions (Sykes *et al.*, 2009) (α = 0.829, McDonald's omega (ω) = 0.832)			
• Proper technical infrastructure and organizational support are available when a problem occurs (fa1)	0.834	0.696	0.000
• The government has provided financial facilities for the use of solar energy technologies (fa2)	0.816	0.666	0.000
• Specific individuals or companies are available to solve solar energy technology problems (fa3)	0.720	0.518	0.000

Notes: AWA: Awareness, SOI: Social influence, USI: Usage intention, EXP: Effort expectancy, PEX: Performance expectancy, FAC: Facilitating conditions.

Table 3. Validity and validity indices and Fornell–Larcker criterion.

	Fit Indices					Fornell and Larcker Criterion					
	CR	AVE	MSV	MaxR(H)		AWA	SOI	USI	EXP	PEX	FAC
AWA	0.906	0.659	0.335	0.913	**AWA**	**0.812**					
SOI	0.823	0.608	0.342	0.829	**SOI**	0.346***	**0.780**				
USI	0.833	0.556	0.506	0.842	**USI**	0.522***	0.585***	**0.745**			
EXP	0.898	0.698	0.322	0.907	**EXP**	0.452***	0.479***	0.520***	**0.830**		
PEX	0.847	0.648	0.506	0.848	**PEX**	0.503***	0.515***	0.711***	0.568***	**0.805**	
FAC	0.834	0.627	0.335	0.843	**FAC**	0.578***	0.489***	0.568***	0.536***	0.525***	**0.792**

Table 4. Heterotrait-Monotrait ratio of correlations (HTMT).

	AWA	SOI	USI	EXP	PEX	FAC
AWA						
SOI	0.351					
USI	0.520	0.577				
EXP	0.441	0.501	0.529			
PEX	0.406	0.514	0.713	0.575		
FAC	0.582	0.488	0.581	0.534	0.521	

The combination of high reliability coefficients and strong factor loadings, together with these additional indices, ensures that the measurement model not only meets reliability standards but also demonstrates solid discriminant and convergent validity, further supporting the robustness of the model's underlying constructs.

Composite Reliability (CR) assesses the internal consistency of each latent variable. A CR value above 0.7 is typically considered acceptable, and all constructs (AWA, SOI, INT, EXP, PEX, and FAC) exceed this threshold, indicating strong internal consistency. AWA has the highest CR at 0.906, while SOI has the lowest at 0.823, but both values are well within acceptable ranges.

The Average Variance Extracted (AVE) measures the variance captured by a construct relative to the variance due to error, with a value above 0.5 indicating adequate convergent validity. All constructs surpass this threshold, with AVE values ranging from 0.556 (INT) to 0.689 (EXP), demonstrating good convergent validity across the model.

Maximum Shared Variance (MSV) compares the variance shared between constructs to the variance explained by the construct itself (AVE). To establish discriminant validity, the AVE of a construct should be greater than its MSV. While INT and PEX have MSV values equal to their respective AVE values (0.506), which could indicate some overlap, other constructs, like AWA (AVE = 0.659, MSV = 0.335), show clearer discriminant validity.

Maximum Reliability (MaxR(H)) provides an upper-bound estimate of reliability for each construct. All constructs display MaxR(H) values exceeding 0.8, confirming the reliability of the measurement model. AWA has the highest MaxR(H) value (0.913), and SOI has the lowest (0.829), but both values support the reliability of the model.

The Fornell–Larcker criterion, which is used to assess discriminant validity, is represented in the table by the diagonal values in bold, which correspond to the square root of the AVE for each construct. For adequate discriminant validity, these diagonal values should be higher than the off-diagonal correlations in their respective rows and columns. In this table, the diagonal values (e.g., AWA = 0.812 and SOI = 0.780) are consistently higher than the correlations with other constructs, confirming discriminant validity for all variables. Although some correlations are moderately high, such as INT and PEX (correlation = 0.711), the square roots of AVE values remain higher, indicating sufficient discriminant validity across the board. Overall, the constructs in the model demonstrate strong reliability and validity, both convergent and discriminant, with only a few areas, such as the potential overlap between INT and PEX, that may warrant further investigation.

The Heterotrait-Monotrait (HTMT) ratio of correlations presented in Table 4 is used to assess discriminant validity in structural equation modeling. Typically, an HTMT value below 0.85 indicates that constructs are sufficiently distinct from one another, while values above this threshold suggest potential issues with discriminant validity.

The HTMT values between AWA and the other constructs range from 0.351 (with SOI) to 0.582 (with FAC), all of which are well below the threshold of 0.85. This suggests that AWA demonstrates good discriminant validity with the other constructs. Similarly, SOI has HTMT values of 0.351 with AWA and 0.577 with USI, both of which are comfortably below the 0.85 threshold. The correlation with EXP is 0.501, also within an acceptable range, supporting the discriminant validity of SOI.

USI has HTMT values with other constructs that range from 0.520 (with AWA) to 0.713 (with PEX). While these values are moderate, they remain below 0.85, indicating that USI has adequate discriminant validity relative to the other constructs. EXP has correlations that range from 0.441 (with AWA) to 0.575 (with PEX), suggesting that it is sufficiently distinct from the other constructs, as all values fall below the critical 0.85 value.

PEX shows relatively higher correlations with other constructs, such as 0.713 with USI and 0.575 with EXP, but these values are still under 0.85, maintaining discriminant validity. FAC demonstrates HTMT values ranging from 0.488 (with SOI) to 0.582 (with AWA). These values are all well within the acceptable range, indicating that FAC also has adequate discriminant validity in relation to the other constructs.

In conclusion, all HTMT values are below the common threshold of 0.85, indicating that discriminant validity is sufficiently supported for all constructs in the model. None of the constructs exhibit problematic overlap, and they appear to be distinct from one another. This finding supports the reliability of the measurement model in terms of discriminant validity.

Table 5 presents the goodness-of-fit indices for a Structural Equation Model (SEM), which are used to evaluate how well the model aligns with the data.

The CMIN (Chi-Square Minimum Discrepancy) value is 226.197 with 194 degrees of freedom (DF). While the chi-square statistic can be sensitive to sample size, the CMIN/DF ratio is 1.166, which falls within the ideal range of 1–3, indicating a good model fit.

The Comparative Fit Index (CFI) is 0.992, exceeding the threshold of 0.95, which signifies excellent fit. Values closer to 1 are preferred, and this high value confirms a

Table 5. Goodness-of-fit indices of the SEM model.

	CMIN	DF	CMIN/DF	CFI	SRMR	RMSEA	PClose	PNFI	NFI	TLI
Estimate	226.197	194	1.166	0.992	0.027	0.023	1	0.796	0.947	0.988
Threshold	–	–	Between 1 and 3	>0.95	<0.08	<0.06	>0.05	>0.5	>0.9	>0.9
Interpretation	–	–	***	***	***	***	***	***	***	***

strong fit between the model and the observed data. The Standardized Root Mean Square Residual (SRMR) is 0.027, well below the maximum acceptable threshold of 0.08, indicating that the model's residuals are minimal and the fit is strong.

The Root Mean Square Error of Approximation (RMSEA) is 0.023, which is significantly lower than the threshold of 0.06, suggesting a very good fit. The associated PClose value is 1, which is far greater than the required minimum of 0.05, further supporting the interpretation that the model's approximation error is close to zero and the fit is excellent.

The Parsimony Normed Fit Index (PNFI) stands at 0.796, which exceeds the 0.5 threshold, indicating that the model strikes a good balance between fit and parsimony. The Normed Fit Index (NFI) is 0.947, just above the 0.9 threshold, demonstrating strong evidence that the model fits the data well. Finally, the Tucker–Lewis Index (TLI) is 0.988, which, like the CFI, is close to 1, further confirming that the model's fit is exceptionally good.

Overall, the indices presented in this table strongly indicate that the model fits the data well, with values consistently meeting or exceeding the accepted thresholds for good model fit. The combination of a low CMIN/DF ratio, high CFI and TLI values, and low SRMR and RMSEA values demonstrates that the model is robust and reliable in explaining the relationships within the dataset.

4.2. *Structural model and hypothesis results*

The results revealed the measurement model's reliability, validity, and goodness of fit. A structural model was performed to evaluate the significance, intensity, and direction of the hypotheses. The standardized structural model and the test of the model hypotheses are presented in Fig. 2 and Table 6.

The standardized regression coefficient (β) represents the strength and direction of the relationship between two variables. A positive β indicates a direct positive relationship, meaning as one variable increases, the other also tends to increase. The magnitude of β shows the strength of this relationship, with larger values indicating a stronger effect.

For H1, the path from awareness to usage intention has a β value of 0.130, which means there is a modest positive relationship between AWA and USI. The p-value of 0.039 indicates that this relationship is statistically significant, and thus, the hypothesis is accepted.

In H2, social influence has a standardized regression coefficient (β) of 0.235, indicating a stronger positive relationship with usage intention. The p-value of 0.000 means this

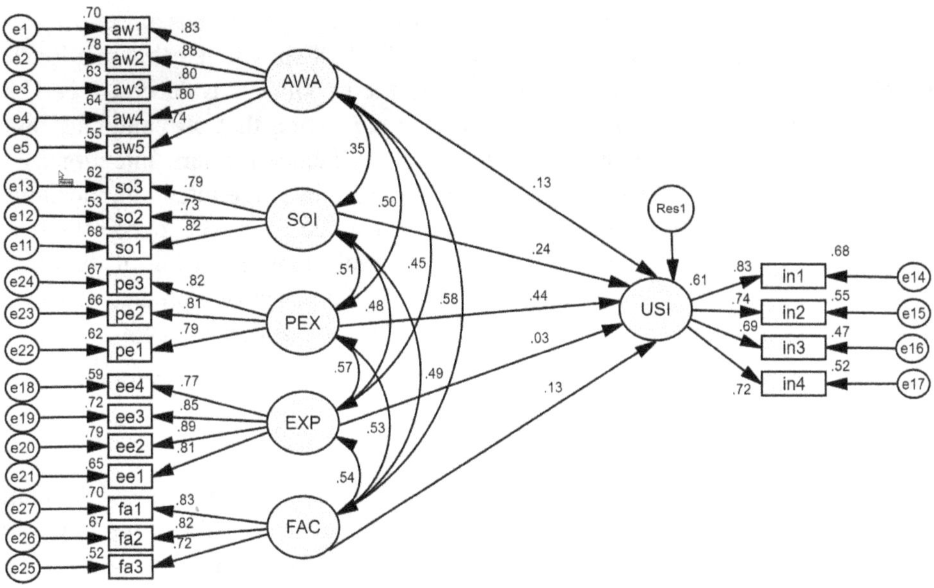

Figure 2. Standardized structural model.

Table 6. Structural paths and hypothesis results.

Hypotheses	Structural Paths			β	*P*-value	Conclusion	R^2
H1	AWA	--->	USI	0.130	0.039	Accepted	
H2	SOI	--->	USI	0.235	0.000	Accepted	Usage intention: 0.610
H3	PEX	--->	USI	0.439	0.000	Accepted	
H4	EXP	--->	USI	0.028	0.664	Rejected	
H5	FAC	--->	USI	0.132	0.048	Accepted	

relationship is highly significant, and the hypothesis is accepted. SOI has a moderate influence on USI, showing that social factors play an important role in shaping people's intention to use solar water pumps.

H3 presents the strongest effect, with performance expectancy showing a β of 0.439, indicating a strong positive relationship with usage intention. This means that when farmers expect the solar water pumps to perform well, they are more likely to intend to use them. The *p*-value of 0.000 confirms that this is a highly significant relationship, and the hypothesis is accepted. PEX is the most influential factor in predicting USI in this model, as reflected by the highest β value.

In contrast, H4 shows a very weak relationship between effort expectancy and usage intention, with a β of 0.028 and a *p*-value of 0.664. The hypothesis is rejected, as the *p*-value indicates that this relationship is not statistically significant. This suggests that the perceived effort required to use the solar water pumps does not have a meaningful impact on usage intention in this case.

For H5, the path from facilitating conditions to usage intention has a β of 0.132, indicating a small positive relationship. The p-value of 0.048 shows that this relationship is statistically significant, though marginally so, and the hypothesis is accepted. FAC has a modest but significant impact on Usage Intention, suggesting that providing an environment or resources that facilitate usage can positively influence farmers' intentions.

The model explains 61% ($R^2 = 0.610$) of the variance in usage intention, meaning that the combined effects of awareness, social influence, performance expectancy, effort expectancy, and facilitating conditions account for a substantial portion of the observed variation in usage intention. This suggests that the model has strong predictive power for understanding what influences people's intention to use a particular system or service.

5. Discussions and Conclusion

This chapter utilized an extended Unified Theory of Acceptance and Use of Technology (UTAUT) model to examine the essential factors influencing the adoption of solar water pumps in the agricultural sector. The model incorporated key constructs such as awareness, social influence, performance expectancy, and facilitating conditions to assess their impact on farmers' intention to adopt solar water pumps. The findings showed that these factors accounted for 61% of the variance in usage intention, with performance expectancy emerging as the most significant predictor, followed by social influence. Awareness and facilitating conditions also had an influence, though to a lesser degree. Notably, effort expectancy did not significantly affect usage intention in this context. The extended UTAUT model effectively captured the relationships among these factors and provided valuable insights into the drivers of solar water pump adoption in agriculture.

Performance expectancy was the strongest determinant of usage intention, aligning with earlier research (Lau *et al.*, 2021; Yun and Lee, 2015; Zhou and Abdullah, 2017). Farmers' intention to adopt solar water pumps is driven by their expectation of increased productivity, efficiency, and cost savings. This finding supports the notion that when farmers believe that a technology will enhance their farming operations, their intention to adopt it rises significantly. Similarly, Aggarwal *et al.* (2020) emphasized that the perceived performance of smart energy technologies is often the decisive factor in adoption decisions. The policy implications derived from these findings are as follows:

- *Emphasize performance benefits through demonstration projects*: Governments and agricultural organizations should organize demonstration projects in which solar water pumps are installed and showcased on selected farms. These projects can highlight the benefits of the technology in terms of energy efficiency, cost savings, and improved agricultural output. Real-life examples of performance success can help build trust and motivate adoption among other farmers.
- *Create performance certification programs*: To further encourage adoption, performance certification programs for solar water pumps should be introduced. These certifications should focus on ensuring reliability, efficiency, and long-term durability, which will help boost farmers' confidence in the technology. Solar water pumps that

meet certification standards should be marketed as premium, high-performance products, backed by technical guarantees.

- *Implement government-backed performance subsidies*: Governments could introduce performance-based subsidies, where farmers receive financial support based on the proven performance of their solar water pumps. For example, additional financial incentives could be provided when the pumps meet energy-saving benchmarks, motivating farmers to adopt high-performance, energy-efficient technologies.

This study also found that Social Influence (SOI) had a significant impact on farmers' intention to adopt solar water pumps, consistent with previous research (Kaur *et al.*, 2024; Nguyen and Hoang, 2023; Rezaei and Ghofranfarid, 2018). In rural agricultural communities, decisions regarding the adoption of new technologies are often influenced by peers, family members, and local leaders. Farmers are more likely to adopt solar water pumps if they observe positive experiences and endorsements from others in their social networks. This reflects Venkatesh *et al.* (2003), who noted that social influence plays a crucial role during the early stages of technology adoption, particularly in close-knit rural communities. The policy implications related to social influence are as follows:

- *Leverage social influence through local leaders and community programs*: Governments and NGOs should engage local community leaders, cooperative heads, and influential farmers to promote solar water pumps. These leaders can serve as advocates, providing trusted testimonials that can encourage adoption within their communities. By organizing community-driven awareness programs, these influential figures can demonstrate the practical benefits of solar water pumps, thus leveraging social validation.
- *Create peer-learning networks*: Policymakers should establish peer-learning platforms where farmers can share their experiences with solar water pumps. These platforms could be organized as community meetings or online forums supported by agricultural agencies. By fostering an environment where farmers can learn from each other, the positive impact of social influence can be amplified, making adoption decisions more comfortable for those who are hesitant.
- *Support word-of-mouth marketing and success stories*: Governments can encourage word-of-mouth marketing by promoting the success stories of early adopters through local media, radio, and community events. Farmers who have experienced positive outcomes from using solar water pumps should be showcased as examples of how the technology can lead to better yields and cost savings, further reinforcing the social validation needed for widespread adoption.

The study confirmed that awareness is a key factor influencing the intention to adopt solar water pumps, which is consistent with the findings of studies conducted in Malaysia, India, Pakistan, and Iran (Kardooni *et al.*, 2016; Liu *et al.*, 2013; Parsad *et al.*, 2020; Rezaei and Ghofranfarid, 2018; Zainudin and Ishak, 2017; Zhou and Abdullah, 2017; Zyadin *et al.*, 2012). When farmers are more informed about the benefits, cost savings, and practicalities of using solar water pumps, their likelihood of adoption increases. Lack of awareness has long been recognized as a major barrier to the adoption of sustainable energy technologies (SETs) in rural areas. The policy implications related to awareness are as follows:

- *Launch comprehensive educational campaigns*: Governments, NGOs, and agricultural agencies should develop comprehensive awareness campaigns that target rural farmers. These campaigns could utilize various channels such as local radio stations, television, social media, and agricultural fairs to inform farmers about the economic, environmental, and practical benefits of solar water pumps.
- *Integrate solar energy education into agricultural training programs*: To build long-term awareness, policymakers should integrate solar energy education into existing agricultural training programs. This could include teaching farmers about renewable energy technologies in vocational schools or extension programs, helping build a foundation of knowledge that supports future adoption.
- *Conduct on-the-ground workshops and demonstrations*: In addition to media campaigns, hands-on training and informational sessions should be conducted in rural communities. Governments should partner with NGOs and local agricultural extension services to hold workshops and live demonstrations of solar water pumps, providing farmers with practical, on-the-ground knowledge about how the technology works and how they can access it.

Facilitating conditions were also found to have a positive influence on Usage Intention. Farmers are more likely to adopt solar water pumps if they have access to the necessary financial resources, infrastructure, and technical support. This aligns with findings from previous research (Kumar *et al.*, 2020; O'Shaughnessy *et al.*, 2021) that highlight the importance of financial incentives and infrastructural support in driving the adoption of SETs. The policy implications related to facilitating conditions are as follows:

- *Provide financial incentives and subsidies*: Governments should offer financial incentives to reduce the initial costs of adopting solar water pumps. These could include subsidies, tax exemptions, or low-interest loans for farmers who invest in renewable energy technologies. By lowering the financial barrier, farmers will be more inclined to adopt solar water pumps.
- *Create tailored financial products for solar energy adoption*: Policymakers should work with financial institutions to develop tailored loan products designed for solar energy adoption. These products should include low-interest rates or deferred payment options that allow farmers to finance solar water pumps through the energy savings they generate, making the investment more feasible for farmers with limited capital.
- *Expand technical support and maintenance networks*: To ensure the long-term success of solar water pumps, governments should invest in expanding infrastructure and technical support services. This includes building maintenance networks and providing training programs for technicians who can assist farmers with installation and maintenance issues. Accessible technical support will increase farmers' confidence in the technology and ensure that the pumps function properly over time.

Interestingly, effort expectancy was not found to have a significant impact on farmers' intention to adopt solar water pumps in this study. This contrasts with findings from studies in rural Iran and Malaysia (Rezaei and Ghofranfarid, 2018; Aravindan *et al.*, 2022), which found that ease of use can influence adoption in contexts where technology is more complex. In this case, the ease of using solar water pumps does not appear to be a significant barrier, possibly because the technology is perceived as user-friendly or because farmers have prior experience with similar systems. The policy implications related to effort expectancy are as follows:

- *Provide technical assistance and simplify installation processes*: Even though effort expectancy was not a significant factor, policymakers should still ensure that the adoption of solar water pumps is as seamless as possible. Technical assistance programs should be made available to farmers, helping them with the installation, operation, and maintenance of solar water pumps.
- *Design user-friendly solar water pump*: Manufacturers should produce user-friendly designs that are easy to install and maintain. This would reduce any potential concerns about technical complexity and ensure that farmers can quickly integrate solar water pumps into their existing irrigation systems with minimal effort. Designers and developers of solar energy technologies need to consider effort expectancy as an essential factor when designing user interfaces and providing installation and maintenance services (Lau *et al.*, 2021; Rahmani and Bonyadi Naeini, 2023).

References

Aggarwal, A.K., Syed, A.A., and Garg, S. 2020. Diffusion of residential RT solar – is lack of funds the real issue? *Int. J. Energy Sect. Manag.* 14, 316–334. https://doi.org/10.1108/IJESM-02-2019-0004.

Aghdam, F.H., Taghizadegan Kalantari, N., and Mohammadi-Ivatloo, B. 2020. A stochastic optimal scheduling of multi-microgrid systems considering emissions: A chance constrained model. *J. Clean. Prod.* 275, 122965. https://doi.org/10.1016/j.jclepro.2020.122965.

Aklin, M., Cheng, C.-Y., and Urpelainen, J. 2018. Social acceptance of new energy technology in developing countries: A framing experiment in rural India. *Energy Policy* 113, 466–477.

Amutha, W.M. and Rajini, V. 2016. Cost benefit and technical analysis of rural electrification alternatives in southern India using HOMER. *Renew. Sustain. Energy Rev.* 62, 236–246.

Apfel, D. and Herbes, C. 2021. What drives senegalese SMEs to adopt renewable energy technologies? Applying an extended UTAUT2 model to a developing economy. *Sustainability* 13, 9332. https://doi.org/10.3390/su13169332.

Aravindan, K.L., Thurasamy, R., Raman, M., Ilhavenil, N., Annamalah, S., and Rathidevi, A.S. 2022. Modeling awareness as the crux in solar energy adoption intention through unified theory of acceptance and use of technology. *Mathematics* 10, 2045. https://doi.org/10.3390/math10122045.

Ding, L., Shi, Y., He, C., Dai, Q., Zhang, Z., Li, J., and Zhou, L. 2021. How does satisfaction of solar PV users enhance their trust in the power grid? - Evidence from PPAPs in rural China. *Energy Sustain. Soc.* 11, 1–19. https://doi.org/10.1186/s13705-021-00306-4.

Dwivedi, A., Dwivedi, P., Joshi, K., Sharma, V., Sengar, A., Agrawal, R., Sharma, P.K., Dixit, G., and Barthwal, M. 2022. Local leader's impact on adoption of renewable energy generation technology by rural communities in the Himalayan region. *J. Clean. Prod.* 352, 131479. https://doi.org/10.1016/j.jclepro.2022.131479.

Gimpel, H., Graf, V., and Graf-Drasch, V. 2020. A comprehensive model for individuals' acceptance of smart energy technology – A meta-analysis. *Energy Policy* 138. https://doi.org/10.1016/j.enpol.2019.111196.

Hoyle, R.H. 2012. *Handbook of Structural Equation Modeling*. Guilford Press.

Irfan, M., Hao, Y., Ikram, M., Wu, H., Akram, R., and Rauf, A. 2021. Assessment of the public acceptance and utilization of renewable energy in Pakistan. *Sustain. Prod. Consum.* 27, 312–324. https://doi.org/10.1016/j.spc.2020.10.031.

Jaafar, N.I., Sulaiman, A., Moghavvemi, S., Tajudeen, F.P., and Dehdar, F. 2020. Factors affecting the intention to adopt light-emitting diode lighting at home. *Light. Res. Technol.* 52, 1020–1039.

Kardooni, R., Yusoff, S.B., and Kari, F.B. 2016. Renewable energy technology acceptance in Peninsular Malaysia. *Energy Policy* 88, 1–10.

Kaur, P., Ritu, R.K., and Kaur, A. 2024. Unraveling consumer behavioral intentions to adopt solar water heaters in India using UTAUT model. *Built Environ. Proj. Asset Manag.* 14, 312–328. https://doi.org/10.1108/BEPAM-07-2023-0118.

Kesari, B., Atulkar, S., and Pandey, S. 2021. Consumer purchasing behaviour towards eco-environment residential photovoltaic solar lighting systems. *Glob. Bus. Rev.* 22, 236–254. https://doi.org/10.1177/0972150918795550.

Kumar, V., Syan, A.S., Kaur, A., and Hundal, B.S. 2020. Determinants of farmers' decision to adopt solar powered pumps. *Int. J. Energy Sect. Manag.* 14, 707–727. https://doi.org/10.1108/IJESM-04-2019-0022.

Lau, L.-S., Senadjki, A., Ching, S.-L., Choong, C.-K., Seow, A.-N., Choong, Y.-O., and Wei, C.-Y. 2021. Solar photovoltaic as a means to sustainable energy consumption in Malaysia: the role of knowledge and price value. *Energy Sources Part B Econ. Plan. Policy* 16, 303–323. https://doi.org/10.1080/15567249.2021.1922545.

Lau, L.S., Choong, Y.O., Wei, C.Y., Seow, A.N., Choong, C.K., Senadjki, A., and Ching, S.L. 2020. Investigating nonusers' behavioural intention towards solar photovoltaic technology in Malaysia: The role of knowledge transmission and price value. *Energy Policy* 144, 111651. https://doi.org/10.1016/j.enpol.2020.111651.

Li, B., Ding, J., Wang, J., Zhang, B., and Zhang, L. 2021. Key factors affecting the adoption willingness, behavior, and willingness-behavior consistency of farmers regarding photovoltaic agriculture in China. *Energy Policy* 149. https://doi.org/10.1016/j.enpol.2020.112101.

Liang, X., Hu, X., Islam, T., and Mubarik, M.S. 2021. Social support, source credibility, social influence, and solar photovoltaic panels purchase intention. *Environ. Sci. Pollut. Res.* 28, 57842–57859. https://doi.org/10.1007/s11356-021-14750-4.

Liu, W., Wang, C., and Mol, A.P.J. 2013. Rural public acceptance of renewable energy deployment: The case of Shandong in China. *Appl. Energy* 102, 1187–1196.

Lu, J., Yu, C., Liu, C., and Yao, J.E. 2003. Technology acceptance model for wireless internet. *Internet Res.*

Nandal, V., Kumar, R., and Singh, S.K. 2019. Barriers identification and analysis of solar power implementation in Indian thermal power plants: An interpretative structural modeling approach. *Renew. Sustain. Energy Rev.* 114, 109330. https://doi.org/10.1016/j.rser.2019.109330.

Nguyen, Q.N. and Hoang, T.H.L. 2023. Acceptance of solar technology by enterprises in the Mekong delta region, Vietnam. *J. Law Sustain. Dev.* 11, e428–e428.

O'Shaughnessy, E., Barbose, G., Wiser, R., Forrester, S., and Darghouth, N. 2021. The impact of policies and business models on income equity in rooftop solar adoption. *Nat. Energy* 6, 84–91. https://doi.org/10.1038/s41560-020-00724-2.

Parsad, C., Mittal, S., and Krishnankutty, R. 2020. A study on the factors affecting household solar adoption in Kerala, India. *Int. J. Product. Perform. Manag.* 69, 1695–1720. https://doi.org/10.1108/IJPPM-11-2019-0544.

Qiao, H., Zheng, F., Jiang, H., and Dong, K. 2019. The greenhouse effect of the agriculture-economic growth-renewable energy nexus: evidence from G20 countries. *Sci. Total Environ.* 671, 722–731.

Rahmani, A., Aboojafari, R., Taghizadeh-Hesary, F., Naeini, A.B., and Mashayekh, J. 2024a. Consumers' behavioral economics in renewable energy. In: *A Modern Guide to Energy Economics*. Edward Elgar Publishing, pp. 28–55.

Rahmani, A. and Bonyadi Naeini, A. 2023. Predicting intention in applying solar energy technologies in agriculture industry: A moderated and mediated model. *Clean. Responsible Consum.* 8, 100102. https://doi.org/10.1016/j.clrc.2023.100102.

Rahmani, A., Bonyadi Naeini, A., Mashayekh, J., Aboojafari, R., Daim, T., and Yalcin, H. 2024b. Green innovation for a greener future: A meta-analysis of the impact on environmental performance. *J. Clean. Prod.* 460, 142547. https://doi.org/10.1016/j.jclepro.2024.142547.

Rahmani, A., Mashayekh, J., Aboojafari, R., and Bonyadi Naeini, A. 2023. Determinants of households' intention for investment in renewable energy projects. *Renew. Energy* 205, 823–837. https://doi.org/10.1016/j.renene.2023.01.096.

Rezaei, R. and Ghofranfarid, M. 2018. Rural households' renewable energy usage intention in Iran: Extending the unified theory of acceptance and use of technology. *Renew. Energy* 122, 382–391. https://doi.org/10.1016/j.renene.2018.02.011.

Rode, J. and Weber, A. 2016. Does localized imitation drive technology adoption? A case study on rooftop photovoltaic systems in Germany. *J. Environ. Econ. Manage.* 78, 38–48. https://doi.org/10.1016/j.jeem.2016.02.001.

Sadatshojaie, A. and Rahimpour, M.R. 2020. CO2 emission and air pollution (volatile organic compounds, etc.)–related problems causing climate change. In: *Current Trends and Future Developments on (Bio-) Membranes*. Elsevier, pp. 1–30.

Shahbaz, M., Balsalobre-Lorente, D., and Sinha, A. 2019. Foreign direct Investment–CO2 emissions nexus in Middle East and North African countries: Importance of biomass energy consumption. *J. Clean. Prod.* 217, 603–614.

Sharvini, S.R., Noor, Z.Z., Chong, C.S., Stringer, L.C., and Yusuf, R.O. 2018. Energy consumption trends and their linkages with renewable energy policies in East and Southeast Asian countries: Challenges and opportunities. *Sustain. Environ. Res.* 28, 257–266. https://doi.org/10.1016/j.serj.2018.08.006.

Sykes, T.A., Venkatesh, V., and Gosain, S. 2009. Model of acceptance with peer support: A social network perspective to understand employees' system use. *MIS Q.* 371–393.

Tanveer, A., Zeng, S., Irfan, M., and Peng, R. 2021. Do perceived risk, perception of self-efficacy, and openness to technology matter for solar pv adoption? An application of the extended theory of planned behavior. *Energies* 14. https://doi.org/10.3390/en14165008.

Tarka, P. 2018. An overview of structural equation modeling: its beginnings, historical development, usefulness and controversies in the social sciences. *Qual. Quant.* 52, 313–354. https://doi.org/10.1007/s11135-017-0469-8.

Tavana, A., Emami Javid, A., Houshfar, E., Mahmoudzadeh Andwari, A., Ashjaee, M., Shoaee, S., Maghmoomi, A., Marashi, F. 2019. Toward renewable and sustainable energies perspective in Iran. Renew. *Energy* 139, 1194–1216. https://doi.org/10.1016/j.renene.2019.03.022.

Tsaur, R.-C. and Lin, Y.-H. 2018. Exploring the consumer attitude of building-attached photovoltaic equipment using revised technology acceptance model. *Sustainability* 10, 4177.

Venkatesh, V., Morris, M.G., Davis, G.B., and Davis, F.D. 2003. User acceptance of information technology: Toward a unified view. *MIS Q. Manag. Inf. Syst.* 27, 425–478. https://doi.org/10.2307/30036540.

Venkatesh, V., Thong, J.Y.L., and Xu, X. 2012. Consumer acceptance and use of information technology: extending the unified theory of acceptance and use of technology. *MIS Q.* 157–178.

Wall, W.P, Khalid, B., Urbański, M., and Kot, M. 2021. Factors influencing consumer's adoption of renewable energy. *Energies* 14. https://doi.org/10.3390/en14175420.

Wang, Z., Ali, S., Akbar, A., and Rasool, F. 2020. Determining the influencing factors of biogas technology adoption intention in Pakistan: The moderating role of social media. *Int. J. Environ. Res. Public Health* 17. https://doi.org/10.3390/ijerph17072311.

Yang, L., Danwana, S.B., and Yassaanah, F.-L.I. 2021. An empirical study of renewable energy technology acceptance in ghana using an extended technology acceptance model. *Sustainability* 13. https://doi.org/10.3390/su131910791.

Yun, S. and Lee, J. 2015. Advancing societal readiness toward renewable energy system adoption with a socio-technical perspective. *Technol. Forecast. Soc. Change* 95, 170–181. https://doi.org/10.1016/j.techfore.2015.01.016.

Zainudin, W.N.R.A. and Ishak, W.W.M. 2017. Measuring public acceptance on renewable energy (RE) development in Malaysia using ordered probit model. *J. Phys. Conf. Ser.* (IOP Publishing) 12137. https://doi.org/10.1088/1742-6596/890/1/012137.

Zhou, D. and Abdullah. 2017. The acceptance of solar water pump technology among rural farmers of northern Pakistan: A structural equation model. *Cogent Food Agric.* 3, 1280882. https://doi.org/10.1080/23311932.2017.1280882.

Zyadin, A., Puhakka, A., Ahponen, P., Cronberg, T., and Pelkonen, P. 2012. School students' knowledge, perceptions, and attitudes toward renewable energy in Jordan. *Renew. Energy* 45, 78–85.

https://doi.org/10.1142/9789819812608_0005

Chapter 5

Energy Security, Pollution, and Health in Selected Developing Asian Economies[#]

FARHAD TAGHIZADEH-HESARY[*], EHSAN RASOULINEZHAD[†,**], NAOYUKI YOSHINO[‡], YOUNGHO CHANG[§], FARZAD TAGHIZADEH-HESARY[¶], and PETER J. MORGAN[|]

[*]*Tokai University Research Institute for Environment and Sustainability, Tokai University, Tokyo, Japan*
[†]*Faculty of World Studies, University of Tehran, Tehran, Iran*
[‡]*Faculty of Economics, Keio University, Tokyo, Japan*
[§]*School of Business, Singapore University of Social Sciences, Singapore*
[¶]*The Five Senses Health Institute, School of Medicine, Iran University of Medical Sciences, Tehran, Iran*
[|]*Asian Development Bank Institute, Tokyo, Japan*
[**]*e.rasoulinezhad@ut.ac.ir*

Increased dependence on nonrenewable energy sources contributes to greater air pollution, which in turn leads to negative health outcomes. This chapter examines the relationship between fossil fuel consumption (FFC) and health issues using the generalized method of moments (GMM) for data from 18 developing Asian economies spanning 1991 to 2022. The findings show that fossil fuel use elevates the risk of lung and respiratory diseases (LRD), with CO_2 emissions and FFC significantly affecting undernourishment and mortality rates. Additionally, higher gross domestic product (GDP) per capita and healthcare expenditure are found to reduce undernourishment and death rates (UDR). The chapter concludes that transitioning from fossil fuels to renewable energy can improve energy security and reduce greenhouse gas emissions.

Keywords: Energy consumption, health issues, energy insecurity, developing Asian economies, panel data estimation.

1. Introduction

One of the major relations between energy insecurity and health is that in many low-income countries, burning indoor biomass (wood, dung, and animal residual) is a major source of household energy used for cooking. This is one of the major causes of indoor air pollution and has significant health impacts. Improving energy security means increasing access to modern fuels such as natural gas for cooking or renewable energy for generating electricity that will reduce indoor and ambient air pollution and reduce negative health

[#]The chapter is an updated version of the paper published in the *Singapore Economic Review*, Vol. 66, No. 2 (2021) 435–455; DOI: 10.1142/S0217590820430043.

impacts (Farabi-Asl *et al.*, 2019; Khan *et al.*, 2024). Fossil fuel consumption may be considered as a factor influencing a country's health security. For instance, a lack of clean energy, especially in low- and middle-income countries, can potentially expose populations to various noxious gases from the combustion of fossil fuels, leading to an increase in energy insecurity. Furthermore, energy consumption — particularly fossil fuel energy sources — can directly or indirectly affect human health by inducing air pollution, a shortage of safe water, and poor medical care infrastructure. Fossil fuel energy consumption increases energy insecurity (Le *et al.*, 2019; Chu *et al.*, 2023; Rasoulinezhad and Eksi, 2024) and threats to human health, future costs associated with climate change, and other forms of environmental damage, which are considered together as the health–environmental security of a country (e.g., Machol and Rizk 2013, and Phung *et al.*, 2023). This issue is most serious in low- and middle-income countries due to their lack of health infrastructure, poor energy efficiency, and greater contribution of FFC in their total energy consumption basket. Figure 1 illustrates the share of FFC in the total energy consumption basket of low- and middle-income countries. According to the data displayed in Figure 1, fossil fuel contributions to total energy consumption in such countries increased between 1991 and 2018. The share of FFC in these countries reached nearly 90% in 2018, which is greater than the share of the world's upper middle-income countries.

The increased share of FFC and air pollutant emissions in these countries may constitute the main cause of their high death rates compared with upper middle-income countries. As reported in a Stanford University Report (2008), carbon dioxide (CO_2) emissions have a significant association with human mortality.

Despite previous studies like Newborough and Probert (1987), Lambert *et al.* (2014), Chaabouni *et al.* (2016), Nasre Esfahani and Rasoulinezhad (2016), Sirag *et al.* (2017), Apergis *et al.* (2018), Hanif (2018), and Wang and Azam (2024), there has been little focus on the relationship between FFC, air pollution, and health in low- and middle-income

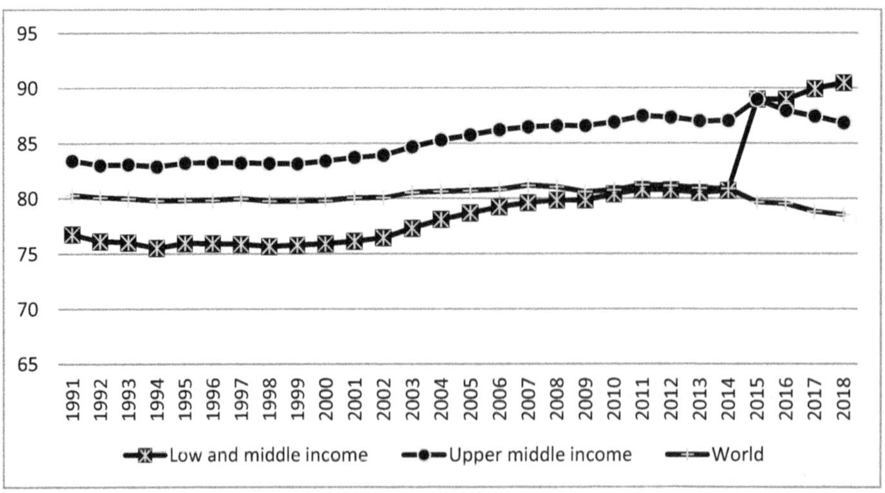

Figure 1. FFC (% of total).

Asian countries. This chapter aims to assess the negative impact of FFC and air pollution on human health in Asia, highlighting the crucial role of energy insecurity and its health consequences, particularly in these regions.

This chapter makes a valuable contribution to the literature on energy insecurity and human health by demonstrating that higher FFC increases the risk of LRD. It also shows that rising GDP per capita and healthcare spending can help lower undernourishment and mortality rates. The conclusion suggests that diversifying energy sources in developing Asian economies, shifting away from heavy reliance on fossil fuels toward renewable energy, can enhance energy security while reducing greenhouse gas emissions.

The remainder of this chapter is organized as follows. Section 2 reviews the related literature. Section 3 describes the data and specifies the model. Section 4 presents the empirical findings, and finally Section 5 concludes the chapter.

2. Energy, Pollution, and Health Impacts

Air pollution consists of a mixture of various gases and particulate matter (PM). The latter is usually classified based on its size to better characterize its pathogenicity. Fine PM with a diameter of 2.5 micrometers ($PM_{2.5}$) is the main subgroup that can enter small airways, can be inhaled (Chen *et al.*, 2018), and can cause toxicity (Dominici *et al.*, 2006). The gaseous components are mainly composed of polycyclic aromatic hydrocarbons, ozone, carbon monoxide (CO), nitrogen oxides (NOx), and sulfur dioxide (Fetterman *et al.*, 2017). According to a World Health Organization (WHO) report, 92% of the global population lives in areas with poor air quality (WHO, 2016). In 2010, ambient (outdoor) and household (indoor) air pollution constituted the fourth and ninth leading risk factors behind the global disease burden, respectively (Lim *et al.*, 2012a). In South Asia, household air pollution arising from solid fuels (e.g., wood, coal, and other biomass) is ranked among the top four risk factors for human health (Lim *et al.*, 2012a). High concentrations of PM from anthropogenic sources can affect the pulmonary system, the cardiovascular system, the psychoendocrine system, and the reproductive system (Fetterman *et al.*, 2017). Various studies have assessed the mechanisms underlying these effects. Accordingly, a large number of previous studies have focused on the reactive oxygen species (ROS) that are produced in response to the components of air pollution (e.g., PM or NOx) (Fetterman *et al.*, 2017). In addition, other components of air pollution such as CO and carbon dioxide (CO_2) are major sources of the negative health impacts of FFC (Raub, 1999; Chaabouni *et al.*, 2016; Can *et al.*, 2019). These are chemically reactive molecules that contain oxygen. ROS are highly reactive with cellular elements, especially DNA. By interacting with cellular and mitochondrial DNA molecules, they cause changes that eventually result in human diseases. In addition to air pollution, energy insecurity can affect human health as a result of the shortage of safe water. Energy insecurity may affect water sources through global warming. The shortage of safe and clean water could expose populations to various communicable (or infectious) and noncommunicable diseases (e.g., micronutrient deficiencies). Even, according to Taghizadeh-Hesary *et al.* (2019), the lack of the existence of clean water may lead to the threat of food security for the population of a country. Hence, energy insecurity may have a relationship with health and food security of a society. Last but not least, the availability of modern energy sources plays a major role in determining access to standard healthcare facilities. Women and children are the most vulnerable demographic groups. According to a WHO factsheet, over 289,000 women globally die from pregnancy or delivery complications every year, and approximately 24% of these deaths occur in South Asia (WHO, 2014). Most of these deaths are preventable with simple lighting, operating facilities, and blood transfusion services (Mills, 2012). In the following sections, the connecting channels between energy insecurity and human health are presented in detail. These interconnections can be categorized into environmental effects, household effects, and medical care effects.

2.1. *Health impacts of air pollution*

Air pollution can affect human health in several ways. Therefore, a few mechanisms are proposed. For instance, PM can directly target mitochondria (the main actor of cellular metabolism) and cause cellular dysfunction (Meyer *et al.*, 2013). It can also induce genetic and epigenetic alterations, and lead to cancer formation (DeMarini, 2015).

PM and ozone are the two main components of air pollution that can affect the pulmonary system (USGCRP, 2016). They may either cause or exacerbate pulmonary disorders. Indeed, various pulmonary disorders are linked to exposure to air pollution. First, prolonged exposure to household air pollution (e.g., using traditional stoves for baking bread in developing Asian economies) can induce prolonged inflammation in airways and cause chronic obstructive pulmonary disease. This is mediated by inducing systemic ROS production (Golshan *et al.*, 2002). Second, air pollution plays a major role in the development of asthma and recurrent wheezing in children with hyperactive airways (Padhi and Padhy, 2008; Modig *et al.*, 2009). Third, air pollution may exacerbate the symptoms of patients suffering from rhinosinusitis (WHO, 2013). Relatedly, air pollution can induce pneumonia by impairing the immune system (Kreyling *et al.*, 2004). PM and nitric oxide (NO) are the two key components of air pollution that are associated with the cardiovascular system. According to a meta-analysis, each 10 microgram per cubic meter ($\mu g/m^3$) increase in $PM_{2.5}$ concentration can escalate annual cardiovascular mortality by 11% (Hoek *et al.*, 2013). The equivalent rate for NO is equal to 13% (Faustini *et al.*, 2014). Coronary artery disease, cardiac failure, stroke, and arrhythmia are all cardiovascular disorders that are causally linked to air pollution. These effects are mainly caused by the pro-atherogenic feature of resultant ROS (Bourdrel *et al.*, 2017).

A number of studies have postulated a convergence between air pollution and mental disorders, including depression and anxiety (Szyszkowicz *et al.*, 2009; Szyszkowicz *et al.*, 2010; Lim *et al.*, 2012b). Dubos (1969) highlighted the impact of poor indoor air quality on people's insufficient adaptation. Colligan (1981) found that indoor air pollution can affect psychological reactions in two ways: firstly, through affecting mental efficacy (e.g., memory status, interpersonal relations, or mood status) and, secondly, through sympathetic arousal and increasing heart and breathing rates. The latter may induce an unconscious sense of anxiety, fear, or panic. According to a study in the Republic of Korea, air pollution might be a risk factor for a number of psychological disorders, ranging from anxiety to suicidal ideation (Shin *et al.*, 2018). Similarly, Costa *et al.* (2017) have labeled air pollution as a risk factor for autistic disorders in children. In all the studies reviewed here, air pollution is recognized as a risk factor for a wide range of mental disorders.

Furthermore, several prospective studies have explored the relationship between long-term exposure to air pollution and type 2 diabetes mellitus (Andersen *et al.*, 2012; Wang *et al.*, 2014). This might be mediated by the systemic inflammatory effect of ROS, which in turn causes insulin resistance in peripheral tissues. Another proposed mechanism pertains to mitochondria impairment, which leads to glucose intolerance (Xu *et al.*, 2011). Although there is little information available on this notion, the existing evidence distinguishes air pollution as a risk factor for type 2 diabetes mellitus. A number of studies have established that air pollution is a risk factor for cancer. Certainly, almost all organs are at risk from exposure to air pollution. The evidence reviewed by Fetterman *et al.* (2017) has demonstrated the key role played by air pollution in inducing cancer in the lungs, kidneys, bladder, prostate, central nervous system, endocrine system, oropharynx, skin, cervix, ovary, liver, and rectum. Many mechanisms have been proposed in the literature for this relationship. To better understand how air pollution acts as a carcinogen, it is advisable to first define one of the most crucial organelles of human cells, the mitochondria. These represent the central regulator of cellular metabolism. They are the main cellular organelles that extract energy packs [i.e., adenosine triphosphate (ATP) from organic compounds, including fatty acids]. Furthermore, they are the major cellular component to organize biosynthetic pathways (i.e., the production of amino acids, lipids, nucleotides). In other words, mitochondria are the key bioenergetic and biosynthetic organelles of human cells. ROS interconnect air pollution to cancer by impairing the function of cellular mitochondria (Fetterman *et al.*, 2017). Targeting mitochondria with ROS may induce cancer formation by preventing genome stability (Ishikawa *et al.*, 2008). Several studies have demonstrated the relationship between air pollution and infertility. Indeed, recent systematic reviews such as that conducted by Carre *et al.* (2017) have clearly shown the negative impact of air pollution on fertility. Both male and female gametogenesis are at risk of this effect. Various components of air pollution can affect either the quality or the quantity of gametes. Moreover, they can compromise fetal development, leading to increased miscarriage rates. Systemic oxidative stress, hormonal disturbance, and genetic and epigenetic alterations are four proposed mechanisms for air pollution-induced reproductive disorders (Carre *et al.*, 2017). Given the impacts of air pollution on the genetic and epigenetic features of gametes, its negative effects on fetal development are to be expected. A number of studies have attempted to explore this relationship. For instance, Pederson *et al.* (2013) highlighted the effect of air pollution on low birth weight. Moreover, Suades-Gonzales *et al.* (2015) found a negative effect of perinatal exposure to polycyclic aromatic hydrocarbons, nitrogen dioxide (NO_2), and PM on children's neuropsychiatric development. For further information, also see the review by Costa *et al.* (2017) regarding its crucial impact on the development of autistic disorders.

On the other hand, an increase in CO_2 concentration can result in many health impacts through hypercapnia (defined as an increase in bloodstream CO_2). Prolonged exposure to low CO_2 concentrations may result in cardiopulmonary failure, intracranial hemorrhage, immune defects, miscarriages, and behavioral disorders (Rice, 2004; Shigemura *et al.*, 2017). Moreover, the increase in intrapulmonary CO_2 is a documented risk factor for the development of lung cancer in smokers and nonsmokers (Merryman *et al.*, 1997). Several mechanisms are proposed for this effect. In 2019, Akbari *et al.* provided a hypothesis that links cancer evolution with a decrease in ATP (Akbari *et al.*, 2019). Considering their findings, an increase in intrapulmonary CO_2 can induce lung cancer by interfering with cellular respiration and a decrease in cellular ATP.

In the empirical part of this chapter, we use CO_2 as a proxy for other hazardous emissions such as NOx and particulates, due to data availability.

2.2. *Energy insecurity and health impacts*

Energy insecurity interconnects with medical care infrastructure in several ways. First, it can provide basic necessities to acquire safe medical care (e.g., lighting, sterilizers, air conditioners). Moreover, energy plays an important role in performing various diagnostic procedures (e.g., laboratories, clinical imaging, electrocardiography). Another application of energy in medical care pertains to therapeutic procedures (e.g., radiotherapy). It is also central to the cold chain in refrigerating blood, vaccines, and medicines (Porcaro *et al.*, 2017).

Another important factor is water insecurity. This condition plays a direct role in both the outbreak of various infectious diseases (e.g., cholera) and the development of food insecurity. The latter may in turn induce growth defects, developmental abnormalities, or micronutrient deficiency, causing various chronic disorders (e.g., anemia, osteoporosis, immune deficiency) (Maggini *et al.*, 2018). In addition, food insecurity during pregnancy may result in anxiety and depression (Laraia *et al.*, 2010).

3. Data and Model Specification

The empirical part of this chapter aims to assess the impact of FFC and pollution on health in 18 selected developing Asian economies[1] over the period 1991–2022 (Taghizadeh-Hesary *et al.*, 2021).[2]

A review of the literature (e.g., Sirag *et al.* (2017), Apergis *et al.* (2018) and Hanif (2018)) recognizes four major health effects of ambient air pollution: tracheal, bronchial, and lung cancer (TLC), respiratory diseases (RD), prevalence of undernourishment (PU), and death rates due to exposure to outdoor and household air pollution (DR). These outcomes have a high correlation that will result in multicollinearity in regression and spurious regression. We used principal component analysis (PCA) to reduce these health issues to the minimum number of components that capture information from all four variables. Unlike other linear transformation methods, PCA does not have a fixed set of basis vectors. Rather, it depends on the dataset, and PCA has the additional

[1]The 18 countries in the study are Afghanistan, Bangladesh, Cambodia, the People's Republic of China, Indonesia, India, Iran, Kazakhstan, the Kyrgyz Republic, Malaysia, Myanmar, Pakistan, the Philippines, Sri Lanka, Tajikistan, Thailand, Uzbekistan and Vietnam. Low- and middle-income countries from the World Bank's classification at https://datahelpdesk.worldbank.org/knowledgebase/articles/906519-world-bank-country-and-lending-groups.

[2]The model and the empirical study of this chapter are based on Taghizadeh-Hesary *et al.* (2021).

Table 1. PCA technique results.

	Initial Eigenvalues			Extraction Sums of Squared Loadings		
Component	Total	% of Variance	Cumulative (%)	Total	% of Variance	Cumulative (%)
1	1.830	45.760	45.760	1.830	45.760	45.760
2	1.210	30.238	75.998	1.210	30.238	75.998
3	0.529	13.231	89.228			
4	0.431	10.772	100.000			

Table 2. Component matrix of PCA.

	Component	
	1	2
TLC	–0.549	–0.677
RD	–0.280	0.859
PU	0.858	–0.058
DR	0.845	–0.096

advantage of indicating what is similar and different about the various models created (Bruce-Ho and Dash-Wu, 2009). Through the results of this method, shown in Table 1, we can reduce the four health variables (*TLC*, *RD*, *PU*, *DR*) into two components of LRD and UDR.

Table 1 shows that only two components are significant as their Eigenvalue is larger than 1 (Yoshino and Taghizadeh-Hesary, 2015). These two components explain 75.998 of the variance of the results, which is statistically significant according to the literature. Table 2 shows the component matrix. Component 1 receives its major loading from PU and DR and component 2 gains its main loading from TLC and RD.

Besides arranging the dependent variable, we need to explore explanatory variables. Following earlier studies such as Chaabouni *et al.* (2016), we choose CO_2 emissions (metric tons per capita), FFC (% of total energy basket), GDP per capita (current USD), healthcare expenditure per capita (current USD), and urban population growth (URB) (annual %), collected from the World Bank database[3] and British Petroleum's *Statistical Review of World Energy* 2019 (BP, 2019).

Tables 3 and 4 present the variables' information and the primary descriptive characteristics of our data, respectively. TLC is measured as a percentage, with our sample of 18 developing Asian economies yielding a mean of 0.02% over the period 1991–2022. The mean of our sample's RD is 190,328 people lost per day, with a maximum and a minimum of 352,912 and 8,093 lost per day during 1991–2018, respectively. The PU and DR in the 18 selected countries during the period have means of 17.3% and 20.19%, respectively. The average CO_2 emissions per capita and share of FFC in the total energy basket in our selected sample are 9.19 metric tons per capita and 95.39%, respectively, whereas the GDP

[3] https://data.worldbank.org/ (accessed on 14.12.2023).

Table 3. Variables' information.

Variables	Unit	Symbol	Source of Variables
TLC	%	TLC	WHO
RD	People lost per day	RD	WHO
PU	%	PU	WHO
DR	%	DR	WHO
CO_2	Metric tons per capita	CO_2	BP Statistical Review of World Energy, 2019
FFC	%	FFC	World Bank database
GDP	Current USD	GDP	World Bank database
URB	%	URB	World Bank database
HEX	Current USD	HEX	World Bank database

Table 4. Variables' descriptive statistics.

Variables	Unit	Obs.	Mean	Std. Dev.	Max.	Min.
TLC	%	504	0.027	1.92	0.411	0.0012
RD	People lost per day	504	19,0328	5.9	35,2912	8,093
PU	%	504	17.3	32.39	19.29	12.06
DR	%	504	20.19	41.02	39.44	11.03
CO_2	Metric tons per capita	504	9.19	12.23	21.94	6.12
FFC	%	504	95.39	140.39	100	24.55
GDP	Current USD	504	5,627.39	1,302.93	11,238.64	43.29
URB	%	504	12.49	40.29	17.33	1.24
HEX	Current USD	504	415.90	1,921.44	2,913.92	32.91

per capita has a maximum of \$11,238.64 and a minimum of \$43.29. Urbanization in the selected countries presents an average of 12.49%, with a maximum and a minimum of 17.33% and 1.24%, respectively. Health expenditure (HEX) per capita presents an average of \$415.90 over the period.

We empirically investigate the following models based on our two components of dependent variables and the five above-mentioned explanatory variables:

Model I based on the first dependent variable (Component 1: LRD):

$$lnLLRD_{it} = \alpha_1 LnCO_{2it} + \alpha_2 LnFFC_{it} + \alpha_3 LnGDP_{it} + \alpha_4 LnURBit + \alpha_5 LnHEX_{it} + \varepsilon_{it} \quad (1)$$

Model II based on the second dependent variable (Component 2: UDR):

$$lnLURD_{it} = \alpha_1 LnCO_{2it} + \alpha_2 LnFFC_{it} + \alpha_3 LnGDP_{it} + \alpha_4 LnURBit + \alpha_5 LnHEX_{it} + \varepsilon_{it} \quad (2)$$

In this study, we use CO_2 as a proxy for hazardous emissions of fossil fuel combustion. The coefficients α_1, α_2, α_3, α_4, and α_5 represent the long-run elasticity estimates of health problems with respect to CO_2 emissions per capita, FFC, GDP per capita, URB, and HEX

Table 5. Expected signs of variables.

Variables	Expected Sign of Coefficient
CO_2	+
FFC	+
GDP	–
URB	+
HEX	–

per capita. Based on the relevant literature, we expect that increased CO_2 emissions, FFC, and urbanization lead to an increase in different diseases, while the impacts of GDP per capita and HEX per capita as tools that can facilitate progress are expected to reduce diseases. Table 5 lists the expected coefficients of the variables.

In order to estimate the coefficients based on Model I and Model II, the GMM is utilized in a panel gravity framework for FFC–environment pollution–health issues among the 18 selected developing Asian economies in Asia. The reliability of the GMM method has been proved by many scholars, such as Arellano and Bond (1991), Martinez-Zarzoso *et al.* (2009), Kahouli and Maktouf (2015), and Lin (2015). Arellano and Bond (1991) argued that the GMM estimator, including the lagged endogenous variable as an explanatory variable, is more convenient for panel data because it yields more consistent and robust results in the presence of arbitrary heteroskedasticity. In general, a regression model in the form of GMM is written as follows:

$$Y_{it} = \alpha + \beta Y_{it-1} + \gamma X_{it} + \eta_{it} + \varepsilon_{it} \tag{3}$$

where Y indicates the dependent variable (LRD in Model I; UDR in Model II) and X represents all explanatory variables (CO_2 emissions per capita, FFC, GDP per capita, URB, HEX per capita). η_{it} represents the country-specific effects and ε_{it} is the error term.

To attain reliable empirical estimations, we need to conduct some preliminary tests. As the first pre-estimation test, the variance inflation factor (VIF) will be performed to ascertain whether there is any multicollinearity among the series. The second preliminary test is the Hausman test to check for the existence of heterogeneity, which would clarify the presence of random or fixed effects in our panel. Given that the economies of the selected sample have experienced various exogenous and endogenous shocks, the next pre-estimation test is to check cross-section dependency among the series. The second-generation unit root test will constitute the last preliminary test to identify whether the series are I(1) stationary or I(0) nonstationary.

Furthermore, we conducted two different diagnostics tests after running the GMM estimations. The first is the Arellano–Bond test for zero autocorrelation in the first-differenced errors and the second is the Sargan test to verify the overidentifying restrictions.

4. Empirical Results

The VIF (checking multicollinearity among series) and Hausman (checking the nature of the panel data series) tests were conducted to identify the consistency of the GMM approach. Tables 6 and 7 present their findings.

Table 6. VIF and Hausman test results (Model I).

Samples	Independent Variables	Explanatory Variables					
		LLRD	LCO_2	*LFFC*	*LGDP*	*LURB*	*LHEX*
18 developing Asian economies	*LLRD*	—	1.10	1.42	1.02	1.18	1.53
	LCO_2	1.11	—	1.10	1.21	1.10	1.51
	LFFC	1.29	1.53	—	1.39	1.39	1.40
	LGDP	1.31	1.33	1.39	—	1.42	1.21
	LURB	1.01	1.15	1.21	1.30	—	1.31
	LHEX	1.19	1.61	1.40	1.29	1.32	—
	Mean VIF	1.18	1.34	1.30	1.24	1.28	1.39
	$Chi^2(5)$	13.21					

Note: *L* indicates variables in the natural logarithms.

Table 7. VIF and Hausman test results (Model II).

Samples	Independent Variables	Explanatory Variables					
		LLRD	LCO_2	*LFFC*	*LGDP*	*LURB*	*LHEX*
18 developing Asian economies	*LUDR*	—	1.42	1.53	1.19	1.29	1.02
	LCO_2	1.19	—	1.47	1.32	1.19	1.35
	LFFC	1.43	1.42	—	1.29	1.04	1.28
	LGDP	1.39	1.12	1.30	—	1.38	1.44
	LURB	1.12	1.26	1.32	1.03	—	1.13
	LHEX	1.23	1.11	1.14	1.21	1.43	—
	Mean VIF	1.27	1.26	1.35	1.20	1.26	1.24
	$Chi^2(5)$	12.14					

Note: *L* indicates variables in the natural logarithms.

Based on Tables 6 and 7, we conclude that there is low multicollinearity between the cross-sections. Moreover, the findings of the Hausman test (Chi^2) depict the panel data with random effects. Next, we should check the existence of cross-section dependence (CSD) in the series. Table 8 presents the results of the CSD test for our variables.

The results of the CSD test, presented in Table 8, confirm that cross-sections are present in all series, meaning that our samples share the same characteristics. Generally, in situations where there is low multicollinearity and cross-section dependence in the series, it is necessary to check if the variables are stationary. Thus, here we conduct the second-generation panel unit root test (Pesaran's, 2007 cross-sectional augmented IPS (CIPS) test) with the null hypothesis of all series being I(1). The findings of the test are reported in Table 9 and affirm that all series are I(0).

By considering the results of the preliminary tests, the Arellano–Bond dynamic GMM estimations for two models (Model I and Model II) are conducted (with four instruments).

Table 8. CSD test results.

Samples	Variables	CSD Test	Corr.	Abs. (Corr.)	Significant at 1% Level
18 developing Asian economies	*LLRD*	7.14	0.363	0.363	Yes
	LUDR	9.19	0.413	0.413	Yes
	LCO_2	10.01	0.392	0.392	Yes
	LFFC	8.43	0.488	0.488	Yes
	LGDP	9.28	0.317	0.317	Yes
	LURB	9.15	0.349	0.349	Yes
	LHEX	8.18	0.418	0.418	Yes

Note: *L* indicates variables in the natural logarithms.

Table 9. Pesaran (2007) panel unit root test results.

Samples	Variables	Without Trend	With Trend
18 developing Asian economies	*LLRD*	0.501	1.419
	LUDR	0.482	1.432
	LCO_2	0.422	–0.814
	LFFC	0.366	–0.728
	LGDP	0.318	–0.782
	LURB	0.441	–0.681
	LHEX	0.512	1.482

Note: *L* indicates variables in the natural logarithms.

The results of the GMM estimations for the 18 developing Asian economies are reported in Tables 10 and 11.

According to Table 10, CO_2 emissions per capita in developing Asian economies lead to increased LRD. Indeed, a 1% increase in CO_2 emissions per capita leads to an increase in such diseases by approximately 1.73%. With regard to FFC, the estimation proves that this variable leads to greater LRD. A 1% increase in FFC may accelerate LRD in these countries by nearly 1.38%.

Table 11 reports the estimated coefficients of variables with regard to the undernourishment and death ratio. The results demonstrate that greater CO_2 emissions and FFC lead to increases in UDR. A 1% increase in CO_2 emissions increases the undernourishment and death ratio by nearly 1.24%. Furthermore, GDP per capita and healthcare expenditure lead to reduced undernourishment and death ratio. The estimation reveals that through a 1% increase in GDP per capita and healthcare expenditure, UDR in developing Asian economies may decline by approximately 0.39% and 0.21%, respectively. Furthermore, the Hansen J-test (with a null hypothesis of correct model specification and valid overidentifying restrictions) results for both models have p-values of 0.808 and 0.784, which do not reject the null at any level of significance. Therefore, our GMM estimations have valid instrumentation.

Table 10. Estimation result for Model I (dependent variable: LRD).

Explanatory Variables	Coefficients	Significant at 1% Level
Constant	0.19	No
LCO_2	1.73	Yes
LFFC	1.38	Yes
LGDP	–0.11	Yes
LURB	0.58	Yes
LHEX	–0.41	Yes
No. of observations	504	
Range	1991–2018	
Cross-sections included	18	
Hansen J-Statistic test	Chi^2 = 13.432, P-value = 0.784	
Wald Chi^2 (5)	616.28	Yes

Note: *L* indicates variables in the natural logarithms.

Table 11. Estimation result for Model II (dependent variable: URD).

Explanatory Variables	Coefficients	Significant at 1% Level
Constant	1.29	No
LCO_2	1.24	Yes
LFFC	1.19	Yes
LGDP	–0.39	Yes
LURB	0.19	Yes
LHEX	–0.21	Yes
No. of observations	504	
Range	1991–2022	
Cross-sections included	18	
Hansen J-Statistic test	Chi2 = 14.648, P-value = 0.808	
Wald Chi^2 (5)	702.39	Yes

Note: *L* indicates variables in the natural logarithms.

5. Robustness Analysis

To ascertain the estimation results from the GMM technique, reported in Tables 10 and 11, we next carry out an alternative panel data technique, namely fully modified least squares (FM–OLS), to check the robustness of our major findings. As shown in Tables 12 and 13, the estimation findings do not significantly differ, suggesting the robustness of our results.

Table 12. Robustness check with FM–OLS for Model I (dependent variable: LRD).

Sample	Independent Variables				
	LCO_2	*LFFC*	*LGRO*	*LURB*	*LHEX*
Developing Asian economies group	1.01***	0.98***	–0.01***	0.14***	–0.04***

Notes: *L* indicates variables in the natural logarithms. ** and *** indicate statistically significant at 1% and 5% levels, respectively.

Table 13. Robustness check with FM–OLS for Model II (dependent variable: URD).

Sample	Independent Variables				
	LCO_2	*LFFC*	*LGRO*	*LURB*	*LHEX*
Developing Asian economies group	1.32***	1.19***	–0.02***	0.05**	–0.13***

Notes: *L* indicates variables in the natural logarithms. ** and *** indicate statistically significant at 1% and 5% levels, respectively.

6. Concluding Remarks

In this empirical study, we have attempted to analyze the energy–pollution–health nexus in 18 developing Asian economies (Afghanistan, Tajikistan, Bangladesh, Indonesia, India, the Kyrgyz Republic, Cambodia, Myanmar, Pakistan, the Philippines, Uzbekistan, Vietnam, the People's Republic of China, Iran, Kazakhstan, Sri Lanka, Malaysia, and Thailand), based on annual data over the period 1991–2018. With regard to the methodology, through the use of the PCA technique, we reduced the four health variables (*TLC*, *RD*, *PU*, *DR*) into two components — LRD and undernourishment and death ratio (UDR) — as dependent variables. Furthermore, the GMM was utilized to estimate the coefficients of the dependent variables (CO_2, *FFC*, *GDP*, *URB*, *HEX*).

Based on the results, we have found that CO_2 emissions per capita in developing Asian economies have led to increased LRD. Moreover, the estimation has proved that FFC stimulates LRD. In addition, we found a significant impact of population growth in urban areas on an increase of LRD. The results have demonstrated the role of CO_2 emissions and FFC in increasing the undernourishment and death ratio. Furthermore, GDP per capita and health care expenditure have been found to reduce the undernourishment and death ratio.

Our findings about the effects of CO_2 emissions on accelerating the spread of disease in countries are in line with Chaabouni *et al.* (2016), Aung, Saboori, and Rasoulinezhad (2017), Chaabouni and Saidi (2017), Rasoulinezhad and Saboori (2018), Bi and Hansen (2018), and Apergis *et al.* (2018). Furthermore, the positive relationship between urbanization and the spread of disease has been confirmed by Moore *et al.* (2003), although this result contradicts the findings of Geobel *et al.* (2010) regarding the role of urbanization in affecting women's health in a South African city. In terms of the positive association between GDP per capita and health satisfaction, our result is in line with Ettner (1996) and Frijters *et al.* (2005), while it is in contrast with Pickett and Wilkinson (2015), who discussed the effects of income inequality as opposed to GDP per capita.

Consequently, we suggest that developing Asian economies adopt various policies to improve energy transition, indicating the need to shift from fossil fuel energy sources to renewable ones, which increases a country's energy security (Mata Perez *et al.*, 2019). Using more fossil fuel energy sources may become a potential threat to energy security, destroy human living environments, and lead to an increase in the number of serious diseases such as cancer. Moreover, we recommend that these countries carry out new policies to provide easy access to electricity from green sources as well as increased renewable supply through improved technologies, sustainable economic growth, and the greater incorporation of green sources in daily social life. To this end, these countries must receive scientific, financial, and technological assistance from developed countries or countries with successful histories of energy transition. In addition, given the negative implications of urbanization for human health, improving urban lifestyles is highly recommended, which may lead to better human health in cities. In addition, the diversification of energy in developing Asian economies from too much reliance on fossil fuels to more renewable energy can improve energy insecurity and at the same time reduce greenhouse gas emissions and the negative impacts of ambient air pollution on health.

However, it needs to be noted that the development of renewable energy projects also has several obstacles, such as lack of long-term financing, a low rate of return, the existence of various risks, and the lack of capacity of market players. Governments, especially in developing economies, need to take the right policy actions for supporting this sector, which are out of the scope of this study. (See Taghizadeh-Hesary and Yoshino 2019, 2020; Yoshino *et al.*, 2019, for more information on the challenges and practical solutions for the development of renewable energy projects.)

Despite some limitations such as data access, and weakness of sensitivity to normalizations of the GMM approach, and using components of diseases, we believe that the contents of this chapter make an important contribution to the existing literature on the relationship between FFC and health issues in developing Asian economies. We encourage the development of future studies that employ different control variables such as trade openness, interest rates, and inflation as part of an econometric model that considers direct and indirect effects and that conducts causality tests in order to distinguish short- and long-run linkages between dependent and independent variables. In addition, carrying out research to compare the results for developing economies is recommended.

References

Akbari, H, F Taghizadeh-Hesary, Y Heike and M Bahadori (2019). Cell energy: A new hypothesis in decoding cancer evolution. *Archives of Iranian Medicine*, 22(12), 733–735.

Andersen, ZJ *et al.* (2012). Diabetes incidence and long-term exposure to air pollution: A cohort study. *Diabetes Care*, 35(1), 92–98.

Apergis, N, M Ben Jebli and S Ben Youssef (2018). Does renewable energy consumption and health expenditure decrease carbon dioxide emissions? Evidence for sub-Saharan Africa countries. *Renewable Energy*, 127, 1011–1016.

Arellano, M and S Bond (1991). Some tests of specification for panel data: Monte Carlo evidence and an application to employment equations. *Review of Economic Studies*, 58, 277–297.

Aung, T, B Saboori and E Rasoulinezhad (2017). Economic growth and environmental pollution in Myanmar: An analysis of environmental Kuznets curve. *Environmental Science and Pollution Research*, 24(25), 20487–20501.

Bi, P and A Hansen (2018). Carbon emissions and public health: An inverse association? *The Lancet Planetary Health*, 2(1), E8–E9, https://doi.org/10.1016/S2542-5196(17)30177-8.

Bourdrel, T, MA Bind, Y Bejot, O Morel and JF Argacha (2017). Cardiovascular effects of air pollution. *Archives of Cardiovascular Diseases*, 110(11), 634–642.

British Petroleum (2019). Statistical Review 2019, https://www.bp.com/en/global/corporate/energy-economics/statistical-review-of-world-energy.html.

Bruce-Ho, CT and D Dash-Wu (2009). Online banking performance evaluation using data envelopment analysis and principal component analysis. *Computers & Operations Research*, 36(6), 1835–1842.

Can, G *et al.* (2019). Mapping of carbon monoxide related death risk in Turkey: A ten-year analysis based on news agency records. *BMC Public Health*, 19(9), https://bmcpublichealth.biomedcentral.com/articles/10.1186/s12889-018-6342-4#citeas.

Carré, J, N Gatimel, J Moreau, J Parinaud and R Léandri (2017). Does air pollution play a role in infertility? A systematic review. *Environmental Health*, 16(1), 82.

Chaabouni, S and K Saidi (2017). The dynamic links between carbon dioxide (CO_2) emissions, health spending and GDP growth: A case study for 51 countries. *Environmental Research*, 158, 137–144.

Chaabouni, S, N Zghidi and M Ben Mbarek (2016). On the causal dynamics between CO_2 emissions, health expenditures and economic growth. *Sustainable Cities and Society*, 22, 184–191.

Chen, Y *et al.* (2018). Summer–winter differences of PM2.5 toxicity to human alveolar epithelial cells (A549) and the roles of transition metals. *Ecotoxicology and Environmental Safety*, 165, 505–509.

Chu, L, S Ghosh, B Dogan, N Nguyen and M Shahbaz (2023). Energy security as new determinant of renewable energy: The role of economic complexity in top energy users. *Energy*, 263(Part C), 125799, https://doi.org/10.1016/j.energy.2022.125799.

Colligan, MJ (1981). The psychological effects of indoor air pollution. *Bulletin of the New York Academy of Medicine*, 57(10), 1014.

Costa, LG, YC Chang and TB Cole (2017). Developmental neurotoxicity of traffic-related air pollution: Focus on autism. *Current Environmental Health Reports*, 4(2), 156–165.

DeMarini, DM (2015). Abstract CN08-03: How does air pollution cause cancer? *Cancer Prevention Research*, 8(10), https://aacrjournals.org/cancerpreventionresearch/article/8/10_Supplement/CN08-03/30962/Abstract-CN08-03-How-does-air-pollution-cause.

Dominici, F *et al.* (2006). Fine particulate air pollution and hospital admission for cardiovascular and respiratory diseases. *Jama*, 295(10), 1127–1134.

Dubos, R (1969). The human environment. *Science Journal*, 5A, 75–80.

Ettner, SL (1996). New evidence on the relationship between income and health. *Journal of Health Economics*, 15(1), 67–85.

Farabi-Asl, H, F Taghizadeh-Hesary, A Chapman, SM Bina and K Itaoka (2019). Energy challenges for clean cooking in Asia, the background, and possible policy solutions. ADBI Working Paper 1007, Tokyo: Asian Development Bank Institute.

Faustini, A, R Rapp and F Forastiere (2014). Nitrogen dioxide and mortality: Review and meta-analysis of long-term studies. *European Respiratory Journal*, 44(3), 744–753.

Fetterman, JL, MJ Sammy and SW Ballinger (2017). Mitochondrial toxicity of tobacco smoke and air pollution. *Toxicology*, 391, 18–33.

Frijters, P, JP Haisken-DeNew and M Shields (2005). The causal effect of income on health: Evidence from German reunification. *Journal of Health Economics*, 24(5), 997–1017.

Geobel, A, B Dodson and T Hill (2010). Urban advantage or urban penalty? A case study of female-headed households in a South African city. *Health & Place*, 16(3), 573–580.

Golshan, M, M Faghihi and MM Marandi (2002). Indoor women jobs and pulmonary risks in rural areas of Isfahan, Iran, 2000. *Respiratory Medicine*, 96(6), 382–388.

Hanif, I (2018). Energy consumption habits and human health nexus in Sub-Saharan Africa. *Environmental Science and Pollution Research*, 25(22), 21701–21712.

Hoek, G, RM Krishnan, R Beelen, A Peters, B Ostro, B Brunekreef and JD Kaufman (2013). Long-term air pollution exposure and cardio-respiratory mortality: A review. *Environmental Health*, 12(1), 43.

Ishikawa, K *et al.* (2008). ROS-generating mitochondrial DNA mutations can regulate tumor cell metastasis. *Science*, 320(5876), 661–664.

Kahouli, B and S Maktouf (2015). The determinants of FDI and the impact of the economic crisis on the implementation of RTAs: A static and dynamic gravity model. *International Business Review*, 24(3), 518–529.

Khan, K, A Khurshid, J Cifuentes-Faura and D Xianjin (2024). Does renewable energy development enhance energy security? *Utilities Policy*, 87, 101725, https://doi.org/10.1016/j.jup.2024.101725.

Kreyling, WG, M Semmler and W Möller (2004). Dosimetry and toxicology of ultrafine particles. *Journal of Aerosol Medicine*, 17(2), 140–152.

Lambert, JG, C Hall, S Balogh, A Gupta and M Arnold (2014). Energy, EROI and quality of life. *Energy Policy*, 64, 153–167.

Laraia, BA, AM Siega-Riz and C Gundersen (2010). Household food insecurity is associated with self-reported pregravid weight status, gestational weight gain, and pregnancy complications. *Journal of the American Dietetic Association*, 110(5), 692–701.

Le, TH, Y Chang, F Taghizadeh-Hesary and N Yoshino (2019). Energy insecurity in Asia: A multi-dimensional analysis. *Economic Modelling*, 83, 84–95.

Lim, SS *et al.* (2012a). A comparative risk assessment of burden of disease and injury attributable to 67 risk factors and risk factor clusters in 21 regions, 1990–2010: A systematic analysis for the global burden of disease study 2010. *The Lancet*, 380(9859), 2224–2260.

Lim, YH, H Kim, JH Kim, S Bae, HY Park and YC Hong (2012b). Air pollution and symptoms of depression in elderly adults. *Environmental Health Perspectives*, 120(7), 1023–1028.

Lin, F (2015). Estimating the effect of the Internet on international trade. *The Journal of International Trade & Economic Development*, 24(3), 409–428.

Machol, B and S Rizk (2013). Economic value of U.S. fossil fuel electricity health impacts. *Environment International*, 52, 75–80.

Maggini, S, A Pierre and P Calder (2018). Immune function and micronutrient requirements change over the life course. *Nutrients*, 10(10), 1531.

Martinez-Zarzoso, I, D Nowak-Lehmann and N Horsewood (2009). Are regional trading agreements beneficial? Static and dynamic panel gravity models. *The North American Journal of Economics and Finance*, 20(1), 46–65.

Mata Perez, M, D Scholten and K Stegen (2019). The multi-speed energy transition in Europe: Opportunities and challenges for EU energy security. *Energy Strategy Reviews*, 26, 100415.

Meyer, JN *et al.* (2013). Mitochondria as a target of environmental toxicants. *Toxicological Sciences*, 134(1), 1–17.

Mills, E (2012). Technical report 10: Health impacts of fuel-based lighting. The Lumina Project, http://light.lbl.gov/pubs/tr/lumina-tr10-summary.html.

Modig, L, K Torén, C Janson, B Jarvholm and B Forsberg (2009). Vehicle exhaust outside the home and onset of asthma among adults. *European Respiratory Journal*, 33(6), 1261–1267.

Merryman, JI, PG Park and HM Schuller (1997). Carbon dioxide, an important messenger molecule for small cell lung cancer. *Chest*, 112(3), 779–784.

Moore, M, P Gould and B Keary (2003). Global urbanization and impact on health. *International Journal of Hygiene and Environmental Health*, 206(4–5), 269–278.

Nasre Esfahani, M and E Rasoulinezhad (2016). Will be there new CO_2 emitters in the future? Evidence of long-run panel co-integration for N-11 countries. *International Journal of Energy Economics and Policy*, 6(3), 463–470.

Newborough, M and SD Probert (1987). Relating energy-consumption and health-care concerns to diet choices. *Applied Energy*, 27(3), 169–201.

Padhi, BK and PK Padhy (2008). Domestic fuels, indoor air pollution, and children's health: The case of rural India. *Annals of the New York Academy of Sciences*, 1140(1), 209–217.

Pedersen, M *et al.* (2013). Ambient air pollution and low birthweight: A European cohort study (ESCAPE). *The Lancet Respiratory Medicine*, 1(9), 695–704.

Phung, T *et al.* (2023). How are FDI and green recovery related in Southeast Asian economies? *Economic Change and Restructuring*, 56(6), 3735–3755.

Pickett, KE and G Wilkinson (2015). Income inequality and health: A causal review. *Social Science & Medicine*, 128, 316–326.

Porcaro, J *et al.* (2017). Modern energy access and health, http://documents.worldbank.org/curated/en/756131494939083421/Modern-energy-access-and-health.

Rasoulinezhad, E and B Saboori (2018). Panel estimation for renewable and non-renewable energy consumption, economic growth, CO_2 emissions, the composite trade intensity, and financial openness of the Commonwealth of Independent States. *Environmental Science and Pollution Research*, 25(18), 17354–17370.

Rasoulinezhad, E and IH Eksi (2024). The economic development of the Russian Federation. *Countries Studies*, 2(2), 279–289.

Raub, JA (1999). Health effects of exposure to ambient carbon monoxide. *Chemosphere- Global Change Science*, 1(1–3), 331–351.

Rice, SA (2004). Human health risk assessment of CO_2: Survivors of acute high-level exposure and populations sensitive to prolonged low-level exposure. Third Annual Conference on Carbon Sequestration, Alexandria, Virginia, http://www.netl.doe.gov/publications/proceedings/04/carbon-seq/169.pdf.

Sirag, A, N Mohamed Nor, S Law, N Raja Abdullah and M Lacheheb (2017). The impact of health financing and CO_2 emission on health outcomes in Sub-Saharan Africa: A cross-country analysis. *Geo Journal*, 82(6), 1247–1261.

Shigemura, M, E Lecuona and JI Sznajder (2017). Effects of hypercapnia on the lung. *The Journal of Physiology*, 595(8), 2431–2437.

Shin, J, JY Park and J Choi (2018). Long-term exposure to ambient air pollutants and mental health status: A nationwide population-based cross-sectional study. *PloS One*, 13(4), e0195607.

Suades-Gonzalez, E, M Gascon, M Guxens and J Sunyer (2015). Air pollution and neuropsychological development: A review of the latest evidence. *Endocrinology*, 156(10), 3473–3482.

Stanford University (2008). Carbon dioxide emissions linked to human mortality. *Science Daily*, www.sciencedaily.com/releases/2008/01/080103135757.htm.

Szyszkowicz, M, B Rowe and I Colman (2009). Air pollution and daily emergency department visits for depression. *International Journal of Occupational Medicine and Environmental Health*, 22(4), 355–362.

Szyszkowicz, M, JB Willey, E Grafstein, BH Rowe and I Colman (2010). Air pollution and emergency department visits for suicide attempts in Vancouver, Canada. *Environmental Health Insights*, 4, 79–86.

Taghizadeh-Hesary, F, E Rasoulinezhad and N Yoshino (2019). Energy and food security: Linkages through price volatility. *Energy Policy*, 128(C), 796–806.

Taghizadeh-Hesary, F and N Yoshino (2019). The way to induce private participation in green finance and investment. *Finance Research Letters*, 31, 98–103.

Taghizadeh-Hesary, F and N Yoshino (2020). Sustainable solutions for green financing and investment in renewable energy projects. *Energies*, 13, 788.

Taghizadeh-Hesary, F, E Rasoulinezhad, N Yoshino, Y Chang, F Taghizadeh-Hesary and PJ Morgan (2021). The energy–pollution–health nexus: A panel data analysis of low- and middle-income Asian countries. *The Singapore Economic Review*, 66(2), 435–455, https://doi.org/10.1142/S0217590820430043.

United States Global Change Research Program (2016). *The Impacts of Climate Change on Human Health in the United States: A Scientific Assessment*. Washington, DC: US Global Change Research Program.

Wang, B, D Xu, Z Jing, D Liu, S Yan and Y Wang (2014). Effect of long-term exposure to air pollution on type 2 diabetes mellitus risk: A systemic review and meta-analysis of cohort studies. *European Journal of Endocrinology*, 171(5), R173–R182.

Wang, J and W Azam (2024). Natural resource scarcity, fossil fuel energy consumption, and total greenhouse gas emissions in top emitting countries. *Geoscience Frontiers*, 15(2), 101757, https://doi.org/10.1016/j.gsf.2023.101757.

World Health Organization (2013). Review of evidence on health aspects of air pollution—REVIHAAP project: Technical report. Copenhagen: WHO Regional Office for Europe.

World Health Organization (2014). Mortality from household air pollution for 2012, http://www.who.int/phe/health_topics/outdoorair/databases/en/.

World Health Organization (2016). Ambient air pollution: A global assessment of exposure and burden of disease, https://www.who.int/phe/publications/air-pollution-global-assessment/en/.

Xu, X *et al.* (2011). Long-term exposure to ambient fine particulate pollution induces insulin resistance and mitochondrial alteration in adipose tissue. *Toxicological Sciences*, 124(1), 88–98.

Yoshino, N and F Taghizadeh-Hesary (2015). Analysis of credit risk for small and medium-sized enterprises: Evidence from Asia. *Asian Development Review*, 32(2), 18–37.

Yoshino, N, F Taghizadeh-Hesary and M Nakahigashi (2019). Modelling the social funding and spill-over tax for addressing the green energy financing gap. *Economic Modelling*, 77, 34–41.

Section 2

Country-Level Studies

https://doi.org/10.1142/9789819812608_0006

Chapter 6

Green Finance for Energy Efficiency, Sustainable Transition, and Emission Reduction: Insights from the Top 10 Green Finance-Supporting Countries

EHSAN RASOULINEZHAD[*,‡] and FARHAD TAGHIZADEH-HESARY[†,§]

[*]*Faculty of World Studies, University of Tehran, Tehran, Iran*

[†]*Tokai Research Institute for Environment and Sustainability, Tokai University, Tokyo, Japan*

[‡]*e.rasoulinezhad@ut.ac.ir*

[§]*farhad@tsc.u-tokai.ac.jp*

This study examines the critical role of green energy deployment in advancing energy security, enabling energy transition, and contributing to environmentally sustainable development goals (SDGs). Utilizing the stochastic impact model (STIRPAT), which considers population, affluence, and technology, the analysis explores the relationships between CO_2 emissions, energy efficiency, the green energy index (GEI), and green finance in the top ten countries supporting green finance. Results indicate that green bonds are an effective tool for promoting green energy projects and achieving substantial CO_2 reduction, though no short-term causal link is observed among these variables. To foster sustainable economic growth and address environmental challenges, governments are encouraged to implement long-term policies that support private sector involvement in green energy investments.

Keywords: Energy efficiency, energy security, environmental efficiency, green finance.

1. Introduction

The global shift toward sustainable energy has elevated green energy, green finance, and energy efficiency as critical pillars in achieving SDGs, particularly those targeting affordable and clean energy, climate action, and ecological preservation. These elements play crucial roles not only in reducing carbon footprints but also in enhancing energy security—a priority for nations as they strive to maintain stable energy supplies amidst the volatility of global energy markets and escalating environmental risks (Gielen *et al.*, 2019; Taghizadeh-Hesary & Yoshino, 2020).

Energy security, defined by the reliability and resilience of energy systems to meet current and future needs, is increasingly intertwined with the broader goals of the energy transition (Ang *et al.*, 2015). The COVID-19 pandemic underscored vulnerabilities in traditional energy systems, highlighting the need for resilient, secure energy infrastructure (Khanna, 2020; Meo & Karim, 2021). Expanding green energy capacity, particularly through renewable sources, addresses energy security by reducing dependency on fossil fuel imports, often subject to price volatility and geopolitical risks (Ren *et al.*, 2020; Charfeddine & Kahia, 2019). Studies show that countries investing in renewable energy see significant improvements in their energy security indexes by diversifying their energy portfolios and reducing import dependencies (Sovacool & Mukherjee, 2011; IRENA, 2021).

Green finance, especially through green bonds, is pivotal in advancing energy security by channeling funds into renewable energy projects. Taghizadeh-Hesary *et al.* (2021) emphasized the role of green finance in catalyzing investment for energy transition, noting that targeted financial policies encourage private sector participation in green projects. In regions with established financial markets, green bonds have been shown to effectively mobilize capital for energy projects, fostering both economic resilience and environmental sustainability (Sachs *et al.*, 2019; Gielen *et al.*, 2019). In contrast, emerging economies face barriers such as underdeveloped financial infrastructures and limited investor confidence, which can stymie the growth of green finance (Hafner *et al.*, 2020; Fu & Ng, 2021).

Enhanced energy efficiency further supports energy security by lowering overall energy demand, making systems less susceptible to supply shocks. Efficiency gains, often financed through green finance mechanisms, contribute to both emission reductions and economic stability, enabling countries to manage energy demand more sustainably and cost-effectively (Gielen *et al.*, 2019; Meo & Karim, 2021). A significant body of research underscores the need for integrated policies that leverage green finance to achieve energy security and climate goals simultaneously (Amir & Khan, 2021; Jin *et al.*, 2021; Sovacool & Brown, 2010). For instance, Naeem *et al.* (2021) found that green bonds provided greater stability compared to conventional bonds during the pandemic, highlighting their value as secure investments for the energy transition.

Given these complex interconnections, understanding the dynamic interactions between green finance, green energy consumption, energy efficiency, and CO_2 emissions is essential. This study utilizes the STIRPAT to analyze these linkages among "Green Leaders"—economies at the forefront of green finance support. The empirical insights aim to assist policymakers in formulating long-term strategies that bolster energy security, foster sustainable economic growth, and mitigate emissions. This work contributes to the ongoing discourse by illustrating how green finance and energy policies can collectively reinforce energy security, resilience, and sustainable growth (Holdren & Ehrlich, 1974; Wang *et al.*, 2021).

This paper aims to make several unique contributions to the existing literature:

1. Firstly, it is the first to explore the dynamic relationships among CO_2 emissions, green energy, green finance, and energy efficiency, specifically within the context of the "green leaders" economies (Figure 1).
2. This analysis employs the stochastic impacts by regression on population, affluence, and technology (STIRPAT) model, recognized as a suitable theoretical framework for examining environmental impact factors (Ji & Chen, 2017; Debone *et al.*, 2021). This model is utilized here for the first time to assess these particular variables and contexts.

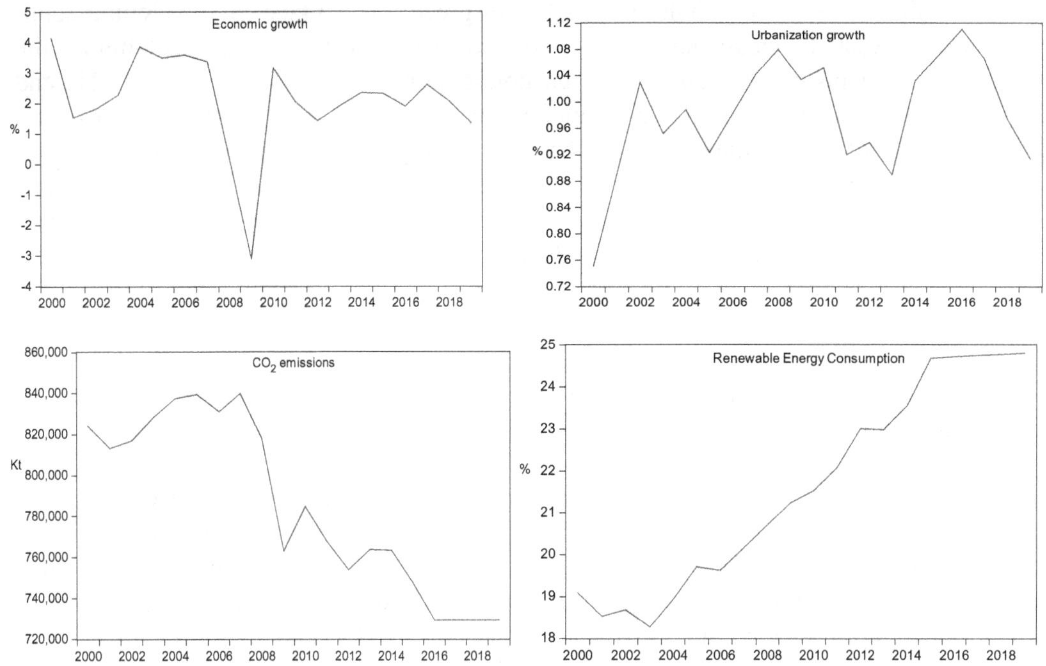

Figure 1. Green Leaders' economic situation.

Source: Compiled by the authors based on the data from the World Bank and British Petroleum Statistical Review of World Energy 2020.

3. Additionally, the study constructs a GEI using the principal component analysis (PCA) method, which serves as an integral part of the empirical model.

The paper is organized into six sections: Section 2 reviews the existing literature and highlights the research gap. Section 3 provides details on the data and model specifications. Section 4 presents the empirical results, followed by Section 5, which includes robustness checks to validate these findings. Finally, Section 6 summarizes key outcomes and offers practical policy recommendations.

2. Literature Review

The nexus of green finance, energy efficiency, and energy security has attracted significant scholarly attention, given their combined importance in addressing climate goals and ensuring economic stability. Research has increasingly focused on the effectiveness of green finance tools like green bonds, especially in supporting clean energy transitions and improving energy security. While some scholars argue that green finance is not universally effective, particularly in emerging economies, others have documented positive impacts on both economic and environmental indicators, albeit under certain conditions (Yadav *et al.*, 2024).

A number of studies highlight the challenges green finance faces in developing countries, where weak financial markets and limited private-sector engagement hinder the effectiveness of instruments such as green bonds. For example, Fu and Ng (2021) and Hafner *et al.* (2020) note that in less-developed regions, inadequate financial infrastructure and limited institutional support reduce the efficacy of green finance, making it challenging to mobilize private capital toward sustainable projects. Hammoudeh *et al.* (2020) also explored the causal relationships between green bonds and various economic and environmental factors, concluding that green bonds had limited impact in certain cases. Similarly, Prakash and Mahdvi (2021) found that structural issues like financing gaps and insufficient regulatory frameworks prevent green bonds from effectively contributing to the SDGs in India. Research by Gibon *et al.* (2020) on green bonds issued by the European Investment Bank for renewable energy projects from 2015–2018 highlighted inefficiencies in fund allocation, which diluted the intended environmental benefits.

In contrast, recent studies illustrate the potential for green finance to positively influence sustainable development in economies with more mature financial systems. Naeem *et al.* (2021) found that green bonds performed better than conventional bonds during the COVID-19 pandemic, largely due to their transparency and perceived stability, which enhanced investor confidence. Nguyen *et al.* (2021) examined the relationship between green bonds, clean energy, and emissions from 2008 to 2019, uncovering a strong link between green bonds and clean energy adoption. Taghizadeh-Hesary *et al.* (2021) examined the green bond market across Asia and the Pacific, finding that while green bonds in Asia deliver higher returns, they also carry increased risks and volatility. This trend, they argue, calls for risk management policies and public-sector involvement to sustain the market post-COVID-19. Wan (2020) further emphasizes that state support is essential in cultivating green finance markets in emerging economies, as government backing can attract private investors and drive the growth of renewable energy sectors.

Beyond green finance, studies have shown that energy efficiency directly contributes to energy security by reducing the reliance on fossil fuels and lowering energy demand (Alemzero *et al.*, 2021). The International Renewable Energy Agency (IRENA, 2021) argues that improvements in energy efficiency can mitigate energy import dependency, strengthening a nation's resilience to external shocks. Tolliver *et al.* (2020) highlight that when directed toward energy efficiency projects, green bond can significantly decrease investment risks, increase returns, and attract global investment to energy-saving technologies. Likewise, Liu *et al.* (2021) show that enhanced risk management in green bond markets fosters investor trust, allowing more funds to flow into green energy and efficiency projects. In developing countries, Meo and Karim (2021) suggest that supportive market conditions and well-designed green finance mechanisms are critical for realizing the benefits of green finance in promoting small-scale renewable projects and energy security.

Energy security, as an essential aspect of the energy transition, has also gained importance in the literature. A secure and diversified energy mix ensures consistent energy supply and buffers against price fluctuations and geopolitical risks (Feng *et al.*, 2024). Sovacool and Mukherjee (2021) argue that energy security and green finance are interdependent, with green bonds acting as vehicles to fund renewable energy projects that reduce fossil fuel dependency. In India, for instance, Sarangi (2018) found that green finance significantly contributes to expanding the renewable energy sector, particularly through solar and wind projects, which enhances energy security by reducing reliance on imported fossil fuels. Similarly, Wang and Zhi (2016) argue that robust financial policies are needed to support renewable energy, which, in turn, strengthens energy security by fostering local energy resources and reducing exposure to global energy market volatility.

These studies collectively underscore that green finance outcomes vary significantly across contexts, influenced by factors such as financial market maturity, regulatory support, and the strength of public-private partnerships (PPPs). Accordingly, it is valuable to study green finance within economies that actively support it, such as the Green Leaders. Insights from these economies can guide other countries as they develop green finance markets tailored to their specific needs and constraints. This study distinguishes itself from prior research in several ways. It uniquely examines the simultaneous causal relationships between green finance, green energy consumption, and energy efficiency, all of which contribute to long-term energy security. Unlike other studies, this research analyzes these relationships within top green finance-supporting nations, which offers insights into successful frameworks and policies. Additionally, the empirical model includes a GEI, created using PCA, to comprehensively represent various green energy sources. The study employs the STIRPAT model as an analytical framework, validating it as a robust approach within energy economics and environmental research.

3. Data and Model Specification

The development of theoretical frameworks to assess the environmental impacts of various factors has been extensively explored by researchers. One of the earliest comprehensive models, the IPAT framework, was introduced by Holdren and Ehrlich (1974) to examine the environmental impact driven by population, affluence, and technology. Later, in 2002, Waggoner and Ausubel expanded on this model with the ImPACT framework, incorporating consumption per unit of gross domestic product (GDP) to offer a more nuanced perspective. Despite these advancements, both IPAT and ImPACT face limitations, such as a lack of dynamic analysis capabilities and inconsistencies in measuring factor impacts (York *et al.*, 2003).

Dietz and Rosa (1994, 1997) developed the STIRPAT model, an enhanced framework that uses regression analysis to examine the effects of various factors on environmental outcomes to address these limitations. STIRPAT is widely regarded as a robust model for evaluating the relationship between environmental pollution and explanatory variables, as Bargaoui *et al.* (2014) and Gani (2021) noted. The theoretical equation underpinning the STIRPAT model is represented by Eq. (1) (Rasoulinezhad and Taghizadeh-Hesary, 2022).[1]

$$I_i = \alpha \,.\, P_i^b \,.\, A_i^c \,.\, T_i^d \,.\, e_i \tag{1}$$

In this model, I represent the environmental impact in a given country i, with P and A denoting population and affluence, respectively. The variable T stands for technology, while e represents the error term. The parameter α serves as the scaling factor for the

[1]The model and empirical study of this chapter is based on Rasoulinezhad and Taghizadeh-Hesary (2022).

model, and the exponents *b*, *c*, and *d* capture the estimated influence of each factor—population, affluence, and technology—on environmental impact.

Building on the work by Wang *et al.* (2017), the STIRPAT model in Eq. (1) can be reformulated in a logarithmic form, as shown in Eq. (2).

$$ln\,I_{it} = ln\alpha + b(\ln P_{it}) + c(\ln A_{it}) + d(\ln T_{it}) + ln e_{it} \qquad (2)$$

In this formulation, α denotes a constant, while *b*, *c*, and *d* are the exponents for population, affluence, and technology, respectively. The error term is represented by *e*, and *t* refers to time. For the dependent variable *I*, we adopt the approach of Zheng *et al.* (2016) and Wang *et al.* (2020), using CO_2 emissions per capita as the measure. Population is used to represent *P*, while *A* stands for GDP per capita and energy intensity (EI). Finally, issued green bonds and the GEI are incorporated into the model as proxies for *T*. Table 1 provides an overview of the variables included in the model.

The GEI, which reflects green energy consumption, is created using PCA and includes nuclear, hydro, solar, wind, and biofuel energy consumption data. Prior to performing the PCA, the dataset's suitability for factor analysis was verified using the Kaiser–Meyer–Olkin (KMO) test and Bartlett's test. The KMO and Bartlett values, calculated at 0.83 and 0.001 respectively, confirmed that the PCA could be applied to these variables. The results of the PCA are displayed in Table 2.

Table 1. Variables of model.

Variables (Symbols)		Unit	Sources
Carbon emission per capita (COPC)		Metric tons per capita	World Bank, Knoema
Population (POP)		Number	World Bank
GDP per capita (GDPPC)		Current USD	World Bank
Energy intensity (EI)		MJ/$ 2011 PPP GDP	IEA, World Bank
Green bonds (GB)		USD	Climatebonds.net
GEI	Nuclear consumption	Million tonnes oil equivalent	BP, IEA
	Hydro consumption	Million tonnes oil equivalent	BP, IEA
	Solar consumption	Million tonnes oil equivalent	BP, IEA
	Wind consumption	Million tonnes oil equivalent	BP, IEA
	Biofuels consumption	Thousand barrels per day	BP, IEA, Knoema

Table 2. PCA results.

Component	Eigenvalue	% of Variance	Cumulative Variance (%)
A1	3.54	78.04	78.04
A2	0.82	7.19	85.23
A3	0.76	5.87	91.1
A4	0.61	4.95	96.05
A5	0.39	3.95	100

Table 3. Factor loadings of green energy consumptions in component A1.

Variable	Component A1
Nuclear consumption	0.014
Hydro consumption	0.082
Solar consumption	–0.051
Wind consumption	0.749
Biofuels consumption	0.009

The analysis indicates that component A1 has an eigenvalue greater than 1, accounting for 67.4% of the total variance in green energy consumption across the ten Green Leaders. Consequently, A1 is incorporated into our model as the GEI. To further illustrate the contribution of each energy source within A1, the factor loadings are detailed in Table 3.

As shown in Table 3, hydro and wind energy consumption exhibit higher factor loadings than other green energy sources within component A1.

The generalized method of moments (GMM) estimation method is applied to investigate Granger causality relationships among the variables, utilizing Eq. (3) with annual data spanning from 2002 to 2018.

$$\Delta lCOPC_{it} = \gamma_0 + \sum_{j=1}^{m} \delta_1 \Delta lPOP_{it-j} + \sum_{j=1}^{m} \delta_2 \Delta lGDPPC_{it-j} + \sum_{j=1}^{m} \delta_3 \Delta lEI_{it-j}$$
$$+ \sum_{j=1}^{m} \delta_4 \Delta lGB_{it-j} + \sum_{j=1}^{m} \delta_5 \Delta lGEI_{it-j} + u_{it} \tag{3}$$

In Eq. (3), the variables are defined as follows: *COPC* denotes CO_2 emissions per capita, *POP* represents population size, *GDPPC* is GDP per capita, *EI* stands for energy intensity, *GB* represents issued green bonds, and *GEI* is the green energy index. To ensure robustness of the empirical results, a series of panel unit root and co-integration tests were conducted. This study applied first-generation unit root tests, including the augmented Dickey–Fuller (ADM) (Dickey and Fuller, 1979), Phillips and Perron (1988), Breitung (2000), and Levin–Lin–Chu (LLC) test (Levin *et al.*, 2002). To validate these results, we also utilized the unit root test with structural breaks by Carrion-i-Silvestre *et al.* (2002). Subsequently, panel co-integration analysis was conducted to examine potential long-term equilibrium among the variables, employing the Westerlund (2007) and Maddala and Wu (1999) tests. Where a long-term relationship was identified, the augmented mean group (AMG) estimator was used to determine the long-run coefficients of the explanatory variables.

The panel-error correction model (P-ECM) was applied to analyze causal relationships among the variables. For robustness checks, the coefficients were re-estimated using the fully modified-ordinary least squares (FM-OLS) estimator and the common correlated effects mean group (CCEMG) estimator. The empirical findings are detailed in Section 4. Furthermore, the conceptual framework in Figure 2 outlines the methodological steps undertaken in this study.

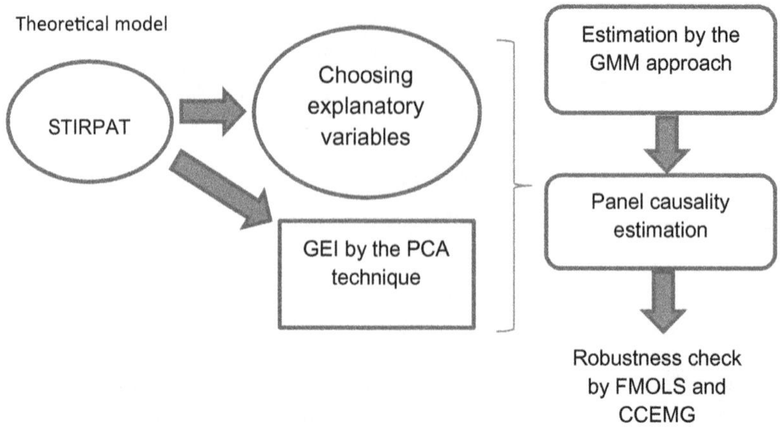

Figure 2. Conceptual framework of empirical research progress.

Table 4. The results of ADF, PP, Breitung and LLC tests.

		Variables					
Test	At	COPC	POP	GDPPC	EI	GB	GEI
ADF	Level	61.43 (0.243)	56.94 (0.419)	60.59 (0.349)	70.84 (0.116)	45.55 (0.866)	44.10 (0.940)
	Δ	547.39 (0.00)	419.59 (0.00)	444.09 (0.00)	167.44 (0.00)	204.50 (0.00)	138.78 (0.00)
PP	Level	19.59 (1.00)	70.44 (0.144)	30.59 (0.695)	0.317 (1.00)	30.59 (0.985)	18.86 (1.00)
	Δ	933.59 (0.00)	500.45 (0.00)	359.05 (0.00)	96.14 (0.001)	80.94 (0.133)	975.33 (0.00)
Breitung	Level	6.076 (1.00)	−1.048 (0.158)	−0.019 (0.455)	−0.993 (0.160)	1.654 (0.855)	5.068 (1.00)
	Δ	−10.39 (0.00)	−9.043 (0.00)	−18.053 (0.00)	−5.694 (0.00)	−8.594 (0.00)	−16.59 (0.00)
LLC	Level	2.60 (0.990)	−0.960 (0.179)	−0.010 (0.500)	−0.349 (0.351)	3.400 (0.995)	−0.618 (0.270)
	Δ	−20.58 (0.00)	−18.59 (0.00)	5.604 (0.00)	−16.04 (0.00)	−3.594 (0.00)	−3.756 (0.00)

Notes: COPC, POP, GDPPC, EI, GB and GEI indicate CO_2 emissions per capita, population, GDP per capita, energy intensity, issued green bonds and GEI, respectively. ADF = Augmented Dickey-Fuller; PP = Phillips–Perron test; LLC) test. Δ is at the first difference, p-values are in ().

4. Empirical Results

First, the panel unit root tests were performed, and the results have been reported in Tables 4 and 5.

The findings of the panel unit root tests, shown in Table 3, conclude that all the variables have unit roots at levels while they become stationary at the first level.

Table 5. Panel unit root test with structural breaks.

Variables	–	Bartlett Kernel	Quadratic Kernel	Bootstrap Critical Values 5%	2.5%	1%
COPC	Ho	8.758**	8.761**	7.713	8.100	8.853
	He	5.600***	5.673***	5.405	6.813	7.239
POP	Ho	18.230*	18.607*	17.112	17.439	18.100
	He	20.329**	20.670**	18.794	20.200	21.014
GDPPC	Ho	9.439*	9.501*	7.800	8.132	8.809
	He	8.099*	8.165*	5.498	6.514	7.093
EI	Ho	15.655***	16.119*	15.400	15.684	16.019
	He	16.301***	16.718***	16.055	16.788	17.490
GB	Ho	7.301**	7.419**	6.817	7.001	7.519
	He	6.839*	6.909*	5.480	5.947	6.384
GEI	Ho	7.918*	7.958*	6.817	7.001	8.109
	He	8.304**	8.694*	5.483	5.911	8.897

Notes: COPC, POP, GDPPC, EI, GB and GEI indicate CO_2 emissions per capita, population, GDP per capita, energy intensity, issued green bonds and GEI, respectively. Ho and He stand for homogeneous and heterogeneous, respectively; *, ** and *** denote the significance at 1% , 2.5%, and 5%.

Considering the structural breaks, the panel unit root test results presented in Table 4 prove the rejection of **H0** of the stationary series.

The panel unit root tests, as summarized in the tables above, indicate that the variables are non-stationary at their levels but achieve stationarity upon first differencing, confirming integration at I(1). This finding permits the use of panel co-integration testing to investigate the presence of any long-term equilibrium relationships. Accordingly, both the Westerlund and Johansen Fisher tests were conducted, with the results detailed in Tables 5 and 6. The evidence presented in Tables 6 and 7 suggests the existence of a long-term association between CO_2 emissions per capita and the explanatory variables.

Next, regression estimations are carried out using the AMG estimator. The results are presented in Table 8.

The estimated coefficients demonstrate that population size and GDP per capita positively impact CO_2 emissions per capita among the Green Leaders, indicating that as these factors rise, CO_2 emissions and, consequently, air pollution increase. This positive association between GDP per capita, population, and CO_2 emissions aligns with findings from Tucker (1995), Akalpler and Hove (2019), and Aslam *et al.* (2021) for the emissions-GDP link, as well as Knapp and Mookerjee (1996), Yeh and Liao (2017), and Rehman *et al.* (2021) regarding emissions-population correlations. The primary reason for this positive impact is the higher energy demand associated with economic and population growth, leading to elevated CO_2 emissions.

Additionally, the results indicate that greater EI—a measure linked to energy efficiency—leads to increased CO_2 emissions. Specifically, among the Green Leaders, a 1%

Table 6. Panel co-integration test (Johansen Fisher).

—	Stat. from the Trace Test	Stat. from the Max Eigenvalue Test
None	1495.1*	613.2*
At most 1	1230.4*	439.5*
At most 2	938.5*	215.4*
At most 3	411.9*	141.9*
At most 4	287.5*	121.0*
At most 5	179.4*	98.3*
At most 6	104.7*	98.1*

Notes: the optimal lag length selection is based on the Schwarz Information Criterion (SIC); * shows that the statistics are significant at the 5% level.

Table 7. Panel co-integration test (Westerlund test).

Stat.	Value	Probability
Group-t	–3.813	0.00
Group-a	–12.055	0.766
Panel-t	–15.039	0.00
Panel-a	–7.115	0.740

Table 8. AMG estimation results.

Variables	Coefficient	Statistics
POP	0.04	13.49*
GDPPC	0.118	13.68*
EI	0.09	4.983**
GB	−1.01	17.59*
GEI	−0.92	10.29*

Notes: POP, GDPPC, EI, GB and GEI indicate population, GDP per capita, energy intensity, issued green bonds and GEI, respectively; * and ** show significance at 5% and 10%, respectively.

increase in EI correlates with a roughly 0.09% rise in CO_2 emissions in the long run, consistent with studies by Shahbaz *et al.* (2015) and Namahoro *et al.* (2021) on selected African nations.

Green bond issuance, representing green finance, positively supports green energy initiatives and reduces CO_2 emissions per capita. The estimated coefficient suggests that a 1% increase in green bonds issued leads to approximately a 1% reduction in CO_2 emissions in these countries. Similar outcomes were observed by Gianfrate and Peri (2019),

Table 9. Results of panel causality test.

	Short-Run				Long-Run		
	ΔlCOPC	ΔlPOP	ΔlGDPPC	ΔlEI	ΔlGB	ΔlGEI	ECT
ΔlCOPC	—	0.14*	0.05*	1.20*	–0.05	–0.14	–0.67*
ΔlPOP	–0.08	—	0.19*	0.41**	0.13*	0.03**	–0.73*
ΔlGDPPC	0.15	0.17**	—	0.04*	0.36**	0.12*	–0.66**
ΔlEI	0.01	0.09**	0.11*	—	–0.19*	–0.03*	–0.71*
ΔlGB	0.19	0.03	0.34**	0.16	—	0.46**	–0.61**
ΔlGEI	0.07	0.18*	0.42**	–0.23*	0.37**	—	0.70*

Notes: COPC, POP, GDPPC, EI, GB and GEI indicate CO_2 emissions per capita, population, GDP per capita, energy intensity, issued green bonds, and GEI, respectively; * and ** shows the significance at 5% and 10%, respectively.

Wang *et al.* (2021), Loffler *et al.* (2021), and Meo *et al.* (2021), while Mensi *et al.* (2021) found green bonds to be less effective in some contexts.

The GEI also shows promise in curbing CO_2 emissions, with the coefficient indicating that a 1% increase in the GEI (reflecting green energy consumption) could reduce emissions by about 0.92% in the long term. Previous studies similarly document the beneficial effects of renewable energy on reducing emissions, as seen in works by Lysen (1989) for solar energy, Hanaki and Portugal-Pereira (2018) for biofuels, Li *et al.* (2020) for wind energy, and Hassan *et al.* (2020) for nuclear energy.

Furthermore, the Granger causality test, implemented using the P-ECM, was used to examine the direction of relationships among variables. Table 9 presents these findings. Results indicate that population, GDP per capita, and EI influence CO_2 emissions per capita. However, no causal relationship was found between green bonds and CO_2 emissions per capita or between the GEI and CO_2 emissions per capita. There is, however, a bidirectional causality between green bonds and the GEI in the short term, as well as a bidirectional link between green bonds and GDP per capita, which may be of interest to policymakers. Support for green finance mechanisms could enhance GDP per capita, a key aspect of national welfare.

5. Robustness Check

Several robustness checks were performed to validate the empirical findings. First, the model was re-estimated using the FMOLS and CCEMG estimators to confirm the reliability of the results. As indicated in Table 10, the direction of the estimated coefficients remained consistent, though the magnitude of the effects differed from those obtained with the AMG estimator.

A second robustness check involved substituting the dependent variable. CO_2 emissions per capita were replaced with CO_2 emissions from fossil fuels, and the model was re-estimated using the AMG estimator to assess the robustness of the estimated coefficients for green bonds (as a proxy for green finance), the GEI, and EI (as a proxy for energy efficiency). The results, detailed in Table 11, demonstrate that both green bond

Table 10. Robustness check (FMOLS and CCEMG estimators).

	FMOLS	CCEMG
Variable	Coefficient	Coefficient
POP	0.23**	0.18*
GDPPC	0.09*	0.15*
EI	0.11**	0.23*
GB	–0.19*	–0.06*
GEI	–0.24**	–0.33*

Notes: POP, GDPPC, EI, GB and GEI indicate population, GDP per capita, energy intensity, issued green bonds and GEI, respectively. * and ** denote the significance at 5% and 10%, respectively.

Table 11. Robustness check (dependent variable of CO_2 emission from fossil fuels).

Variable	Coefficient	Statistics
POP	0.18	16.49*
GDPPC	0.09	12.17**
EI	0.27	14.38*
GB	–0.67	18.03*
GEI	–0.19	17.59*

Notes: POP, GDPPC, EI, GB and GEI indicate population, GDP per capita, energy intensity, issued green bonds, and GEI, respectively; * and ** denote the significance at 5% and 10%, respectively.

issuance and an increase in the GEI effectively reduce CO_2 emissions from fossil fuels. Additionally, the positive relationship between EI and CO_2 emissions from fossil fuels was confirmed.

6. Conclusions and Policy Implications

The ongoing discourse surrounding the interplay between green finance, green energy adoption, and energy efficiency underscores the complexity of achieving sustainable growth while reducing carbon emissions. This study employs the STIRPAT model to investigate these relationships within leading green finance economies, or "Green Leaders," using annual data from 2002 to 2018 within a panel framework. The findings emphasize that while green finance instruments like green bonds significantly support green energy deployment and emissions reduction, population growth and GDP increases continue to drive CO_2 emissions without a committed transition toward cleaner energy sources.

In the long run, higher levels of population and GDP per capita can escalate CO_2 emissions if energy transition efforts lag. The analysis indicates that expanding green finance access, particularly through green bonds, plays a crucial role in reducing emissions by facilitating green energy projects. Specifically, a 1% rise in green bond issuance corresponds to an approximate 1% reduction in per capita CO_2 emissions. Likewise, the GEI serves as a positive indicator, where each 1% increase in GEI is linked to a 0.92% decrease in emissions, highlighting the significance of renewable energy consumption in achieving sustainable emission reductions. Short-term results reveal that rising population, GDP, and EI are associated with increased CO_2 emissions. However, there is no immediate causal relationship between green bond issuance and CO_2 reduction, nor between the GEI and CO_2 emissions, although a bidirectional relationship exists between green bond issuance and GDP per capita.

Given the findings, effective policy recommendations should focus on regulatory frameworks, financial incentives, and technological investments to bolster long-term sustainability:

To promote sustained reductions in CO_2 emissions, governments should establish regulatory frameworks that prioritize green finance and incentivize the issuance of green bonds. These frameworks could include tax benefits for green bond investors, expedited regulatory approvals for green projects, and requirements for financial institutions to allocate a portion of their portfolios to green investments. As green bond issuance has shown a positive impact on reducing emissions, governments can also consider subsidizing green bond interest rates to make them more attractive to investors, thereby accelerating the green transition. Investment in energy efficiency technologies is essential, as increased EI is shown to raise emissions. National programs could promote advanced energy-saving technologies and industry-specific efficiency standards, particularly in high-emission sectors like manufacturing and transport. Implementing energy efficiency standards, inspired by successful international models like the EU's Energy Efficiency Plan and Thailand's Energy Efficiency Development Plan, can be instrumental. Programs that support retrofitting buildings, incentivize low-emission manufacturing, and promote efficient energy usage across sectors will help reduce EI and pollution. Financial mechanisms such as PPPs and blended finance should be used to mitigate the risks for private investors in green energy projects. Blended finance structures can leverage public funds to attract private investment by absorbing some of the financial risks associated with early-stage green projects. By developing PPPs that offer credit guarantees, governments can reduce barriers to entry for private investors in green energy, making it easier to finance renewable projects that contribute to the energy security and sustainability goals.

Furthermore, expanding renewable energy adoption requires prioritizing the sectors with the highest CO_2 emissions, particularly electricity generation and heavy industry. Policymakers should encourage a shift to green energy sources, such as solar and wind, through long-term power purchase agreements (PPAs) and incentives for utilities to integrate renewable sources. To further enhance the transition, investments in grid infrastructure for renewable energy integration, storage solutions, and smart grid technologies are crucial. These investments will reduce reliance on fossil fuels and stabilize renewable energy supply, supporting both emissions reduction and energy security. Post-COVID-19 economic recovery offers an ideal moment for governments to integrate sustainability into growth strategies by boosting green finance tools. Stimulus packages aimed at economic recovery can include dedicated funding for renewable projects, job training programs in green technology sectors, and support for energy-efficient public infrastructure, thereby aligning short-term economic recovery with long-term environmental goals. In summary, while this study provides substantial insights, future research could benefit from examining these dynamics at the country level to capture more specific regional variations. A country-specific analysis would offer tailored policy implications, supporting a more precise approach to promoting green finance and sustainable energy practices across diverse economic and environmental contexts.

References

Akalpler, E and S Hove (2019). Carbon emissions, energy use, real GDP per capita and trade matrix in the Indian economy-an ARDL approach. *Energy*, 168, 1081–1093.

Alemzero, DA, H Sun, M Mohsin, N Iqbal, M Nadeem and XV Vo (2021). Assessing energy security in Africa based on multi-dimensional approach of principal composite analysis. *Environmental Science and Pollution Research*, 28, 2158–2171.

Amir, M and S Khan (2021). Assessment of renewable energy: Status, challenges, COVID-19 impacts, opportunities, and sustainable energy solutions in Africa. *Energy and Build Environment*, 3(3), 348–362, https://doi.org/10.1016/j.enbenv.2021.03.002.

Ang, BW, WL Choong and TS Ng (2015). Energy security: Definitions, dimensions and indexes. *Renewable and Sustainable Energy Reviews*, 42, 1077–1093.

Apergis, N and J Payne (2010). Renewable energy consumption and economic growth: Evidence from a panel of OECD countries. *Energy Policy*, 38(1), 656–660.

Aslam, B, J Hu, S Shahab, A Ahmad, M Saleem, S Shah, M Javad, M Aslam, S Hussain and M Hassan (2021). The nexus of industrialization, GDP per capita and CO_2 emission in China. *Environmental Technology & Innovation*, 23, 101674, https://doi.org/10.1016/j.eti.2021.101674.

Bargaoui, S, N Liouane and F Nouri (2014). Environmental impact determinants: An empirical analysis based on the STIRPAT model. *Procedia – Social and Behavioral Sciences*, 109, 449–458.

Breitung, J (2000). The local power of some unit root tests for panel data. *Advanced Econometrics*, 15, 161–178.

Carrion-i-Silverstre, JI, T Del Barrio and E Lopez-Bazo (2005). Breaking the panels: An application to the GDP per capita. *Econometrics Journal*, 8, 159–175.

Charfeddine, L and M Kahia (2019). Impact of renewable energy consumption and financial development on CO_2 emissions and economic growth in the MENA region: A panel vector autoregressive (PVAR) analysis. *Renewable Energy*, 139, 198–213.

Debone, D, V Leite and S Miraglia (2021). Modelling approach for carbon emissions, energy consumption and economic growth: A systematic review. *Urban Climate*, 37, 100849, https://doi.org/10.1016/j.uclim.2021.100849.

Dickey, DA and WA Fuller (1979). Distribution of the estimators for autoregressive time series with a unit root. *Journal of American Statistical Association*, 74, 427–431.

Dietz, T and EA Rosa (1994). Rethinking the environmental impacts of population, affluence and technology. *Human Ecology Review*, 42, 3–6.

Dietz, T and EA Rosa (1997). Effects of population and affluence on CO_2 emissions. *Proceedings of the National Academy of Sciences of the United States of America*, 94, 175–179.

Feng, Y, Y Pan, S Lu and J Shi (2024). Identifying the multiple nexus between geopolitical risk, energy resilience, and carbon emissions: Evidence from global data. *Technological Forecasting and Social Change*, 208, 123661.

Fu, J and A Ng (2021). Scaling up renewable energy assets: Issuing green bond via structured public-private collaboration for managing risk in an emerging market. *Energies*, 14, 3076, https://doi.org/10.3390/en14113076.

Gani, A (2021). Fossil fuel energy and environmental performance in an extended STIRPAT model. *Journal of Cleaner Production*, 297, 126526, https://doi.org/10.1016/j.jclepro.2021.126526.

Gianfrate, G and M Peri (2021). The green advantage: Exploring the convenience of issuing green bonds. *Journal of Cleaner Production*, 219, 127–135.

Gibon, T, L Popescu, C Hitaj, C Petucco and E Benetto (2020). Shades of green: Life cycle assessment of renewable energy projects financed through green bonds. *Environmental Research Letters*, 15, 104045, https://doi.org/10.1088/1748-9326/abaa0c.

Gielen, D, D Saygin, N Wagner, K Petrichenko and A Tsakiris (2015). Synergies between renewable energy and energy efficiency. IRENA Working Paper, Copenhagen, Denmark.

Goldstein, D (2001). Financial sector reform and sustainable development: The case of Costa Rica. *Ecological Economics*, 37(2), 199–215.

Hafner, S, A Jones, A Anger-Kraavi and J Pohl (2020). Closing the green finance gap – a systems perspective. *Environmental Innovation and Societal Transitions*, 34, 26–60.

Hammoudeh, S, A Ajmi and K Mokni (2020). Relationship between green bonds and financial and environmental variables: A novel time-varying causality. *Energy Economics*, 92, 104941, https://doi.org/10.1016/j.eneco.2020.104941.

Hanaki, K and J Portugal-Pereira (2018). The effect of biofuel production on greenhouse gas emission reductions. In: K Takeuchi, H Shiroyama, O Saito, M Matsuura (eds), *Biofuels and Sustainability. Science for Sustainable Societies*. Springer, Tokyo, https://doi.org/10.1007/978-4-431-54895-9_6.

Hassan, S, S Khan, M Baloch and Z Tarar (2020). Is nuclear energy a better alternative for mitigating CO_2 emissions in BRICS countries? An empirical analysis. *Nuclear Engineering and Technology*, 52(12), 2969–2974.

Holdren, JP and PR Ehrlich (1974). Human population and the global environment. *American Scientist*, 62(3), 282–292.

International Renewable Energy Agency (2021). *World Energy Transitions Outlook: 1.5°C Pathway*. IRENA, https://www.irena.org/publications/2021/Jun/World-Energy-Transitions-Outlook, accessed on 24.12.2024.

Ji, X and B Chen (2017). Assessing the energy-saving effect of urbanization in China based on stochastic impacts by regression on population, affluence and technology (STIRPAT) model. *Journal of Cleaner Production*, 163(1), S306–S314.

Jin, Y, X Gao and M Wang (2021). The financing efficiency of listed energy conservation and environmental protection firms: Evidence and implications for green finance in China. *Energy Policy*, 153, 112254, https://doi.org/10.1016/j.enpol.2021.112254.

Khanna, M (2020). COVID-19: A cloud with a silver lining for renewable energy? *Applied Economic Perspectives and Policy*, 43(1), 73–85.

Knapp, T and R Mookerjee (1996). Population growth and global CO_2 emissions: A secular perspective. *Energy Policy*, 24(1), 31–37.

Levin, A, C Lin and C Chu (2002). Unit root tests in panel data: Asymptotic and finite sample properties. *Journal of Econometrics*, 108, 1–124.

Li, J, S Li and F Wu (2020). Research on carbon emission reduction benefit of wind power project based on life cycle assessment theory. *Renewable Energy*, 155, 456–468.

Liu, N, Ch Liu, B Da, T Zhang and F Guan (2021). Dependence and risk spillovers between green bonds and clean energy markets. *Journal of Cleaner Production*, 279, 123595, https://doi.org/10.1016/j.jclepro.2020.123595.

Loffler, K, A Petreski and A Stephan (2021). Drivers of green bond issuance and new evidence on the greenium. *Eurasian Economic Review*, 11, 1–24.

Lysen, EH (1989). The potential of renewable energy to reduce CO_2 emissions. In: PA Okken, RJ Swart, S Zwerver (eds), *Climate and Energy: The Feasibility of Controlling* CO_2 *Emissions*. Springer, Dordrecht, https://doi.org/10.1007/978-94-009-0485-9_6.

Maddala, GS and S Wu (1999). A comparative study of unit root tests with panel data and a new simple test. *Oxford Bulletin of Economics and Statistics*, 61, 631–652.

Maji, I (2015). Does clean energy contribute to economic growth? Evidence from Nigeria. *Energy Reports*, 1, 145–150.

Mensi, W, X Vo and S Kang (2021). Upside-downside multifractality and efficiency of green bonds: The roles of global factors and COVID-19. *Finance Research Letters*, 43(C), 101995, https://doi.org/10.1016/j.frl.2021.101995.

Meo, M and M Karim (2021). The role of green finance in reducing CO_2 emissions: An empirical analysis. *Borsa Istanbul Review*, 22(1), 169–178, https://doi.org/10.1016/j.bir.2021.03.002.

Naeem, M, S Farid, R Ferrer and SJ Shahzad (2021). Comparative efficiency of green and conventional bonds pre- and during COVID-19: An asymmetric multifractal detrended fluctuation analysis. *Energy Policy*, 153, 112285, https://doi.org/10.1016/j.enpol.2021.112285.

Namahoro, JP, Q Wu, N Zhou and S Xue (2021). Impact of energy intensity, renewable energy, and economic growth on CO_2 emissions: Evidence from Africa across regions and income levels. *Renewable and Sustainable Energy Reviews*, 147, 111233, https://doi.org/10.1016/j.rser.2021.111233.

Nguyen, T, M Naeem, F Balli, H Balli and X Vo (2021). Time-frequency comovement among green bonds, stocks, commodities, clean energy, and conventional bonds. *Finance Research Letters*, 40, 101739, https://doi.org/10.1016/j.frl.2020.101739.

Phillips, PCB and P Perron (1988). Testing for a unit root in time series regression. *Biometrica*, 75, 335–346.

Polzin, F and M Sanders (2020). How to finance the transition to low-carbon energy in Europe? *Energy Policy*, 147, 111863, https://doi.org/10.1016/j.enpol.2020.111863.

Prakash, N and S Mahdvi (2020). Green bonds driving sustainable transition in Asian economies: The case of India. *The Journal of Asian Finance, Economics and Business*, 8(1), 723–732.

Rasoulinezhad, E and F Taghizadeh-Hesary (2022). Role of green finance in improving energy efficiency and renewable energy development. *Energy Efficiency*, 15, 14, https://doi.org/10.1007/s12053-022-10021-4.

Rehman, A, H Ma, M Ahmad, M Irfan, O Traore and A Chandio (2021). Towards environmental sustainability: Devolving the influence of carbon dioxide emission to population growth, climate change, forestry, livestock and crops production in Pakistan. *Ecological Indicators*, 125, 107460, https://doi.org/10.1016/j.ecolind.2021.107460.

Ren, X, Q Shao and R Zhong (2020). Nexus between green finance, non-fossil energy use, and carbon intensity: Empirical evidence from China based on a vector error correction model. *Journal of Cleaner Production*, 277, 122844, https://doi.org/10.1016/j.jclepro.2020.122844.

Sachs, J, W Thye, N Yoshino and F Taghizadeh-Hesary (2019). Why is green finance important? ADBI Working Paper Series, No. 917, Asian Development Bank Institute (ADBI), Tokyo.

Sarangi, GK (2018). Green energy finance in India: Challenges and solutions. ADBI Working Paper Series, No. 863, Tokyo, Japan.

Shahbaz, M, S Solarin, R Sbia and S Bibi (2015). Does energy intensity contribute to CO_2 emissions? A trivariate analysis in selected African countries. *Ecological Indicators*, 50, 215–224.

Sovacool, BK and MA Brown (2010). Competing dimensions of energy security: An international perspective. *Annual Review of Environment and Resources*, 35, 77–108.

Sovacool, BK and I Mukherjee (2011). Conceptualizing and measuring energy security: A synthesized approach. *Energy*, 36(8), 5343–5355.

Taghizadeh-Hesary, F and N Yoshino (2019). The way to induce private participation in green finance and investment. *Finance Research Letters*, 31, 98–103, https://doi.org/10.1016/j.frl.2019.04.016.

Taghizadeh-Hesary, F and N Yoshino (2020). Sustainable solutions for green financing and investments in renewable energy projects. *Energies*, 13(4), 788, https://doi.org/10.3390/en13040788.

Taghizadeh-Hesary, F, N Yoshino and H Phoumin (2021). Analyzing the characteristics of green bond markets to facilitate green finance in the post-COVID-19 world. *Sustainability*, 13(10), 5719, https://doi.org/10.3390/su13105719.

Tolliver, C, A Keeley and S Managi (2020). Policy targets behind green bonds for renewable energy: Do climate commitments matter? *Technological Forecasting and Social Change*, 157, 120051, https://doi.org/10.1016/j.techfore.2020.120051.

Tucker, M (1995). Carbon dioxide emissions and global GDP. *Ecological Economics*, 15(3), 215–223.

Waggoner, PE and JH Ausubel (2002). A framework for sustainability science: A renovated IPAT identity. *Proceedings of the National Academy of Sciences of the United States of America*, 99(12), 7860–7865.

Wan, J (2020). Green finance and sustainable development goals: The case of China. *The Journal of Asian Finance, Economics and Business*, 7(7), 577–586.

Wang, M, X Li and Sh Wang (2021). Discovering research trends and opportunities of green finance and energy policy: A data-driven scientometric analysis. *Energy Policy*, 154, 112295, https://doi.org/10.1016/j.enpol.2021.112295.

Wang, Sh, T Zhao, H Zheng and J Hu (2020). The STIRPAT analysis on carbon emission in Chinese cities: An asymmetric Laplace distribution mixture model. *Sustainability*, 9, 2237, https://doi.org/10.3390/su9122237.

Wang, Y and Q Zhi (2016). The role of green finance in environmental protection: Two aspects of market mechanism and policies. *Energy Procedia*, 104, 311–316.

Westerlund, J (2007). Testing for error correction in panel data. *Oxford Bulletin of Economics and Statistics*, 69, 709–748.

Yadav, A, BA Gyamfi, SA Asongu and DK Behera (2024). The role of green finance and governance effectiveness in the impact of renewable energy investment on CO_2 emissions in BRICS economies. *Journal of Environmental Management*, 358, 120906.

Yeh, J and C Liao (2017). Impact of population and economic growth on carbon emissions in Taiwan using an analytic tool STIRPAT. *Sustainable Environment Research*, 27(1), 41–48.

York, R, EA Rosa and T Dietz (2003). STIRPAT, IPAT and ImPACT: Analytic tools for unpacking the driving forces of environmental impacts. *Ecological Economics*, 46, 351–365.

Zhang, B and Y Wang (2019). The effect of green finance on energy sustainable development: A case study in China. *Emerging Markets Finance and Trade*, 57(12), 3435–3454, https://doi.org/10.1080/1540496X.2019.1695595.

Zheng, H, J Hu, R Guan and S Wang (2016). Examining determinants of CO_2 emissions in 73 cities in China. *Sustainability*, 8, 1296.

https://doi.org/10.1142/9789819812608_0007

Chapter 7

Investigating Cost-Effective Policy Incentives for Renewable Energy in Japan[#]

MICHAEL C. HUANG[*,‡] and CHUL JU KIM[†]

[*]*Senior Research Fellow, Ocean Policy Research Institute*
The Sasakawa Peace Foundation
1-15-16 Toranomo, Minato-ku, Tokyo 105-8524, Japan
[†]*Chairman and CEO, Korea Life Insurance Association, Seoul, Republic of Korea*
[‡]*michael-huang@spf.or.jp*

The Great East Japan Earthquake (GEJE) and Fukushima nuclear disaster that occurred in 2011 gave a sharp reminder to Japan's energy security to reconsider the reduction of nuclear power dependence with a better energy mix. We use a recursive CGE model based on Japan's renewable energy input–output model to analyze the energy composite of power generation and consumption to investigate cost-effective policy incentives to achieve an optimal energy mix to reduce the nuclear power dependence to less than 5% within 10 years. Moreover, we create scenarios of: (1) nuclear power decommission, (2) renewable energy promotion and (3) virtual power plant (VPP) implementation with public R&D expenditure and power infrastructure investment. The simulation results show that renewable energy could gradually replace nuclear power with capital-use subsidies. Under the direction of nuclear power decommission, the VPP installation could reduce the fiscal cost of wind power by 13%, solar energy by 8% and the social cost by 36%. We provide empirical evidence that the implementation of VPP should be promoted in addition to the renewable policy promotion policy to facilitate power allocation and overcapacity problems better.

Keywords: Recursive CGE model; renewable energy; Japan; optimal energy mix.

JEL Classification: C68, L94, Q42, Q48.

1. Introduction

The Fukushima nuclear disaster triggered by the Great East Japan Earthquake (GEJE) in 2011 gave a sharp reminder to people around the world and gave governments and society a greater incentive to advocate the use of renewable energy for power generation. The energy insecurity has always been Japan's concern because its self-sufficiency ratio was 9.6%, with the rank of 34 among 35 OECD members. Most of the energy sources such as

---

[‡]Corresponding author.

[#]This Chapter is the updated version of the paper published in the *Singapore Economic Review*, Vol. 66, No. 2, doi: 10.1142/S0217590820430067. © 2021 World Scientific Publishing.

oil, coal, natural gas and other fossil fuels are imported from overseas. Following the Great East Japan Earthquake, Japan's dependence on fossil fuels increased and was 87.4% in 2017. According to METI (2019), Japan wanted to reduce the 25.1% nuclear power dependence, in 2010, Japan actively employed various policies to encourage household and electricity sectors to use more renewable power, such as solar power, wind power, and geothermal power. These policy incentives include subsidizing the implementation of power generation equipment and better electricity buy-in rates.

In order to reduce the risk of nuclear disaster, the government of Japan and society at large began a prudent reconsideration of advocating the use of renewable energy for power generation. Japan temporarily suspended all nuclear reactors for technical inspection after the GEJE. Nuclear power generation was at one point reduced to zero in the year 2014 (METI, 2019) but gradually increased afterward. As a consequence, the share of Japan's nuclear power generation dropped to 2.8% of the total power generation. At the same time, 22 reactors were scheduled for decommissioning, the cost of which would be a vital issue for power companies. On the other hand, the renewable energy source for power regeneration increased from 9.5% (2010) to 16.1% (2017) (Table 1). Despite a satisfactory trend for renewable energy, the overcapacity of solar power in the Kyushu region of Japan resulted in a shutdown of solar power generation facilities for several days. Such issues highlight that the key to renewable energy lies in not only power generation but also allocation.

The unprecedented compound disaster as GEJE gave sharp advice for Japan to reconsider the energy mix of nuclear power to reduce energy security under the environmental concern of greenhouse gas emission (Fesharaki and Hosoe, 2011). Empirical studies showed that energy insecurity has been fluctuating but improved in Japan (Le *et al.*, 2019). Up to 2019, Japan actively employed various policies to encourage household and energy sectors to change their power use from fossil to renewable sources such as solar, wind and geothermal power. These policy incentives included subsidizing the implementation of power generation equipment and legislating electricity buy-in rates. The energy composite path is illustrated with a review of various indicators, such as changes in sectoral output, price and external trade. The primary reason for a substantial increase in the number of household solar power generation facility implantation is Feed-in-Tariff (FIT) regulation, which could be considered a production subsidy at a fixed price for a power generation company to buy electricity generated by households. However, this FIT system faced termination in 2019, and therefore the regulations for promoting renewable energy should be changed to a cost-effective policy.

The objective of this study is to provide an evidence-based empirical study on the implementation of renewable energy to substitute nuclear power and examine the fiscal and social costs are cost-effectiveness analysis. It was found that a nuclear power

Table 1. Japan's Energy Mix Before and After the GEJE

Year	Nuclear	Hydro	Oil	Coal	Natural Gas	Renewable
2010 (before GEJE)	25.1%	7.3%	8.6%	27.8%	29.0	2.2%
2017 (after GEJE)	3.1%	7.9%	8.4%	32.7%	39.8%	8.1%

Source: METI (2019).

phase-out policy would decrease the GDP with more greenhouse gas emissions. Japan's energy-intensive system that generates negative externalities should be carefully considered. We try to use a recursive computable general equilibrium (CGE) model focused on energy sectors to create scenarios for policy simulation on nuclear power decommissioning plan while subsidizing renewable power for policy analysis. The structure and data in the study are based on the extended input–output table of renewable energy developed by Washizu *et al.* (2015). The energy composite path is illustrated with a review of various indicators such as changes in sectoral output and price. The fiscal and social costs are examined for cost-effectiveness. The simulation results enable quantitative analysis in order to open the black box of renewable energy subsidy and the cost of nuclear decommissioning through policy incentives. Such a framework could be referred to as policy options to determine an optimal energy mix, assisting power companies in developing appropriate measures to confront critical challenges for energy transmission.

After this introduction, the literature survey part will focus on methodology and the mainstream of modeling methodology of renewable energy and virtual power plant (VPP). The model structure part will illustrate our CGE model structure, parameter calibrations and its dynamic framework, followed by the data introduction and demonstration of policy scenarios and results. Finally, we will further interpret their implications and make policy recommendations as concluding remarks.

2. Literature Survey

The economic development has thus provided emerging Asian states with incentives to diversify their energy sources for renewable energy to reinforce energy security with growing environmental concerns (Peimani and Taghizadeh-Hesary, 2019). As for China, the advancement of technology on a larger scale of renewable energy is desirable for emission control and energy security (Yao and Chang, 2014). The diversification of energy sources and its affordability with social factors could strengthen energy security from a national to a greater region (Taghizadeh-Hesary *et al.,* 2019). In ASEAN states, such as Indonesia, Malaysia, and Thailand, higher energy consumption on GDP also implied the concern to reduce the energy insecurity to stabilize economic development (Yildirim *et al.*, 2014). The same trend could also be found In Vietnam through an empirical study of GMM that higher economic growth could help transfer to the cleaner energy source (Anh *et al.,* 2019). Furthermore, strong institutional and political factors also play critical roles in renewable energy policy implementation worldwide (Apergis and Eleftheriou, 2015).

Japan's energy policy and structure have changed significantly from increasing energy self-sufficiency to diversifying the energy sources after the GEJE. Yamazaki and Takeda (2017) analyze the environmental impacts of Japan's energy circumstance with examinations on renewable energy in the "New policy scenario" suggested by the International Energy Agency (IEA). For simulation studies, issues regarding the optimal Japanese energy composite of renewable energy from an engineering perspective (Komiyama *et al.,* 2013) and its consequences of social impact (Ban, 2016). The power grid is the critical infrastructure for providing reliable and sustainable power supply in the face of continuous growth in demand. In the rapid growth of Photovoltaics (PV) installation in Japan under FIT after GEJE in 2011, based on the simulations on the power networks, the integrated grid system could effectively economize the power transaction cost from the power plant (Komiyama and Fujii, 2017). Such an energy grid system requires the transition to support the integration of renewable energy sources, while several aspects are essential for modeling a grid-based multi-energy system (Kriechbaum *et al.*, 2018). With spatial consideration of necessary data, the resolutions of energy infrastructure could be identified, and such work is expected to contribute to more efficient electricity converters in a grid-based energy system. Their findings provide the conceptualized support for VPP through various renewable energy sources. The economic assessment remains desirable to provide policy analysis on incentive setting for implementing the system and evaluating its cost-effectiveness.

Modeling an energy mix optimization has always been required along with the transition of energy sources and infrastructure. Economic assessments and regulatory reform on power suppliers toward market prices and costs in electricity consumption have been conducted to illustrate the potential pathway of the post-Fukushima energy scenarios in Japan (Hosoe and Tanaka, 2012). The effectiveness of the FIT policy is examined and found successful in diversifying the energy sources in India (Sarangi *et al.*, 2019). There are also critics on the rebound effects for consumer service that would restrict the analysis and reduce efficiency. To respond to it, Allan *et al.* (2009) use a CGE model to analyze system-wide ramifications of policy intervention for industrial energy efficiency in the UK; the household utility and satisfaction could also be quantified in various scenarios. As for Japan, the trend of solar power installation grew up significantly after the GEJE in 2011 (Komiyama and Fujii, 2017). When analyzing the cost-effectiveness of renewable energy sources and the impact of technology use, the dynamic stochastic general equilibrium (DSGE) model is also used (Argentiero *et al.*, 2018; Punzi, 2019). Whereas the impact on other manufacturing sectors or households could not be identified, and the projection through DSGE could provide policy implications for public investment, the over-simplified model scope could not illustrate the impact for various production sectors and energy sources. Instead, recursive CGE has the capability to analyze multiple industries simultaneously to identify the gaps between policy intervention and business-as-usual (BAU) (Babatunde *et al.*, 2017). In contrast, the predetermined parameters in the model may not perfectly tackle the random walk like market situation. Nevertheless, CGE modeling could provide informative consequences in specific scenarios.

In other mathematical model application, the Fuzzy multi-objective linear programming (MOLP) interprets Turkey's 2018 — 35 power generation plan with policy suggestions aimed at improving pollution levels to fulfill the commitment to the Kyoto Protocol (Incekara, 2019). Nevertheless, the costs of energy infrastructure and technology advancement were not discussed, and this could lead to questions on policy feasibilities. Spatial analysis and geographic information systems (GIS) are applied for identifying transmission, distribution and generation sites for Canada (Gabbar and Zidan, 2016). Their modeling results have provided an informative key performance index (KPI) as the aspects of cost, quality, reliability, and environmental friendliness may serve as vital references for grid system implementation and design for regional implementation plans.

While the renewable energy source is used as backup energy after reaching the peak, such a variable could enable the flexible operation and reduce uncertainty. Despite the fact that the feature of zero marginal cost for power generation by renewable energy, the

Table 2. Methodology Highlight

Authors	Methods	Findings
Punzi (2019)	DSGE, Panel VAR model	Increasing demand or supply uncertainty affects the energy price with a positive impact on GDP in the short-run.
Argentiero *et al.* (2018)	DSGE, Technology-push measures and demand-pull measures	Technology-push measures may produce better dynamic effects than demand-pull measures on environmental policy based on a subsidy policy of equal monetary amount.
Allan *et al.* (2009)	CGE	Economy–energy–environment CGE model of the UK to identify the likely system-wide ramifications of a stimulus to industrial energy efficiency and social utility.
Hosoe (2014); Huang and Hosoe (2017)	Dynamic CGE, nuclear power substitutes	Capital-use subsidy works more cost-effectively than production subsidy; energy good price volatility affects social welfare.
Komiyama *et al.* (2013); Komiyama and Fujii (2017); Kriechbaum *et al.* (2018)	Engineering grid simulation; optimal power generation mix	Renewable energy promotion desirable for capacity expansion of inter/intra-regional power transmission lines; profitability is affected by massive renewable implementation with decreasing the capacity factor of the power plant, including ramp generator.
Yu *et al.* (2019)	Comprehensive review; mathematical description	Mathematical descriptions quantize uncertainties; the uncertainties of VPP were classified and demonstrated with various projections.
Pandžić *et al.* (2013)	Stochastic programming; linear modeling	Mixed-integer linear programming applied to mid-term dispatch scheduling; the maximization of operation profit may defer bilateral contracts and the day-ahead market.
Lima *et al.* (2018)	Optimal programming	Risk-neutral/averse stochastic programming formulations ensembles to characterize uncertainty; risk management analysis made available through extensive computational results for performance and parallel solutions to obtain efficient methods.

(continued)

Table 2. (*Continued*)

Authors	Methods	Findings
Sarangi *et al*. (2019)	Sustainable development framework	Economic, environmental, and social indicators are applied to analyze 12 regions in India; deviations in sustainability performance; nonlinear trend on economic dimension with multiple ups and downs; FIT policy examined to improve the electricity accessibility.
Babatunde *et al*. (2017)	A systematic review of models	Vital themes including carbon tax, emission reduction target, emission trading, renewable energy, energy efficiency, and carbon capture and storage as primary drivers of low carbon economy; more CGE model applications provide to the macroeconomic policy.
Incekara (2019)	Mathematical model	Energy generation cost minimization of energy production considering all energy-related costs in Turkey; greenhouse gas emission's reduction; maximizing efficiency of power plants and the use of fossil fuels in power plants could be projected.
Gabbar and Zidan (2016)	Spatial analysis	Provide KPIs to analyze economic, power quality, reliability, and environmental friendliness; a graphical user interface is used to define the desired geographic area, generation percentage via gas technology and system parameters.
Le *et al*. (2019)	Principal component analysis	Empirical results depict the trend of increasing energy insecurity in South and Southeast Asia; improving energy security was observed in Hong Kong, Japan, Mongolia, Singapore, South Korea and the United Arab Emirates.

Source: Summarized by authors.

variable nature and uncertainty of the power supply is the main concern for the energy mix. Given the increasing popularity of renewable energy use among regional households, the implementation of VPP has become an important issue. The high penetration of renewable energy sources such as wind and solar power still causes uncertainty as regards a steady power supply. Thus, such variable outputs should aggregate through collections of other power generators and storage systems to control the load for a better energy management system such as VPP (Kasaei *et al.,* 2017). The weekly self-scheduling of a VPP of energy sources could use storage system with a conventional power plant to construct the optimal power allocation based on a linear programming model (Pandžić *et al.,* 2013) or stochastic programming method (Lima *et al.,* 2018) to address the optimal operation of a VPP with forecast data in the European Centre for Medium-Range Weather Forecasts. Such results could be applied to calculate the utilization of renewable resources with decomposition methods, and risk management to allocate the efficiency of decomposition methods is determined by parallel solutions.

Along with the technology advancement, the downstream communication protocols between VPP, transmission, and a distribution system would lead the electricity market to make optimal energy mix choices to enable VPP to overcome the stochastic nature of distributed energy resources. To solve the problem, the smart grid implementation is the key power infrastructure (Adu-Kankam and Camarinha-Matos, 2018; Zajc *et al.,* 2019). With such a trend, strategic and dynamic collaborative network principles need to be formed, market price and power load demand are the major uncertainty factors for VPP. The optimization with a mathematical descriptive could help identify the stochastic uncertainty systematically (Yu *et al.,* 2019). The price could substantially affect the incentive for implementing renewable energy infrastructure, while the system should be designed based on evidence of the overall social welfare improvement evaluated by stakeholders. Table 2 presents the highlight of the methodology.

3. CGE Model Structure

Based on Huang and Hosoe (2016), we revise the CGE model structure with more renewable energy sources. The activities within a period with nested constant elasticity of substitution/transformation (CES/CET) functions (1) substitution between capital and labor, (2) intermediate input and composite factor input with energy composite input for a production function of gross output, (3) transformation for domestic goods supply and exports and (4) substitution between domestic goods and imports (Armington, 1969). (5) Armington's composite goods are used by a representative household and government for investment and intermediate input. (6) Household utility depends on the consumption of various nonenergy goods and an energy composite. We assume a Cobb-Douglas type utility function. Social welfare costs are measured by Hicksian equivalent variations (EVs), based on the consumption losses of the representative household. In the analysis of energy incidence, the substitution of electricity with other energy sources is crucial. It is assumed that (7) the energy composite for nonenergy sectors is developed from the five energy goods (crude oil and natural gas, coal, petroleum, electricity and town gas), while conventional Leontief's fixed coefficient technology for the five energy sectors is assumed,

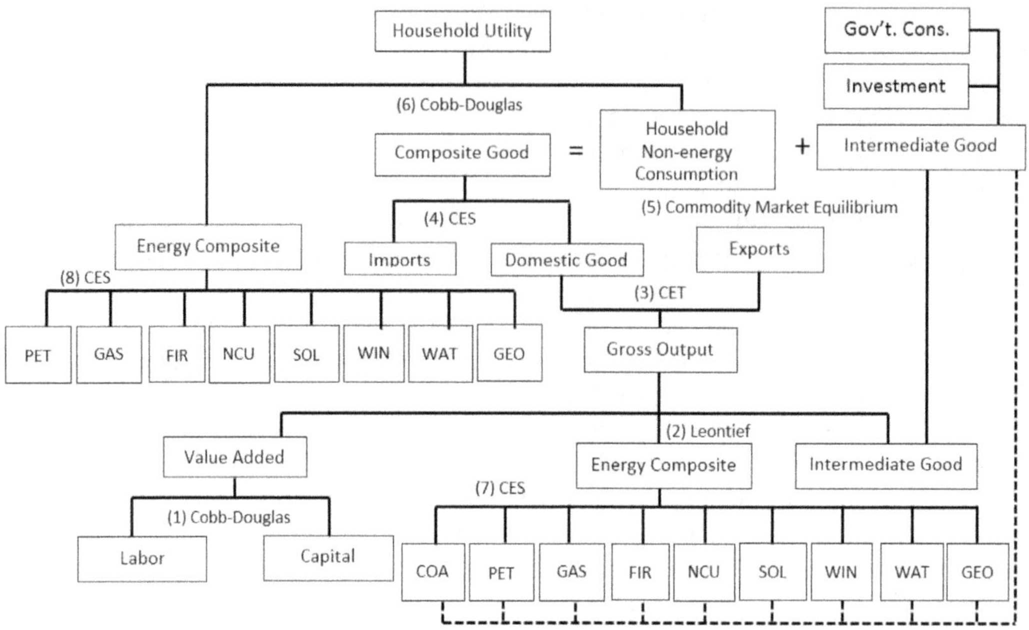

Notes: COA (coal), PET (petroleum), GAS (natural gas), FIR (thermal power), NCU (nuclear power), WIN (wind power), WAT (hydropower), SOL (solar power), GEO (geothermal power).

Figure 1. CGE Model Structure

i.e., no substitution among energy sources. (8) In the energy composite for households, petroleum, natural gas, electricity, natural gas and other renewable energies (without coal) are used (Figure 1).

Our recursive dynamic CGE model was developed on the basis of the static model by Huang and Hosoe (2016). Based on the extended input–output table of renewable energy developed by Washizu *et al.* (2015), the study uses a dynamic CGE model to create scenarios for simulating policy on abolishing nuclear power while subsidizing renewable power. In Table 3, we aggregate the 134 sectors of the renewable energy input–output table into 18 sectors by distinguishing power generation from conventional fossil fuel (COA, GAS, PET) and renewable energy (SOL, WIN, GEO, WAT). Other sectors (AGR, MAN, MCH, TEQ, STL, TEQ, SRV) are also listed to review the impact on economic activity. In this input–output table, separation of power generation and transmission helps us distinguish electricity sectors (FIR, NCU, SOL, WIN, WAT, GEO) and electricity transmission system (ETS) to analyze the implementation of VVP under the installation policy through government expenditure on research and development (R&D) and power infrastructure investment.

Table 4 shows the model system, and the formula used in the dissertation are stated in the following section. For the dynamic model, the time suffix t is not shown for simplicity unless needed.

The model structure demonstrates a multisectoral economy from activities of production, consumption, and capital accumulation through policy intervention. For domestic

Table 3. Sector Abbreviation

Sector	Description	Sector	Description
AGR	Agriculture	COA	Coal
MAN	Manufacture	GAS	Natural gas
ETS	Electricity transmission	PET	Petroleum
STL	Steel	FIR	Thermal power
MCH	Machinery	NCU	Nuclear power
TEQ	Transportation equipment	SOL	Solar power
RAD	Research and development	WIN	Wind power
TRS	Transportation	WAT	Hydropower
SRV	Service	GEO	Geothermal power

Source: Categorized by authors.

Table 4. Model System Suffix

Type of Goods/Factors in Suffix	Syntax	Abbreviations
Energy goods	ei, ej	COA, PET, GAS, FIR, NCU, SOL, WIN, WAT, GEO
Nonenergy goods for industries	ni, nj	{i}{ei}
Energy goods for households	ei2, ej2	PET, GAS, FIR, NCU, SOL, WIN, WAT, GEO
Nonenergy goods for households	ni2, nj2	{i}{ci2}
Nonelectricity goods	ne	{i}
Electricity goods	el	FIR, NCU, SOL, WIN, WAT, GEO
Factor	h, k	CAP, LAB
Mobile factor	h_mob	LAB
Immobile factor	FF	CAP
Time period	t	0, 1, 2, ..., 15

Source: Developed by authors.

production, Y_j is the composite factor used by the *j*th sector composite factor production function (Cobb–Douglas), while $F_{h,j}$ is the *h*th factor input by the *j*th sector.

$$Y_j = b_j \prod_h F_{h,j}^{\beta_{h,j}} \quad \forall j, \tag{1}$$

$$F_{h,j} = \frac{\beta_{h,j} p_j^y}{\left(1+\tau_{h,j}^f\right) p_{h,j}^f} Y_j \quad \forall h, j. \tag{2}$$

The factor demand function of labor and capital is determined as $F_{h,j}$, while for household consumption, the goods are distinguished into energy and nonenergy goods X^{p}_{ni2} and X^{pe}, and the household demand for nonenergy goods, S^{p}, is private saving, and T^{d} is the direct tax revenue.

$$X^{p}_{ni2} = \frac{\alpha_{ni2}}{p^{q}_{ni2}}\left(\sum_{h,j} p^{f}_{h,j} FF_{h,j} - S^{p} - T^{d}\right) \quad \forall ni2, \tag{3}$$

$$X^{pe} = \frac{\alpha^{e}\left(\sum_{h,j} p^{f}_{h,j} FF_{h,j} - S - T^{d}\right)}{p^{xpe}}. \tag{4}$$

The household demand for the energy composite good is determined as X^{pe}, while in regard to energy composite aggregation from other energy resources, the energy composite aggregation function for nonelectricity sectors is defined as X^{e}_{ne}; the energy good demand function for nonelectricity sectors is $X_{ei,ne}$, and the energy composite aggregation function for the household is X_{pe}.

$$X^{e}_{ne} = o_{ne}\left(\sum_{ei} \kappa_{ei,ne} X^{\chi}_{ei,ne}\right)^{1/\chi} \quad \forall ne, \tag{5}$$

$$X_{ei,ne} = \left(\frac{o^{\chi}_{ne}\kappa_{ei,ne} p^{xe}_{ne}}{p^{g}_{ei}}\right)^{1/(1-\chi)} X^{e}_{ne} \quad \forall ei, ne, \tag{6}$$

$$X^{pe} = o^{p}\left(\sum_{ei2} \kappa^{p}_{ei2} X^{p\chi}_{ei2}\right)^{1/\chi}. \tag{7}$$

Further, the energy goods demand for the household X^{p}_{ei2} are the function from the goods production function, while nonelectricity goods $ax_{ni,ne}$, the ax indicates the production function coefficient, which helps us to adjust the power generation efficiency increase by the technology improvement.

$$X^{p}_{ei2} = \left(\frac{o^{p\chi}\kappa^{p}_{ei2} p^{xpe}}{p^{q}_{ei2}}\right)^{1/(1-\chi)} X^{pe} \quad \forall ei2, \tag{8}$$

$$ax_{ni,ne} = \frac{X^{0}_{ni,ne}}{Z^{0}_{ne}}. \tag{9}$$

The electricity good is denoted as $ax_{i,el}$, while the intermediate energy good ax^{e}_{ne} input requirement coefficient, and intermediate good $X_{ni,ne}$ serve the demand function for nonelectricity sectors; the energy composite good X^{e}_{ne} is in the demand function for nonelectricity sectors, while the intermediate good $X_{i,ELY}$ determines the demand function for the electricity sector with the unit cost p^{z}_{ne} function for the nonelectricity and electricity sector.

$$ax_{i,el} = \frac{X^{0}_{i,el}}{Z^{0}_{el}}, \tag{10}$$

$$ax^e_{ne} = \frac{X^{e0}_{ne}}{Z^o_{ne}} \quad \forall j, \tag{11}$$

$$X_{ni,ne} = ax_{ni,ne} Z_{ne} \quad \forall ni, ne, \tag{12}$$

$$X^e_{ne} = ax^e_{ne} Z_{ne} \quad \forall ne, \tag{13}$$

$$X_{i,ELY} = ax_{i,ELY} Z_{ELY} \quad \forall i, \tag{14}$$

$$p^z_{ne} = ay_{ne} p^y_{ne} + \sum_{ni} ax_{ni,ne} p^q_{ne} + ax^e_{ne} p^{xe}_{ne} \quad \forall ne, \tag{15}$$

$$p^z_{ELY} = ay_{ELY} p^y_{ELY} + \sum_i ax_{i,ELY} p^q_i . \tag{16}$$

Finally, the felicity/composite consumption good production function CC is defined in the form of dynamic model

$$CC = a * \left(\prod_i X_i^{p^{\alpha_i}} \right) * (X^{pe} * \alpha^e). \tag{17}$$

For the investment activity performed by government, based on Huang and Hosoe (2017), the consumption is exogenous while the growth at the assumed population growth rate (pop), that is, in terms of the collection of taxes, import tariffs, and a lump-sum direct tax on households, provides subsidies for recursive change.

The government budget is balanced by a lump-sum direct tax. The aggregate investment good for the *j*th sector $II_{j,t}$ is made of various investment goods purchased from the *i*th sector $X^v_{i,t}${ with a Cobb–Douglas type production function.

The recursive dynamics are instilled in the original CGE model structure, which links economic activities *between* periods. In the *t*th period, private savings S^p_t are generated with a constant saving propensity ss^p growing overtime at the population growth rate pop. Following Hosoe (2014), these savings are endogenously allocated among investment for the *j*th sector $II_{j,t}$ according to its expected relative profitability in the next period:

$$II_{j,t} = \frac{p^f_{CAP,j,t+1} \zeta F_{CAP,j,t+1}}{\sum_j p^f_{CAP,i,t+1} \zeta F_{CAP,i,t+1}} \frac{S^p_t + \varepsilon_t S^f_t}{p^k_t}, \tag{18}$$

where P^k_t denotes the price of the investment good $II_{j,t}$, and $P^f_{CAP j,t+1}$ and $F_{CAP j,t+1}$ denote the price and the amount of capital service in the *j*th sector in the next period, respectively. The last two variables can be replaced by the *t*th period variables $P^f_{CAP j,t}$ and (1 + pop)$F_{CAP j,t}$ by assuming a myopic expectation. An elasticity parameter ζ determ ines the sensitivity of sectoral investment allocation to a gap of profitability among sectors. The putty-clay type is assumed in capital installed in the *j*th sector in the *t*th period $KK_{j,t}$.

The capital is assumed to be immobile between sectors but could be accumulated depreciating at the rate of dep, $KK_{j,t+1} = (1 - dep)\, KK_{j,t} + II_{j,t}$. That is, lost capital in a disaster cannot be rebuilt immediately by being mobilized from other sectors. Labor

Table 5. Parameter Calibrations

Parameter	Value
Rate of return of capital (ror)	0.05
Depreciation rate (dep)	0.04
Depreciation rate (dep) for nuclear power	0.52
Population growth rate (pop)	0.01
Armington elasticity parameters (σ, ψ)	1.9–12.0
The elasticity of substitution among energy sources (σ^e)	1.1
Elasticity parameter for investment allocation (ζ)	1.0

Source: Hosoe (2014), Huang and Hosoe (2017).

endowment is exogenously growing at the population growth rate pop and is mobile among sectors. Thus, capital accumulation is calculated as

$$\mathrm{KK}_{j,t+1} = (1-\mathrm{dep})\mathrm{KK}_{j,t} + II_{j,t} \quad \forall j, t. \tag{19}$$

Finally, welfare is determined by equivalent variations (dynamic model), which are the consequences of household consumption after the new equilibrium of output price change

$$\mathrm{EV}_t = \left[\frac{(\mathrm{CC}_t^1 - \mathrm{CC}_t^0)/a}{\left(\prod_{\mathrm{ni2}} \alpha_{\mathrm{ni2}}{}^{\alpha_{\mathrm{ni2}}}\right) * \alpha^{e^{\alpha^e}}}\right]. \tag{20}$$

In the model structure, the parameters serve as an adjustment to cope with the real situation (Table 5). The calibration of the parameters is sourced from existing literature (Hosoe, 2014; Huang and Hosoe, 2017). The depreciation rate for nuclear power is set at eight times more than the setting for other sectors, indicating the decommission policy after the GEJE to reduce power dependence share by 2030. The Armington elasticity parameters are sourced from the GTAP Database version 10.0, while other parameters are assumed by the authors.

4. Data and Scenarios

For constructing a CGE model to make simulations on Japan's renewable energy policy and consequences, we use Japan's renewable input–output table developed by Washizu *et al.* (2015). The data we use for policy simulation is the version 2011 table released in 2019. The extended table contains 134 sectors, including aggregated sectors of renewable energy such as solar, wind, hydro, and geothermal power. Moreover, power generation and transmission systems are disaggregated. This feature helps us in analyzing the potential VPP system with the inclusion of specific R&D investment, which could increase electricity transmission efficiency. Regarding the estimate of production efficiency and Japan's R&D expenditure, we calibrate from the SciREX Policy Intelligence Assistance System — Economic Simulator (SPIAS-e), which is developed through collaboration between several government science agencies, ministries, and universities (Kuroda *et al.*, 2018).

Table 6. Policies and Capital-use Subsidy Rates

	NCU	SOL	WIN	GEO	RAD	ETS
Scenario 1: Nuclear power decommission	500%	n.a.	n.a.	n.a.	n.a.	n.a.
Scenario 2: Renewable energy promotion	500%	96%	96%	96%	n.a.	n.a.
Scenario 3: VPP installation	500%	95%	95%	95%	4.2%*	10%
Efficiency improvement rates	n.a.	7.6%*	7.6%*	7.6%*	n.a.	10%

Note: *estimated based on SPIAS-e.

To examine the energy mix coping with the target of reducing nuclear power dependence below 5% within 10 years, we use capacity-use subsidy as an incentive to reduce nuclear power generation (NCU) as Scenario 1 — the base scenario. The capital-use subsidy is also used as the incentive to promote renewable energy as Scenario 2. The target we set for renewable power dependence is 30% in 15 years. Given such a target, a very high subsidy rate of 96% is made for renewable energy such as solar power (SOL), (WIN), (WAT), and geothermal (GEO). In Scenario 3, in addition to the capital-use subsidy provision for previous sectors mention, the installation of a VPP will be carried out with a 10% investment in an ETS with 7.6% more productivity from renewable energy contributed by 4.2% government expenditure on R&D of energy sectors. VPP transmission efficiency could also increase transmission by 20%. With this input, the production efficiency is expected to be actualized from the 5th year of the policy based on the assumption in SPIAS-e. A description of three scenarios, along with subsidy and efficiency rates (Table 6) is presented in what follows.

Scenario 1: Nuclear power decommission

Provide capital-use tax as an incentive for the nuclear power sector to gradually reduce the nuclear dependence to 5% within 10 years; increase the depreciation rates as decommission policy.

Scenario 2: Renewable energy promotion

Provide capital-use subsidy on solar (SOL), wind (WIN), and geothermal (GEO) power in order to increase the renewable energy share to 30% within 15 years.

Scenario 3: Virtual power plants (VPP) installation

Provide capital-use subsidy on electricity transmission (ETS) as a power infrastructure investment for VPP installation and increase public R&D expenditure on energy and material sciences. The VPP implantation and efficiency improvement for power generation efficiency improvement will be assumed to be fully actualized from the 5th year.

5. Simulation Results

Figure 2 shows the optimal power generation mix in the scenario of nuclear power decommission policy. The high depreciation rates and capital-use subsidy on nuclear power would reduce nuclear power generation substantially to less than 5% within five years. Nevertheless, without other incentive policies on renewable energy, the share of renewable

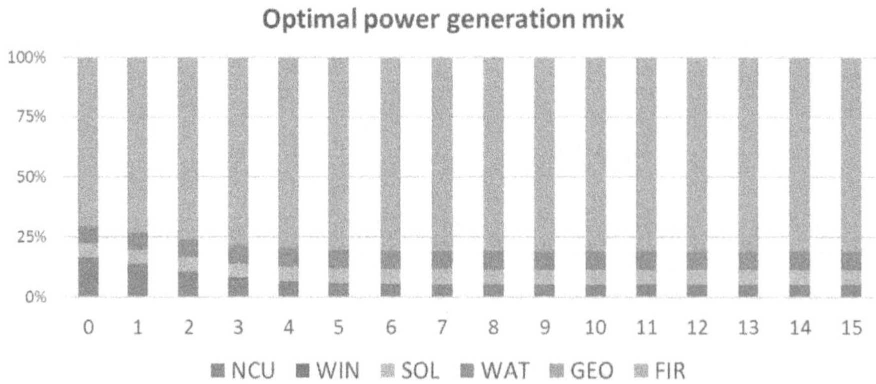

Figure 2. (Color available online) Scenario 1: Nuclear Power Decommission

energy sources does not show much growth and remains from 13% to 15%. The power generation gap is mainly substituted by thermal power sourced from coal, petroleum, and natural gas. The share of thermal power increases from 70% to 80% from the 5th year. Therefore, a nuclear power decommission policy could only is expected to worsen the CO_2 emission due to the use of conventional fossil fuel. The situation actually occurred in 2014, while all the nuclear power plants were temporarily shut down for one year for maintenance, the massive LNG imported to be used as alternative energy to fill the energy gap. Such an energy mix will not only result in energy insecurity but also substantial trade deficits that significantly affect the Japanese economy and social welfare.

With the implementation of the promotion policy on renewable energy through capital-use subsidy in addition to the nuclear power decommission, it could be found that the renewable energy share increased from 13% to 23% within five years and could reach 30% in the 15th year. Among them, the solar power shows the biggest growth from 6% to 21%, while wind power from 0.4% to 0.9% and geothermal power from 0.4% to 1.3% (Figure 3). Geothermal power shows relatively less growth, potentially due to the requirement of appropriate location and greater initial input in facilities. Similarly, the development of wind power also faces geographic constraint and could not reach expansion.

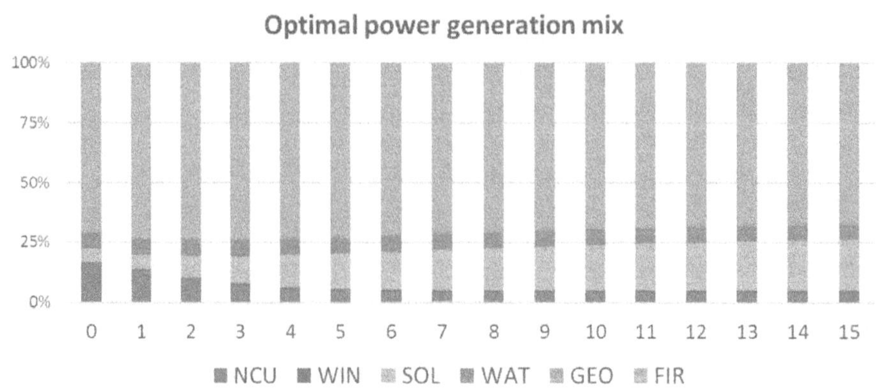

Figure 3. (Color available online) Scenario 2: Renewable Energy Promotion

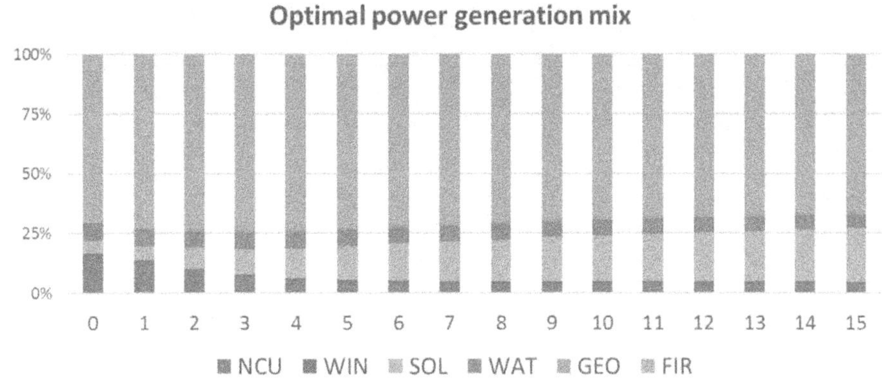

Figure 4. (Color available online) Scenario 3: VPP Installation

On the other hand, thermal power also shows a decrease from 70% to 66%. Also, the hydropower is not included in the renewable energy capital-use scope because of the environmental concern for dam construction in Japan. The flexibility of solar power generation facilities could be implemented in households relatively easier, and thus, solar power becomes the main source for a renewable power generation mix.

While we implement a VPP system by improving the power generation productivity by 7.6% and 10% in transmission efficiency through investing in electricity and R&D based on our assumptions (Figure 4), the power generation mix does not show much difference from the previous two scenarios, notwithstanding, the capital-use subsidy rate is slightly lower than Scenario 2, while the share of nuclear power is also shrinking more from 16% to 4% in the 15th year with a more vibrant development for renewable energy. The impact of higher efficiency for power transmission and its impact on other energy sectors will be demonstrated in the analysis of output and price change. Moreover, the discussion on fiscal and social costs for policy implementation with their cost-effectiveness will be illustrated through equitant variations (EV) from the following figures.

Comparing the output change in Figure 5, the nuclear power generation shows a sharp decrease under the decommission policy, while other conventional fossil fuels such as

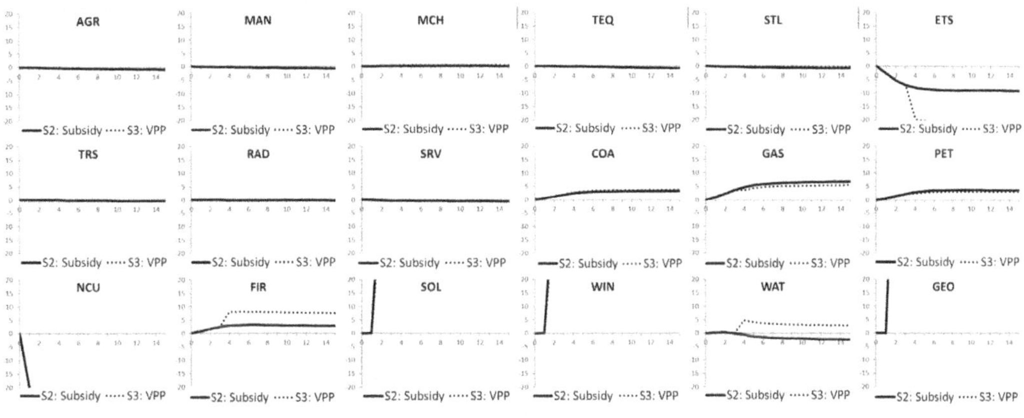

Figure 5. The Output Change

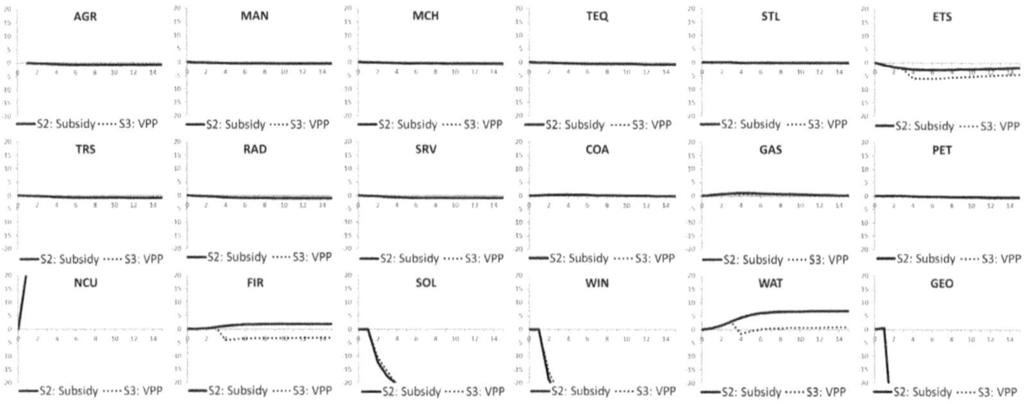

Figure 6. The Output Price Change

coal, petroleum, and gas increase significantly by 3% to 5%. Meanwhile, renewable energy sources such as solar, wind, geothermal, and even water power generation provide an even more significant increase in power generation. After the VPP installation with technology realization in the 5th year, the notable fall of the output of the electricity transmission could function continuously to make more efficient electricity distribution for the household by allocating other energy sources in a more efficient energy composite and storage. Interestingly, the output increase of thermal power could imply the pull to filling the energy gap of nuclear power. However, comparing with the growth of other renewable energy sources, the growth for thermal power is rather marginal.

The indicators of output price change indicate technology improvement and the incentive for using more affordable energy sources (Figure 6). With the policy incentive for renewable energy, the output prices decrease substantially in solar, wind, and geothermal power. As stated previously, the decrease output price of thermal power could be referred to as the decreased demand for fossil fuel for power generation. Due to the limitation of dam construction, hydropower is not the target sector for capital-use subsidy. However, it is interesting to find the decrease in output prices of an electricity transmission system, electricity, and hydropower generation, implying that the investment in a VPP could further facilitate a higher energy mix performance from all sorts of power generation.

When we compare the annual fiscal costs of capital-use subsidy on renewable energy and implementation of VPP in Figure 7, simulation results show that the VPP installation would actually reduce the fiscal cost in wind power by 13% and solar power by 8%, respectively. The reason why geothermal power is slightly costly due to their limited implementation geographically in power generation. On the other hand, the cost of wind power is extraordinarily high, mainly because of constraint as onshore type in Japan. Comparing with the installation fee, the fiscal costs of R&D and power infrastructure investment are rather marginal as JPY 130 billion and JPY 40 billion respectively, whereas their spillover impact and connectivity for a different type of energy sources is highly expected.

The welfare analysis uses the concept of equivalent variations between the policy interventions that cause changes in the price and the quantity of consumption for

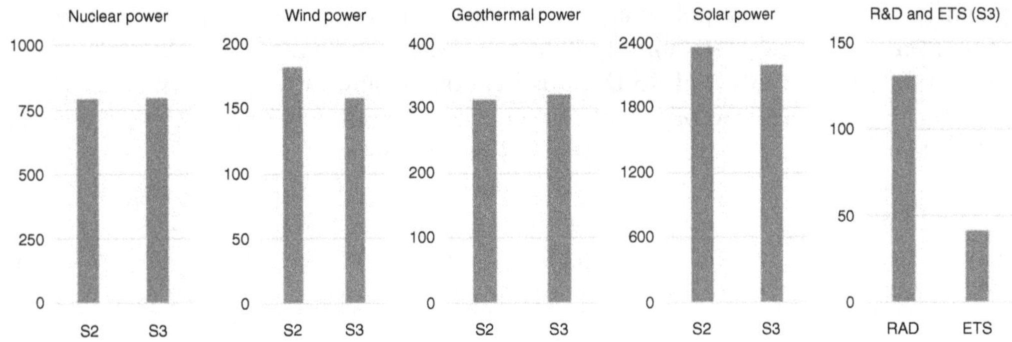

Figure 7. Annual Fiscal Costs of Policy Incentives (Unit: Billion JPY)

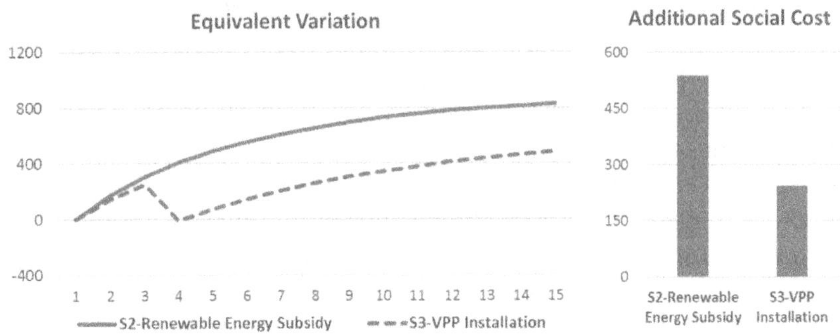

Figure 8. Welfare Analysis (Unit: Billion JPY)

household utility (Figure 8). Based on the simulation results of output and price, the implementation of a VPP could increase the power generation efficiency so that the allocation of electricity from energy sources could be better facilitated. Taking the nuclear power decommission scenario as the basement, the VPP installation could ease the social costs of renewable promotion by 36%. The VPP and technology input also show lower social cost than the renewable energy capital-use subsidy. Such consequences imply that the VPP system could lead to higher cost-effectiveness than simply providing incentives for renewable energy.

6. Concluding Remarks

The research provides policy assessments and visualized policy options with potential costs and paths to achieve the policy target of less than 5% nuclear dependence while increasing the share of renewable energy to 30% within 15 years. By using a dynamic CGE model with Japan's renewable energy input–output table, we demonstrated the policy simulations of three scenarios for optimal energy mixes in scenarios of nuclear decommission policy, capital-use subsidies to energy sectors, and VPP installation. We provided a quantified analysis of the policy and visualization consequences of energy mix, output, price, fiscal and social costs impact on various sectors and households. Also, the assessment of the spillover effect of R&D sheds light on the innovative platform for electricity platform. Such a methodology could provide a comprehensive perspective for energy stakeholders to make holistic management of policy options.

Simulation results show that renewable energy would need policy intervention to fill the gap of nuclear power decommissions. The capital-use subsidy policies were examined in order to abandon nuclear power with the promotion of renewable energy. Without a policy incentive, renewable energy cannot grow while the share of nuclear power is being reduced. R&D investment could improve the efficiency of power generation, accelerating the reduction of nuclear power dependence. With regard to the output and price change, the simulation results show that the policy could stimulate renewable energy output while its price is substantially reduced. Meanwhile, other manufacturing sectors reveal no substantial change, indicating that such a policy could help facilitate the energy structure with affordable energy prices. Given the direction of nuclear decommission policy, the implementation of VPP could further facilitate renewable energy allocation with a reduction of the fiscal cost of wind power by 13%, solar power by 8%, and social costs by 36% compared with the scenario of renewable energy promotion, thereby easing the overcapacity problem of renewable energy sources.

Nevertheless, the simulation results provide visualized consequences and impact the social economy as regards the policy implementation on nuclear decommissioning, renewable-energy promotion, and VPP installation. The cost-effectiveness examined in the scenarios suggests that the power transmission system could help reduce both fiscal and social costs, indicating comprehensive plans for promoting renewable energy. While confronting the overcapacity and inefficiency of power generation from renewable energy sources, it would be indispensable for governments at all levels to help the energy sector to develop a VPP system to strengthen the power resilience. The VPP system includes a storage system that could also be of importance against large-scale natural disasters.

7. Limitations and Future Research

The recursive CGE model based on Japan's 2011 renewable energy input-output table enabled us to provide evidence-based analysis on setting incentives for renewable energy and the implementation costs to the government and the society. These informative outcomes could also provide policy implications for the development of a renewable energy input–output table in many other countries. However, the single-country model scope may not have captured the regional and geographic features precisely to provide more realistic and adequate insights. The application of the renewable energy input-out table serves a vital instrument for renewable energy analysis. It would be desirable to develop the regional version to further investigate the volume flow of electricity transmission. Also, if the compilation of making renewable input-output table could be made available to other countries which are eager for the development of renewable energy, the expansion is highly expected to contribute to the research on a global grid system.

Appendix A. Sensitivity Test

We conduct sensitivity test to robust the simulation results. We multiple the parameters used in the model by 1.5 times, 1.05 times for Armington elasticity parameters and 1.3 times for Elasticity parameter for investment allocation due to model feasibilities. The new parameters for sensitivity test are stated in Table A.1. The welfare analyses are demonstrated in Figures A.1–A.6. The results of sensitivity test show a change in values, respectively, but consistent trend with the simulation results. We could thus indicate that the simulation results are robust.

Table A.1. Parameter Calibrations

Parameter	Value	S-test
Rate of return of capital (ror)	0.05	0.075
Depreciation rate (dep)	0.04	0.06
Population growth rate (pop)	0.01	0.015
Armington elasticity parameters (σ, ψ)	1.9–12.0	2.0–12.6*
The elasticity of substitution among energy sources (σ^e)	1.1	1.65
Elasticity parameter for investment allocation (ζ)	1.0	1.3**

Note: * multiple by 1.05 times; ** multiple by 1.3 times.

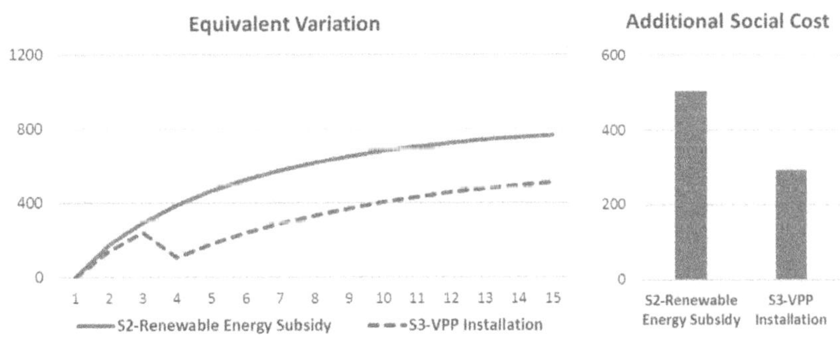

Figure A.1. Welfare Analysis (ror)

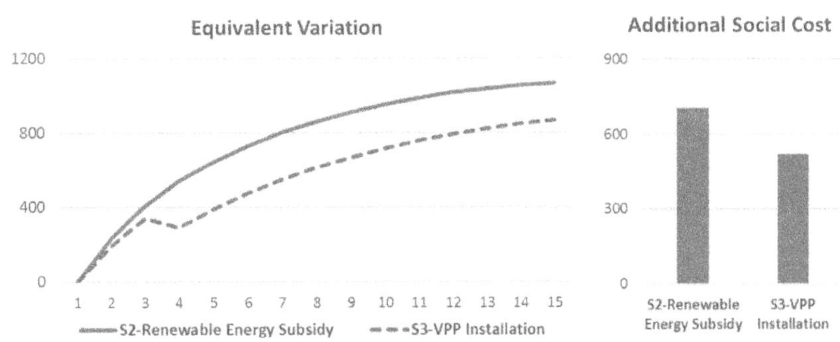

Figure A.2. Welfare Analysis (dep)

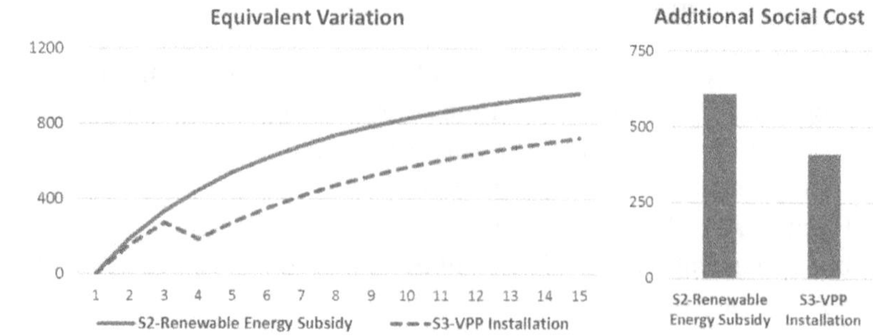

Figure A.3. Welfare Analysis (pop)

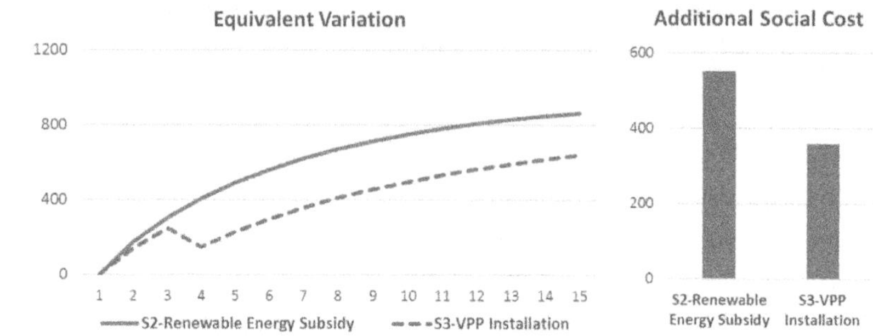

Figure A.4. Welfare Analysis (σ, ψ)

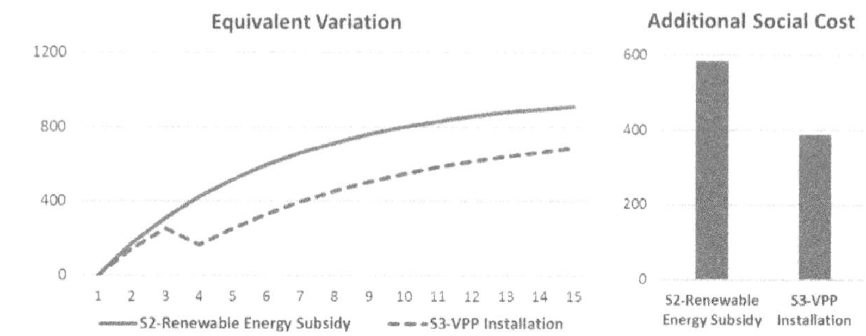

Figure A.5. Welfare Analysis (σ^e)

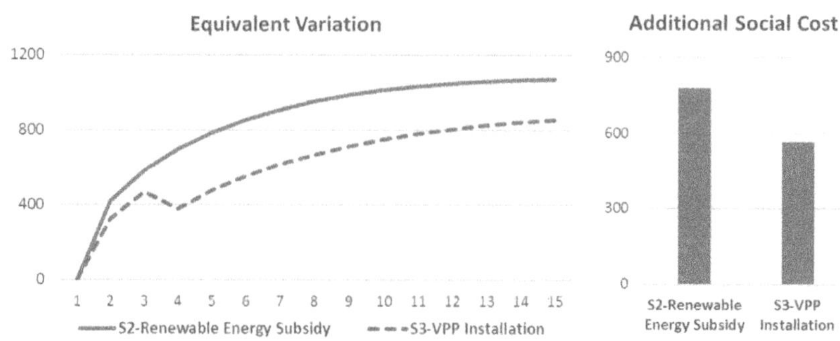

Figure A.6. Welfare Analysis (ζ)

References

Adu-Kankam, K and L Camarinha-Matos (2018). Towards collaborative virtual power plants: Trends and convergence. *Sustainable Energy, Grids and Networks,* 16, 217–230.

Allan, G, M Gilmartin, P McGregor, J Swales and K Turner (2009). Modelling the economy-wide rebound effect. In *Energy Efficiency and Sustainable Consumption: The Rebound Effect,* H Herring and S Sorrell (eds.), pp. 69–98. London: Palgrave Macmillan.

Anh, TC, E Rasoulinezhad, TNGO Chi, HLH Ba and HH Thanh (2019). Modeling energy security-exchange rate linkage: Evidence of GMM approach. *Singapore Economic Review*, pp. 1–16. Available at https://doi.org/10.1142/S0217590819430021.

Argentiero, A, CA Bollino, S Micheli and C Zopounidis (2018). Renewable energy sources policies in a Bayesian DSGE model. *Renewable Energy,* 120, 60–68.

Apergis, N and S Eleftheriou (2015). Renewable energy consumption, political and institutional factors: Evidence from a group of European, Asian and Latin American countries. *Singapore Economic Review*, 60, 1.

Armington, P (1969). A theory of demand for products distinguished by place of production. *International Monetary Fund Staff Papers*, 16, 159–178.

Babatunde, KA, RA Begum and FF Said (2017). Application of computable general equilibrium (CGE) to climate change mitigation policy: A systematic review. *Renewable and Sustainable Energy Reviews,* 78, 61–71.

Ban, K (2016). Economic modeling for assessing/evaluating the relationship between environmental policy and economy. *Environmental Economics and Policy Studies*, 9(1), 1–13. (in Japanese)

Fesharaki, F and T Hosoe (2011). The Fukushima crisis and the future of Japan's power industry. *Asia Pacific Bulletin No.* 106. Available at https://www.files.ethz.ch/isn/128537/apb.106.pdf.

Gabbar, H and A Zidan (2016). Modeling, evaluation, and optimization of gas-power and energy supply scenarios. *Frontiers in Energy,* 10(4), 393–408.

Hosoe, N (2014). Japanese manufacturing facing post-Fukushima power crisis: A dynamic computable general equilibrium analysis with foreign direct investment. *Applied Economics*, 46(17), 2010–2020.

Hosoe, N and M Tanaka (2012). Divestiture of TEPCO for reparation for the Fukushima nuclear accident-A path to vertical unbundling. *Energy Policy,* 51, 207–212.

Huang, M and N Hosoe (2016). Computable general equilibrium assessment of a compound disaster in northern Taiwan. *Review of Urban & Regional Development Studies,* 28(2), 89–106.

Huang, M and N Hosoe (2017). Investigating fiscal and social costs of recovery policy: A dynamic general equilibrium analysis of an earthquake disaster in Northern Taiwan. *Journal of Asian Economics*, 53, 1–17.

Incekara, C (2019). Use of an optimization model for optimization of Turkey's energy management by inclusion of renewable energy sources. *International Journal of Environmental Science Technology,* 16, 6617–6628.

Kasaei, M, M Gandomkar and J Nikoukar (2017). Optimal management of renewable energy sources by virtual power plant. *Renewable Energy,* 114, 1180–1188.

Komiyama, R and Y Fujii (2017). Assessment of post-Fukushima renewable energy policy in Japan's nation-wide power grid. *Energy Policy,* 101, 594–611.

Komiyama, R, S Shibata and Y Fujii (2013). Simulation analysis for massive deployment of variable renewables employing an optimal power generation mix model. *Journal of Energy and Power Engineering,* 7, 1604–1615.

Kriechbaum, L, G Scheiber and T Kienberger (2018). Grid-based multi-energy systems-modelling, assessment, open source modelling frameworks and challenges. *Energy, Sustainability and Society,* 8(35), 1–19.

Kuroda, M, K Ikeuchi, Y Hara and M Huang (2018). Assessments of ICT policy options: The framework of input-output table linked with intangible knowledge stock. In *Applications of Input-Output Model,* K Mukhopadhyay (ed.), pp. 65–110. Singapore: Springer.

Le, TH, Y Chang, F Taghizadeh-Hesary and N Yoshino (2019). Energy insecurity in Asia: A multi-dimensional analysis. *Economic Modelling,* 83, 84–95.

Lima, R, A Conejo, S Langodan, I Hoteit and O Knio (2018). Risk-averse formulations and methods for a virtual power plant. *Computers & Operations Research*, 96, 350–373.

Ministry of Economy, Trade and Industry (METI) (2019). Japan's energy 2019. Available at https://www.enecho.meti.go.jp/en/category/brochures/pdf/japan_energy_2019.pdf, Agency for Natural Resources and Energy (accessed on 30 March 2020).

Pandžić, H, I Kuzle and T Capuder (2013). Virtual power plant mid-term dispatch optimization. *Applied Energy*, 101, 134–141.

Peimani, H and F Taghizadeh-Hesary (2019). The role of renewable energy in resolving energy insecurity in Asia. *ADBI Working Paper Series No. 1010.* Asian Development Bank Institute.

Punzi, MT (2019). The impact of energy price uncertainty on macroeconomic variables. *Energy Policy,* 129, 1306–1319.

Sarangi, GK, A Mishra, Y Chang and F Taghizadeh-Hesary (2019). Indian electricity sector, energy security and sustainability: An empirical assessment. *Energy Policy,* 135, 110964.

Taghizadeh-Hesary, F, N Yoshino, Y Chang and AD Rillo (2019). Introduction. In *Achieving Energy Security in Asia: Diversification, Integration and Policy Implications*, F Taghizadeh-Hesary, N Yoshino, Y Chang and AD Rillo (eds.), pp. v–iv. Singapore: World Scientific. Available at https://www.worldscientific.com/doi/pdf/10.1142/9789811204210_fmatter

Nakano S, S Arai and A Washizu (2015). Economic impacts of Japan's renewable energy sector and the feed-in tarfif system: Using an input-output table to analyze a next-generation energy system. *Environ Econ. Policy Stud* 19, 555–580, https://doi.org/10.1007/s10018-016-0158-1.

Yamazaki, M and S Takeda (2017). A computable general equilibrium assessment of Japan's nuclear energy policy and implications for renewable energy. *Environment Economic Policy Studies*, 19, 537–554.

Yao, L and Y Chang (2014). Energy security in China: A quantitative analysis and policy implications. *Energy Policy*, 67, 595–604.

Yildirim, E, A Aslan and I Ozturk (2014). Energy consumption and GDP in ASEAN countries: Bootstrap-corrected panel and time series causality tests. *Singapore Economic Review*, 59(2), 1450010.

Yu, S, F Fang, Y Liu and J Liu (2019). Uncertainties of virtual power plant: Problems and countermeasures. *Applied Energy,* 239(45), 4–470.

Zajc, M, M Kolenc and N Suljanovic (2019). Virtual power plant communication system architecture. In *Smart Power Distribution Systems*, Q Yang, T Yang and W Li (eds.). Australia: Academic Press.

https://doi.org/10.1142/9789819812608_0008

Chapter 8

Energy Security and Economic Drivers in Lao PDR: Insights on Electricity Consumption and Transition[#]

NISIT PANTHAMIT[*], CHUKIAT CHAIBOONSRI[†], and GUOWEI TIAN[‡]

Faculty of Economics, Chiang Mai University, Chiang Mai, Thailand
[*]*nisit.p@cmu.ac.th*
[†]*chukiat1973@gmail.com*
[‡]*361723810@qq.com*

This chapter investigates the links between electricity consumption (EC) and key factors—gross domestic product (GDP), population, and foreign direct investment (FDI)—in the Lao People's Democratic Republic (Lao PDR) from 1998 to 2018, using ARDL-based Bayesian inference. The findings provide empirical evidence of a long-term linear relationship between EC and these economic indicators in Lao PDR. In the short run, these factors have both positive and negative effects on EC, indicating persistent energy insecurity. To achieve long-term energy security, Lao PDR must invest in substantial infrastructure and alternative renewable energy sources.

Keywords: Laos, energy security, electricity, renewable energy, ASEAN, battery of Asia.

1. Introduction

Nowadays, energy systems in countries that have no access to the outside market through open seas, namely landlocked countries, may suffer from the inability to export or import energy in fair conditions, which can result in a lack of energy for local use and/or in the inability to sell surplus energy (Mezaa *et al.*, 2013). UN-OHRLLS (2016) cited three disadvantages of geographical location: (i) limitation from critical infrastructure deficiencies and poor trade facilitation, (ii) overall trade costs that erode their competitive edge, and (iii) constraints on sustainable resource utilization, leading to elevated transportation costs (United Nations Office of the High Representative for the Least Developed Countries, Landlocked Developing Countries (LLDC) and Small Island Developing Countries (UN-OHRLLS, 2016).

Lao PDR, officially the Lao PDR, located at the heart of the Indochinese peninsula, is the only landlocked country in Southeast Asia (LMEC, 2021). Laos is a fast-growing emerging country, with a high GDP growth rate that has averaged 7.7% over the last

[#]This chapter is the updated version of the paper published in *Singapore Economic Review*, Vol. 66, No. 2 (2021) 595–619; DOI: 10.1142/S0217590820430080.

decade, with income per capita reaching $2,460 in 2018. Economic growth in Lao PDR was expected to be 6.5% according to the World Bank (World Bank, 2019). Empirically, the main factors which will influence EC in the long term are GDP, population, FDI, and other economic factors in the LLDC. In fact, there are few studies on the electricity security of Laos. The studies on energy consumption are varied across countries and regions, depending on the scope of the samples, time periods, and models. Since the last decade, studies on energy consumption can be divided into two aspects: *forecasting and predicting energy behavior based on the theory of consumption* versus *the growth hypothesis*.

From 2011–2016, the GDP growth rose by 7.5% steadily in Laos. Much of this growth was driven by the natural resource sector, including mining, timber extraction, and hydropower. Mining represented 34% of total exports in 2016 and the export of hydropower electricity represented 21% (USAID, 2020). Laos primarily generates its electricity from hydropower, contributing 0.70% to the global total recorded hydro capacity of 1,407 GW (Power Technology, n.d.). From the economic perspective, Lao PDR's electricity sector has long been one of its key growth drivers. As of 2020, Lao PDR had already built 10,021 MW of electricity generation capacity, of which 80 percent is sourced from hydropower. The share of the electricity sector in the Lao PDR's GDP nearly doubled from 6.5% in 2012 to 12.8% in 2022. Externally, electricity exports quadrupled in the same period (Inayoshi & Nejime, 2023).

Before the pandemic, in late 2019, Lao PDR began shifting away from its traditional economic structure. Lao PDR has been transitioning from an agriculture-based economy to manufacturing and, subsequently, the service sector. However, unlike other developing countries, its export sector follows a different trajectory. In comparison, during Thailand's industrialization period—often considered its economic golden era—the country became a major exporter of manufactured goods, with the share of manufactured exports rising from just one-third of total exports in 1980 to over 80% today. Thailand's share of exports in GDP has grown from 20% in the 1980s to almost 70% today (OECD, OECD Investment Policy Reviews: Thailand, n.d.).

In the case of Lao PDR, the major export sector is energy and mining. The country's biggest export in 2017 was electricity, accounting for more than 17% of the country's exports. The export of electricity increased from USD189 in 2010 to USD637 in 2017 (Oum, 2019). According to a 2010 assessment by the International Centre for Environmental Management, if all proposed dams on the main Mekong River were to go ahead, Laos would earn up to USD 2.6 billion per year in export revenue (UNCTAD, n.d.). However, Handayani *et al.* (2023) mentioned that Laos is one of the three countries (Cambodia, Laos, and Myanmar) that has the lowest annual electricity usage per capita in ASEAN, with 0.6 MWh, 0.9 MWh, and 0.4 MWh, respectively, below the ASEAN average of 1.6 MWh, let alone the global average of 3.3 MWh (IEA, 2021). Phoumin & Kimura (2019) state that each person must consume at least 1.4 MWh of electricity per year to be considered above the energy poverty line. Thus, Laos is then considered to be below the energy poverty line (Handayani *et al.* (2023).

After Laos reopened its borders in 2022, the World Bank lowered Laos's 2022 economic growth rate to 2.5% from its initial prediction of 3.6%. Limited fiscal and foreign currency buffers have posed a challenge to the government's ability to mitigate the economic impacts of COVID-19 and global economic disruptions, such as Russia's war in Ukraine and conflicts in Middle East. The Lao currency, the kip, depreciated more than 45% against the USD at one point during 2022, according to the Economist Intelligence Unit, and year-on-year inflation exceeded 40% in December 2022. These factors have exacerbated the country's macroeconomic vulnerabilities. Compared to other countries in the region, FDI inflows to Laos have been relatively stable, driven primarily by infrastructure construction and power projects. The utilization of natural resources and the expansion of hydropower have driven rapid economic growth in Laos over the past decade, with both sectors largely dominated by foreign investors. However, this reliance has also created energy vulnerabilities, posing risks to the country's economic security.

Against this backdrop, ensuring energy security in Laos—a small open economy—remains a critical challenge. The power sector must address the growing mismatch between rising electricity demand and supply reliability while simultaneously adhering to climate commitments and diversifying clean energy sources. This chapter will analyze the future security of the electricity supply in Laos. It could provide some policy recommendations on the investment of electricity infrastructure in Lao PDR and encourage other ASEAN countries to adjust their electricity policies based on both short-term and long-term visions.

This chapter is organized as follows: Section 1 introduces the importance of energy for Laos. Section 2 reviews the existing literature on energy consumption, while Section 3 presents an econometric model. Section 4 discusses the existence of energy insecurity in Laos. Section 5 outlines the methodology, including the variables and data used. Section 6 presents the estimation results, followed by a summary, conclusion, and policy recommendation.

2. Theorical and Empirical Review

There are many studies related to EC based on the forecasting model. Most of the works show the forecasting methods for specific countries. To name a few, Zaid Mohamed and Pat Bodger (2003) developed a multiple linear regression (MLR) model to analyze the EC of New Zealand. All the independent variables were highly correlated to the dependent variables according to the calculation of the correlation. It is also mentioned that the accuracy of the forecasts made by the model is heavily dependent on the accuracy of the forecasts used to explain the variables. Chenthur Pandian *et al.* (2005) used a fuzzy approach to improve short-term forecasting in India. For Lao PDR's energy consumption, Santisouk Phimphachan *et al.* (2004) analyzed Vientiane's (capital of Laos) energy and peak load forecast using artificial neural networks (ANN) with multilayer perceptron and a back-propagation learning algorithm. The absolute maximum temperature, average maximum humidity, wind speed, GDP, population growth rate, and consumer growth rate were taken into account. The method used correlation to select the input variables and devise measures for selecting the training sets. The MAPE was applied to check the accuracy of the model.

Vincenzo Bianco *et al.* (2009) applied the MLR method to long-term EC forecasting in Italy. The authors used GDP, GDP per capita, price, and population as the selected variables. The first part estimated the GDP, GDP per capita, and price elasticities of domestic and non-domestic EC. In the second part, different regression models based on cointegrated or stationary data were presented. Different statistical tests were employed to check the validity of the proposed models. According to the Lagrange Multiplier (LM) test and the root mean square error (RMSE) result, the model performed well on the forecasting. However, Vincenzo Bianco *et al.* (2010) presented an analysis and two forecasting models for nonresidential EC in Romania. The first method was the trigonometric grey model with rolling mechanism (TGMRM) and the second method was Holt–Winters exponential smoothing method. GDP and price were considered in the models, and the authors analyzed the elasticities of EC in terms of two factors in the long term and short term. The result showed that EC was more elastic in the long term. The knowledge of price and income elasticities allowed electricity companies to design convenient policies and helped policymakers to formulate policies to reform the electricity sector. Whereas demand forecasting was important for potential investors in the electricity sector and for the companies involved in the electricity business, there was still some need to make plans for future strategies. Sackdara *et al.* (2010) proposed Neural Networks with backpropagation learning algorithm and regression analysis approaches for Laos's electricity demand forecasting. They compared these two methods using MAPE to measure the forecasting performance. They used populations, number of households, electricity price, and GDP as the determinants. The result illustrated that the accuracy of neural networks was better than MLR. This paper was useful for system expansion planning and financial analysis in Laos.

Kandananond (2011) used three methodologies—ARIMA, ANN, and MLR method—to formulate prediction models on the electricity demand in Thailand based on the historical data from 1986 to 2010. Population, GDP, stock index, and revenue from exporting industrial products were considered in the models. The author selected the mean absolute percentage error (MAPE) as the performance indicator to check the models. ANN outperformed the ARIMA and MLR. But the paired test showed that there was no significant difference among the three models. Mostafavi *et al.* (2013) provided a prediction equation that was developed for electricity demand using an integrated search method of genetic programming and simulated annealing, called GSA. A sensitivity analysis was conducted to investigate the contribution of the parameters affecting the EC. This result was able to show that EC was formulated in terms of population, GDP, stock index, and total revenue from exporting industrial products. Atsawathawichok *et al.* (2014) presented the forecast for the monthly peak electricity demand from 2014 to 2024 for Thailand using the Gaussian process. The study proposed pattern learning by using multiple kernel functions with hyper-parameters. The authors considered climate, temperature, population, GDP, and GNP as the influencing factors for the simulation technique. At the same time, the traditional MLR and ANN models were also applied to the forecasting procedure, thus resulting in proposed models that produced better outcomes. Kleebrang (2015) studied the household electricity demand forecast and energy savings potential for Vientiane, Lao PDR. The paper used survey data on household electricity demand from five districts of Vientiane, Lao PDR, for a demand projection on up to 2030 using an end-use model. Scenario analysis was used to verify the potential of an energy-saving program by alternating selected appliances with more energy-efficient ones following the labeling standard of Thailand. The demographic structure of electrified households and the energy efficiency of electrical appliances were considered the dominant factors affecting electricity demand. Kaynar *et al.* (2017) forecasted Turkey's EC with Support Vector Regression and the Chaotic Particle Swarm Algorithm. Their study found that energy is a very important factor in terms of sustaining the economic development of developing and industrialized countries. Sang Guun Yoo and Myriam Hernandez Alvarez (2018) forecasted residential EC using a neural network in Korea. They found that electricity demand prediction plays an essential role in short-term load allocation and long-term planning for new generation and transmission infrastructure. An accurate prediction also allows one to take better decisions in terms of cost and energy efficiency. Using the extracted variables, the paper could forecast residential EC and it could also demonstrate how the elderly population was the major influential parameter at the moment of forecasting residential EC. Lastly, Lei Tang *et al.* (2019) studied long-term EC forecasting based on expert prediction and fuzzy Bayesian theory. Their work found that long-term EC forecasting is a very important in expansion planning of power systems.

For EC based on a theorical model, there are fewer studies compared to the first approach. Theologos Dergiades *et al.* (2010) examined the main determinants of aggregate residential demand for electricity in Greece. The autoregressive distributed lag (ARDL) method was applied. The result suggested that if electricity saving constituted a major concern for the reduction of pollution, then the government must turn to regulations that encouraged consumers to use power-saving features in all electrical appliances. Philip Kofi Adom and William Bekoe (2012) identified the factors that affected aggregate electricity demand in Ghana for both short-run and long-run periods based on two econometric approaches—the ARDL model and partial adjustment model (PAM). These approaches were applied to obtain electricity demand prediction. The industrial value-added, as a share of GDP, degree of urbanization, industrial efficiency, and real per capita GDP were considered in the model. The paper recommended that substantial capital investment would have to be made in terms of plant capacity to generate the amount of electricity that was commensurate with future demand requirements to prevent any potential serious load shedding in the future. Aslan (2014) examined the nexus between EC and economic growth in Turkey using the ARDL bounds test. Both short-run and long-run Granger causality were investigated. The bounds test was used to determine whether a long-run relationship exists between the variables by testing the significance of the lagged levels of the variables. Ibrahiem (2015) investigated the relationship among renewable EC, FDI, and economic growth in Egypt by using ARDL and complementing techniques, namely unit root test, bounds test, and diagnostic test statistics, and the stability of the model was checked by applying CUSUM and CUSUMQ tests. The empirical findings show that the variables in the study are cointegrated, indicating the existence of long-run relationships among them. Furthermore, renewable EC and FDI have a long-run positive effect on economic growth. Pham Dinh Long *et al.* (2018) investigated the causal relationship between EC, FDI, and economic growth in Vietnam during the period 1990–2015. By applying the ARDL approach, empirical results showed strong statistical evidence that EC and FDI have positive impacts on economic growth in Vietnam in both the short-run and long-run periods. Fukuyo and Hirohata (2019) compared energy consumption in the Asian landlocked countries of Nepal and Lao PDR by focusing on the present and future residential energy consumption in both countries. Although Laos and Nepal are classified as the least developed countries (LDCs) and share many similarities in terms of geographical and socioeconomic features, energy use, especially electricity use, is very different. Regression analysis and the Granger causality test showed that there is a quantitative and causal relationship between economic growth and residential EC. The difference in the EC was able to be illustrated by their economic disparity.

Building on the points mentioned above, this paper aims to fill the gap in the existing literature by using the Bayesian method to analyze and predict electricity consumption (EC). As a developing country with a high economy growth rate, Laos's EC has been increasing rapidly. Empirically, the EC has an inertia characteristic, and the current consumption is highly related to the last period of consumption. Besides, in the long term, the EC is usually influenced by economic factors and sometimes those influences will be continuous or delayed. The purpose of this chapter is to study the influence of GDP, population, and FDI on the long-term EC in Lao PDR by checking the future electricity phenomena of a country that is both domestically and internationally landlocked. By applying the ARDL method, we are not only able to check whether there is a long-run relationship between EC and other economic factors but we can also study the duration of the influence and then predict the future EC precisely. This chapter is going to analyze and predict Laos's EC via a new Bayesian model that still in its infancy. The research gap is because most of the previous works have applied the classical model to energy consumption by using fixed parameters. However, this study will try to make it more suitable by using the Bayesian ARDL model which is capable of making parameter changes randomly and can enable the ARDL to perform better.

Most of the time series data, such as Laos's EC, GDP, and also FDI, did not stay constant during the period from 1998 to 2018 (see Table 2). Therefore, this research paper will employ the unit root test with a structural break for the confirmation of time series data that were not stable over time.

3. Energy Insecurity in Lao PDR

As the only landlocked country in ASEAN, Lao PDR has no access to global trade over the open seas.[1] There are many obvious disadvantages as lacking direct access to the sea means a landlocked country isolated from the outside world market. Seaborne trade makes up a large portion of international trade. This is why coastal regions tend to be wealthier and more populated than inland areas. Since 1971, Laos has been classified as belonging to a group of LDCs in the world (Kaewkhunok, 2018). However, Lao PDR is a developing country with a high economic growth rate; recently, Laos's EC has been increasing rapidly. Empirically, the EC has an inertia characteristic and the current consumption is highly

---

[1]The global community has acknowledged the extreme vulnerability of landlocked countries by means of the Article 125 (1) of the United Nation Convention on the Law of the Sea (UNCLOS), [2], which states that "Land-locked States shall have the right of access to and from the sea for the purpose of exercising the rights provided for in this Convention including those relating to the freedom of the high seas and the common heritage of mankind. To this end, land-locked States shall enjoy freedom of transit through the territory of transit States by all means of transport" (Article 125 (1), of the United Nation Convention on the Law of the Sea).

related to the last period of consumption. In the long term, the EC is usually influenced by economic factors and sometimes these influences will be continuous or delayed. While hydropower development is expected to drive future economic growth in the Lao PDR, the establishment of new power exchange arrangements will be an important prerequisite to help earn export revenue and dispatch excess capacity. The Lao government views the development of the country's vast hydro power resources as having significant potential for achieving sustainable economic growth and addressing domestic electrification needs through highly appropriate methods. In addition, the country exports surplus electrical energy to its neighboring countries of Thailand, Vietnam, Cambodia, and China. Lao PDR has signed a power exchange agreement to export 20,000 MW to Thailand and 2,000 MW to Vietnam before 2020 (Raju & Kumar, 2023).

This means that nearly half of the forthcoming hydropower projects in Lao PDR are earmarked for cross-border exports. The country's central location within the neighboring countries, namely, "the Great Mekong Subregion (GMS)," allows Lao PDR to supply electricity to sizable neighboring markets such as Thailand and Vietnam, and to a lesser extent to Cambodia and Myanmar (ADB, 2023).

In recent years, as the Laos government has continuously strengthened its reform and opening-up policy and expanded foreign cooperation, foreign-funded enterprises have entered Lao PDR to find investment opportunities. Among them, hydropower resource development has become one of the key areas of foreign investment. While the rapid increase in energy generation is crucial for achieving future goals, a significant challenge arises from the heavy reliance on foreign capital, particularly through borrowing from abroad. A report by the OECD (2019) said that its geographical features, together with the country's relatively high annual rainfall, grants Lao PDR advantages in hydropower and makes it possible to export electricity to neighboring countries, which can be the driving force for its economic growth. As a result, hydro plants currently produce most of the country's electricity. Data from the state power company, Électricité du Laos (EDL), show that, prior to 2013, all of the country's electricity was produced by hydropower plants. Since 2013, biomass has also been used to produce electricity and accounts for roughly 0.02–0.03% of Lao PDR's overall energy portfolio. As of 2015, when the Hongsa power plant came online, coal has also been used, and it accounts for 14% of total electricity production. The use of solar power was first recorded in 2014, but its overall footprint remains tiny (OECD, 2019).

Other countries accumulate energy from a variety of resources. While other countries derive energy from a variety of resources, in Lao PDR, energy usage is almost synonymous with electricity consumption (OECD, 2019). Electricity in Lao PDR plays an increasingly important role in helping the nation's economy develop and grow. A shortage of electricity will lead to a decrease in national welfare and a delay in its economic development. Furthermore, an electricity shortage will have a negative impact on society's stability. An insufficient electricity supply will translate to energy insecurity, which is considered a critical issue for a poor country like Lao PDR. Laos is an electricity export country at present as it exports (Table 1) its commodity to its neighbors in the region. The electricity exportation amount was 11,549 GWh in 2015. Because the electricity generation amount is greater than the EC amount, Laos is usually regarded as the

Table 1. Countries with Electricity Export Agreements with Laos.

Country	Exports Capacity (MW)	Year
Thailand	9,000	2030
Vietnam	5,000	2030
Malaysia	300	2020
Cambodia	200	2020
Myanmar	100	2020

Source: Lao PDR Energy Statistics (2018) and Ministry of Energy and Mines of Lao PDR.

"battery of ASEAN." By using this campaign, this is worth to see the reason why it is so important to investigate Laos electricity whether it is capable on ensuring that there is sufficient supply not only for the ASEAN region but also for the Laotian people.

4. Methodology

The first part of the analysis tested for unit roots with structural breaks in all variables included in the study, such as electricity consumption (EC), GDP, foreign direct investment (FDI), and population in Lao PDR. The analysis of the long-run and short-run relationships between macro variables factors based on the Bayesian ARDL approach will be applied for this testing. The analysis process for EC in Laos will be presented as a flowchart in the following.

4.1. *Research design*

Based on the studies we reviewed and according to the electricity demand theory, Laos's EC, GDP, population, and FDI were selected as the influence factors. The EC function can be described by Eq. (1):

$$E\_CONS_t = a + bGDP_t + cPOP_t + dFDI_t + \varepsilon_t \tag{1}$$

where *E_CONS* comes from electricity consumption, *GDP* stands for log of gross domestic product, *POP* represents population of Lao PDR, and *FDI* is for foreign direct investment. All are in natural logarithm value (log), and ε is an error term. As far as the expected signs of coefficients are concerned, we would expect estimated parameters b, c, and d to be > 0, indicating that a growth in GDP, population, and FDI in Laos will result in an increase in energy consumption.

4.2. *Unit root test with structural break*

In econometrics, most models are developed based on the fundamental concept that the relationship between variables remains constant over the estimation period. However, when time series data, particularly on the electricity consumption (EC) of Lao PDR, presents a structural break, it may not be suitable for testing using a basic unit root model. The unit root test with structural break was adopted in this research for time series data that were manipulated by the structural break model which had been developed as a concept by Bai and Perron (1998) and Dickey and Fuller (1979) (see Eq. 2):

$$y_t = \mu + \beta t + \theta DU_t(T_b) + \gamma DT_t(T_b) + wD_t(T_b) + \alpha y_{t-1} + \sum_{i=1}^{k} c_i \Delta y_{t-i} + u_t \tag{2}$$

From Eq. (1), the unit root test with a structural break, based on the model developed by Perron (1989), is combined with the DF-test model developed by Dickey and Fuller (1979) as the full model for this analysis. Rationally, both the electricity consumption (EC) of Lao PDR and several other determining factors were found to be non-stationary with a structural break.

4.3. *ADRL approach to cointegration based on Bayesian inference*

According to the electricity demand theory, Laos's EC, GDP, population, and FDI were selected as the influence factors, and the EC function can be described by Eq. (3):

$$E\_CONS_t = a + bGDP_t + cPOP_t + dFDI_t + \varepsilon_t \tag{3}$$

where *E_CONS* comes from electricity consumption, *GDP* stands for log of gross domestic product, *POP* represents the population of Lao PDR, and *FDI* is for foreign direct investment. All are in natural logarithm value (log), and ε is an error term.

As far as the expected signs of coefficients are concerned, we would expect the estimated parameters b, c, and d to be > 0, indicating that growth of GDP, population, and FDI in Laos will result in an increase in energy consumption.

The energy consumption model represented by Eq. (3) outlines the long-run relation between the energy consumption and its determinants [see latest model studies in Chor Foon Tang *et al.* (2015), Pham Dinh Long *et al.* (2018), and Ha Minh Nguyen *et al.* (2019)].

Thus, following Pesaran *et al.*'s (2001) ARDL approach, Eq. (2) is expressed in its general form, with the ARDL model based on Bayesian inference used to conduct the co-integration test for long-run model estimation. We express the EC of Lao PDR by starting with Eq. (4):

$$\begin{aligned} \Delta E_{CONSt} = a_0 &+ \sum_{i=1}^{n1} b_j \Delta GDP_{t-j} + \sum_{i=1}^{n2} c_j \Delta POP_{t-j} + \sum_{i=1}^{n3} d_j \Delta FDI_{t-j} + \delta_1 E_{CONSt-1} \\ &+ \delta_2 GDP_{t-1} + \delta_3 POP_{t-1} + \delta_4 FDI_{t-1} + \mu_t \end{aligned} \tag{4}$$

To account for the short-run dynamics and the convergence of energy consumption in Lao PDR over time, the error correction term (EC_{t-1}) was also included. This captures the speed of adjustment that measures the response of the energy consumption per period against any deviations between the actual energy consumption and its long-run equilibrium level. Specifically, if there is a shock to the energy consumption, this will raise its value relative to the equilibrium relationship with other series belonging to the cointegration vectors. Then, the coefficient on EC_{t-1} measures how much of the divergence is

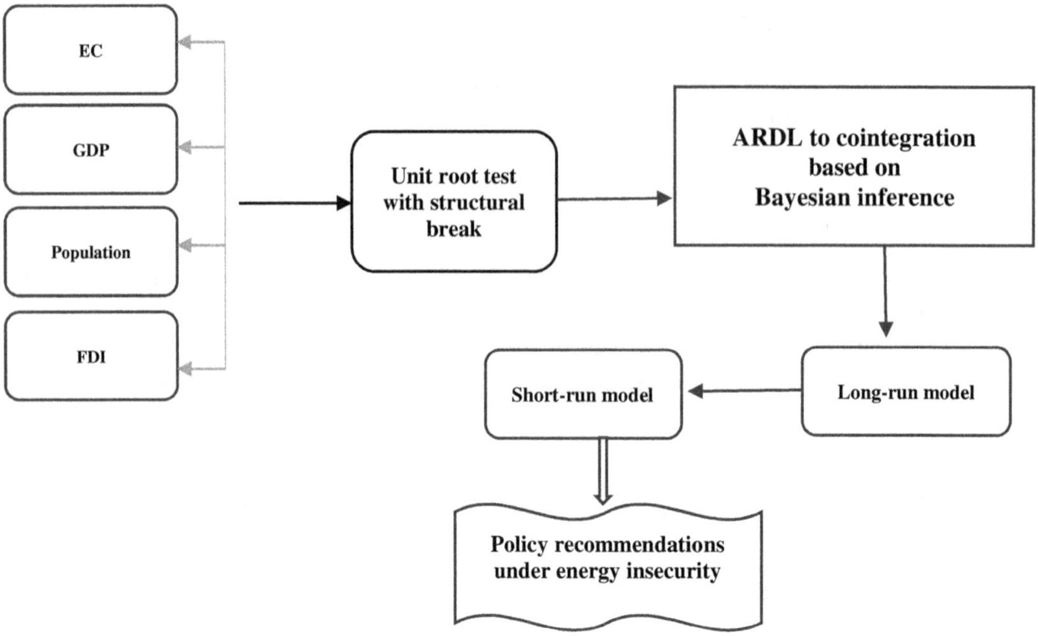

Figure 1. Theoretical model and its research process design.

eliminated in the following period. Convergence of the cointegrating system in its long-run equilibrium is assured when $-1 < EC_{t-1} < 0$, where the deviation of variables, the parameters, and δ_1, δ_2, δ_3, δ_4 function as the long-run multipliers, while the a_j, b_j, c_j, parameters function as the short-run dynamic coefficients of the underlying ARDL (see research methodology in Fig. 1).

The ARDL model based on Bayesian inference requires the application of Bayes' theorem and Bayes' rule for a smoother and more comprehensive understanding. Bayes' rule is the fundamental or essential learning point for understanding Bayesian inference. This rule involves setting events A and B under the conditional probability of A given B, which can be expressed clearly in Eq. (5) as follows:

$$P(A|B) = \frac{P(B|A)P(A)}{P(B)} \tag{5}$$

On the contrary, this rule has a new setting of events for *B* and *A* under conditional probability of *B* given that *A* would also be expressed clearly in Eq. (5) as follows:

$$P(B|A) = \frac{P(A|B)P(B)}{P(A)} \tag{6}$$

This rule says that either Eq. (5) equals Eq. (6) or Eq. (6) equals Eq. (5) in terms of mathematical process. However, Bayesian inference applies Bayes' rule or Bayes' theorem to compute the linear regression model, particularly in the ARDL approach to cointegration, starting with the formula presented in Eq. (7) as follows:

$$P(\theta|y) \propto P(y|\theta)P(\theta) \tag{7}$$

By definition,
$P(\theta|y)$ = posterior
$P(y|\theta)$ = likelihood
$P(\theta)$ = prior

The core concept of Bayesian computation involves combining prior knowledge with likelihood (new data) to obtain the posterior distribution for statistical probabilities. In the process of computing econometric models, Bayesian inference is typically used, which requires the application of the MCMC algorithm for estimation. This algorithm consists of three parts that are accepted in the Bayesian inference. The first part is the Monte Carlo simulation, the second part is the Markov Chains, and the last part is the Metropolis–Hastings algorithm. The steps of the MCMC algorithm for Bayesian inference would proceed as follows:

Step 1: Generate random numbers using the following formula.

$$\text{Draw } \theta_t \sim N(\mu,\sigma)$$

Step 2: Generate random numbers using the extended formula version of Markov Chain Monte Carlo (MCMC)

$$\text{Draw } \theta_t \sim N(\theta_{t-1},\sigma)$$

Step 3: Metropolis–Hastings algorithm

$$\gamma(\theta_{new},\theta_{t-1}) = \frac{\text{Posterior Probalility of } \theta_{new}}{\text{Posterior Probalility of } \theta_{t-1}}$$

$$\begin{aligned} \text{Acceptance probability} &= \alpha(\theta_{new},\theta_{t-1}) \\ &= \min\,[\gamma(\theta_{new},\theta_{t-1}),1] \end{aligned}$$

Draw $\mu <$ Uniform (0,1)
If $\mu < \alpha(\theta_{new},\theta_{t-1})$
then $\theta_t = \theta_{new}$,
otherwise $\theta_t = \theta_{t-1}$

The steps of the MCMC algorithm for Bayesian inference proceed through all the previously outlined stages, with the process continuing in a loop until the target number of iterations, as defined by the researchers, is reached.

4.4. *Data sources*

All of the data used in the consumption part are secondary data from 1998 to 2018. The EC from 2000 to 2015 is from the Ministry of Energy and Mines of Laos; 1998 to 1999 and 2016 to 2018 is from the department of Électricité du Laos. The GDP, population, and FDI

Table 2. Data description and data manipulation.

	E_CONS	*FDI*	*GDP*	*POP*
Mean	2272.34	424000000.00	7170000000.00	6044877.00
Median	1915.69	279000000.00	5440000000.00	6052190.00
Maximum	5416.63	1600000000.00	18100000000.00	6961210.00
Minimum	516.26	4451297.00	1280000000.00	5150763.00
Std. dev.	1597.94	474000000.00	5760000000.00	561157.70
Skewness	0.59	1.07	0.62	0.01
Kurtosis	2.03	3.03	1.92	1.77
Jarque–Bera	2.05	4.00	2.39	1.33
Probability	0.36	0.14	0.30	0.51
ADF unit root test	-2.21^{ns}	-3.12^{ns}	-4.30^{ns}	-24.4234^{*}
(structural break point)	2011	2002	2010	None
Observations	21	21	21	21

data are from the World Bank data source. The data used in the generation part are the total installed capacity, which is the secondary data from 2019 to 2022, from the Ministry of Energy and Mines of Laos.

4.5. *Data descriptive and unit root test with structural break*

In Table 2, the data manipulation under simple statistics calculation is shown. The key considerations for time series data before applying them to econometric models are determining whether the data exhibit non-stationary or stationary properties.

However, most of the time series data that were adopted for the econometrics model estimation for explaining Laos's EC during the period of 1998–2018 are presented as non-stationary and mixed with structural break points except for the population of this country. The structural break points were identified as follows: 2011 for electricity consumption (E_CONS), 2002 for foreign direct investment (FDI), and 2010 for gross domestic product (GDP). Hence, the classical statistics of econometrics model estimation is not quite suitable for this case. While classical statistics in econometric model estimation yield fixed parameters, Bayesian statistics update the parameters based on prior distributions defined by the researchers' subjective viewpoint.

4.6. *Selection of lag length for the ARDL model*

Table 3 shows that the Bayesian Information Criterion (BIC), also known as the Schwarz Information Criterion, is used as the selection criterion for the ARDL model. The model with the lowest BIC value is considered the optimal ARDL model for explaining Laos's electricity consumption (EC) model. Nevertheless, Table 4 displays the many statistics values, especially BIC criterion statistics, which suggests that the ARDL (1, 0, 3, 2) is the best model to be utilized in testing for the cointegration of Laos's EC model.

Table 3. Display of all statistical values implemented to find the best ARDL model.

Model	Log L	AIC	BIC*	HQ	Adj. R-sq.	Specification
50	–99.7615	12.19572	12.69037	12.26393	0.657286	ARDL (1, 0, 3, 2)
49	–98.9837	12.22041	12.76452	12.29543	0.640757	ARDL (1, 0, 3, 3)
64	–107.842	12.53796	12.78528	12.57206	0.482413	ARDL (1, 0, 0, 0)
51	–102.38	12.37555	12.82074	12.43694	0.592495	ARDL (1, 0, 3, 1)
52	–104.075	12.45275	12.84847	12.50732	0.557251	ARDL (1, 0, 3, 0)
34	–99.7599	12.30665	12.85077	12.38168	0.608398	ARDL (1, 1, 3, 2)
3	–98.3392	12.25992	12.8535	12.34176	0.609843	ARDL (1, 3, 3, 1)
18	–98.408	12.26756	12.86114	12.34941	0.60685	ARDL (1, 2, 3, 2)
33	–98.5647	12.28497	12.87855	12.36682	0.599945	ARDL (1, 1, 3, 3)
36	–102.905	12.43392	12.87911	12.49531	0.568002	ARDL (1, 1, 3, 0)
19	–100.497	12.38852	12.93264	12.46355	0.574989	ARDL (1, 2, 3, 1)
17	–97.7039	12.30044	12.94348	12.38911	0.563721	ARDL (1, 2, 3, 3)
63	–107.827	12.64742	12.94421	12.68834	0.440206	ARDL (1, 0, 0, 1)
60	–107.831	12.64791	12.9447	12.68883	0.43993	ARDL (1, 0, 1, 0)
48	–107.84	12.64891	12.9457	12.68983	0.43937	ARDL (1, 1, 0, 0)
35	–102.328	12.48088	12.97553	12.54908	0.544201	ARDL (1, 1, 3, 1)
32	–106.7	12.63331	12.97957	12.68106	0.461188	ARDL (1, 2, 0, 0)
2	–98.2816	12.36462	13.00767	12.45329	0.534802	ARDL (1, 3, 3, 2)
11	–102.628	12.5142	13.00885	12.58241	0.528757	ARDL (1, 3, 1, 1)
16	–105.662	12.62913	13.02485	12.6837	0.471849	ARDL (1, 3, 0, 0)
62	–107.166	12.68506	13.03132	12.73281	0.43257	ARDL (1, 0, 0, 2)
20	–102.844	12.53827	13.03292	12.60648	0.517275	ARDL (1, 2, 3, 0)
56	–107.217	12.6908	13.03706	12.73854	0.429307	ARDL (1, 0, 2, 0)
27	–104.673	12.63036	13.07554	12.69174	0.474233	ARDL (1, 2, 1, 1)
12	–104.752	12.63916	13.08434	12.70054	0.469586	ARDL (1, 3, 1, 0)
1	–97.6187	12.40208	13.09459	12.49757	0.459789	ARDL (1, 3, 3, 3)
28	–106.294	12.69937	13.09509	12.75393	0.433421	ARDL (1, 2, 1, 0)
47	–107.765	12.75167	13.09793	12.79941	0.393489	ARDL (1, 1, 0, 1)
44	–107.822	12.75799	13.10425	12.80573	0.389644	ARDL (1, 1, 1, 0)
59	–107.823	12.75812	13.10438	12.80586	0.389564	ARDL (1, 0, 1, 1)
4	–102.077	12.56416	13.10827	12.63918	0.493385	ARDL (1, 3, 3, 0)
31	–106.414	12.71262	13.10834	12.76719	0.42586	ARDL (1, 2, 0, 1)
61	–106.583	12.73139	13.12711	12.78596	0.414981	ARDL(1, 0, 0, 3)
40	–106.634	12.73711	13.13283	12.79167	0.411629	ARDL (1, 1, 2, 0)
7	–102.497	12.61079	13.15491	12.68582	0.469201	ARDL (1, 3, 2, 1)
15	–105.462	12.71804	13.16323	12.77943	0.42605	ARDL (1, 3, 0, 1)

(*Continued*)

Table 3. (*Continued*)

Model	Log L	AIC	BIC*	HQ	Adj. R-sq.	Specification
10	−102.614	12.62378	13.1679	12.69881	0.46226	ARDL (1, 3, 1, 2)
24	−105.52	12.72445	13.16964	12.78584	0.42236	ARDL (1, 2, 2, 0)
55	−107.068	12.78533	13.18105	12.83989	0.382562	ARDL (1, 0, 2, 1)
23	−104.192	12.68797	13.18262	12.75617	0.439326	ARDL (1, 2, 2, 1)
26	−104.249	12.69429	13.18894	12.76249	0.435771	ARDL (1, 2, 1, 2)
46	−107.149	12.79432	13.19005	12.84889	0.376981	ARDL (1, 1, 0, 2)
58	−107.155	12.79504	13.19076	12.8496	0.376537	ARDL (1, 0, 1, 2)
30	−105.873	12.76363	13.20881	12.82501	0.399279	ARDL (1, 2, 0, 2)
54	−106.037	12.78194	13.22712	12.84332	0.38818	ARDL (1, 0, 2, 2)
6	−101.761	12.64013	13.23371	12.72198	0.429355	ARDL (1, 3, 2, 2)
8	−104.74	12.74885	13.24351	12.81706	0.404127	ARDL (1, 3, 2, 0)
43	−107.745	12.86061	13.25633	12.91517	0.334288	ARDL (1, 1, 1, 1)
22	−103.553	12.72812	13.27224	12.80315	0.403121	ARDL (1, 2, 2, 2)
57	−106.489	12.83209	13.27727	12.89347	0.356716	ARDL (1, 0, 1, 3)
45	−106.56	12.84002	13.28521	12.90141	0.35159	ARDL (1, 1, 0, 3)
39	−106.589	12.84326	13.28844	12.90464	0.349489	ARDL (1, 1, 2, 1)
53	−105.215	12.80161	13.29626	12.86982	0.371845	ARDL (1, 0, 2, 3)
14	−105.372	12.81909	13.31374	12.8873	0.360771	ARDL (1, 3, 0, 2)
9	−102.524	12.72485	13.31843	12.8067	0.378905	ARDL (1, 3, 1, 3)
25	−104.044	12.78265	13.32677	12.85768	0.369667	ARDL (1, 2, 1, 3)
38	−105.641	12.84902	13.34367	12.91722	0.341352	ARDL (1, 1, 2, 2)
42	−107.128	12.9031	13.34828	12.96448	0.309374	ARDL (1, 1, 1, 2)
29	−105.87	12.87448	13.36913	12.94269	0.324364	ARDL (1, 2, 0, 3)
5	−101.624	12.73603	13.37908	12.8247	0.325565	ARDL (1, 3, 2, 3)
21	−103.438	12.82642	13.42	12.90827	0.312507	ARDL (1, 2, 2, 3)
41	−106.337	12.92634	13.42099	12.99454	0.288405	ARDL (1, 1, 1, 3)
37	−105.205	12.91161	13.45573	12.98664	0.282907	ARDL (1, 1, 2, 3)
13	−105.36	12.92884	13.47296	13.00387	0.270443	ARDL (1, 3, 0, 3)

5. Empirical Analysis

5.1. *Bayesian ADRL approach to co-integration*

According to the strong point of Bayesian inference, it tries to display a variety of updated parameters under prior distribution defined by the subjective viewpoint of the researchers. Most of the time, it has been found that the macroeconomic variables that have a relationship between them do not stay constant over a period of time. The extreme case, as identified previously, was that many variables were found to be non-stationary with a

Table 4. Display of the full ARDL model for cointegration estimated using the Bayesian approach.

Bayesian Normal Regression	***MCMC Iteration =***		***12,500***
Random-Walk Metropolis–Hasting Sampling	**Burn-In =**		**2,500**
	MCSC Sample Size =		**10,000**
	Number of Obs. =		**18**
	Acceptance Rate =		**0.8591**
	Efficiency:	**Min. =**	**0.001118**
		Avg. =	**0.001297**
Log Marginal Likelihood = 49463.785		**Max. =**	**0.001935**

d_e_cons	Mean	Std. Dev.	MCSE	Median	**Equal-Tailed** (95% Cred. Interval)	
fdi	2.78e-08	4.67e-10	1.4e-10	2.77e-08	2.70e-08	2.85e-08
gdp	1.56e-08	2.31e-10	6.4e-11	1.56e-08	1.52e-08	1.62e-08
*gdp*1	1.09e-07	3.14e-10	9.2e-11	1.09e-07	1.08e-07	1.09e-07
*gdp*2	1.31e-07	1.81e-10	4.9e-11	1.31e-07	1.31e-07	1.31e-07
*gdp*3	−2.66e-07	2.82e-10	8.4e-11	−2.66e-07	−2.67e-07	−2.66e-07
pop	0.016236	1.78e-10	4.9e-11	016236	.016236	0.016236
*pop*1	−0.0269569	4.34e-10	1.3e-10	−0.0269569	−0.0269569	−0.026569
*pop*2	.0107155	2.18e-10	6.0e-11	−0.0107155	0.0107155	0.0107155
*d_e_cons*1	−0.5303373	2.07e-10	5.6e-11	−0.5303373	−0.5303373	−0.5303373
d_fdi	−1.31e-08	2.38e-10	6.4e-11	−1.30e-08	−1.36e-08	−1.27e-08
d_gdp	−2.23e-10	1.62e-10	3.7e-11	−2.38e-10	−5.41e-10	1.07e-10
d_pop	5.86e-10	2.88e-10	8.3e-11	−6.12e-10	−1.40e-10	9.72e-10
_cons	−357.6407	4.08e-10	1.2e-10	−0.357.6407	−345.6407	−357.6407

structural break. From the Table 4, these were utilized in the estimation of Laos' EC model. Therefore, this research attempts to utilize the Bayesian statistics or inference for testing the cointegration between dependent variable (Laos's Electrics consumption) and independents variables such as GDP, FDI, and Population of Laos during the period of 1998 to 2018. The cointegration test based on the Bayesian ARDL approach will proceed as follow. The estimation of the short-run ARDL model for co-integration using the Bayesian approach is shown in Table 5:

Step 1: Define the full ADRL model and estimate this model by Bayesian statistics method.

$$\Delta E_{CONS\,t} = a_0 + \sum_{i=1}^{n1} b_j \Delta GDP_{t-j} + \sum_{i=1}^{n2} c_j \Delta POP_{t-j} + \sum_{i=1}^{n3} d_j \Delta FDI_{t-j} + \delta_1 E_{CONS\,t-1} + \delta_2 GDP_{t-1} + \delta_3 POP_{t-1} + \delta_4 FDI_{t-1} + \mu_t \tag{8}$$

Table 5. Short-run ARDL model for co-integration estimated using the Bayesian approach.

Bayesian Normal Regression				***MCMC Iteration =***		***12,500***
Random-Walk Metropolis-Hasting Sampling				**Burn-In =**		**2,500**
				MCSC Sample Size =		**10,000**
				Number of Obs. =		**19**
				Acceptance Rate =		**0.8561**
				Efficiency:	**Min. =**	**0.001199**
					Avg. =	**0.005812**
Log Marginal Likelihood = –81544.453					**Max. =**	**0.02186**
					Equal-Tailed	

d_e_cons	Mean	Std. dev.	MCSE	Median	[95% Cred.	Interval]
*d_e_cons*1	0.669676	3.34e-09	9.0e-10	0.669676	0.0669676	0.0669676
d_fdi	1.39e-07	1.43e-09	2.5e-10	1.39e-07	1.36e-07	1.42e-07
d_gdp	1.58e-07	3.24e-10	2.2e-11	1.58e-07	1.58e-07	1.59e-07
d_pop	0.004302	4346e-09	1.3e-09	0.004302	0.004302	0.004302
_cons	–297.7707	5.04e-09	1.4e-09	–297.7707	–297.7707	–297.7707

Step 2: Define the short-run ARDL model and estimate this model by Bayesian statistics method.

$$\Delta E_{CONSt} = a_0 + \sum_{i=1}^{n1} b_j \Delta GDP_{t-j} + \sum_{i=1}^{n2} c_j \Delta POP_{t-j} + \sum_{i=1}^{n3} d_j \Delta FDI_{t-j} \tag{9}$$

Step 3: Model Selection Based on Deviance Information Criterion (DIC) Statistics.

This research tries to bring Bayesian inference or subjective statistics through conventional approaches to estimate Laos's EC. Because most of the time series data were implemented in model estimation, Laos's EC is non-stationary which included a structural break. It was already mentioned that objective statistics or classical statistics may not be good enough because the parameters received from the model estimation were fixed. In terms of model selection, deviance information criterion (DIC), which was invented by Spiegelhalter *et al.* (2002), was utilized for the best model selection. All the analytical steps for the cointegration test under the Bayesian ADRL model need to follow the process, which had already been mentioned. The DIC (Table 6) suggests that the full model is the best model for an explanation of Laos's EC. It is implying that this consumption has a long-run relationship between dependent variables (Laos's EC) and independent variables such as GDP, FDI, and the population of Laos. In the theorem of cointegration analysis, it has been pointed out that if the model has a long-run relationship, then it will have a short-run relationship as well.

Table 6. Display the DIC statistics criterion for model selection.

Types of Models	DIC	Log (ML)
The full model	34378.07	–49463.79
The short-run model	118555	–81544.45
The best model	The full model	ML*/

Source: authors, */Marginal likelihood (ML) is computed using Laplace–Metropolis approximation.

Table 7. Display the ECM model of short-run model.

Bayesian Normal Regression	***MCMC Iteration =***		***12,500***
Random-Walk Metropolis–Hasting Sampling	**Burn-in =**		**2,500**
	MCSC Sample Size =		**10,000**
	Number of Obs. =		**11**
	Acceptance Rate =		**0.2396**
	Efficiency:	**Min. =**	**0.005004**
		Avg. =	**0.01415**
Log Marginal Likelihood = –21.627662		**Max. =**	**0.02563**

1d_e_cons	Mcan	Std. Dev.	MCSE	Median	Equal-Tailed [95% Cred. Interval]	
*1d_e_cons*1	–0.102906	0.5241624	0.044482	0.1148135	–1.123608	0.9692994
1d_fdi	0.3836457	0.3811149	0.034548	0.3841615	–0.3377237	1.129212
1d_gdp	0.0491672	0.5530615	0.034549	0.0416621	–1.041755	1.163568
1d_pop	–0.1978774	0.0858022	0.062461	–0.2324053	–1.732464	1.486596
_cons	0.3098777	1.361949	0.192531	0.3150126	–2.316272	2.941058
ecml	–0.2067069	1.3376	0.124455	–0.2079312	–2.796688	2.482675

Note: There is a high autocorrelation after 500 lags.

5.2. *ECM model for explanation of short-run model*

Table 7 presents the Error Correction Model (ECM) used to estimate the short-run dynamics of Laos's electricity consumption (EC) using the Bayesian approach. The model was run with 12,500 MCMC iterations, discarding the first 2,500 as a burn-in period to ensure more accurate results. However, the MCMC sample size is 10,000 and the log marginal likelihood is equal to –21.627662. The acceptance rate is equal to 0.2396 and the efficiency on average is equal to 1% to 3% for the fast convergence of the MCMC chain. In terms of inefficiency for MCMC convergence, which was displayed, the model estimation would have a higher autocorrelation. On the other hand, the efficiency for MCMC convergence was displayed by a low autocorrelation.

In the short run, Laos's electricity consumption (EC) is positively influenced by FDI and GDP, but negatively by its previous EC and population. This creates a challenge for both the private and public sectors to balance these opposing factors. Specifically, GDP's influence on EC ranges from –1.04% to 1.16%, with an average of 0.04% based on MCMC posterior estimates. Similarly, FDI's impact on EC varies from –0.33% to 1.12%, with an average of 0.38%. On the other hand, the previous EC's effect on current EC ranges from –1.12% to 0.96%, averaging –0.10%, while the population's influence is between –1.73% and 1.48%, with an average of –0.19%. The speed of adjustment coefficient for the short-run model ranges from –2.79 to 2.48, with an average of –0.20, indicating the necessary negative sign for equilibrium between the long-run and short-run models.

5.3. *Nonlinear NARDL model estimation results*

This model is very useful for estimating the long-run and short-run models, as it can take into account asymmetric situations that affect the long-run and short-run periods. This NARDL model was introduced by Shin *et al.* (2014); the general equation form of this model is described as follows:

$$lnE_{CONSt} = a_0 + \sum_{i=1}^{p} b_j lnE_{CONSt-i} + \sum_{i=1}^{p} c_j lnGDP_{t-j} + \sum_{i=0}^{p} d_j \Delta GDP^{+}_{t-j} + \sum_{i=1}^{p} e_j \Delta GDP^{-}_{t-i} + \epsilon_t$$

$$lnE_{CONSt} = f_0 + \sum_{i=1}^{p} g_j lnE_{CONSt-i} + \sum_{i=1}^{p} h_j lnFDI_{t-j} + \sum_{i=0}^{p} i_j \Delta FDI^{+}_{t-j} + \sum_{i=1}^{p} k_j \Delta FDI^{-}_{t-i} + \epsilon_t \quad (10)$$

The impact of the macroeconomic sector on Lao PDR's energy usage is depicted in the first model. The impact of the international sector on Lao PDR's EC is depicted in the second model. On the other hand, we estimated two models based on annual data covering the 25-year period from 1998 to 2022.

Table 8 attempts to present the NARDL Model Estimation Results for the Macroeconomic Sector's Effect on EC in the Lao PDR, which is quite an interesting topic. The GDP of Lao PDR plays an important role in driving EC in both the long run and short run. Additionally, this model can confirm that the GDP of Lao PDR influences EC by asymmetric phenomena more than systematic phenomena in both the long run and short run. In the short run, when Lao PDR experiences negative economic shocks, such as GDP decreasing faster than increasing, electricity consumption (EC) will decrease by approximately –0.28%. However, in the long run, the impact may differ. Despite GDP slowing down and decreasing faster than it increases, EC in Lao PDR is expected to increase by approximately 5.68%. Furthermore, this research result found that population might play an important role in controlling the long-run increasing trend of EC in Lao PDR, by

Table 8. Display NARDL model estimation results for the macroeconomic sector's effect on EC in the Lao PDR.

lnEC	Variable	Coefficient	Std. Error	t-Statistic	Prob.
Long-run model	**C**	**–52.904**	**20.088**	**–2.634**	**0.025**
	LN_EC(-1)	**–0.934**	**0.286**	**–3.270**	**0.008**
	LN_R_GDP(-1)	**0.669**	**0.251**	**2.660**	**0.024**
	R_GDP_POS(-1)	4.612	3.059	1.508	0.163
	R_GDP_NEG(-1)	**5.685**	**3.107**	**1.830**	**0.097**
	LN_POP(-1)	**2.879**	**1.263**	**2.280**	**0.046**
Short-run model	D(LN_EC(-1))	0.345	0.216	1.601	0.140
	D(LN_R_GDP)	1.311	1.967	0.666	0.520
	D(LN_R_GDP(-1))	**–5.147**	**1.854**	**–2.777**	**0.020**
	D(R_GDP_POS)	–0.835	2.111	–0.395	0.701
	D(R_GDP_NEG)	–0.167	2.037	–0.082	0.936
	D(R_GDP_NEG(-1))	**–0.282**	**0.123**	**–2.295**	**0.045**
	D(LN_POP)	–3.810	2.235	–1.704	0.119
			R-squared		0.855
			Adjusted R-squared		0.787
			Akaike info criterion		–3.995
			Schwarz criterion		–3.600
			Durbin–Watson stat		2.012

approximately 2.78%. Nevertheless, in the short run, there is no statistical evidence to suggest that the population of Lao PDR controls electricity consumption (EC).

For Table 9, the NARDL Model Estimation Results for the International Sector's Effect on EC in Lao PDR indicate that Foreign Direct Investment (FDI) plays a significant role in driving EC, with its influence showing more pronounced asymmetric effects than symmetric effects in both the long-run and short-run periods. In the short run, EC in Lao PDR is influenced by negative FDI of approximately –0.025%. It might be interpreted that when FDI flow in Lao PDR increases, it does not support EC in Lao PDR to move in the same direction. Additionally, the long-run results are also quite interesting because only the FDI inflow will be a positive important factor that influences EC in Lao PDR. It can be implied that the government of Lao PDR needs to plan electricity storage based on FDI inflow to ensure that this country does not lag behind or experience a shortage of electricity in the long-term period. Furthermore, the NARDL Model will be used to predict EC in Lao PDR depending on FDI inflow, which confirms that the trend to predict long-term EC in Lao PDR will be increasing at approximately 0.03%–0.10%, depending on the systematic phenomena of FDI or asymmetric phenomena of FDI.

Table 9. Display NARDL Model Estimation Results for the International Sector's Effect on EC in Lao PDR.

lnEC	Variable	Coefficient	Std. Error	t-Statistic	Prob.
	C	–2.353	15.247	–0.154	0.879
Long-run model	**LN_EC(-1)**	**–0.075**	**0.004**	**–18.568**	**0.000**
	LN_R_FDI	**0.028**	**0.015**	**1.908**	**0.074**
	R_FDI_POS	**0.104**	**0.023**	**4.578**	**0.000**
	R_FDI_NEG(-1)	0.007	0.041	0.182	0.858
	LN_POP	0.157	1.032	0.152	0.881
Short-run model	**D(R_FDI_NEG)**	**–0.025**	**0.013**	**–1.943**	**0.069**
				R-squared	0.742
				Adjusted R-squared	0.731
				Akaike info criterion	–3.990
				Schwarz criterion	–3.891
				Durbin–Watson stat	1.838

6. Conclusion, Policy Implication, and Future Studies

Based on the findings, Laos's EC has a positive relationship both with the FDI and GDP. But the previous EC and population of Laos have a negative relationship with this consumption for the period of 1998–2018. The results precisely show several issues and policies that have become a challenge to Laos's policymakers:

(1) The challenge of Laos's hydropower development and investment is the concern that these large-scale hydropower projects may damage the environment, especially the Mekong River and its tributaries. In addition to the Nam Ngum River project, China is also involved in several other hydropower projects, including projects in Don Sahong, Pak Beng, and Xayaburi.

(2) Neighbors of Laos are also worried that these hydropower projects will have an impact on the water flow. The governments of Thailand, Vietnam, and Cambodia have publicly opposed the expansion of hydropower projects in Laos. After a period of government economic liberalization, Myanmar has rapidly grown into a strong competitor in the field of energy infrastructure financing. Myanmar claims that its potential hydropower capacity is about 100 million kilowatts, far exceeding the current level of Laos. A large number of potential projects may steal funds for hydropower development that may have flowed into Laos.

(3) China's large investment in Laos, which is undoubtedly the largest foreign investor in Laos, has caused Laos to face a large amount of debt. According to the figures of the Laos government, as of the end of 2016, the total value of construction projects undertaken by Chinese companies in Laos reached USD6.7 billion, accounting for about 30.1% of the total budgetary expenditure for the Laos Infrastructure Upgrade

Program. These huge contracts have made Laos a member of the ASEAN Group and China's third largest contractor service export market.

(4) China's economic slowdown may not make it easier for the region to obtain low-cost hydropower construction funds. For several years, the planning department of the Chinese government has been encouraging foreign investment in strategic industries such as Southeast Asian hydropower projects. However, as the Chinese government's concerns about the bad loans of major banks have increased, the funds obtained by the Laos hydropower project seem to be gradually diminishing. The growing awareness of the social and environmental costs of dam construction by local residents has become another risk for such projects, which has affected investors' interest in projects in the region.

The most important point is that the energy planning capacity in Southeast Asia seems to far exceed the energy needs of the region. China was once considered to be a potential market for Laos's electricity, but today China's domestic electricity market has already "taken a step ahead" into overcapacity. At present, Thailand is still the main investor in the Laos's hydropower project, but Thailand has consistently overestimated its country's EC level, and there is still ample room for the country to reduce domestic electricity demand through energy-saving measures. At the same time, both Cambodia and Vietnam plan to reduce their dependence on imported electricity, and Vietnam has invested heavily in thermal power plants.

6.1. *Policy recommendation*

The future energy outlook in Laos is still unknown. Despite the many risks, the Lao Energy Planning Department still insists that prioritizing the development of energy is for the best of national security and stability. Last but not least, the AEC 2025 Blueprint (AEC, 2025) envisions an integrated, competitive, and resilient region and "a more dynamic and resilient ASEAN" that can address challenges, including energy security issues, which incorporate "a sustainable growth agenda" by promoting green technologies (ASEAN Secretariat, 2015). ASEAN's power connectivity from Laos seems too far to achieve. Our findings propose that Laos develops alternative energy from renewable energies such as solar, wind, and biomass which could be considered crucial topics to explore for energy enterprises for Laos in the near future.

References

ADB (2023). Lao People's Democratic Republic: Fact sheet. Asian Development Bank Member Fact Sheet.

Adom, PK and W Bekoe (2012). Conditional dynamic forecast of electrical energy consumption requirements in Ghana by 2020: A comparison of ARDL and PAM. *Energy*, 44(1), 367–380.

Aslan, A (2013). Causality between electricity consumption and economic growth in Turkey: An ARDL bounds testing approach. *Energy Sources, Part B: Economics, Planning, and Policy*, 9(1), 25–31.

Atsawathawichok, P, P Teekaput and T Ploysuwan (2014). Long term peak load forecasting in Thailand using multiple kernel Gaussian Process. *2014 11th International Conference on Electrical Engineering/Electronics, Computer, Telecommunications and Information Technology (ECTI-CON)*.

Bai, J and P Perron (1998). Estimating and testing linear models with multiple structural changes. *Econometrica*, 66(1), 47, https://doi.org/10.2307/2998540.

Bianco, V, O Manca and S Nardini (2009). Electricity consumption forecasting in Italy using linear regression models. *Energy*, 34(9), 1413–1421.

Bianco, V *et al.* (2010). Analysis and forecasting of nonresidential electricity consumption in Romania. *Applied Energy*, 87(11), 3584–3590.

Dergiades, T and L Tsoulfidis (2010). Revisiting residential demand for electricity in Greece: New evidence from the ARDL approach to cointegration analysis. *Empirical Economics*, 41(2), 511–531.

Fukuyo, K and N Hirohata (2019). Comparative study on energy consumption in the Asian landlocked countries. *IOP Conference Series: Earth and Environmental Science*, 294, 1–10.

Handayani, K, I Overland, B Suryadi and R Vakulchuk (2023). Integrating 100% renewable energy into electricity systems: A net-zero analysis for Cambodia, Laos, and Myanmar. *Energy Reports*, 10, 4849–4869.

IEA (2021). Analysis. World Energy Outlook 2021, https://www.iea.org/reports/world-energy-outlook-2021.

Ibrahiem, DM (2015). Renewable electricity consumption, foreign direct investment and economic growth in Egypt: An ARDL approach. *Procedia Economics and Finance*, 30, 313–323.

Inayoshi, N and S Nejime (2023). Lao PDR's electricity sector: Risk or opportunity? https://amro-asia.org/lao-pdrs-electricity-sector-risk-or-opportunity/.

Kaewkhunok, S (2018). The battery of ASEAN: The opportunity and lesson of India's energy security. *SADF Focus*, 39.

Kandananond, K (2011). Forecasting electricity demand in Thailand with an artificial neural network approach. *Energies*, 4, 1246–1257.

Kaynar, O, H Özekicioğlu and F Demirkoparan (2017). Forecasting of Turkey's electricity consumption with support vector regression and chaotic particle swarm algorithm. *Journal of Administrative Sciences*, 15(29), 211–224.

Kleebrang, W, P Bunditsakulchai and W Wangjiraniran (2017). Household electricity demand forecast and energy savings potential for Vientiane, Lao PDR. *International Journal of Sustainable Energy*, 36(4), 344–367.

Kyophilavong, P, D Souphonphacdy, S Komany and K Tounalom (2021). *Decarbonization in Lao PDR: The Options and Challenges*.

LMEC (2021). Lancang-Mekong Environmental Cooperation Center, http://en.lmec.org.cn/countries/202109/t20210907_123524.html.

Mezaa, C, C Li, L Koodlurc, M Goel, M Khujamberdierv and T Mumtaz (2013). Energy policy for landlocked countries. 1–6.

Mohamed, Z and P Bodger (2005). Forecasting electricity consumption in New Zealand using economic and demographic variables. *Energy*, 30(10), 1833–1843.

Mostafavi, ES *et al.* (2013). A novel machine learning approach for estimation of electricity demand: An empirical evidence from Thailand. *Energy Conversion and Management*, 74, 548–555.

OECD (2019). Structure policy country notes: Laos PDR. *Economic Outlook for Southeast Asia, China and India 2019*, 203–209.

OECD (n.d.). *OECD Investment Policy Reviews: Thailand*, https://www.oecd-ilibrary.org/sites/c4eeee1c-en/1/3/2/index.html.

Oum, S (2019). Energy poverty in the Lao PDR and its impacts on education and health. *Energy Policy*, 132, 247–253.

Pandian, SC *et al.* (2006). Fuzzy approach for short term load forecasting. *Electric Power Systems Research*, 76, 541–548.

Perron, P (1989). The great crash, the oil price shock, and the unit root hypothesis. *Econometrica*, 57(6), 1361, https://doi.org/10.2307/1913712.

Pesaran, MH, Y Shin and RJ Smith (2001). Bounds testing approaches to the analysis of level relationships. *Journal of Applied Econometrics*, 16(3), 289–326.

Pham, D, H Bui and T Duong (2018). The relationship between foreign direct investment, electricity consumption and economic growth in Vietnam. *International Journal of Energy Economics and Policy*, 8(3), 267–274.

Phimphachan, S *et al.* (2004). Energy and peak load forecast models using neural network for fast developing area. *IEEE International Symposium on Communications and Information Technology*, 389–393.

Phoumin, H and F Kimura (2019). The impacts of energy insecurity on household welfare in Cambodia: Empirical evidence and policy implications. *Economic Modelling*, 82, 35–41, https://doi.org/10.1016/j.econmod.2019.09.024.

Power Technology (n.d.). Top five hydro power plants in operation in Laos, https://www.power-technology.com/data-insights/top-five-hydro-power-plants-in-operation-in-laos/.

Raju, DV and M Kumar (2023). Laos expands the grid, https://www.tdworld.com/overhead-transmission/article/20963781/laos-expands-the-grid.

Sackdara, V, S Premrudeepreechacharn and K Ngamsanroaj (2010). Electricity demand forecasting of Electricite Du Lao (EDL) using neural networks. *TENCON 2010—2010 IEEE Region 10 Conference*.

Sang, GY and M Hernandez Alvarez (2018). Predicting residential electricity consumption using neural networks: A case study. *Journal of Physics: Conference Series*, 1–13.

Spiegelhalter, DJ, NG Best, BP Carlin and A Van Der Linde (2002). Bayesian measures of model complexity and fit. *Journal of the Royal Statistical Society Series B (Statistical Methodology)*, 64(4), 583–639, https://doi.org/10.1111/1467-9868.00353.

Shin, Y, B Yu and M Greenwood-Nimmo (2014). Modelling asymmetric cointegration and dynamic multipliers in a nonlinear ARDL framework. In Y Shin, B Yu, M Greenwood-Nimmo (eds), *Festschrift in Honor of Peter Schmidt*, 281–314, New York: Springer.

Tang, L *et al.* (2019). Long-term electricity consumption forecasting based on expert prediction and fuzzy Bayesian theory. *Elsevier*, 167, 1144–1154.

UNCTAD (n.d.). UN list of least developed countries, https://unctad.org/topic/least-developed-countries/list.

UN-OHRLLS (2016). Accelerating sustainable energy for all in landlocked developing countries through innovative partnerships. *UN-OHRLLS*, 8–15.

USAID (2020). Lao power sector vulnerability assessment and resilience action plan. In S Stout, N Lee, J Vogel, L Giangola, JE Leisch, *National Renewable Energy Laboratory (NREL)*. Resilient Energy Platform.

World Bank (2019). The World Bank in Lao PDR, https://www.worldbank.org/en/country/lao/overview.

https://doi.org/10.1142/9789819812608_0009

Chapter 9

Oil Prices and Stock Market Impact in Kazakhstan: Boosting Energy Security in the Transition Process[#]

MOLDIR MUKAN[*]

Narxoz University, Kazakhstan
moldir.mukan@narxoz.kz

YESSENGALI OSKENBAYEV

Narxoz University, School of Economics and Management, Zhandossov Str 55., Almaty, Kazakhstan

NIKI NADERI

Azad University Tehran North, Iran

YERGALI DOSMAGAMBET

Atyrau University of Oil and Gas, Kazakhstan

This study investigates the complex relationship between oil price fluctuations and stock market performance in Kazakhstan, a resource-dominant economy heavily dependent on oil exports. Using structural vector autoregression (VAR) analysis, we explore how both global oil supply and demand shocks influence Kazakhstan's stock market. Our findings show that aggregate demand shocks significantly affect stock market volatility, while oil production shocks have a more limited effect on financial stability. Given Kazakhstan's dependence on oil revenue, the country faces significant economic risks when oil prices fluctuate. These risks are further compounded by the ongoing global transition towards cleaner energy sources. This paper argues that to enhance energy security and ensure economic stability during this transition, Kazakhstan must diversify its energy sources, invest in renewable energy, and strengthen financial resilience. The development of green financial instruments and policies that promote energy transition will play a crucial role in safeguarding the country's long-term financial and energy security. Our study contributes to the existing literature by linking oil price volatility with the need for enhanced energy security strategies during Kazakhstan's energy transition.

Keywords: Stock market index; oil price volatility; Kazakhstan; VAR decomposition.

JEL Classification: G01, G32, Q31

[*]Corresponding author.

[#]This chapter is the updated version of the paper published in *The Singapore Economic Review*, Vol. 66, No. 2 (2021) 569–594 DOI: 10.1142/S0217590820430055. © 2021 World Scientific Publishing.

1. Introduction

The global financial crisis was accompanied by a sharp decrease in oil prices that significantly impacted many oil-exporting countries (see, e.g., Blinder and Kilian, 2009; Taghizadeh-Hesary and Yoshino, 2014; Yoshino and Taghizadeh-Hesary, 2014, 2016; Hesse and Poghosyan, 2016). Exports and government revenues have fallen considerably in resource-based economies, which adversely affected GDP growth. In 2008, the world economy entered a period of deep recession due to the most significant financial shock in developed financial markets. As the global economy shifts towards decarbonization and renewable energy adoption, countries like Kazakhstan face increasing pressure to reduce their reliance on fossil fuels. This transition underscores the need for comprehensive policies that integrate green finance tools to support the energy shift and maintain economic stability (Wang *et al.*, 2024).

Kazakhstan, like other oil-exporting nations, faced significant energy security challenges during these times. Movkebayeva *et al.* (2020) stress the importance of sustainability in energy security, especially as Kazakhstan works towards its 2040 energy transition goals. According to the International Monetary Fund (IMF) estimates, global economic growth slowed from 5.2% in 2007 to 3.2% in 2008. August 2007 can be considered the beginning of the crisis for Kazakhstan (National Bank of Kazakhstan, 2009). Listed companies that first felt the crisis consequences and defaulted were mostly from among the medium-sized firms that could not meet the requirements for issuers. In 2009, 16 issuers defaulted, including four large institutes, as well as three banks, even though the requirements for that period were significantly reduced. A buffer category had also been introduced in that period to allow companies to remain on the official list (Kazakhstan Stock Exchange Report, 2009).

In 2017, the trading volume in the money market reached its historical maximum of 151.5 trillion KZT, which is more than half as high as in previous years. The exchange markets showed positive dynamics, and the volume of transactions on the securities market increased as well, while the money market rose by more than 60%, and the foreign exchange market grew 17.6%. Equity market capitalization increased by 20% over the year to its historical maximum value of 17.1 trillion KZT. The volume of corporate debt on the KASE grew 8%. 110 issuers issued 128 shares, which also represented the historical maximum (Kazakhstan Stock Exchange Report, 2017).

The time-fluctuating relationship changed in reaction to oil price shocks in times of world turmoil. Recent research highlights the growing role of green finance as a catalyst for promoting renewable energy and addressing carbon emissions. This transition is critical to safeguarding Kazakhstan's energy security while reducing its dependence on volatile fossil fuel markets (Wang *et al.*, 2024). Warning demand shocks — which were caused by external changes in the world business cycle (e.g., the Asian crisis, worldwide financial crisis) — have considerably more impact on the connection between oil and securities exchange costs, and supply-side shocks appeared as a result of OPEC's development cuts and other different factors (e.g., Filis *et al.,* 2011; Komijani *et al.,* 2013).

Oil-exporting countries usually benefit from high oil prices, and their economies can easily recover from recessions. Furthermore, energy security is about the creation of special policy strategies to ensure the continuous availability of energy sources all over the world. The economies of most of the oil-exporting countries strictly depend on exports of energy resources. So far, most of the deep research on energy security focused on supply security for energy-importing countries. There is a standard definition of energy security which concerns supply security. However, for most of the energy-exporting countries, global energy security means sustainable energy export flows at "reasonable" prices that can ensure not only new energy investment but also general economic development, together with financial stability in the country (Energy Charter Secretariat, 2015).

There are direct and indirect channels through which the price of oil affects the economic situation of a country. Higher oil prices could increase government revenues from oil exports and lead to favorable conditions which boost higher domestic demand that in turn leads to higher confidence in banks, lending and declining non-performing loans. High oil prices also fuel public and private investment and thus increase the productive capacity of economies. This can be observed especially during the pre-crisis boom. With soaring oil prices, oil-exporting countries created investment programs to diversify the domestic economy and improve human capital; at the same time, higher oil prices often lead to increases in the rate of inflation (Taghizadeh-Hesary *et al.,* 2013, 2016).

Due to the availability of the resources in the country, Kazakhstan is mainly dependent on the oil-exporting function. Kazakhstan's energy transition is essential to both its economic stability and its long-term energy security. The increasing global focus on green finance, which supports renewable energy and sustainability projects, underscores the importance of diversifying Kazakhstan's energy sources (Wang *et al*., 2024). This means that when there are good economic conditions and financial stability, domestic demand will gradually increase. The first oil collapse faced by Kazakhstan led to a recession and its negative effects on Kazakhstan. Kazakhstan, as one of the oil-exporting countries, faced energy insecurity when the oil price collapsed, which has underscored the need for green finance mechanisms to ensure a resilient transition to renewable energy sources. The impact of fluctuating oil prices on financial markets, particularly in resource-dependent economies like Kazakhstan, has been well documented. Recent studies indicate that a move toward renewable energy can mitigate these price shocks and bolster energy security during the transition process (Duan *et al*., 2024). As global trends shift towards decarbonization, oil-exporting countries like Kazakhstan face increasing pressure to transition to renewable energy. Green finance mechanisms, such as green bonds, are becoming essential tools to fund this transition, ensuring long-term energy security and economic stability (Taghizadeh-Hesary *et al*., 2023). Oil price since July 2008, peaked at $147 per barrel, has damaged the commodity export-dependent economy. The recent oil price fluctuations further emphasize the importance of diversifying Kazakhstan's energy sources. By promoting renewable energy projects and integrating green finance, Kazakhstan can safeguard its economy against the volatility of global oil markets (Wang *et al*., 2024). According to the Ministry of Statistics, a full 70% of Kazakhstan's export revenue comes from oil, so oil prices are certainly crucial for the Kazakhstan economy and government revenue. When oil prices are rising, most oil-importing countries try to decrease their dependency on oil. In such situations, oil-exporting countries start to worry about "demand stability". In Table 1, it can be seen the same direction for both indicators: total revenue and oil price. When oil prices increase, the percentage of GDP from total government revenue in the

Table 1. Percentage of GDP from Total Government Revenue (Excluding Grants) and Average Oil Price (WTI, Dubai, Brent)

Year	% of GDP, Total Government Revenue (Excluding Grants)	Oil Price (Average, USD)
2009	22.14	61.81
2010	23.94	79.05
2011	27.04	104.06
2012	26.34	104.85
2013	24.75	103.99
2014	23.74	96.27
2015	16.61	50.74
2016	17.01	42.72
2017	20.30	52.68
2018	22.22	68.56

country also rises, which undoubtedly explains the influence of oil prices on the financial system of the oil-exporting country. However, in the years 2015–2016, the lowest oil prices and percentage of GDP from government revenue. In those years, oil prices declined by more than 50% because export revenues were cut by almost a half and there were twin deficits in the fiscal and current-account balances in 2015 (World Bank, 2015).

Thus, the oil price plunge adversely affected oil-exporting countries economic performance since oil price decline causes significant losses in export and fiscal revenues. This leads reassessment by investors of the credit and sovereign risks of oil-exporting countries which is amplified with limited sectoral diversification. The abrupt decline in oil prices is accompanied by capital outflows, losses in reserves, sharp depreciation of the domestic currency. Indeed, lower oil prices weaken the fiscal and external position of the oil-exporting country, and it significantly reduces the economic activity. The decline in oil prices deteriorates the sentiment of the investor about oil-exporting economies and could cause a considerable fluctuation in financial markets, as observed in several oil-exporting countries in the last quarter of 2014.[1]

Given the concentration of exports in resource-based countries in extractive industries, the link between oil prices and financial systems — including the banking sector — is of high policy interest, not only during a period of the financial crisis but also during boom-bust oil cycles. Do oil prices influence the financial system and its performance and if so, what could be the relevant channels through which financial systems are affected?

[1]Baffes *et al.* (2015) investigate the impact of oil price decrease for both oil-importing and oil-exporting countries which occurred in 2014. This was largely led by an increase in oil production of non-OPEC oil-exporting countries. The price decline caused real income shift from oil-exporting countries to oil-importing economies. Supply-driven oil price increase triggered overall GDP per capita increase and lowered inflation. While positive impact for oil importers is observed, this implied negative impact on oil exporters and in some cases underscored financial market pressure.

Energy security and the role of renewables have become critical components in discussions about Kazakhstan's future economic sustainability. As Mouraviev (2021) points out, policymakers are increasingly aware of the need to reduce reliance on fossil fuels to enhance national energy security. The purpose of this study is to provide an empirical investigation of these issues. The role of green finance is becoming increasingly prominent in the context of energy security. Policymakers in oil-exporting countries must not only mitigate the short-term impacts of oil price volatility but also create long-term strategies to transition to renewable energy sources, reducing exposure to the risks associated with fluctuating fossil fuel markets (Taghizadeh-Hesary *et al.*, 2023). Moreover, there is no clear consensus on the existence and the form of the relationship between oil price and stock performance. In this paper, we develop an econometric model of the impact of factors on the stock performance in Kazakhstan. Based on this data, the impact of oil price fluctuations on the financial system of an oil-producing country such as Kazakhstan is investigated. From the energy security perspective, what role does the oil price play in establishing the financial system via its impact on creditworthiness in Kazakhstan? The main objective of this study to show that oil price decline damages the financial markets of oil-exporting economies by deteriorating its creditworthiness. The paper is organized as follows. Section 2 provides a literature review, while Section 3 offers an overview of the Kazakhstan stock market and its current situation. Section 4 describes data and methods, with the results and some robustness checks. Section 5 is dedicated to conclusions and policy implications.

2. Literature Review

Oil prices are really important for economic development as well as the economic performance of oil-exporting countries. The need to develop the stock market in Kazakhstan has been researched for many years. At the same time, it has not become a real factor for economic growth. Meanwhile, the development of the domestic securities market today is becoming the most urgent topic. Recently, the efforts of the government and businesses have been aimed at solving this problem. Kazakhstan's stock market, despite obvious progress in some of its areas (the formation of collective investment institutions, the development of infrastructure, the improvement of the regulatory framework), continues to belong to the least developed sectors of the domestic financial system. In this regard, the foreign experience of the successful formation and growth of stock markets deserves attention. The experience of emerging markets is of great interest for Kazakhstan, since emerging markets are more comparable with Kazakhstan in terms of factors and prerequisites that determine the dynamics of growth.

Throughout the years, the connections between stock markets and oil prices have been the object of research (Sadorsky, 1999; Park and Ratti, 2008; Wang and Wu, 2012). Recent research suggests that green finance mechanisms can mitigate the negative effects of oil price volatility by promoting renewable energy investments and contributing to energy security in oil-exporting nations like Kazakhstan (Taghizadeh-Hesary *et al.*, 2021).

Shadrina (2018) highlights that cooperation in energy policies across Central Asian nations can also improve energy security, a critical consideration for Kazakhstan, which has historically been heavily reliant on oil revenues. There have been various investigative studies about the changes in oil prices and their influence on the stock market. Recent studies demonstrate that oil price shocks can significantly impact green investments, especially during periods of global uncertainty, influencing both the stock market and the green bond market (Liu *et al*., 2024). Most of these studies have concerned oil-exporting countries (Bjørnland, 2009; Bastianin *et al.,* 2016). Duan *et al.* (2024) emphasizes the importance of integrating green finance instruments to stabilize financial markets in oil-exporting countries. By developing frameworks for green bonds and renewable energy investments, countries like Kazakhstan can reduce their dependency on oil revenues and foster a more resilient economic structure. For example, some works have provided detailed descriptions of the interaction between oil prices and economic activity (Guo and Kliesen, 2005). Their results indicate that positive shocks in oil prices lead to a reduction in real stock returns, while shocks to real stock returns lead to a positive effect on interest rates and industry.

Similarly, a number of studies investigate both types of countries: oil-exporting and oil-importing. According to Khalfaoui *et al.* (2019), it can be seen that oil-importing countries may usually not respond similarly to oil price shocks. However, there is less evidence of interdependence between stock markets for both importing and exporting countries. The study reports that lagging volatility in the oil and stock markets has a statistically significant effect on current volatility in the respective markets. However, the results show that in general, an oil asset is relatively more important for oil-exporting countries than for oil-importing countries. Furthermore, some studies prove that in the Asian neighboring countries as India, Pakistan and China, the oil price volatility has negative overflow impacts because of the past shocks (pre-crisis period, after-crisis period). In any case, stock market returns of these emerging markets and fluctuating oil price returns have a less critical impact on each other (Sarwar *et al.,* 2020).

Moreover, there is also evidence that oil price volatility shocks have dissymmetrical effects on the economic activity of a country. In particular, positive oil price shocks have a greater impact on stock returns and economic activity than do negative oil price shocks (Sadorsky, 1999). However, in many countries, the oil price does not have any impact on real stock returns (see, e.g., Sadorsky, 1999; Park and Ratti, 2008). In contrast, green finance initiatives can help stabilize financial markets by integrating sustainable investments into national economic strategies, particularly during periods of oil price shocks (Du *et al*., 2024). Considering the behavior of currency value, some studies argue that a rise in real oil prices leads to a significant depreciation of the dollar against the currencies of the oil exporter, such as Canada, Mexico and Russia. For countries like Kazakhstan, green finance offers a path to stabilize currency values by reducing reliance on oil exports and fostering investments in renewable energy (Chang *et al*., 2023). On the other hand, the currencies of oil importers, such as Japan, depreciate against the dollar when the real price of oil rises (Radhamés and Mollick, 2010).

Bernanke (2016) shows that a positive correlation between reserves and oil may arise because they both respond to underlying changes in global demand. The premise is that commodity prices, long-term interest rates and the dollar are likely to react to investors' perception of global and US demand, and not so much to changes in oil supplies. Arouri *et al.* (2010) examined the relationship between shocks that occurred in oil prices and stock returns within the period 2005–2008 among countries exporting oil. According to the conducted study, stock returns in oil-exporting countries such as Oman, Qatar, Saudi Arabia and the UAE respond to changes in oil prices, although changes that had occurred in oil prices in Bahrain and Kuwait did not affect their stock returns. As oil-exporting nations grapple with the challenges posed by fluctuating oil prices, green finance has emerged as a viable solution to enhance financial stability. These mechanisms not only support energy security but also align with global climate commitments and economic diversification strategies (Taghizadeh-Hesary *et al*., 2024).

Karatayev & Hall (2020) further point out that establishing energy security in resource-exporting nations like Kazakhstan will require significant investment in both energy efficiency and renewable energy infrastructure.

While there is abundant literature on the oil price and stock performance nexus in oil-exporting countries, there is no clear consensus on the impact of oil prices on stock performance. Sadorsky (2001) observed that the oil price is positively associated with Canadian stock returns during the 1990s. Many studies indicate a positive link between oil price and stock performance. For example, Boyer and Filion (2009) find a positive impact of oil price on stick returns in Canada from 1995 to 2002. Mohanty *et al.* (2011) also document the positive relationship between oil price and stock performance in the Gulf Cooperation Council (GCC) countries.

However, Singhal *et al.* (2019) find a negative impact of oil prices on stock performance in Mexico. Although Mexico is an oil-exporting country, crude oil exports account for only 6% and manufacturing items contribute to 70% of total exports. Thus, the oil price impact increase squeezes out manufacturing sector due to high costs of production in that sector. Rahman and Serletis (2019) detect negative and statistically significant effects of increased oil prices on stock market returns using US high-frequency data. This is interesting finding considering that the US is becoming a leading oil-exporting country. More recently, Shahrestani and Rafei (2020) investigate and find that the oil price positively and negatively influences the stock market using VAR model for Tehran stock exchange data. Mokni (2020) also finds the negative reaction of the stock market to oil-supply shocks, while the positive reaction is observed to oil-demand shocks.

While oil-exporting countries often benefit from high oil prices, reliance on oil revenues exposes these economies to significant risks. Green finance offers a pathway to diversify and build resilience in the face of oil price volatility (Taghizadeh-Hesary *et al*., 2024).

For Kazakhstan, which is heavily reliant on fossil fuel exports, Azhari *et al.* (2021) note that fluctuations in oil prices can have a strong impact on financial markets, but green bonds and renewable energy projects offer a pathway to mitigate these risks. Energy-exporting countries place their main emphasis on maintaining "demand stability", while the developed countries pay great attention to sufficient supply at affordable prices (Gallis, 2006) from energy security perspectives. For large industrialized countries, it is the constant supply of energy that stimulates their economies and helps maintain a high quality of life. For countries with low-income populations, this is a vital component for moving out of poverty. Oil and gas exporters were able to make unanticipated profits from high oil and gas prices. However, their trade relations with importers may ultimately suffer as a result of the negative impact of high energy prices on economic growth, although there are still few signs of this (World Bank, 2005). Furthermore, energy security leads to the creation of special policy strategies for the continuous availability of energy sources all over the world. The economies of many countries strictly depend on the export of energy resources. This means that the balance of payments of the oil-exporting countries is affected by the vulnerability value of oil and gas trades (Speight, 2011). Having a good political strategy concerning energy security leads to higher aggregate demand for energy resources. The "stable demand" can directly affect and increase the population's confidence in banks, and they will not fear to take and returning loans.

However, the resilience of renewable energy stock returns to oil price uncertainty effects may stem from the fact that the economics of the renewable energy sector has become very competitive in recent years. Therefore, renewables can compete successfully with oil, even when the price of oil fluctuates around the recent low levels. Furthermore, the resilience of the renewable energy sector can be explained by the fact that developing countries, such as China, India and Middle East countries, experience rapid economic growth that is accompanied by growing energy demand. Finally, the insignificant effect of oil price uncertainty on the stock returns might be a possible explanation for the symmetrical relationship between oil prices and stock returns (Kyritsis and Serletis, 2019).

3. Status of the Stock Market in Kazakhstan

3.1. *Overview of the stock market in Kazakhstan*

The Kazakhstan Stock Exchange (KASE) is a trading platform for Kazakhstan that gives a wide scope of services for trading in shares, corporate and government securities, foreign currencies and so forth. A mix of various markets on one exchanging stage is an interesting advantage of the KASE, and it permits clients of the Exchange to deal with their ventures adequately. KASE businesses include securities listing and the admission of other financial instruments to trading, the arrangement of trading in financial instruments using various appropriate trading methods for various financial instruments (including pre-trading and post-trading procedures), acting as book-runners when offering securities, clearing and settlements on certain exchange markets and market risk management as well as selling market information and providing technological solutions.

The global economic recovery occurred in 2017 at a faster rate than predicted. The world's GDP grew by 3.7%, with an increase in this indicator in 120 countries. This number is three-quarters of the world's gross product. This is the steadiest and synchronized rise that the world economy has seen since 2010. Most international financial institutions made an upward revision of their forecasts for world GDP growth rates in 2017. The forecast was positive for the next year but unfortunately, the barrel price for Brent crude oil fell to \$61.64 in November 2018, which was the lowest since the beginning of that year. WTI crude oil is traditionally cheaper than Brent. The difference in prices between them is determined by local and fundamental market factors, including composition, ease of transportation and speed of delivery. According to the results of trading in shares on the KASE on 29 December 2018, the KASE Index value decreased by 20.51 points (0.88%) from 2,325.45 to 2,304.94 (Bloomberg, 2017).

Table 2. Trading Volume on KASE Market in 2018 Compared to 2017, in Million US$

KASE Market	2018	2017
Securities Market	**13,864.2**	10,575.7
Shares	1,534.5	828.9
Corporate debt securities	6,449.8	3,482.5
Kazakhstan GS	4,722.3	6,137.2
IFI bonds	288.3	124.0
Investment trust securities	1,3	3.2
Foreign exchanges market	**39,065.0**	37,726.3
Money market	**319,180.3**	**419,318.3**
Repo transactions	220,628.5	226,545.8
Currency swap transactions	98,551.8	192,772.5
Derivatives market	0	66.2
Total trading volume	**372,109.5**	467,686.5

Notes: GS — Government securities; IFI bonds — international financial institutional bonds (KASE).

The KASE is one of the least developed sectors of the domestic financial system due to the influence of external factors that hamper its development. In many developed countries, stock markets are very popular and function successfully. Trading platforms become attractive due to the transparency of transactions in the stock market, which attracts not only investors but also issuers. Until recently, for Kazakhstan's stock market, these words did not mean much. If we assess the current state of the KASE, there are still a few tools on the market and the volumes of trade exchanges are weak (see, Table 2). In this paper, we consider the influence of world oil price volatility on the KASE stock index. Unfortunately, on the graph below, there is the anomalous behavior of the two variables. This chart shows the correlation between the oil market and the stock index. From December 2008 to May 2016, there is a negative correlation, which reflects the abnormal reaction of the stock index to the volatility of oil prices. It should be noted that this period includes the global mortgage crisis that began in the United States in 2008. The basic principle recommends the convergence of the trends for shares and oil, the growth of shares alongside the growth of oil and the reduction of shares with a decrease in oil, which confirms the positive relationship during the first half of the period from August 2000 to August 2008. Recently, however, there has been a decline in the stock market, and these movements were recently accompanied primarily by rising oil prices. This trend of falling shares alongside rising oil prices is rather unusual. The basic principle is to raise oil prices, which is seen as a positive factor for the economy, at least for oil-exporting countries like Kazakhstan.

On the eve of the crisis, the country's economy showed very good macroeconomic indicators: a significant surplus in the consolidated budget, a rapid increase in gold and

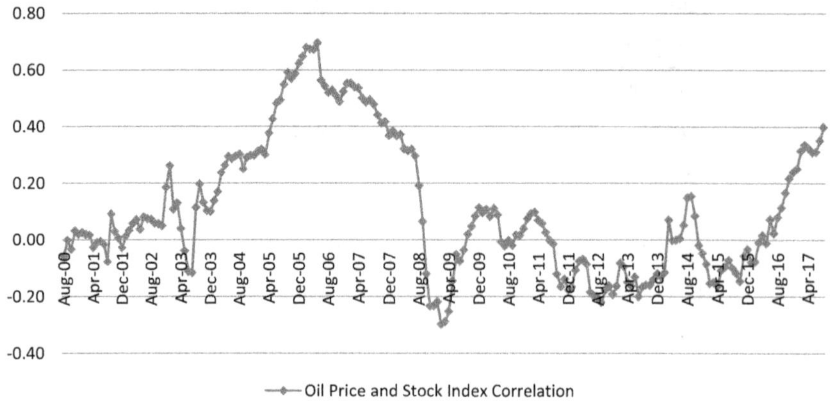

Source: Bloomberg (2017).

Figure 1. Correlation of Oil Prices and Stock Market Index

foreign exchange reserves and funds in the National Fund and accumulating revenues from the oil sector. However, despite good indicators, negative signs were already becoming apparent: rising inflation, growing unemployment, as well as rapid wage growth with low labor productivity. The years of crisis can be considered 2008 and 2009, while 2010 and 2011 can be considered as years of overcoming the crisis and economic recovery. Although the crisis in the financial sector started back in 2007, the whole economy felt it only in 2008. The worst problems in the economy happened in 2009 and all sectors were affected. Only in 2011 was the crisis more or less overcome. However, in Figure 1, from 2011 to 2015, there were also negative correlations between oil prices and the stock market index. The fall in oil prices in 2011 was due to several factors. The key one was the fear of a repeat of the global recession, which would entail a significant weakening in demand for raw materials. Recession leads to a reduction in the production of goods and services, which in turn leads to a decrease in derivative energy carriers and the consumption of oil. Additional pressure on oil prices was exerted by the situation in the international currency market: the dollar was steadily growing against major reserve currencies. On the other hand, after the crisis, the Kazakhstani economy started to develop and grow. Due to Kazakhstan's openness and the impact of the export of raw materials, which make up the lion's share of the country's income, the economy will continue to depend on the situation in international markets. Almost all countries applied unprecedented amounts of stimulation to their economies. On 20 August 2015, the government announced the transition to a floating KZT exchange rate, as a result of which the local currency lost almost 40% of its value against the US dollar the next day. The fall in commodity prices on world markets led to a further devaluation of the Kazakhstan currency. In 2015, the country faced a real crisis stronger than that in the period 2007–2009.

In July 2007, the KASE index reached a record of 2,708 points, and then it maintained a plateau near the historical maximum throughout the year. The KASE index can be considered as a barometer for Kazakhstan's economy. At first glance, it appears that the high level of the KASE from July 2007 until 2008 indicates a period of economic prosperity.

3.2. *Historical trends and current status of the stock market in Kazakhstan*

The history of the KASE began in late 1993. In November 1993, the national currency — the tenge — was first launched in the Kazakhstani economy, and a few days later, the stock market was introduced as well. In the beginning, the KASE was called the Kazakhstan Interbank Currency Exchange. The first role of the exchange was foreign currency trading. From the moment of its launch, the KASE has been the only exchange in Kazakhstan operating the stock and currency markets.

The KASE's traditional partnership with professional participants provides a mutually acceptable balance between the interests of the Exchange as a commercial institution and those of its members, who are the consumers of its services. In 1998, the KASE first introduced the system of "nego" deals, one year after it launched new corporate bond trading. In early 1999, the development of corporate bonds placed on the stock exchange started, and the first corporate bonds were incorporated into the official trading list on 1 February 1999. The year 1999 also saw the beginning of the stock trade's area of repo exchanges on government securities, starting on 5 July, and the holding of the primary sale on government bond flotation on 7 July. Since October 2013, the KASE has achieved membership in the World Federation of Exchanges (WFE). At present, the Exchange is an all-inclusive financial market which can be restrictively separated into five noteworthy segments: the government securities market, shares and corporate securities market, the repo market, the derivatives market and the foreign currency market. As of 1 December 2018, the KASE has 52 shareholders, including banks, broker-dealer organizations, asset management companies and other financial organizations.

According to the latest KASE report, at the end of December 2018, the KASE index fell to 2,280.10 points. Short-term borrowing rates showed a steady decrease, and demand for short-term notes completely failed to achieve the expected results. The growing currency supply was challenged by a negative external background. Meanwhile, by the time of the closing of currency trading on the KASE, Brent oil prices lost more than 10% and began to cost only US$54 per barrel.

As for oil release by Kazakhstan, its share of global oil production in 2015 amounted to 1.82%. In 2000, this proportion was 0.98%. Compared with the countries' of Cooperation of Independent States (CIS) oil producers, the increase in production of oil in Kazakhstan amounted to 224.6% in the period from 2000 to 2015. During these 15 years, oil production in Kazakhstan averaged 80.2 million tons, given the development of existing oil fields. This level is close to the limit (RFCA Rating Agency, 2016). For several years, oil production in Kazakhstan was stagnating and remained at about 80 million tons, but since 2017, there has been a tendency to increase. Kazakhstan ranks eighth in the world in explored oil reserves 11–12 billion tons, and in total, there are 200 fields (RFCA Rating Agency, 2017). Supported by robust oil production, the economy expanded at an annual rate of 4.1% in the first half of 2018, down slightly from a growth rate of 4.3% for the same period in 2017. Oil output rose by 6.2% year-on-year in the first half of 2018, supported by stronger-than-expected production from the Kashagan oil field. However, expansion was below that posted for the same period in 2017 (9.7%) (World Bank, 2018).

3.3. *The financial system of Kazakhstan*

In many developed countries, stock markets are very popular and function successfully. Trading platforms become attractive due to the transparency of transactions in the stock market, thereby attracting not only investors but also issuers. Until recently, these words did not mean much to Kazakhstan's stock market. The Kazakhstan stock market is currently in an evolving stage, although over the past few years, it has gained good ground. The stock market plays an important role in the economy of the country, ensuring the redistribution of capital from investors to issuers operating in various sectors of the economy of Kazakhstan. At present, the infrastructure of the stock market as a whole meets international requirements. The necessary institutions have been created and are successfully functioning to ensure the operation of the market, including the stock exchange, a central depository, a single registrar and a clearing organization. To attract investors to the securities market, Kazakhstan provides various tax incentives, exempting investor income received from trades of stocks and bonds on the Exchange, as well as dividends and other remuneration for securities.

To determine the rankings of the Global Competitiveness Index (GCI), research is provided through 12 pillars of each country's performance. The pillars include the indicators of the infrastructure, health, macroeconomic situation of the country, financial market development, labor productivity, etc. Kazakhstan's competitive performance decreased for four ranks during the past two periods. While from 2016 to 2017 it took the 53rd place, from 2017 to 2018 it took the 57th place (Schwab, 2018). However, growth is still observed. High oil production and expanded movement in trade and assembling led to the economic development in Kazakhstan. Exports have added to an improvement in the external current account. Besides, inflation has been kept in check, and the National Bank of Kazakhstan has undertaken policy rate cuts. Price stability should continue to be the focus of monetary policy going forward, especially because of the potential inflationary effects of recent pressures on the tenge-dollar exchange rate (International Monetary Fund, 2018).

Another factor that can influence the financial system of the country is the currency value on the international exchange. Nomura securities presented an analysis of the susceptibility of developing countries to currency crises (Nomura, 2018). The so-called Damocles index (a reference to the sword of Damocles in ancient Greek mythology) ranks 30 emerging markets (countries) by their degree of exposure to currency crises. The index is based on 13 indicators — taking into account such macroeconomic factors as the size of foreign exchange reserves, external debt, imports, budget deficit and current accounts — that taken together predict the risk of a currency crisis in the country during the next 12 months. Nomura's analysis identifies some countries with very low risk of currency shocks, including Brazil, Indonesia, Russia and Kazakhstan. The authors of the report noted a significant decrease in the risk of currency shocks in Kazakhstan in comparison with the pre-crisis period and against the backdrop of economic recovery and prudent macroeconomic policies. The economy of Kazakhstan recovered from the oil shock of 2014, thanks to a floating exchange rate, prudent macroeconomic policies, the restoration of oil prices and the return of economic growth in Russia. As a result, the value of the Damocles index fell to zero, which indicates an extremely low currency risk.

4. Empirical Analysis

4.1. *Data description and analysis*

This study employs a structural vector autoregression (VAR) model. Firstly, the VAR model was proposed by Sims (1980). In his investigation, he created a model as a simultaneous equation in which there was an exact description of the behavior of variables. In the equations, he suggested that the past movements of the variables could affect the behavior of current variables. VAR or vector autoregression takes the linear combinations of all including time-series variables in econometric models. Moreover, the VAR model is considered as flexible in the forecasting of the variables. We use this model as our paper is based on the previous study of Kilian (2009). In his study, there is shown how we can decompose the price of oil into structural shocks and make the decomposition of forecast error variance. The model is based on monthly time series data for Kazakhstan, during the period from August 2000 to August 2017 (a total of 205 observations). Concerning the empirical strategy, in our regression for the z_t variable, there are included: $prod_t$, rea_t, rpo_t and $kase_t$, where $prod_t$ is the change in percentage of world crude oil production, rea_t is real economic activity, rpo_t is the real oil price and $kase_t$ is the stock index. The data was collected on world oil production from the Bloomberg database to calculate the log-differences in global oil production pumped in millions of barrels per day (averaged monthly). The real economic activity is an index mentioned in the previous works of Kilian (2009). The "real economic activity" component is estimated as a real freight rate index, which indicates the demand for industrial commodities worldwide. The index, as mentioned by Kilian (2009), is calculated from dry cargo ocean freight rates and is deflated by the Consumer Price Index (CPI) to convert it into real terms. To remove the long-term trend and thus single out the global business cycle, the real freight rate index is linearly detrended. See Kilian (2009) for a detailed description of the construction of this global real economic activity measure.

Figure 2 exhibits the historical development of the time series discussed above (log change of crude oil production $\Delta\, prod_t$, the real economic activity rea_t, log of the real price of oil rpo_t, log change of stock index KASE $\Delta\, kase_t$, real exchange rate rer_t) for the period 2000:08 to 2017:08. Interestingly, crude oil prices soared from the beginning of 2000 to 2008. The same pattern is documented for the log detrended index of real economic activity. This was at its highest in 2008, and there was a dramatic decline around 2010. The percentage change in global crude oil production was relatively stable and exhibited high volatility during the period considered.

4.2. *Structural VAR estimates*

The structural vector autoregression estimates are based on Kilian (2009) as follows:

$$Bz_t = \gamma + \sum_{i=1}^{p} \Gamma_i z_{t-i} + \varepsilon_t, \tag{1}$$

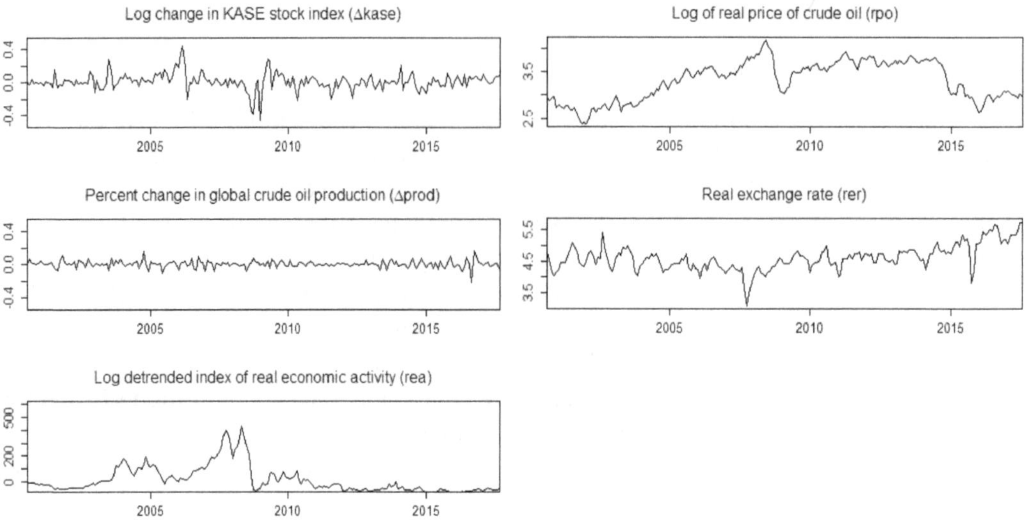

Figure 2. Historical Development for the Time Series 2000:08–2017:08

where $\boldsymbol{\gamma}$ is a vector parameter, $\boldsymbol{\Gamma}_i$ and $\boldsymbol{B}$ denote the lagged and contemporaneous coefficient matrices, respectively, and $\boldsymbol{\varepsilon}_t$ is a vector of mutually and serially uncorrelated structural innovations.

Considering that $\boldsymbol{B}^{-1}$ exists, the reduced-form representation of Equation (1) is

$$z_t = \boldsymbol{\alpha} + \sum_{i=1}^{p} A_i z_{t-i} + \boldsymbol{e}_t, \tag{2}$$

where $\alpha = \boldsymbol{B}^{-1}\boldsymbol{\gamma}$, $\boldsymbol{A}_i = \boldsymbol{B}^{-1}\boldsymbol{\Gamma}_i$, and the reduced form innovations, $\boldsymbol{e}_t$, are linear combinations of the structural shocks, $\boldsymbol{\varepsilon}_t$, $\boldsymbol{e}_t = \boldsymbol{B}^{-1}\boldsymbol{\varepsilon}_t$. The reduced-form Equation (2) is estimated and the structural shocks, $\boldsymbol{\varepsilon}_t$, are recovered by imposing zero (exclusion) restrictions on the elements of $\boldsymbol{B}$. The structural moving average representation is used to infer impulse responses. We follow Kilian (2009) to force a square recursive structure on the contemporaneous connection between the decreased form of VAR innovations and the basic auxiliary structural statics. In particular, it is assumed that $\boldsymbol{B}^{-1}$ has a recursive structure such that the reduced-form innovations, $\boldsymbol{e}_t$, can be decomposed according to $\boldsymbol{e}_t = \boldsymbol{B}^{-1}\boldsymbol{\varepsilon}_t$, as follows:

$$\boldsymbol{e}_t = \begin{pmatrix} e_t^{\Delta\text{prod}} \\ e_t^{\text{rea}} \\ e_t^{\text{rpo}} \\ e_t^{\text{rer}} \end{pmatrix} = \begin{pmatrix} b_{11} & 0 & 0 & 0 \\ b_{21} & b_{22} & 0 & 0 \\ b_{31} & b_{32} & b_{33} & 0 \\ b_{41} & b_{42} & b_{43} & b_{44} \end{pmatrix} = \begin{pmatrix} \varepsilon_t^{\text{oil supply shock}} \\ \varepsilon_t^{\text{aggregate demand shock}} \\ \varepsilon_t^{\text{oil-specific demand shock}} \\ \varepsilon_t^{\text{real exchange rate}} \end{pmatrix}.$$

4.3. *Structural VAR estimates*

To check our variables to see whether they are stationary or not, we use the analysis of the Augmented Dickey–Fuller unit root testing. All our variables are expressed in real terms, meaning that they are deflated by consumer price index. The monthly data from 2000:08 to 2017:08 is used (see, Table 3).

In the next step, we provide the impulse response function for each variable, but first, the cross-equation covariance matrix is built, which is presented in Table 4.

The impulse response function measures the temporal profile of the effect of shock on the behavior of a series (Koop *et al.*, 1996). We take the impulse response functions in our research because they are very useful tools for studying the interactions between variables in a vector autoregressive model. They represent the reactions of the variables to shocks hitting the system. Moreover, the impulse response functions are presented in rates. In Figures 3(a)–3(e), the impulse responses are resulting from the observed variables responding to each other. Figure 3(a) shows the impulse responses resulting from a kase shock to kase, oil prices, industrial production, real economic activity, and real exchange rate. If we take the reaction of the shock to each variable separately, the impulse response function of the kase shock to kase is significantly positive during all periods under review. The kase shock to the real exchange rate is slightly negative during the time profile of 5 to

Table 3. Unit Root Tests

	Series in Level		Series in First Difference	
	Without Trend	With Trend	Without Trend	With Trend
Kase	–9.374***	–0.5868	–7.399***	0.1379
Rea	–1.988	–1.279	–8.937***	–0.4271
Prod	–7.787***	–2.713***	–8.854***	0.3133
Rpo	–1.928	–0.1743	–11.86***	–0.9086
Rer	0.02066	1.873*	–7.955***	1.954*

Notes: ADF: Augmented Dickey-Fuller Test. Rejection of the null hypothesis at the 5% (respectively, 1%) significance level.
*Significant, ***Extremely significant.

Table 4. Cross-Equation Covariance Matrix

	Kase	rea	prod	Rpo	rer
Kase	0.0064	0.2408	–0.0001	0.0020	–0.0016
Rea	0.2408	635.84	0.2039	0.4637	–0.6702
Prod	–0.0001	0.2039	0.0009	0.0100	–0.0005
Rpo	0.0021	0.4637	0.0100	0.0055	–0.0002
Rer	–0.0016	–0.6702	–0.0005	–0.0002	0.0240

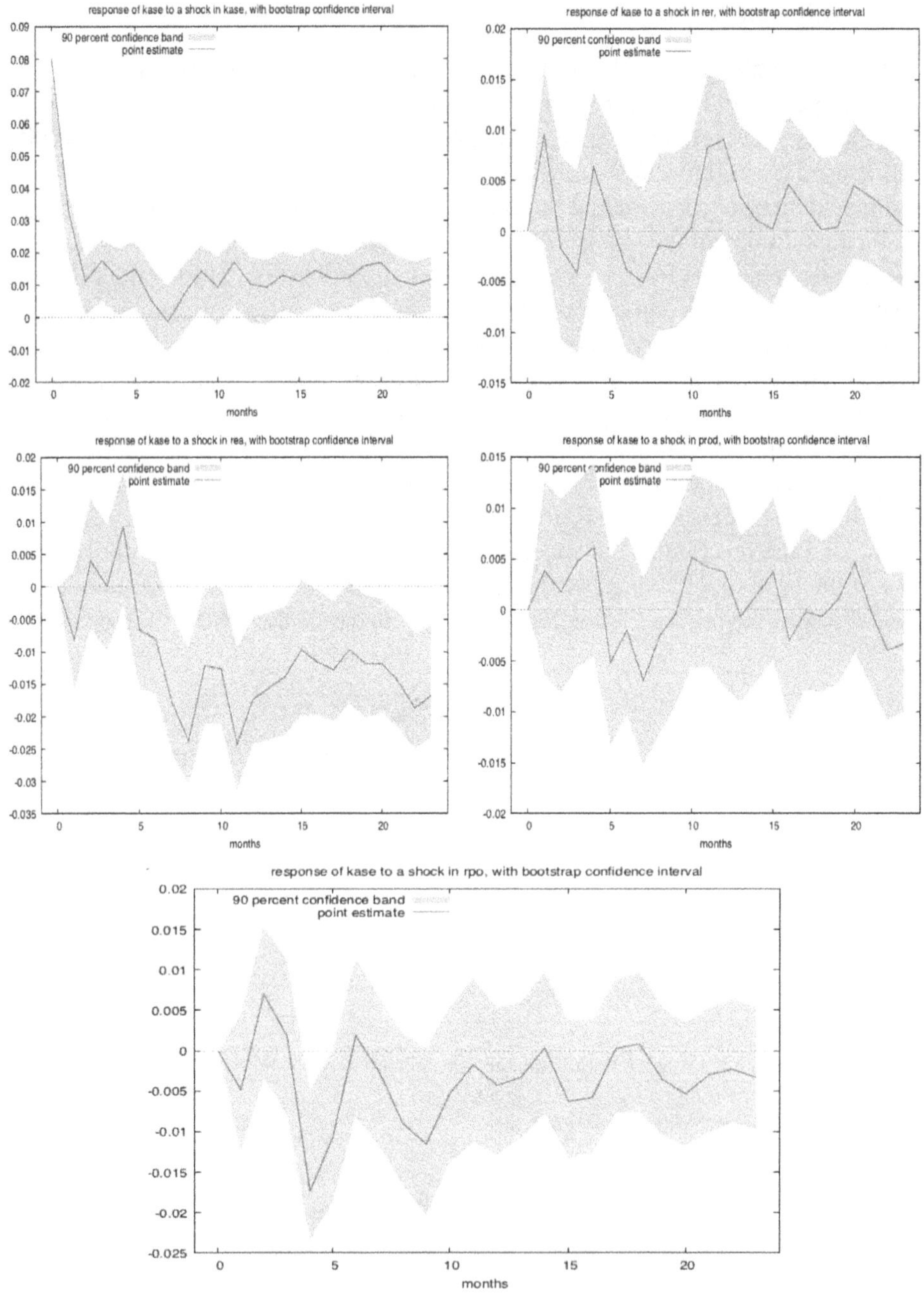

(a)

Source: Authors' compilation.

Figure 3. (a) IRF of *kase*, (b) IRF of *rea*, (c) IRF of *prod*, (d) IRF of *rpo* and (e) IRF of *rer*

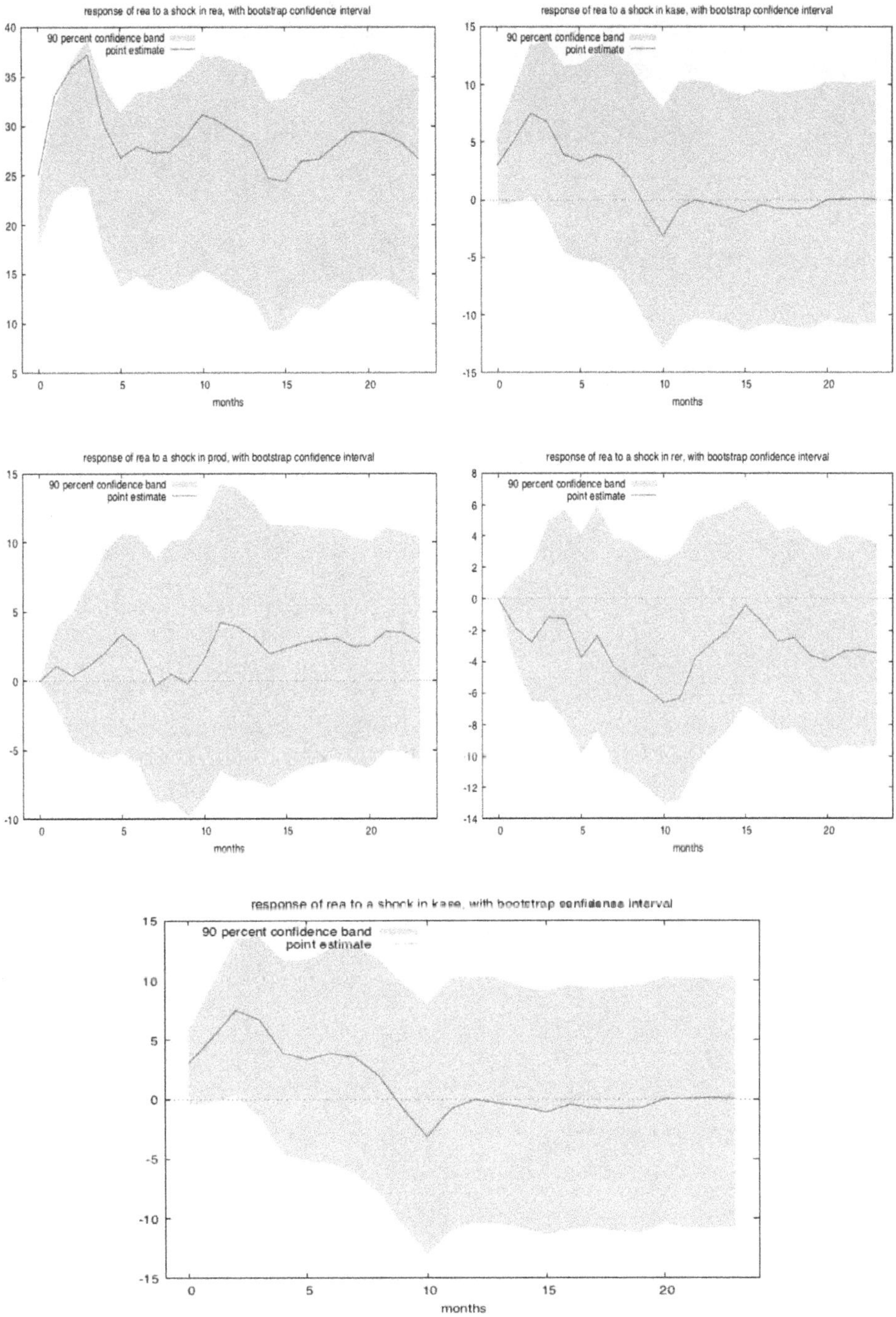

(b)

Figure 3. (*Continued*)

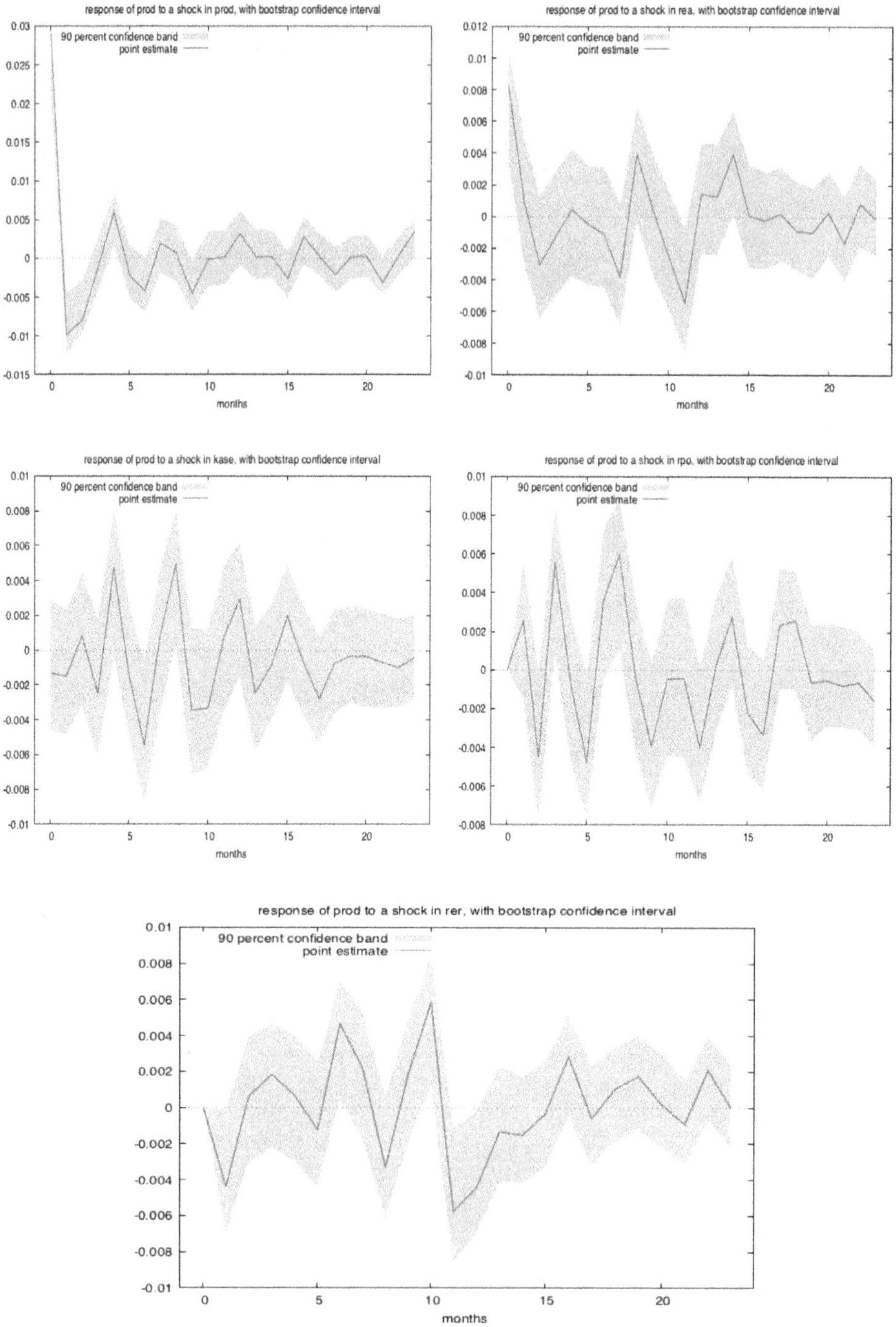

(c)

Figure 3. (*Continued*)

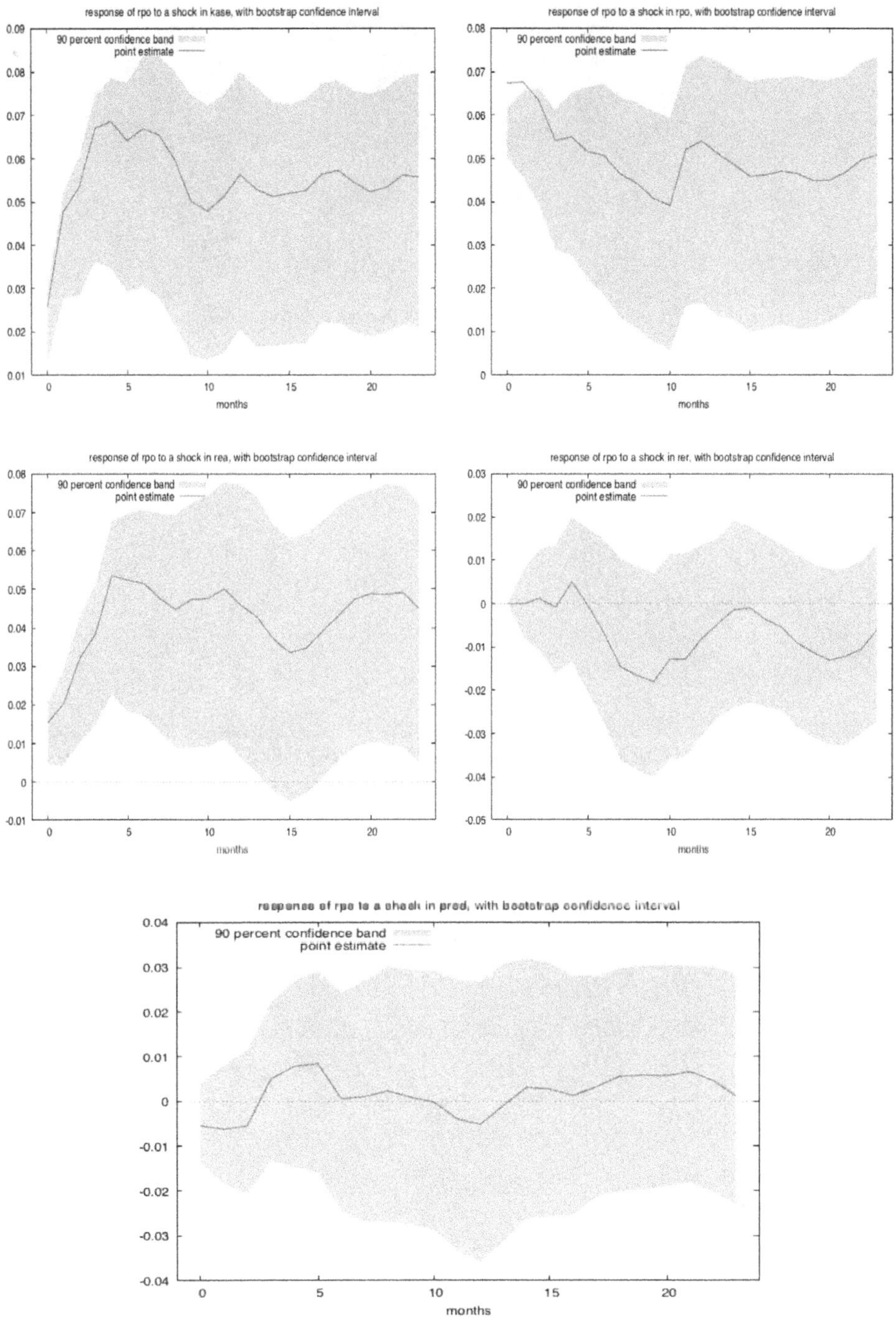

(d)

Figure 3. (*Continued*)

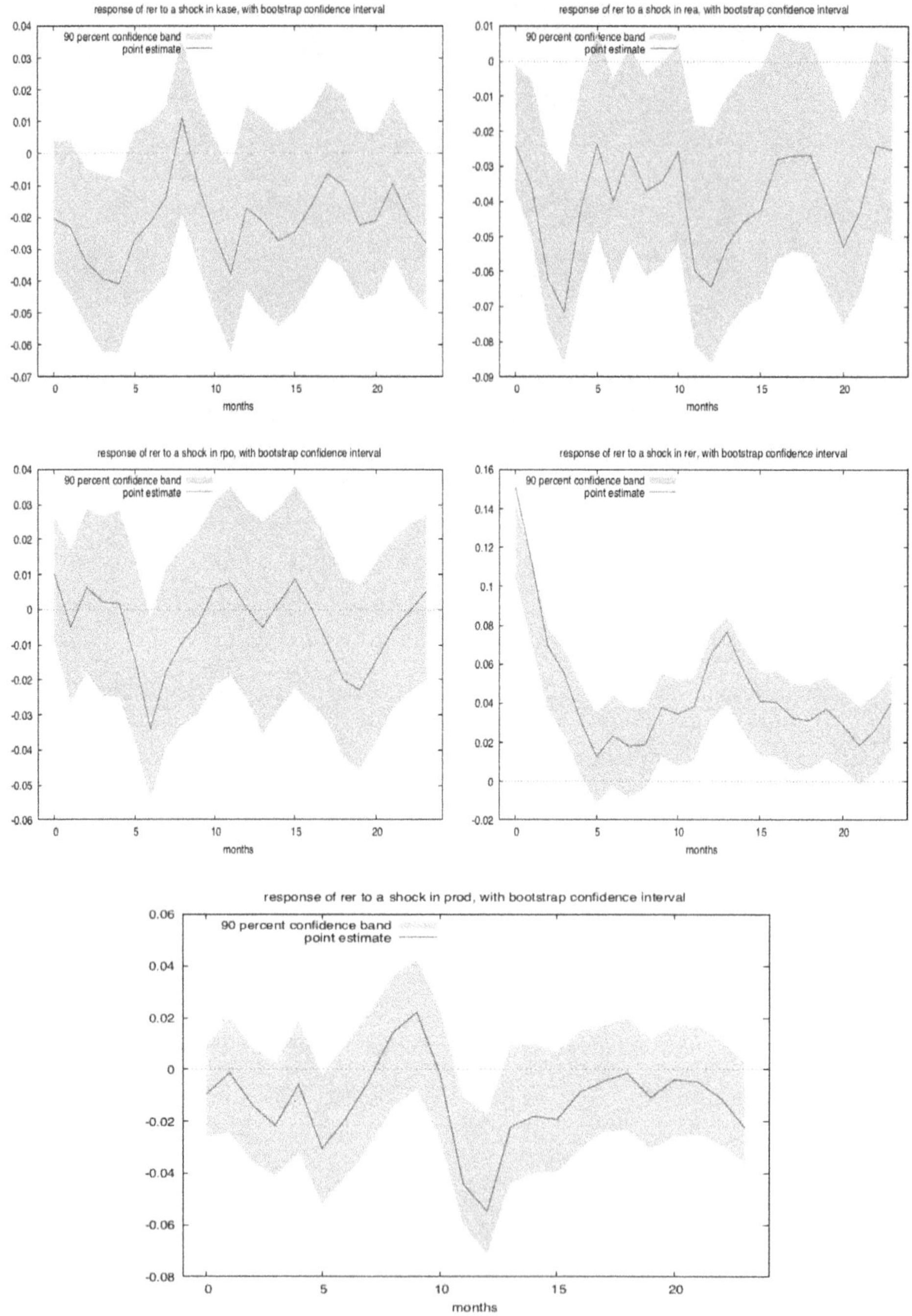

(e)

Figure 3. (*Continued*)

10 months. The stock index is one of the main indicators of the Kazakhstan Stock Exchange, characterized by a moderate decline, an average level of investor confidence and trade in Kazakhstan tenge and US dollars. The impulse response function to real economic activity is negative for nearly all of the proposed period, while negative to production for only a certain timeline. The rapid economic growth in the country should be reflected in the rapid growth of the stock market of this country. As a result, the stock markets of developing countries are attractive to investors because they have a higher expected yield than the markets of developed countries in which the economic growth rate is significantly lower. In this case, it is usually noted that the risk, which is considered as expected volatility, is higher for emerging markets. Furthermore, the liquidity of the stock market and the financial development of the banking sector positively correlate with future economic growth and productivity in the country (Levine and Zervos, 1998). The impulse response function of the kase index to real oil price is also negative during all periods under study. Some studies conclude that the maximum positive stimulating effect on an oil-producing country is reached approximately 14 to 15 months, after which the effect dies out (Bjørnland, 2009).

Figure 3(b) shows that a real economic activity shock has a large and statistically significant positive impact on the kase index, production and real oil price. Changes in real economic activity affect real exchange rates for several reasons. The long-term trend of the tenge exchange rate is influenced by fundamental factors, which mainly include oil prices, the exchange rates of the countries that are the main trading partners, as well as the state of the balance of payments, the inflation rate, the base rate of the National Bank and world interest rates. There is no pressure on the tenge in terms of the real exchange rate index. Moreover, the tenge rate seems undervalued. Now, relatively speaking, buying goods and services in Kazakhstan is more profitable than it was before the last devaluations. So, the demand for tenge should remain quite high, supporting the national currency. Besides, a decrease in the index can positively affect the trade balance and the balance of services, which is also good for the economy. Figure 3(c) indicates the impulse response function of the production shock to other variables. In Figure 3(d), we see the impulse response function of the oil price shock. In this case, it most positively affects the variables except for the real exchange rate. However, in Figure 3(e), the real exchange rate shock has a significantly negative impact on all variables, except for the real exchange rate itself. The monetary policy of Kazakhstan depends on the prices of raw materials as well as the foreign exchange rates. Hence, the real exchange rate depends mainly on the oil price, production in the country, stock market development and the overall economic activity in the country.

The dissociation of forecast error variance in Table 5 allows us to assess the influence of crude oil market structural shocks on the variability of the KASE index, as well as the impact of structural shocks (and volatility) in the crude oil market on exchange rate volatility. In the short term, the effects of the three structural shocks in the crude oil market (shock of crude oil supply, aggregate demand for industrial commodities related to the business cycle and shock in crude oil market demand) are insignificant.

The results of VAR decomposition in Table 5 show that in the previous month, the impact of shocks in the oil market on the stock index was near zero. As the horizon goes

Table 5. Percentage of the Impact of Supply and Demand Shocks in the Crude Oil Market on Total Changes in the KASE Index

Horizon	Aggregate Demand (%)	Oil Supply (%)	Real Oil Price (%)	RER (%)	Other (%)
1	3.03	1.40	8.46	0.83	86.29
2	2.56	1.73	7.33	1.96	86.42
3	3.41	1.65	15.35	1.82	77.77
15	12.33	3.67	19.31	5.90	58.78
∞	2.83	2.21	60.93	33.28	0.74

Source: Authors' compilation based on the variance decomposition of the structural VAR model (1).

up, the effect of shocks to the real price of oil, aggregate demand and the real exchange rate takes on a little more importance, while the impact of supply shocks is insignificant throughout the period under review. For example, the total power of explanation of these shocks at impact is less than 14% of the variance in the real price of the oil market on the variability of the KASE index, less than 3% of the variance in the real price of the oil market on the volatility of the exchange rate and 16% of the variance of volatility in the oil market in the volatility of the exchange rate, but the power of explanation increases as the forecast horizon increases. It is observed that on the 15-month horizon, the real oil price shocks account for 19%, and aggregate demand shocks explain only 12% of stock index volatility. On a horizon of more than 15 months, the impact of real oil price shocks on the stock index is about 61%, followed by about 33% for the real exchange rate.

Structural shocks in the world crude oil market are an important basis for the stock market of Kazakhstan. Historical decomposition of the aggregate effect of structural shocks on the KASE index shows the overall impact of oil prices and the volatility of oil prices on the KASE index. The real price of oil has an impact on the KASE index, but volatility shocks in the real price of oil have the greatest impact, which mainly corresponds to changes in the KASE index since the beginning of 2010. More interestingly, the variable is the only determinant that causes fluctuations in the KASE.

In the long term, the shocks in the supply of crude oil, aggregate demand and oil demand on the market together make up about 99% of the variability of the real price in the crude oil market for changes in the KASE index, 53% of the volatility of the real price in the crude oil market for volatility in the exchange rate and approximately 39% of the variability of the volatility in the crude oil market on overall exchange rate volatility. This suggests that structural shocks in the global crude oil market are an important indicator for the Kazakhstan stock market, with the greatest contribution being from oil demand shocks (accounting for more than 60% of long-term changes in real oil prices), followed by changes in the real exchange rate, which account for more than 33%. In turn, fluctuations in the exchange rate are due to shocks in the crude oil market (which account for about 47%) or other shocks in general (accounting for about 40%).

Figure 4 presents the cumulative impact of each structural shock on the KASE index and shows the overall impact of oil prices on the KASE index. The real price of oil (on the

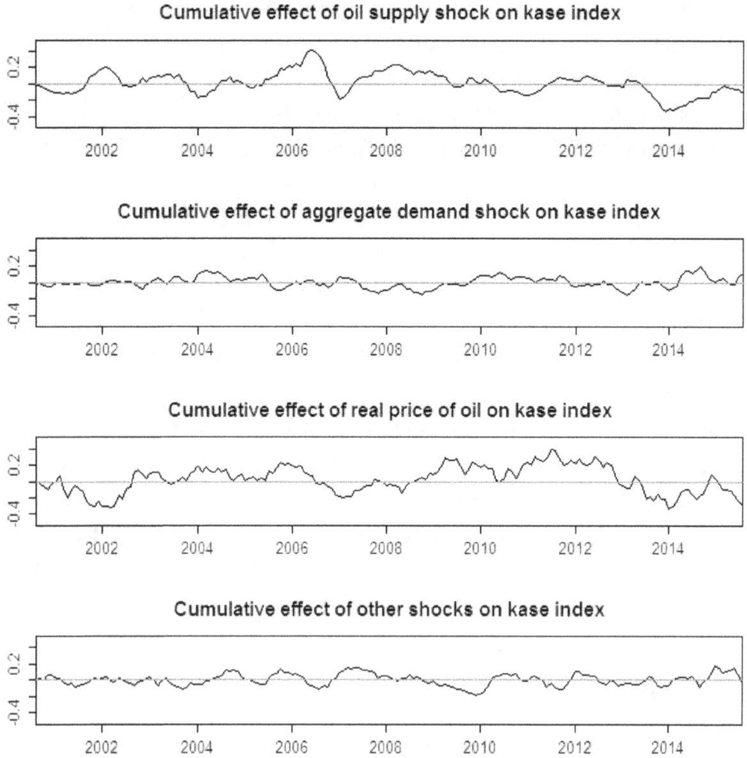

Note: Based on the variance decomposition of the structural VAR model (1).
Source: Authors' compilation.

Figure 4. Historical Decomposition of the KASE Index

first chart) appears to make the largest contribution to the KASE index. Besides, it is also found that shocks in oil supplies caused long fluctuations in the KASE index. Although the results are not presented in this paper, we observe that the volatility shocks in the real price of oil have the greatest impact and have mainly corresponded to changes in the KASE index since the beginning of 2010 when the volatility of the real oil price replaced the real price of oil. More interestingly, the variable is the only determinant that caused fluctuations in the KASE index. The accumulated effect of changes in real oil prices on the variability of the KASE index was the most significant. Although supply and demand shocks in the supply of crude oil caused long fluctuations in the KASE index, the effect of oil price volatility overtime was much more intense.

5. Conclusion and Policy Implications

This study empirically investigates the relationship between oil price fluctuations and stock index movements, focusing on their impact on Kazakhstan's financial market and broader energy security concerns. The results highlight that while oil price fluctuations influence stock market volatility, a clear understanding of the causes behind these shocks — particularly demand-driven versus supply-driven shocks — is crucial for accurately interpreting stock market reactions.

Our findings show that the stock market is less sensitive to oil supply shocks than to demand shocks. Specifically, aggregate demand shocks significantly affect the stock index, contributing to at least 12% of its volatility. Over the long term, oil prices represented about 61% of the total stock index volatility. Investors, risk managers, and policymakers should take into account that oil production shocks have had a negligible impact on financial markets during the period of this study, suggesting that oil supply-driven shocks are less relevant for predicting stock market performance in Kazakhstan.

The policy implications of these findings are significant, particularly for oil-exporting countries like Kazakhstan that are seeking to enhance their energy security during the global transition to renewable energy. The volatility of oil prices, especially demand-driven shocks, poses risks to Kazakhstan's financial markets and its broader economy. As such, a strategic shift toward promoting renewable energy through green finance mechanisms — such as green bonds — could reduce the country's vulnerability to oil price fluctuations while simultaneously supporting long-term energy security (Taghizadeh-Hesary, Yoshino, & Rasoulinezhad, 2023).

Key Policy Implications:

1. Time-Varying Stock Market Reactions: Policymakers must recognize the time-varying reactions of stock markets to oil price shocks. As our study demonstrates, demand-driven oil shocks can have prolonged impacts on financial markets. Thus, regulators should focus on building financial resilience through policies that encourage green investments, which can buffer the economy against future oil demand shocks (Wang *et al.*, 2024).
2. Focus on Demand-Driven Oil Shocks: Kazakhstan's policymakers should focus more on mitigating the impacts of demand-driven rather than supply-driven oil shocks. Given that demand shocks have a more significant effect on stock market volatility, green finance instruments can help diversify investment away from oil reliance, ensuring more stable financial markets and contributing to energy security (Taghizadeh-Hesary *et al.*, 2024).
3. Integrating Green Finance for Energy Transition: To reduce Kazakhstan's dependency on oil and stabilize its financial markets, the government should prioritize green finance mechanisms, such as green bonds and renewable energy investment frameworks. These tools are essential to attract international investment, support renewable energy projects, and ensure a smooth energy transition (Duan *et al.*, 2024). This will ultimately contribute to long-term economic stability and energy security by diversifying the country's energy portfolio.
4. Enhancing Financial Stability: It is crucial for policymakers to monitor and respond to key financial indicators, such as interest rates, exchange rates, inflation, and production levels, particularly in the context of energy market volatility. By adjusting monetary policies to accommodate shifts in energy demand, Kazakhstan can create a more

stable financial environment that supports the country's energy transition efforts (Taghizadeh-Hesary, Yoshino, & Ozturk, 2024).

5. Ensuring Sustainable Aggregate Demand for Energy Resources: From an energy security perspective, maintaining stable aggregate demand for energy resources is vital for Kazakhstan. Ensuring access to affordable, reliable, and modern energy services will enhance socioeconomic well-being and support the country's sustainable development goals. By leveraging green finance to support renewable energy projects, Kazakhstan can secure its energy future while reducing its dependency on oil exports (Taghizadeh-Hesary, Yoshino, & Mollaahmetoğlu, 2024).

In conclusion, Kazakhstan's economic stability and energy security are intrinsically linked to its ability to adapt to global energy transitions. By focusing on green finance and renewable energy investments, policymakers can mitigate the negative effects of oil price volatility on the stock market and ensure a more resilient financial system that supports sustainable development.

References

Arouri, MEH, A Lahiani and M Bellalah (2010). Oil price shocks and stock market returns in oil-exporting countries: The case of GCC countries. *International Journal of Economics and Finance,* 2(5), 132–139.

Azhari, A, MI Azman Aziz, YK Cheah and H Shahiri (2021). Oil Price Shocks and Energy Stock Returns of ASEAN-5 Countries: Evidence from Ready's (2018) Decomposition Technique in a Markov Regime Switching Framework. JSM 50, 1143–1156. https://doi.org/10.17576/jsm-2021-5004-24

Baffes, J, MA Kose, F Ohnsorge and M Stocker (2015). The great plunge in oil prices: Causes, consequences, and policy responses. World Bank Policy Research Note 94725.

Bastianin, A, C Francesca and M Matteo (2016). The impacts of oil price shocks on stock market volatility: Evidence from the G7 countries. *Energy Policy,* 98, 160–169.

Bernanke, BS (2016). The relationship between stocks and oil prices. Available at: https://www.brookings.edu/blog/ben-bernanke/2016/02/19/the-relationship-between-stocks-and-oil-prices/ [Accessed 27 March 2020].

Bjørnland, HC (2009). Oil price shocks and stock market booms in an oil exporting country. *Scottish Journal of Political Economy,* 56(2), 232–254.

Blinder, AS and L Kilian (2009). Causes and consequences of the oil shock of 2007–08. Available at: www.jstor.org/stable/25652720 [Accessed 25 March 2020].

Bloomberg (2017). Kazakhstan Stock Exchange Index KASE. Available at: https://www.bloomberg.com/quote/KZKAK:IND [Accessed 18 September 2018].

Boyer, MM and D Filion (2009). Common and fundamental factors in stock returns of Canadian oil and gas companies. *Energy Economics,* 29, 428–453.

Chang, L, M Mohsin, Z Gao and F Taghizadeh-Hesary (2023). Asymmetric impact of oil price on current account balance: Evidence from oil importing countries. Energy Economics 123, 106749. https://doi.org/10.1016/j.eneco.2023.106749

Du, J, Y Liu, S Xu and F Taghizadeh-Hesary (2024). How does green finance affect the sustainability of mineral resources? Evidence from developing countries. Journal of Cleaner Production 475, 143620. https://doi.org/10.1016/j.jclepro.2024.143620

Duan, K, J Tan, X Ren and F Taghizadeh-Hesary (2024). How does green investment respond differently to decomposed oil shocks? Resources Policy 92, 104997. https://doi.org/10.1016/j.resourpol.2024.104997

Energy Charter Secretariat (2015). Common concept for energy producing, consuming and transit economies. Available at: https://www.energycharter.org/fileadmin/DocumentsMedia/Thematic/International_Energy_Security_2015_en.pdf [Accessed 25 March 2020].

Filis, G, S Degiannakis and C Floros (2011). Dynamic correlation between stock market and oil prices: The case of oil-importing and oil-exporting countries. *International Review of Financial Analysis,* 20, 152–164.

Gallis, P (2006). NATO and energy security. Available at: https://fas.org/sgp/crs/row/RS22409.pdf [Accessed 18 September 2018]. Hesse, H and T Poghosyan (2016). Oil prices and bank profitability: Evidence from major oil-exporting countries in the Middle East and North Africa. Available at: https://www.imf.org/en/Publications/WP/Issues/2016/12/31/Oil-Prices-and-Bank-Profitability-Evidence-From-Major-Oil-Exporting-Countries-in-the-Middle-23337 [Accessed 20 March 2020].

Guo, H and KL Kliesen (2005). Oil price volatility and U.S. macroeconomic activity. *Federal Reserve Bank of St. Louis Review,* 86(5), 669–684.

International Monetary Fund (2018). Republic of Kazakhstan 2018 Article IV Consultation — Press Release; and Staff Report. Available at: https://www.imf.org/en/Publications/CR/Issues/2018/09/14/Republic-of-Kazakhstan-2018-Article-IV-Consultation-Press-Release-and-Staff-Report-46243 [Accessed 18 September 2018].

Karatayev, M and S Hall, (2020). Establishing and comparing energy security trends in resource-rich exporting nations (Russia and the Caspian Sea region). Resources Policy 68, 101746. https://doi.org/10.1016/j.resourpol.2020.101746

Kazakhstan Stock Exchange (2009). KASE Annual Report, 2009. Available at: https://kase.kz/files/reports/2009_en.pdf [Accessed 18 September 2018].

Kazakhstan Stock Exchange (2017). KASE Market Overview as of December 01, 2017. Available at: http://kase.kz/files/presentations/en/17_12_01_KASE_eng.pdf [Accessed 18 September 2018].

Khalfaoui, R, S Sarwar and AK Tiwari (2019). Analysing volatility spillover between the oil market and the stock market in oil-importing and oil-exporting countries: Implications on portfolio management. *Resources Policy*, 62, 22–32.

Kilian, L (2009). Not all oil price shocks are alike: Disentangling demand and supply shocks in the crude oil market. *American Economic Review,* 99(3), 1053–1069.

Koop, G, MH Pesaran and SM Potter (1996). Impulse response analysis in nonlinear multivariate models. *Journal of Econometrics,* 74(1), 119–147.

Komijani, A, NA Gandali and E Naderi (2013). The long-run and short-run effects of crude oil price on methanol market in Iran. *International Journal of Energy Economics and Policy,* 3(1), 43–50.

Kyritsis, E and A Serletis (2019). Oil prices and the renewable energy sector. *The Energy Journal,* 40.

Levine, R and S Zervos (1998). Stock markets, banks, and economic growth. *American Economic Review*, 88(3), 537–558.

Liu, Y, K Dong, K Wang and F Taghizadeh-Hesary (2024). Moving towards sustainable city: Can China's green finance policy lead to sustainable development of cities? Sustainable Cities and Society 102, 105242. https://doi.org/10.1016/j.scs.2024.105242

Mohanty, SK, M Nandha, AQ Turkistani and MY Alaitani (2011). Oil price movements and stock market returns: Evidence from gulf cooperation council (GCC) countries. *Global Finance Journal,* 22(1), 42–55.

Mokni, K (2020). Time-varying effect of oil price shocks on the stock market returns: Evidence from oil-importing and oil-exporting countries. *Energy Reports,* 6, 605–619.

Mouraviev, N (2021). Energy security in Kazakhstan: The consumers' perspective. Energy Policy 155, 112343. https://doi.org/10.1016/j.enpol.2021.112343

Movkebayeva, G, A Aktymbayeva, Y Tyurina, N Baikadamov, K Beketova, M Troyanskaya, S Smagulova and I Imangaliyeva (2020). Energy Security and Sustainability in Eurasian Economic Union in the Terms of Economic Growth: The Case of Kazakhstan's Energy Sector up to 2040 Perspectives. IJEEP 10, 497–503. https://doi.org/10.32479/ijeep.9073

National Bank of Kazakhstan (2009). *Annual Report of the National Bank of the Republic of Kazakhstan for the Year 2008.* Available at: http://www.nationalbank.kz/cont/publish381647_6031.pdf [Accessed 18 September 2018].

Nomura (2018). Damocles: Our early warning indicator of exchange rate crises. Available at: https://www.nomuraconnects.com/focused-thinking-posts/damocles-our-early-warning-indicator-of-exchange-rate-crises/ [Accessed 18 September 2018].

Park, J and R Ratti (2008). Oil price shocks and stock markets in the U.S. and 13 European countries. *Energy Economics*, 30, 2587–2608.

Radhamés, AL and AV Mollick (2010). Oil price fluctuations and U.S. dollar exchange rates. *Energy Economics*, 32(2), 399–408.

Rahman, S and A Serletis (2019). Oil prices and the stock markets: Evidence from high frequency data. *The Energy Journal, International Association for Energy Economics*, Vol. 0 (Special I).

RFCA Rating Agency (2016). *Oil and Gas Sector of the Republic of Kazakhstan.* Available at: https://kase.kz/files/ra_rfca_reports/rfca_oil_and_gas_sector_01_10_16.pdf [Accessed 18 September 2018].

RFCA Rating Agency (2017). *Analysis of the Oil and Gas Sector of Kazakhstan by the Results of 8 Months, 2017.* Available at: https://kase.kz/files/ra_rfca_reports/rfca_oil_and_gas_sector_300817.pdf [Accessed 18 September 2018].

Sadorsky, P (1999). Oil price shocks and stock market activity. *Energy Economics,* 21, 449–469.

Sadorsky, P (2001). Risk factors in stock returns of Canadian oil and gas companies. *Energy Economics,* 23(1), 17–28.

Sarwar, S, AK Tiwari and C Tingqiu (2020). Analyzing volatility spillovers between oil market and Asian stock markets. *Resources Policy,* 66, 101608.

Schwab, K (2018). *The Global Competitiveness Report 2017–2018,* pp. 13–24. Available at: http://www3.weforum.org/docs/GCR2017-2018/05FullReport/TheGlobalCompetitivenessReport2017%E2%80%932018.pdf [Accessed 18 September 2018].

Shadrina, E (2018). Energy Policies of Kazakhstan and Kyrgyzstan: Case for Energy Security through Cooperation.

Shahrestani, P and M Rafei (2020). The impact of oil price shocks on Tehran stock exchange returns: Application of the Markov switching vector autoregressive models. *Resources Policy,* 65, 101579.

Singhal, S, S Choudhary and PC Biswal (2019). Return and volatility linkages among international crude oil price, gold price, exchange rate and stock markets: Evidence from Mexico. *Resources Policy,* 60, 255–261.

Speight, JG (2011). *An Introduction to Petroleum Technology, Economics, and Politics.* New York: Wiley-Scrivener.

Sims, CA (1980). Macroeconomics and reality. *Econometrica,* 48(1), 1–48.

Taghizadeh-Hesary, F, E Rasoulinezhad, M Shahbaz and X Vinh Vo (2021). How energy transition and power consumption are related in Asian economies with different income levels? Energy 237, 121595. https://doi.org/10.1016/j.energy.2021.121595

Taghizadeh-Hesary, F and N Yoshino (2014). Monetary policies and oil price determination: An empirical analysis. *OPEC Energy Review,* 38(1), 1–20, doi: 10.1111/opec.1202.

Taghizadeh-Hesary, F, N Yoshino, MMH Abadi and R Farboudmanesh (2016). Response of macro variables of emerging and developed oil importers to oil price movements. *Journal of the Asia Pacific Economy,* 21(1), 91–102, doi: 10.1080/13547860.2015.1057955.

Taghizadeh-Hesary, F, N Yoshino, G Abdoli and A Farzinvash (2013). An estimation of the impact of oil shocks on crude oil exporting economies and their trade partners. *Frontiers of Economics in China,* 8(4), 571–591, doi: 10.3868/s060-002-013-0029-3.

Wang, Y and C Wu (2012). Forecasting energy market volatility using GARCH models: Can multivariate models beat univariate models? *Energy Economics,* 34(6), 2167–2181. Available at: doi.org/10.1016/j.eneco.2012.03.010 [Accessed 18 September 2018].

Wang, X, K Hong, X Ren and F Taghizadeh-Hesary (2024). Can green finance act as a catalyst to renewable energy deployment? Evidence from China using a spatial econometric approach. Energy 311, 133302. https://doi.org/10.1016/j.energy.2024.133302

World Bank (2005). *Energy Security Issues.* Washington, DC: World Bank. Available at: http://documents.worldbank.org/curated/en/464811468175435408/Energy-security-issues [Accessed 20 November 2018].

World Bank (2015). *World Bank Annual Report 2015.* Available at: http://documents.worldbank.org/curated/ru/880681467998200702/World-Bank-annual-report-2015 [Accessed 27 March 2020].

World Bank (2018). *Kazakhstan — The Challenge of Economic Diversification Amidst Productivity Stagnation.* Available at: http://www.worldbank.org/en/country/kazakhstan/publication/economic-update-fall-2018 [Accessed 18 September 2018].

Yoshino, N and F Taghizadeh-Hesary (2014). Monetary policies and oil price fluctuations following the subprime mortgage crisis. *International Journal of Monetary Economics and Finance,* 7(3), 157–174. doi: 10.1504/IJMEF.2014.066482.

Yoshino, N and F Taghizadeh-Hesary (2016). What's behind the recent oil price drop? In *Monetary Policy and the Oil Prices,* N Yoshino and F Taghizadeh-Hesary (eds.), pp. 1–5. Tokyo: Springer.

https://doi.org/10.1142/9789819812608_0010

Chapter 10

Energy Security and Exchange Rate Dynamics in Vietnam[#]

CHUC ANH TU[*], EHSAN RASOULINEZHAD[†,¶], THANH NGO CHI[‡],
HUYEN LE HOANG BA[‡], and HANH HOANG THANH[§]

[*]*Academy of Finance, Ha Noi, Vietnam*
[†]*Faculty of World Studies, University of Tehran, Tehran, Iran*
[‡]*Hong Duc University, Thanh Hoa, Vietnam*
[§]*Academy of Finance, Ha Noi, Vietnam*
[¶]*e.rasoulinezhad@ut.ac.ir*

This chapter empirically revisits energy insecurity in Vietnam, focusing on the role of the official exchange rate. Using data from 1985 to 2022 and applying the GMM estimator based on the 4A theory of energy security, we found that economic growth positively impacts the official exchange rate. CO_2 emissions negatively affect the exchange rate, indicating an inverse relationship, while inflation negatively influences the exchange rate by increasing the cost of domestic products, which boosts import flows and depreciates the national currency. Additionally, energy intensity is negatively related to the official exchange rate. Our analysis also reveals that a 1% increase in gas imports is linked to a decline in the official exchange rate. This chapter recommends that Vietnam should diversify its gas imports, enhance local energy production, and improve energy efficiency to strengthen its currency against the USD and improve energy security.

Keywords: Energy insecurity, Exchange rate, GMM estimator, Vietnam.

1. Introduction

Energy security has emerged as a critical issue among scholars, defined as the consistent availability of energy sources at affordable prices (IEA, 2018). For many countries, energy is a vital input for production, essential for maintaining local market supply and competing in international markets (Rasoulinezhad and Kang, 2016; Taghizadeh-Hesary *et al.*, 2017; Rasoulinezhad and Jabalameli, 2019; Taghizadeh-Hesary *et al.*, 2019; Misik, 2022; Foss, 2022; Khan *et al.*, 2024). Consequently, nations must pay close attention to their energy security levels. Vietnam, as a key player in the Asian economy, exemplifies this need due to its significant reliance on energy resources. This dependency underscores the critical importance of energy security for the country, highlighting the need for strategies to ensure a stable and affordable energy supply.

[#]This chapter is an updated version of the paper published in the *Singapore Economic Review*, Vol. 66, No. 2 (2021) 529–544; DOI: 10.1142/S0217590819430021.

Generally, the development of the Vietnam's economy has been closely accompanied by the fast-growing energy consumption in the country. According to MoIT 2017, energy demand in Vietnam will go up by an average of 5% every year until 2030, with a higher percentage of import for domestic energy supply; by 2035, the total final energy demand will be approximately 2.5 times higher than the level in 2015. It is estimated that local energy production cannot cater to the needs of energy demand, and in case all energy projects are mobilized at full or nearly full capacity, the import share of the total primary energy supply increases significantly—from below 5% in 2015 to 15% in 2020, 33% in 2025, and 45% in 2030. Table 1 reports the growth rate of the final energy demand by fuel source as forecasted in percent.

According to a report by the Vietnam Oil and Gas Group, Vietnam possesses approximately 4.4 billion barrels of proven oil reserves, placing it 28th globally in terms of oil reserves. The country's oil industry began with the exploitation of the first crude oil at the White Tiger oil field in 1986, and Vietnam commenced crude oil exports in April 1987. Currently, Vietnam ranks 4th in Southeast Asia for oil exports and is expected to sustain an output of around 340,000 barrels per day in the coming years. Figure 1 illustrates the

Table 1. Final energy demand growth rate, (%).

Energy Source	2016–2020	2021–2025	2026–2030	2031–2035	Average 2016–2035
Coal	3.7	3.4	3	1.4	2.9
Oil products	6.1	5.8	5.2	3.4	5.1
Natural gas	10.4	6.4	4.4	1.6	5.7
Electricity	9.8	8.6	7.4	5.9	7.9
Total	5.3	4.9	4.8	3.7	4.7

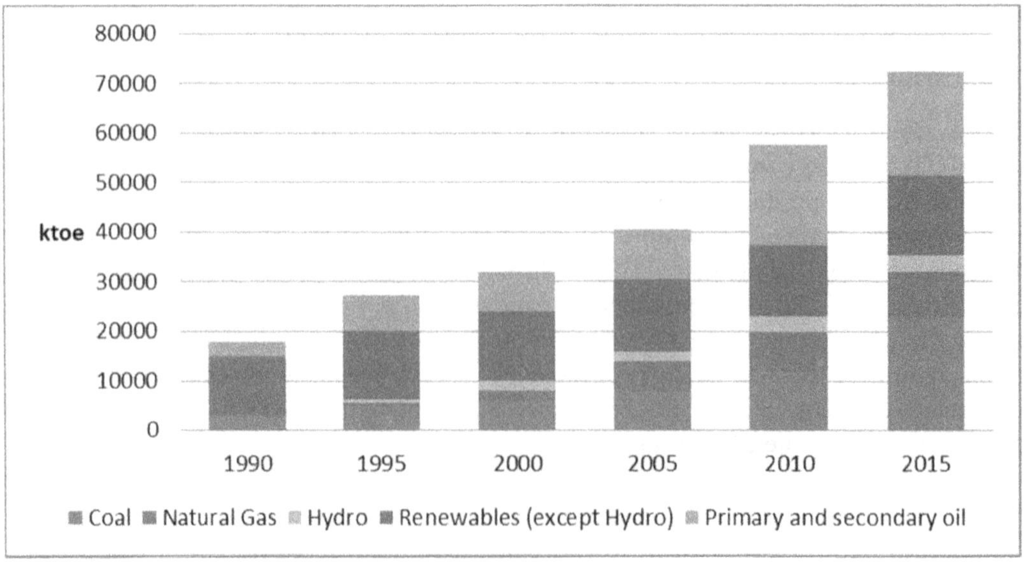

Figure 1. (Color available online) Total primary energy supply in Vietnam.

total primary energy supply in Vietnam, highlighting the nation's achievements in energy production over time.

A highlight about Vietnam's energy market is that the positive growth rate of energy demand and semi-constant production potential have increased the need for energy import by this country. The energy trade balance of Vietnam has been negative since 2010, meaning the energy imports are at a higher level than energy exports in the country. Figure 2 represents the energy import and energy export levels in Vietnam during 2001–2018:

The increased reliance on energy imports to meet local demand in Vietnam underscores the importance of the official exchange rate. In other words, Vietnam's importers need foreign currency (US dollar) to buy energy resource from foreign providers, which creates a high linkage between local energy provision (or energy security) and the exchange rate. Table 2 illustrates the energy resource imports into Vietnam from the world.

Based on Table 2, Vietnam's energy imports have considerably increased in the last decade, which highlights the linkage between the foreign exchange rate and energy

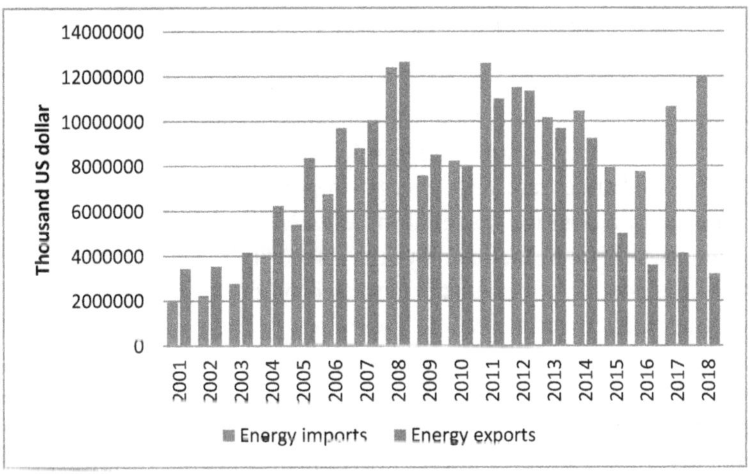

Figure 2. (Color available online) Energy trade of Vietnam, 2001–2018, thousand USD.

Table 2. Total energy resources' imports by Vietnam, 2011–2018, million USD.

	2011	2012	2013	2014	2015	2016	2017	2018
Petroleum oils and oils obtained from bituminous minerals	10341	9356	7392	8028	5972	56646	7308	8576
Coal	227	210	218	236	452	873	1307	1894
Petroleum gas and other gaseous hydrocarbons	672	618	644	782	538	494	688	478
Coke	39	37	45	127	95	85	213	292
Electrical energy	300	158	221	142	142	135	109	93
Petroleum oils and oils obtained from bituminous minerals, crude	566	647	1123	516	99	202	635	206

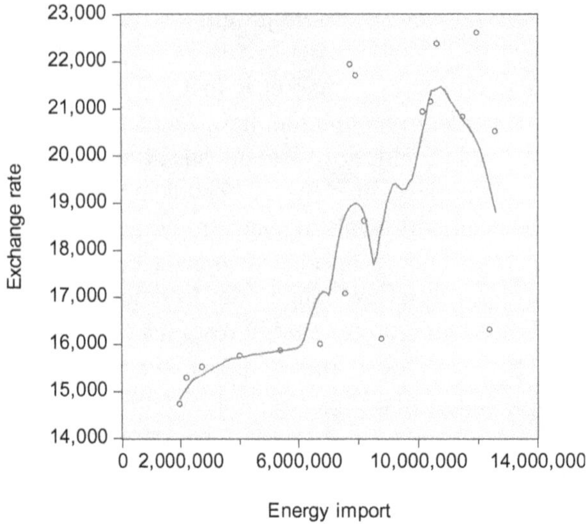

Figure 3. Correlation between official exchange rate and energy imports in Vietnam, 2001–2018.

security of Vietnam. Figure 3 shows scatterplots correlated with the Kernel fit line for Vietnam's official exchange rate and energy import over the period of 2001–2018. It proves the existence of a positive correlation between these two variables in Vietnam.

The main question is how Vietnam's energy security indicators can affect the official exchange rate of the country. Foreign currencies brought from crude oil exports are very important for a trade deficit economy like Vietnam. This helps Vietnam meet a significant portion of foreign currency demand for imports, for international payment transactions as well as repaying foreign loans of the state. This source of foreign currency is also important to stabilize the exchange rate, regulate the macroeconomy, and improve the foreign currency liquidity for the entire economy of Vietnam. Since its exploitation began, crude oil has consistently held a high export value compared to other key export items like footwear, textiles, and seafood. Hence, Petrodollars (income from exporting oil and oil products) can be defined as an important factor influencing the energy insecurity of Vietnam.

Although numerous studies have explored the relationship between official exchange rates and energy security (e.g., Clarida and Gali, 1994; Chaudhuri and Daniel, 1998; Chen and Chen, 2007; Spatafora and Stavrev, 2003; Bjornland and Hungnes, 2008; Akram, 2004; Habib and Kalamova, 2007; Ozsoz and Akinkunmi, 2011; Hassan and Zahid, 2011; Victor *et al.*, 2012; Jahangard *et al.*, 2017; Nguyen *et al.*, 2024), there is a notable lack of empirical research focusing on this linkage, specifically within the context of Vietnam. This chapter aims to address this gap by offering new insights into the interplay between energy security and exchange rates in Vietnam.

This chapter has 5 sections: Section 2 presents a literature review. Section 3 describes the data and research methods. In Section 4, the empirical findings are discussed. We conclude in Section 5 by briefly reviewing the key findings and explaining some results in the light of actual practice, and then we propose a discussion and policy implications.

2. Literature Review

In this literature review, we focus on presenting studies related to the topic of the relationship between energy insecurity and the exchange rate in Vietnam. Theoretically, the relationship between energy price as a proxy for energy insecurity and the exchange rate is well established (see, for example, Golub, 1983; Krugman, 1983a, 1983b; Bloomberg and Harris, 1995; Chen and Chen, 2007; Hem *et al.*, 2014; Baghestani and Toledo, 2019; Wu *et al.*, 2023).

Golub (1983) and Krugman (1983a, 1983b) explain why energy price movements should affect exchange rates. Theoretically, an energy-exporting (importing) country may experience currency appreciation (depreciation) when energy prices rise and depreciation (appreciation) when they fall. For example, an increase in the real oil price will worsen the trade balance for an oil-importing country, which will require real currency depreciation in order to improve the country's competitiveness (Zhou, 1995). Bloomberg and Harris (1995) explain how exchange rates can influence energy prices based on the law of one price. For instance, since oil is fairly homogeneous and internationally traded and priced in the USD, as the USD weakens relative to other currencies, this will reduce oil prices measured in other currencies, which may increase the demand for oil, and thus increase its prices. For example, Zhang *et al.* (2008) and Akram (2009) find that a weaker USD leads to higher energy prices. While previous studies have focused on developed countries, little attention has been devoted to developing countries. Hem *et al.* (2014) explore the long- and short-run movements between energy prices and the real exchange rates of two large oil-exporting countries—Canada and Norway. Cointegration and serial correlation tests were jointly used to identify the long-term common trends and short-term common cycles. It was found that oil prices and the real exchange rates of the Canadian Dollar and the Norwegian Krone have two shared trends and one shared cycle. The trend-cycle decomposition revealed a strong positive correlation between the trend and cyclical components. The two currencies showed economic dynamics very similar to crude oil prices. Baghestani and Toledo (2019) set up a forecasting framework to generate the multi-period random walk predictions of both real broad and narrow effective exchange rates of NAFTA countries (Canada, Mexico, and the US). Another research area is oil-exporting countries, with a study by Usama and Che (2012) investigating the impact of oil price shocks on the real exchange rate, covering the most recent oil shocks from 2000 to 2010 in 12 oil-exporting countries, namely Algeria, Bahrain, Egypt, Indonesia, Kuwait, Nigeria, Oman, Qatar, Saudi Arabia, Sudan, United Arab Emirates, and Venezuela. In this study, the panel model was implemented using six variables, namely the real exchange rate as the dependent variable, and oil price, government consumption expenditure, current account, inflation rate, and gross domestic product based on the purchasing power parity as independent variables. The results showed that the increases in oil prices have caused a real exchange rate appreciation in these countries.

Studies of the relationship between global crude oil prices and real exchange rates have been conducted in Asian countries, such as those by Salah and Khalid, 2014; Hem and Kamal, 2015; Mehmet *et al.*, 2015; and Nandi *et al.*, 2024. Salah and Khalid (2014) studied the long-run relationship between Asian real exchange rates and global oil prices in the presence of structural breaks. The Johansen test clearly demonstrated the importance of considering breaks and provided strong support for a stable long-run relationship in all cases. Moreover, the results proved the evidence of bi-directional causality in Malaysia and Thailand, unidirectional causality from exchange rates to oil prices in Korea, the Philippines, and Singapore, unidirectional causality from oil prices to the exchange rate in Indonesia, and no evidence of causality in Japan. In another study in the Asian region, Hem and Kamal (2015) analyzed the impact of oil price shocks on real output, inflation, and the real exchange rate in Thailand, Malaysia, Singapore, the Philippines, and Indonesia (ASEAN-5) using a structural VAR model. Cointegration tests indicated that the macro-economic variables of these countries are cointegrated and share common trends in the long run. The impulse response functions revealed that oil price fluctuations do not impact the ASEAN-5 economies in the long run and much of the effect is absorbed within five to six quarters. The variance decomposition results further asserted that with a few exceptions, oil price shocks do not explain a significant variation in any of the variables under consideration. The study also identified a very unique pattern of response to oil price fluctuations between Malaysia and Singapore, and between the Philippines and Thailand. A study of Vietnam was conducted by Mehmet *et al.* (2015) who analyzed the impact of global energy prices on several macroeconomic variables (Real GDP per Capita, Government Consumption, Investments, Inflation rate, Real Openness of the economy, Population, and Nominal exchange rate) for 10 developing Asian countries—Bangladesh, PR China, India, Indonesia, Malaysia, Pakistan, the Philippines, Thailand, Turkey, and Vietnam—with annual data from 1960 to 2010. The major results showed that the volatility in world energy prices is negatively associated with the aggregate economic activity. Mansson *et al.* (2014) discussed that volatile energy price can be considered as a threat or risk for energy security of a nation. Haar and Haar (2019) explained that global oil market volatilities can positively and negatively affect the energy security of nations. Both kinds of effects are not good for sustainable development. Mohsin *et al.* (2018) argued that oil suppliers that greatly depend on oil revenues have riskier energy security. Any sharp changes in oil revenues can hit the foreign exchange market and the government's budget deficit. La Rovere *et al.* (2011) proved that oil price fluctuations can have a negative impact on energy security of Brazil; hence, Brazil is trying to develop other sources of energy in its national economy. Toan *et al.* (2011) focused on energy demand and energy supply in Vietnam. They discussed that Vietnam's energy policies are divided into three branches of energy security, energy efficiency, and development of renewable energy sources. To cover all these branches, Vietnam has defined various national energy policies in line with the Asian Energy Security (AES).

As many studies have been conducted on developed countries, there is a dearth of such studies in developing countries, including Vietnam. This is the reason for this chapter.

3. Data and Research Methodology

3.1. *Research data*

In this section, we choose variables based on the theory of 4As for energy security to conduct our empirical analysis and explore the linkages between the exchange rate and different variables for Vietnam. Here, we need the following real variables: Official exchange rate (*EXC*), Economic growth (*GRO*), Global oil price (*OILP*), CO_2 emissions per capita (CO_2), Energy intensity (*ENIN*), Inflation rate (*INF*), Share of oil import in oil supply (*SOI*), Share of import in gas supply (*SGI*), and energy supply per capita (*ENSU*).

The study utilizes a 4A framework to explain energy security, ensuring representation for each component. In the framework, Availability is a dimension that indicates the existence and sufficiency of fossil fuels and other indigenous sources of energy to meet the region's needs. The higher the reserves, potential, and sufficiency of indigenous sources of energy, the higher the region ranks on this dimension. Share of oil import in oil supply (*SOI*) and Share of import in gas supply (*SGI*) are two proposing variables for this energy security dimension. The Applicability dimension reflects the ability of a country to access and increase its reserves of indigenous energy. For example, the ability to use new technologies to reduce energy wastages and increase energy conservation, and hence extending the use of the same energy reserves, improves performance on the applicability scale. Energy Intensity is a representative variable for this dimension. The Acceptability dimension covers the social and environmental aspects of the new sources of energy. For a new source of energy to be adopted, it must clear social and environmental barriers (Tongsopit *et al.*, 2016). Changing the energy mix of a region to increase the share of renewable fuels would improve its energy security. Renewables like nuclear, hydropower, solar, and wind each face their unique set of challenges on the social and environmental fronts. CO_2 emissions per capita is an indicator for this dimension in our model. The affordability dimension represents the ability of an economy or society to access energy resources at a reasonable price (Tongsopit *et al.*, 2016). Moreover, it also covers the equitable access to energy, i.e., energy should be accessible to all income groups. A decreasing affordability level for a country indicates decreasing accessibility to energy by its people and therefore its inability to meet the energy needs of its people. Energy supply per capita is used as an indicator for this variable.

In addition to the theoretical model variables, we added economic growth, global oil price, and inflation rate as three controls.

We gathered annual data from World Bank Development Indicators (WDI). Our annual series covers the period 1985–2022 for Vietnam.

Table 3 shows the primary descriptive characteristics of our data. Economic growth as a change in GDP is measured in percent. Vietnamese economic growth has a mean of 6.03% over the period 1985–2018. Mean global oil price is 42.72 dollars per barrel. It has a maximum and minimum of 111.66 dollars per barrel and 12.71 dollars per barrel during 1980–2018, respectively. CO_2 emissions per capita during the period of 1980–2018 take the mean of 0.89 metric tons per capita. The average share of gas imports in the total gas supply is 0.11%, ranging from a minimum of 0.0006% to a maximum of 0.29% between 1980 and 2018. The energy intensity in Vietnam has a mean of 6.06 MJ/$2011 PPP GDP, while the inflation rate in this country takes an average of 5.98% during 1980–2018. The bilateral exchange rate of Vietnam's Dong during 1980–2018 takes the average of 11873.4. It has a maximum and minimum of 22602.05 and 1.001, respectively.

Figure 4 shows how the correlation between economic growth and the exchange rate in Vietnam is positive. The exchange rate in Vietnam is positively related to economic growth, but its correlations with other variables do not follow a certain movement, and hence its relationships are vague.

Table 3. Variables' descriptive statistics.

Variables	Unit	Obs.	Mean	Std. Dev.	Max.	Min.
GRO	%	39	6.03	1.81	9.54	2.78
OILP	$ per barrel	39	42.72	30.22	111.66	12.71
CO_2	metric tons per capita	39	0.89	0.63	2.18	0.26
SGI	%	39	0.11	0.11	0.29	0.0006
ENIN	MJ/$2011 PPP GDP	39	6.06	0.61	7.54	4.83
INF	%	39	5.98	4.24	23.11	–1.71
SOI	%	39	0.23	0.14	0.50	0.05
ENSU	Tones Oil equivalent per capita	39	0.30	0.20	0.56	0.04
EXC	Vietnamese dong/USD	39	11873.4	7762.6	22602.05	1.001

Notes: GRO = Economic Growth, OILP = Global Oil Price, EX = bilateral exchange rate, CO_2 = CO_2 emissions per capita, SGI = Share of gas import of gas supply, ENIN = Energy Intensity, Inf = Inflation Rate, SOI = Share of oil import of oil supply, ENSU = energy supply per capita.

With regard to the empirical model, we make an econometric equation with the above-mentioned variables:

$$lnLEXC_{it} = \delta_1 ln(GRO_{it}) + \delta_2 ln(OILP_{it}) + \delta_3 ln(CO_{2it}) + \delta_4 ln(SGI_{it}) + \delta_5(ENIN_{it}) + \delta_6 ln(INF_{it}) + \delta_7 ln(SOI_{it}) + \delta_8 ln(ENSU_{it}) + \varepsilon_{it}$$

The coefficients δ_1, δ_2, δ_3, δ_4, δ_5, δ_6, δ_7, and δ_8 represent the long-run elasticity estimates of Vietnam's exchange rate with respect to economic growth (GRO), global oil price (OILP), CO_2 emissions per capita (CO_2), share of gas import to gas supply (SGI), energy intensity (ENIN), inflation rate (INF), share of oil import to oil supply (SOI), and energy supply per capita (ENSU).

To estimate our coefficients, the Generalized Method of Moments (GMM) will be performed for analyzing the variables representing energy security on exchange rate of Vietnam. The reliability of the GMM method has been proved by many scholars such as Arellano and Bond (1991), Martinez-Zarzoso *et al.* (2009), Kahouli and Maktouf (2015), and Lin (2015). In general, the regression model in the form of GMM is written as follows:

$$Y_{it} = \alpha + \beta Y_{it-1} + \gamma X_{it} + \eta_{it} + \varepsilon_{it}$$

where Y indicates the dependent variable (the official exchange rate in Vietnam) and X represents all explanatory variables. η_{it} denotes the country-specific effects and ε_{it} is the error term.

To have reliable empirical estimations, we need to conduct some preliminary tests. As the first pre-estimation test, the presence of structural breakpoints will be checked and then the Variance Inflation Factor (VIF) will be performed to find out whether there is any multicollinearity among the series. The third preliminary test is the Hausman test to check out the existence of heterogeneity to clarify the presence of random or fixed effects in our panel.

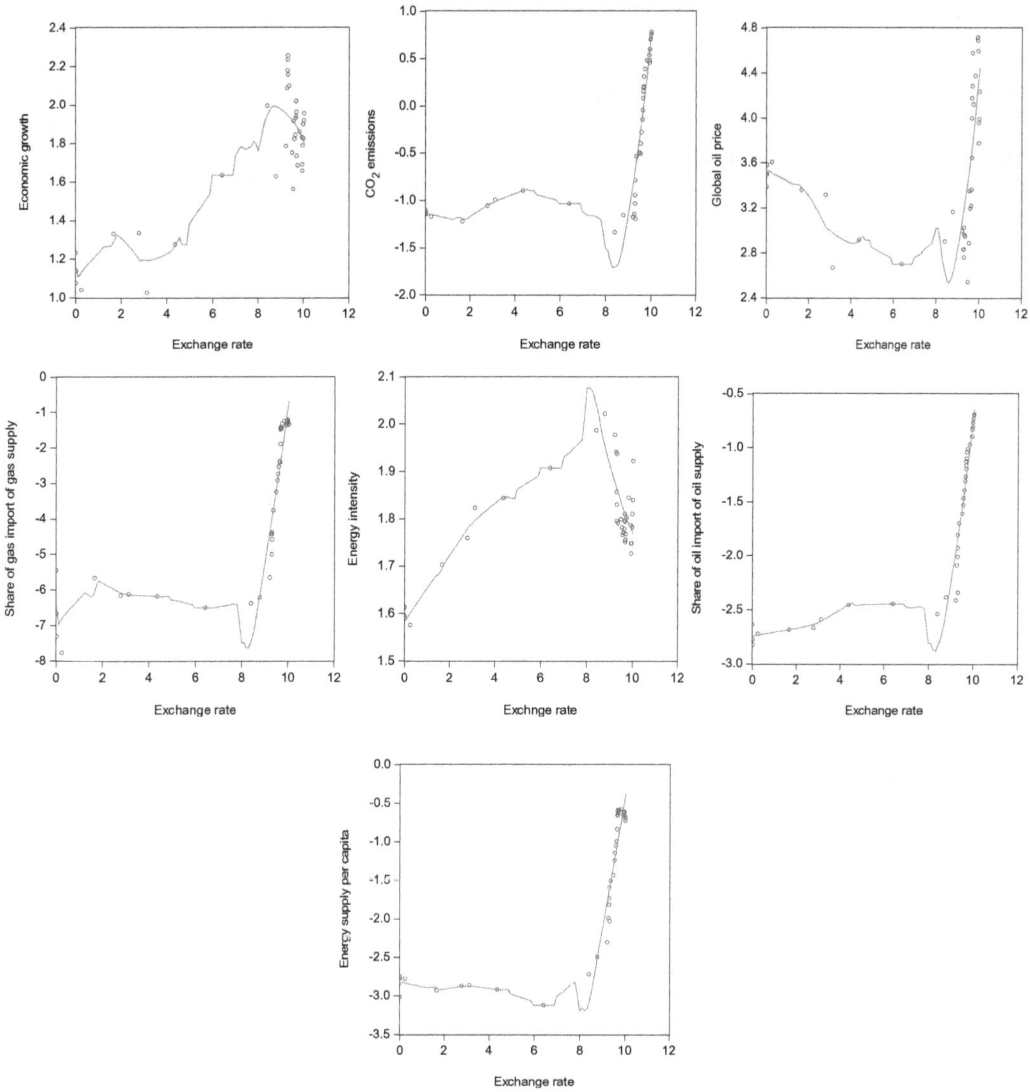

Figure 4. Correlation with Kernel Fit line.

Furthermore, we will conduct two different diagnostics tests after running the GMM estimations. The first is the Arellano–Bond test for zero autocorrelation in the first-differenced errors, while the Sargan test is the second diagnostic test to verify the overidentifying restrictions.

4. Empirical Results

In this section, the results of the empirical model are represented and discussed.

As a first step, we investigated the characteristics of the time series data. The first preliminary task was to find out whether there were any structural changes throughout the period of our survey (a vast number of scholars such as Rapach and Strauss (2008),

Lizardo and Mollick (2010), Mensi *et al.* (2015), Nusair and Kisswani (2015), Wen (2018), and Anjum (2019) have discussed the importance of checking structural breakpoints in econometric models). To this end, we ran the Chow test to check the availability of structural breaks at the two points of the 1997 Asian Financial Crisis and the 2008 Financial Crisis. The results did not confirm structural breaks at these two points. As reported in Table 4, since the p-value is not lower than 5%, the null hypothesis cannot be rejected. This finding is in line with earlier studies. With regard to the financial crisis of 1997, Hoa (2000) discussed that this financial crisis did not heavily affect Vietnam's economy because of its normal transmission mechanism of government revenue and disbursement. According to the World Bank Working Paper (2010), due to the productivity gains and rapid growth of the labor force due to the "demographic dividend," Vietnam was one of the only Southeast Asian emerging economies not to have gone into recession in 2009.

The second preliminary test was checking out the existence of unit root in series. To this end, the Augmented Dicky Fuller test was conducted and the PP (Phillips–Perron) unit root test was also carried out as a robustness check. Table 5 reports the results of these two unit root tests.

Table 4. Structural break test.

Chow Test for Structural Break in 1997			
F-statistic	12.10	Prob. F	0.293
Log likelihood ratio	8.01	Pro. Chi-square	0.190
Wald statistic	7.42	Prob. Chi-square	0.190
Chow Test for Structural Break in 2008			
F-statistic	10.84	Prob. F	0.309
Log likelihood ratio	9.80	Pro. Chi-square	0.480
Wald statistic	9.68	Prob. Chi-square	0.482

Note: Prob. stands for probability.

Table 5. Unit root tests results.

	Augmented Dickey Fuller (ADF)		Phillips–Perron (PP)	
Variables	Level	1st Difference	Level	1st Difference
LEXC	–2.38 (0.15)	–5.932 (0.00)	–2.55 (0.11)	–2.84 (0.04)
LGRO	–2.38 (0.15)	–5.932 (0.00)	–2.30 (0.17)	–6.06 (0.00)
LCO_2	0.359 (0.97)	–5.23 (0.00)	0.29 (0.97)	–5.21 (0.00)
LINF	–2.41 (0.32)	–6.01 (0.00)	0.16 (0.84)	–6.11 (0.00)
LENIN	–2.49 (0.12)	–3.19 (0.02)	–2.21 (0.2)	–3.19 (0.02)
LSOI	–0.46 (0.88)	–6.75 (0.00)	–0.45 (0.88)	–6.76 (0.00)
LSGI	–1.89 (0.33)	–4.30 (0.00)	–1.85 (0.34)	–4.06 (0.00)
LENSU	–0.96 (0.75)	–3.09 (0.03)	–0.94 (0.76)	–4.44 (0.00)
OILP	–0.98 (0.75)	–5.70 (0.00)	–0.98 (0.75)	–5.69 (0.00)

Note: Numbers in parenthesis show P-value.

According to Table 5, all the series are I(1) or first order integrated. The next step is to run a cointegration test to avoid a spurious regression and estimate the long-run linkages between Vietnam's official exchange rate and the explanatory variables, including energy security indicators and control variables To this end, we employed the ADF and KPSS (Kwiatkowski–Phillips–Schmidt–Shin) tests on the GMM residuals from a static regression model. The results of cointegration tests are reported in Table 6.

The findings, listed in Table 6, represent that the GMM residuals are I(0). Therefore, our variables are cointegrated. In other words, we can conclude that our empirical model has meaningful linkages.

After conducting preliminary tests, we can run the GMM model. The GMM estimation's results are shown in Table 7.

According to the estimated coefficients, reported in Table 7, the results are as follows:

- First, economic growth has a positive impact on the official exchange rate. A 1% increase in the economic growth of Vietnam may lead to an appreciation of Vietnam's national currency by nearly 0.92%. In other words, a higher range of economic production means a higher volume of exports which makes national currency stronger in relation to the USDs.

Table 6. Cointegration test results.

Residuals		ADF Test	KPSS Test
Test statistic		–6.1923	0.3492
Critical values	At 0.01 level	–3.4920	0.8127
	At 0.05 level	–2.8384	0.5901

Table 7. GMM estimation results.

Variables' title	Variables' symbol	Coefficients	p-value
Differential of log of exchange rate	LEXC(-1)	0.74	0.00*
Economic growth	LGRO	0.92	0.09**
CO_2 emissions	LCO_2	–0.04	0.07**
Inflation rate	LINF	–0.02	0.08**
Energy intensity	LENIN	–0.04	0.00*
Share of oil import of oil supply	LSOI	0.61	0.45
Share of gas import of gas supply	LSGI	–0.26	0.03*
Energy supply per capita	LENSU	0.14	0.00*
Global oil prices	OILP	0.26	0.06**
AR(2)		0.45	0.00
R^2= 0.98, D.W. = 2.239			
J-Statistic = 0.0253			

Note: *and **indicate significant at 5% and 10% level of significance.

- Second, CO_2 emissions have a negative coefficient which means a negative relationship between this variable and Vietnam's official exchange rate. Since Vietnam is a coal importer, an increase in its coal import flows means more CO_2 emissions. An increase in import flows makes the national currency weaker than the USDs.
- Third, the inflation rate has a negative sign, suggesting that by increasing the price level of commodities in Vietnam's economy, the domestic product will be more expensive than before, which will accelerate commodity import flows leading to a depreciation of Vietnam's national currency.
- Fourth, energy intensity has a negative relationship with the official exchange rate in Vietnam. A 1% increase in Vietnam's energy intensity leads to a decrease in the official exchange rate of this country by approximately 0.04%. In other words, any increase in energy intensity leads to an increase in energy imports, which strengthens the value of the USD against Vietnam's national currency.
- Fifth, the results show that the coefficient for the share of oil imports in Vietnam's oil supply is not statistically significant. However, a 1% increase in gas imports is negatively associated with Vietnam's official exchange rate. This is because Vietnam is a gas importer, and a higher volume of gas imports requires more USD payments to foreign suppliers, leading to a depreciation of the local currency against the USD.
- Sixth, energy supply per capita has a positive impact on Vietnam's official exchange rate. This means that an increase in Vietnam's energy supply per capita leads to a decrease in energy import needs, which means an appreciation of Vietnam's national currency.
- Seventh, the global oil price shows a positive sign of coefficient. A 1% increase in global oil price leads to an increase in Vietnam's official exchange rate by about 0.26%. Since Vietnam is an oil exporter nation, any increase in global oil price helps this country earn more US dollars, which leads to appreciation of the local national currency. This result is in line with Rati and Vespignani (2016) and Aloui *et al.* (2013) who proved that a rise in the price of oil is associated with the depreciation of the dollar because the U.S. trade deficit widens.

5. Concluding Remarks

In this chapter, we tried to analyze Vietnam's energy security through the foreign exchange rate. To this end, annual series over the period 1985–2022 for Vietnam were analyzed in the GMM estimator.

The empirical estimations proved that economic growth has a positive impact on the official exchange rate. A 1% increase in the economic growth of Vietnam may lead to the appreciation of Vietnam's national currency by nearly 0.92% Furthermore, CO_2 emissions have a negative coefficient, which means a negative relationship between this variable and Vietnam's official exchange rate, while the inflation rate has a negative sign, suggesting that by increasing the price level of commodities in Vietnam's economy, the domestic product will be more expensive than before, which accelerates commodity import flows, leading to depreciation of Vietnam's national currency. In addition, we found out that energy intensity has a negative relationship with the official exchange rate in Vietnam. A

1% increase in Vietnam's energy intensity leads to a decrease in the official exchange rate of this country by approximately 0.04%. Moreover, the results revealed that a 1% increase in gas imports has a negative linkage with Vietnam's official exchange rate. The major findings showed that energy supply per capita has a positive impact on Vietnam's official exchange rate, which means a 1% increase in the global oil price leads to an increase in Vietnam's official exchange rate by about 0.26%.

In Vietnam, there is no single, official definition of energy security codified in legal documents. However, various government policies provide extensive regulations related to energy management and strategy. Key documents include Decision No. 18-NQ/TW 2007, which outlines the "National Energy Development Strategy of Vietnam to 2020, with a Vision to 2050," Decision No. 1855/2007, and Decision No. 2068/2015, which approves "Vietnam's Strategy for Renewable Energy Generation by 2030, with a Vision to 2050." Additionally, the Power Development Plan VII and its revised version also address aspects of energy management.

At the national level, energy security in Vietnam is understood as ensuring the availability of sufficient energy for various needs—such as daily living, economic activities, social functions, and defense—at affordable prices. To provide a comprehensive framework for assessing energy security, it is advisable to consolidate these plans and strategies into a single, cohesive document titled "Energy Security of Vietnam." This consolidated document would enable policymakers and economists to better evaluate the country's energy security and compare it with the implementation and effectiveness of existing plans.

Future research on this topic could explore several advanced avenues. For instance, one could investigate the effects of global oil prices on various indicators of energy security in Vietnam using alternative methodologies such as quantile regression, which could reveal how the impact varies across different levels of the oil price distribution. Additionally, applying panel data analysis could provide a broader understanding by examining data across multiple periods or countries, thus offering a comparative perspective. Another promising direction is to continue evaluating the influence of global crude oil prices on Vietnam's real effective exchange rate, particularly from 2016 onward. This period marks the implementation of Vietnam's new central exchange rate policy.

References

Akram, QF (2004). Oil prices and exchange rates: Norwegian evidence. *Econometrics Journal*, 7(2), 476–504, http://dx.doi.org/10.1111/j.1368-423X.2004.00140.x.

Akram, QF (2009). Commodity prices, interest rates and the dollar. *Energy Economics*, 31, 838–851.

Aloui, R, MS Ben Aissa and DK Nguyen (2013). Conditional dependence structure between oil prices and exchange rates: A Copula–GARCH approach. *Journal of International Money and Finance*, 32(1), 719–738.

Anjum, H (2019). Estimating volatility transmission between oil prices and the US dollar exchange rate under structural breaks. *Journal of Economics and Finance*, 43(4), 750–763, https://doi.org/10.1007/s12197-019-09472-w.

Arrelano, M and S Bond (1991). Some tests of specification for panel data: Monte Carlo evidence and an application to employment equations. *Review of Economic Studies*, 58, 277–297.

Baghestani, H and H Toledo (2019). Oil prices and real exchange rates in the NAFTA region. *North American Journal of Economics & Finance*, 48, 253–264, https://doi.org/10.1016/j.najef.2019.02.009.

Bjournland, HO and H Hungnes (2008). The commodity currency puzzle. *The ICFAI Journal of Monetary Economics*, 2, 7–30.

Bloomberg, SB and ES Harris (1995). The commodity-consumer price connection: Fact or fable? *Federal Reserve Board of New York, Economic Policy Review*, October, 21–38.

Chen, SS and HC Chen (2007). Oil prices and real exchange rate. *Energy Economics*, 29, 390–404.

Chaudhuri, K and BC Daniel (1998). Long run equilibrium real exchange rate and oil prices. *Economic Letters*, 58(2), 231–238.

Clarida, R and J Gali (1994). Sources of real exchange rate fluctuations: How important are nominal shocks? *Carnegie-Rochester Conference Series on Public Policy*, 41, 1–56.

Foss, M (2022). The impact of renewables on energy security. *Canadian Foreign Policy Journal*, 28(3), 234–248.

Golub, S (1983). Oil prices and exchange rates. *Economic Journal*, 93, 576–593.

Haar, L and LN Haar (2019). A financial option perspective on energy security and strategic storage. *Energy Strategy Reviews*, 25, 65–74.

Habib, MM and MM Kalamova (2007). Are there oil currencies? The real exchange rate of oil exporting countries. European Central Bank Working Paper 839.

Hassan, S and M Zahid (2011). The real exchange rate of an oil exporting economy: Empirical evidence from Nigeria. FIW Working Paper 72.

Hem, CB, V Puneet and S Subhash (2014). Common trends and common cycles in oil price and real exchange rate. *Global Economy Journal*, 14(2), 249–263, https://doi.org/10.1515/gej-2013-0042.

Hem, CB and PU Kamal (2015). Impact of oil price shocks on output, inflation and the real exchange rate: Evidence from selected ASEAN countries. *Applied Economics*, 47(29), 3078–3091, http://dx.doi.org/10.1080/00036846.2015.1011322.

IEA (2015). World Energy Outlook 2015, https://www.iea.org/newsroom/news/2015/november/world-energy-outlook-2015.html.

IEA (2018). World Energy Statistics 2018, https://webstore.iea.org/key-world-energy-statistics-2018.

Jahangard, S, A Daneshmand and M Tekieh (2017). Oil prices and the real exchange rate in Iran: An ARDL bounds testing approach. *Applied Economics Letters*, 24(15), 1051–1056.

Kahouli, B and S Maktouf (2015). The determinants of FDI and the impact of the economic crisis on the implementation of RTAs: A static and dynamic gravity model. *International Business Review*, 24(3), 518–529.

Khan, K, A Khurshid, J Cifuentes-Faura and D Xianjun (2024). Does renewable energy development enhance energy security? *Utilities Policy*, 87, 101725, https://doi.org/10.1016/j.jup.2024.101725.

Krugman, P (1983a). Oil and the dollar. In *Economic Interdependence and Flexible Exchange Rates*, 179–190, Cambridge: MIT Press.

Krugman, P (1983b). Oil shocks and exchange rate dynamics. In *Exchange Rates and International Macroeconomics*, 281–283, Chicago, IL: University of Chicago Press.

La Rovere, E, A Pereira and A Simoes (2011). Biofuels and sustainable energy development in Brazil. *World Development*, 39(6), 1026–1036.

Lin, F (2015). Estimating the effects of the internet on international trade. *The Journal of International Trade & Economic Development*, 24(3), 409–428.

Lizardo, R and V Mollick (2010). Oil price fluctuations and US dollar exchange rates. *Energy Economics*, 32(2), 399–408.

Mansson, A, B Johansson and LJ Nilsson (2014). Assessing energy security: An overview of commonly used methodologies. *Energy*, 73, 1–14.

Martinez-Zarzoso, I, D Nowak-Lehmann and N Horsewood (2009). Are regional trading agreements beneficial? Static and dynamic panel gravity models. *The North American Journal of Economics and Finance*, 20(1), 46–65.

Mehmet, HB, G Giray and K Gokhan (2015). The impact of world energy price volatility on aggregate economic activity in developing Asian economics. *The Singapore Economic Review*, 60(1), 1550009, https://doi.org/10.1142/S0217590815500095.

Mensi, E, Sh Hammoudeh and D Yoon (2015). Structural breaks, dynamic correlations, asymmetric volatility transmission and hedging strategies for petroleum prices and USD exchange rate. *Energy Economics*, 48, 46–60.

Ministry of Industry and Trade of Viet Nam (2019). https://moit.gov.vn/web/web-portal-ministry-of-industry-and-trade/news.

Misik, M (2022). The EU needs to improve its external energy security. *Energy Policy*, 165, 112930, https://doi.org/10.1016/j.enpol.2022.112930.

Mohsin, M, P Zhou, N Iqbal and SA Shah (2018). Assessing oil supply security of South Asia. *Energy*, 155, 438–447.

Nandi, B, H Kabir and M Nandi (2024). Crude oil price hikes and exchange rate volatility: A lesson from the Bangladesh economy. *Resources Policy*, 91, 104858, https://doi.org/10.1016/j.resourpol.2024.104858.

Nguyen, H, P Nguyen and V Ngo (2024). Energy security and the shift to renewable resources: The case of Russia-Ukraine war. *The Extractive Industries and Society*, 17, 101442, https://doi.org/10.1016/j.exis.2024.101442.

Nusair, SA and Kh Kisswani (2015). Asian real exchange rates and oil prices: A cointegration analysis under structural breaks: Asian real exchange rates and oil prices. *Bulletin of Economic Research*, 67(S1), S1–S25.

Ozsoz, E and M Akinkunmi (2011). An evaluation of price based determinants of Nigeria's real exchange rate. *SSRN elibrary*.

Rapach, DE and JK Strauss (2008). Structural breaks and GARCH models of exchange rate volatility. *Journal of Applied Econometrics*, 23(1), 65–90.

Rasoulienezhad, E and F Jabalameli (2019). Russia-EU gas game analysis: Evidence from a new proposed trade model. *Environmental Science and Pollution Research*, 26(24), 24482–24488.

Rasoulinezhad, E and GS Kang (2016). A panel data analysis of South Korea's trade with OPEC member countries: The gravity model approach. *Iranian Economic Review*, 20(2), 203–224.

Ratti, RA and JL Vespignani (2016). Oil prices and global factor macroeconomic variables. *Energy Economics*, 59, 198–212.

Report of the Vietnam Oil and Gas Group (2019). https://pvoil.com.vn/Upload/media/cbtt2020/eng/annual_report-2019_eng_v1.pdf, accessed on 20.12.2024.

Salah, AN and MK Khalid (2014). Asian real exchange rates and oil prices: A cointegration analysis under structural breaks. *Bulletin of Economic Research*, 67(S1), 1–25, https://doi.org/10.1111/boer.12027.

Spatafora, N and VE Staurev (2003). The equilibrium real exchange rate in a commodity exporting country: The case of Russia. IMF Working Paper 03/93.

Taghizadeh-Hesary, F, E Rasoulinezhad and Y Kobayashi (2017). Energy and food security: Linkages through price volatility. *Energy Policy*, 128, 796–806.

Taghizadeh-Hesary, F, E Rasoulinezhad and N Yoshino (2019). Oil price fluctuations and oil consuming sectors: An empirical analysis of Japan. *Economics and Policy of Energy and the Environment*, 2, 33–51.

Tangsopit, S, N Kittner, Y Chang, A Aksomkij and W Wangjiranian (2016). Energy security in ASEAN: A quantitative approach for sustainable energy policy. *Energy Policy*, 90, 60–72.

Toan, Kh, P Minh Bao and HD Nguyen (2011). Energy supply, demand, and policy in Viet Nam, with future projections. *Energy Policy*, 39(11), 6814–6826.

Trademap (2019). https://trademap.org/Index.aspx.

Usama, A and NBC S Che (2012). Oil prices and the real exchange rate in oil-exporting countries. *OPEC Energy Review*, 36(4), 375–382.

Van Hoa, T (2000). Vietnam: Economic and social impact of the Asia crisis. In: T Van Hoa (ed), *The Social Impact of the Asia Crisis*, London: Palgrave Macmillan.

Victor, EO and OE Nathanael (2012). Oil prices and the real exchange rate in Nigeria. *International Journal of Economics and Finance*, 4(6), 198–205, https://doi.org/10.5539/ijef.v4n6p198.

Wen, F, J Xiao, Ch Huang and X Xia (2018). Interaction between oil and US dollar exchange rate: Nonlinear causality, time-varying influence and structural breaks in volatility. *Applied Economics*, 50(3), 319–334.

World Bank (2010). How deep was the impact of the economic crisis in Vietnam? A focus on the informal sector in Hanoi and Ho Chi Minh City. Washington, DC: World Bank.

Wu, A, J Chen and Y Zhang (2023). Natural resources and energy resources prices an answer to energy insecurity? The role of mineral, forest, coal resources and financial development. *Resources Policy*, 87(Part A), 104275, https://doi.org/10.1016/j.resourpol.2023.104275.

Zhang, Y, Y Fan, H Tsai and Y Wei (2008). Spillover effect of US dollar exchange rate on oil prices. *Journal of Policy Modeling*, 30, 973–991.

Zhou, S (1995). The response of real exchange rates to various economic shocks. *Southern Economic Journal*, 61, 936–954.

www.ingramcontent.com/pod-product-compliance
Lightning Source LLC
Chambersburg PA
CBHW082056141225
36468CB00006B/391
* 9 7 8 9 8 1 9 8 1 2 5 9 2 *